SOCIAL STUDY:

Inquiry in Elementary Classrooms

SOCIAL STUDY:
Inquiry in Elementary Classrooms

H. Millard Clements
UNIVERSITY OF WISCONSIN

William R. Fielder
CLAREMONT GRADUATE SCHOOL

B. Robert Tabachnick
UNIVERSITY OF WISCONSIN

THE BOBBS-MERRILL COMPANY, INC.

A SUBSIDIARY OF HOWARD W. SAMS & CO., INC.

PUBLISHERS • INDIANAPOLIS • NEW YORK • KANSAS CITY

TO
FANNIE SHAFTEL
TEACHER, FRIEND

Preface

Helping students reach some understanding of the meaning of their own lives should be the goal of a social studies program. This book is written for teachers who are interested in stimulating youngsters to think about the things they encounter that tell them about themselves and their world, its past and its present.

While lesson plans may supply orderly arrangements of material to feed students, they seldom concern themselves with the development of ideas. Study takes place only when children are encouraged to question and pursue the implications of ideas and events. Even the very young can ask, "How do you know that?"

We think, then, that the fundamental problem of instruction is not to tell children "facts", but to teach them how to pursue answers to their own questions. Social study occurs when a student engages in inquiry about social phenomena in a way that challenges his imagination, his capacity to observe and his ability to think. In essence, the goal of social study is to give children the greatest possible opportunity to behave as social scientists.

Experienced teachers may find ideas here that will lead them to re-evaluate their approach to social studies instruction and to re-appraise conventional avenues and materials. For new teachers, conceptions and illustrations for challenging students to examine the social world are abundantly offered.

The question that a teacher might profitably pose while reading this text is: How can I inspire my students to ask meaningful questions and motivate them to seek a greater understanding of the world?

October 1965

Contents

ix

PART FOUR

Introduction

Social study is both art and skill: there is art in conceiving possible explanations for what one observes; there is skill involved in translating possibilities into testable notions and in carrying out the appropriate tests. Intuition and an appeal to experience are essential features of social study.

In the elementary classroom, the art and skill of social study may be nurtured by confronting students with a fair sample of the residue of social activity. There are two kinds of social residue that students may confront: natural residue and induced residue.

Residue and Study

Natural residue is what remains now of what happened then. A student can only seek out this residue and make of it what he can. He may explore textbooks, works of art, ships' logs, poems, letters, and newspapers. The student is in no way responsible for the existence of natural residue. He can only devise strategies of inquiry that may compel a painting or a newspaper to tell him what he wants to know. In order to invent such a strategy, he must identify what it is that he wants to know.

Induced residue is what remains now of a student's deliberate efforts to observe and interact with living people. This interaction may involve writing a letter, watching a trial in court, sending out a questionnaire, engaging in an experiment, or interviewing people. The student is not only responsible for the social interaction in which he has engaged, he is responsible for the existence of whatever residue remains. Answers to his letters or questionnaires would not exist had he not contrived to bring them into existence; his memories of watching the trial could not exist had he not decided to go.

Students must not only develop strategies for interaction, they must devise strategies for recording their experience, so that, at some later date, they will have satisfactory residue to examine. Thus, two skills of the inquiring person are: a certain flair for obtaining the remnants bearing on his questions, and a certain cunning in making stable and public the remnants of social interaction he obtains.

The range of arts and skills that should be nurtured in the elementary school is determined by the variety of residue that a student can confront. Students must learn how to make use of this residue to further their inquiry.

Newspapers, for example, are extremely interesting social documents. Students should discover that newspapers are made by men; that different newspapers are made by different men; that newspapermen report what is news in the light of the prejudices and the passions that are part of their lives. Southern and Northern newspaper accounts of racial troubles provide easy illustrations of the various ways in which news may be reported. Democratic newspaper accounts of Republican affairs, and Republican newspaper reports of Democratic affairs provide another illustration of the ways in which passions influence what appears in newspapers as news. It is possible to get foreign, English-language newspapers that report on American happenings and to compare them with different sorts of American newspaper accounts of the same event. The purpose of this comparison is to help children gain skill in appraising the reports they hear and read. The ability to evaluate reports is an essential art and skill of social study.

Examples of *natural* residue are: telephone books and letters; such artifacts as paintings and coins; the commonplace attitudes, beliefs, and linguistic skills that children bring to the classroom. Developing the ability to confront each kind of natural residue appropriately is an important feature of social study in the elementary classroom.

Examples of *induced* residue that students should learn how to produce and evaluate are: written messages that are responses to students' inquiries, such as letters and completed questionnaires; artifacts that students may request, such as the photographs that a cooperating student might take in Mitla, Mexico, at specified hours during the course of the day; records of interviews, observations, and experiments in which students may engage. The ability to work with induced residue is essential in effective study of the contemporary world.

The Plan of the Book

In this book, we suggest and illustrate how one can study ancient times, far-away peoples, and the communities in which students live. We believe, with John Dewey, that the problem of instruction is to give students *something to do* that challenges their imagination, their capacity to observe, and their ability to think. The problems with which students should work are the problems of study. There are specific difficulties that must be overcome in order to study any particular time, place, or social situation. It is with these problems that we are primarily concerned, problems in posing questions about social events, observing carefully, and formulating explanations or guesses about the meanings of what has been observed.

The book has four major parts. Part I, "Social Study," includes Chapters One through Five. It explores the intellectual space within which social study can take place: what content is characteristically *social* content; what thoughtful behavior is typical of *study*. Special attention is given to skills of inquiry relevant to studying social events and to the way in which the language we use may block or facilitate the discovery or invention of useful social concepts.

Part II, "The Challenge of Teaching," consisting of Chapters Six through Nine, explores the social and political space within which teachers can maneuver. Study goes on within a socio-political context, as well as within an intellectual context. This socio-political context is woven out of the interrelations of people, powers, roles, and prerogatives found in schools. The purpose of the second part of the book is to help teachers to know about this, and to use their knowledge to the advantage of study.

Part III, "Tasks of Instruction," containing Chapters Ten through Fourteen, describes specific problems encountered in teaching and learning about social events. These chapters describe ways to work with children that are well within the bounds of the "politically" possible and the educationally practical, yet they stress an encounter with study that is powerful in its intellectual significance.

Part IV, "Speculative Resources," presents what we consider to be thoughtfully provocative statements by social scientists and schoolmen about the problems of social studies. Although the articles themselves are collected at the back of the book, references to them are scattered throughout the text when specific articles are relevant to points under discussion.

SOCIAL STUDY:

Inquiry in Elementary Classrooms

PART ONE

Social Study

———

Social studies are often said to be the study of man's relationship to his environment. This notion seems to make sense. But does it really? *Man's relationship to his environment* is a complex idea. *Man* must mean all men. What is the relationship of all men to their various environments? Who could hope to seek to answer such a question? The problem is no simpler if one thinks of *man* as being *mankind*. What is the relationship that mankind has had with its terrestrial environment? To think of social studies in these terms is to invite a lack of precision that is dangerous for instruction.

In Chapters One and Two we have sought to explain what we think of as *social* and as *study*. Study we define as the art and skill of asking and answering questions. *Social study* we regard as an activity: it is the effort to pose and answer questions about people as they may be, or have been, found in the various cities, villages, nations, and territories on our planet.

In Chapter Three, we discuss the relationships between social study and the social sciences, and Chapter Four we devote to the discipline of study.

A student of social study must become aware of the influence of language on the conduct of inquiry. Chapter Five will introduce some of the problems of working with languages.

How does one go about studying people? How much of such studying can children in school do? These questions are our first concern.

3

I

What Is *Social?*

The statement, "I teach social studies," is deceptively simple. It is often difficult to agree upon what teachers should teach or children learn as they engage in social studies. Under the heading of social studies, children may spend most or all of a school year reading about United States history (with some geography included); studying one or more non-Western cultures, possibly with an anthropological emphasis; taking an hour a week to discuss a weekly newsletter; investigating variety and discovering similarities in family make-up and values; searching out and interpreting old documents in an attempt to learn how their town developed. Is each of these a social study? Is each of these an appropriate way for elementary children to spend some of their school time?

It is reasonable to expect a book about the teaching of social studies to define "social studies" in some precise way. In view of disagreements about what the term should mean, it is even more important that we make clear what *we* mean when *we* use the phrase "social studies."

The History of Social Studies

Before 1916, the term "social studies" was rarely heard. When it was used in the late nineteenth century, it referred typically to collections of diverse studies of society. Mrs. Bolton's *Social Studies in England*[1] records mainly her impressions of the place of women in English life, but includes comments on profit-sharing and a workingmen's college. *Social Studies,* by R. Heber Newton, presents the clergyman's thinking on such topics as socialism, the free kindergarten in church work, and the prevention of intemperance.[2]

"Social studies" was used to refer to a part of the school curriculum at least as early as 1905. An article by Thomas Jones, entitled "Social Studies," appeared in the magazine *Southern Workman* in that year. It was included as part of a longer statement published in 1908 under the title "Social Studies

[1] SARAH K. BOLTON, *Social Studies in England* (Boston: Lathrop, 1885).
[2] R. HEBER NEWTON, *Social Studies* (New York: G. P. Putnam, 1886).

5

in the Hampton Curriculum."[3] Jones pointed out the value of such social studies as civics, social welfare, and economics for helping Negro and Indian young men at Hampton Institute become acquainted with the wider American society.

The report, in 1916, of the Committee on Social Studies of the Commission on Reorganization of Secondary Education of the National Education Association gave the sanction of official usage to the term. It was perhaps no accident that the chairman of the committee was the same Mr. Jones who was instructor in social studies at Hampton Institute. With the formation of the National Council for the Social Studies in 1921, and with the term's consistent use in professional writing and by professional organizations, "social studies" came almost universally to refer to the school treatment of any and all of those sciences called social sciences.[4]

Social Studies and Social Sciences

Material from each of the social sciences may be used in some systematic way to solve "persistent problems of living," such as "communicating ideas," or "transporting people and goods," or "earning a living." Or all of the social sciences may be focused on different geographical entities, such as the "school community," or the "region-of-states community," or the "Atlantic community." ·

Typically, one or a few of the social sciences is expected to make the major contribution at any particular time, while the other social sciences are given only minor emphasis. For example, material from sociology and economics is widely used in studies of family, school, and neighborhood in primary grades. The major emphasis tends to become historical and geographical in the middle grades, but it may lean heavily on anthropology in the study of cultures outside the United States. Even when school districts teach only history and geography, and teach these as separate subjects, they will usually refer to their "social-studies program."

Social studies thus refers to a field of studies rather than to a single discipline of some sort. These several studies do not contribute equally at any particular time. Social studies is *not* a fancy way to say history and geog-

---

[3] THOMAS J. JONES, *Social Studies in the Hampton Curriculum* (Hampton, Virginia: Hampton Institute Press, 1908).

[4] The Library of Congress lists anthropology, economics, education, geography, history, law, political science, regionalism, and sociology as social sciences. *The Encyclopaedia of the Social Sciences* details eight "purely" social sciences (politics, economics, history, jurisprudence, anthropology, penology, sociology, social work); four "semi-" social sciences (ethics, education, philosophy, and psychology); and five "natural and cultural" sciences with social implications (biology, geography, medicine, linguistics, art). E. R. A. Seligman, "What Are the Social Sciences?" *Encyclopaedia of the Social Sciences* (New York: Macmillan, 1951), Vol. I, 3-7.

raphy; we are easily able to say history and geography, and we would if we intended to. History and geography may contribute to, or be considered separately among, social studies undertaken in school. The field of related social studies is fed by the social sciences.

The Content of School Social Studies

"Social studies is the study of man's relationships to his human and physical environments." This most commonly offered definition seems straightforward enough, yet it has a curiously opaque quality, as though a handful of words, like a handful of brightly colored beads, were put into a cup, shaken, and poured out upon a tabletop. They look pretty, but how much do we know about what they mean? Suppose we look into some classrooms.

Mrs. Claridge turns from the blackboard to face her second grade and ask:

TEACHER: Who can read what is on the board? Jill?
CHILD: Com——com——
TEACHER: Community . . .
CHILD: Community Helpers.
TEACHER: Community Helpers. That's right. We are going to learn about Community Helpers. What do you think a Community Helper is?
CHILD: Good boys and girls.
TEACHER: Yes, they are nice and they certainly help. But who helps everyone in a community?
CHILD: What is a community?
TEACHER: A community is a place where people live. It is like a neighborhood. All the children who go to Marcy School live in the same community. It could be like a big neighborhood or many little neighborhoods put together.
TEACHER: Let me give you a hint. The policeman helps everyone in our community to be safe, so he is one of our Community Helpers. (Writes "Policeman" on board under "Community Helpers.") Can you think of someone else? Charles?
CHILD: The snowplow-man? He helps by plowing off the snow.
TEACHER: He helps *us*. But suppose we lived in Florida; would we need a snowplow-man?
CLASS: No.
TEACHER: No. Billie?
CHILD: The fireman?
TEACHER: (Writes "Fireman" on board) Yes, the fireman is a Community Helper.

Miss Shelton has assigned the "housekeeping" tasks for the next two weeks. She has all the class helpers come to the front of the room and asks if someone will count them. A child counts twelve helpers. She thanks them and they are seated.

TEACHER: My, so many helpers! Do you think we really need so many?

CHILD: We have a lot of jobs to do.

TEACHER: I suppose each of us could take care of himself and do any job that he saw that needed doing.

CHILD: How about the milk money? Should each of us go down to the office?

CHILD: And blackboards. There aren't enough erasers.

CHILD: And it's no fun.

TEACHER: What is no fun, Brian?

CHILD: Not to have helpers.

TEACHER: You mean you like being a helper?

CLASS: Yes!

TEACHER: What would you call being a helper; is it work or play?

CLASS: It's play. . . . It's work. . . . It's work and play too. . . . (answering together)

TEACHER: Wait a minute, please! You have many different ideas, I see. Some people say one thing and some people say another. How can we find out what we want to know?

CHILD: Look it up in the dictionary.

TEACHER: (uncertainly) Look what up in the dictionary?

CHILD: Look up "work" and look up "play" and then decide what it is.

TEACHER: Well, you can try looking in the dictionary. What else can you do? Do you know anyone who works?

CHILD: My daddy works.

CLASS: Let's ask our daddies what work is.

CLASS: Yes, yes, let's ask our daddies. . . .

If you were to ask Mrs. Claridge and Miss Shelton what they were teaching at ten in the morning, they might answer in unison, "social studies." They might even agree that they were concerned about children's learning how man relates to the environments (human or social, and natural or physical) in which he lives. Clearly, their problems are similar: What is the network of human interdependencies that pattern a community? The two *styles* of teaching differ markedly; differences in teaching style are responsible for the different ideas and events that make up the content of instruction in each room. Mrs. Claridge knows exactly where she is going and how she will get there. Children will at least go through the motions of accompanying her, with few detours allowed. They will become acquainted with a category of people, labeled "Community Helpers," that includes some special types and excludes others. Miss Shelton seems not quite so sure of precisely what children will learn. Is work different from play? Are they alike? Identical? These are open questions, open to a variety of "correct" answers. This group of children, and dissenting individuals in the group, have yet to commit themselves to answers.

For our immediate purpose, it is enough to establish that two different, even conflicting, modes of teaching can huddle under the same defining umbrella. Social studies deals with man's relationships to his social and physical environments. We might find that this statement perfectly well describes the social studies—if only we knew what the statement meant. Does it include Mrs. Claridge? Miss Shelton? Both of them? What kind of studies are *social* studies?

The Meaning of *Social* in Social Study

Men are notoriously gregarious beings. They rarely live alone. Those ascetics who voluntarily remove themselves from human contact make a choice so unusual and difficult that it underscores the necessity most of us feel to be constantly in interaction with other people. Among the most severe penalties for criminal acts is a confinement that prevents communication with other people.

Human Variety

Variety is an attribute of all organisms. Even within physiological limits, men exhibit an endless variety in their beings and in their behavior. The part that symbols play in the conduct of human affairs extends the possibilities for variety and autonomy in human behavior beyond that which is observable in nonhuman organisms (such as beavers or bees) that also live in groups. If, in the remote prehistory of human existence, families developed out of the physiological interdependence of their members, these needs cannot explain the network of economic arrangements and feelings of deference and responsibility, anxiety, and joy which enfold the roles of eldest son, father, bride, or child. Nor do physiological needs explain the variation in behavior from one culture to another that these roles produce. Men's dependence on the manipulation of symbols might account for some of these differences.

The Use of Symbols

The fact of variety and the fact of the use of symbols complicates the fact of living in groups. Peoples who are different from one another may find it difficult to live together without friction, especially if the symbols with which they communicate arouse different meanings, even though they may once have referred to the same actions or objects. (The word "co-operation," for example, can refer to obedient behavior for some persons, at the same time that it causes others to think of shared power and shared responsibility.) In order to ease the strain of living together and make the experience of living in a group an asset to the individuals who undergo it, men invent certain patterned ways of behaving. Marrying, governing, and buying and selling are examples of human inventions for reducing some of the abrasive effects of living in groups.

Children engage in *social* studies when they are encouraged to study[5] evidences of human variety: people, their acts, and their arrangements for living by, with, in spite of, because of, one another.

If we erect such abstractions as nation, society, democracy, government, we remember that the reality of our study is people. Human beings decide to make war, devise tariff regulations, build factories. It is people, not "a people," who tell lies, work hard, build ingenious machines, or write lilting poetry. It is people, not "a people," who move to cities, stay on farms, get rich, or starve.

Social Change

The compelling constant in this drama of human action and interaction is change. All societies are, and have always been, in process of changing. Sometimes change is so slight as to be hardly noticeable, in so-called highly stable societies. Sometimes change comes with explosive suddenness—in social, or economic, or political revolutions. One of the puzzling facts of contemporary life is that certain traditionally stable societies have entered upon processes of change so rapid that social, economic, and political patterns form and shift with the speed (if not the regularity) of a kaleidoscope. Children can understand little about social institutions and social behavior if they cannot appreciate the importance of the process of change in social events.

Method as a Part of Content

While course content is highly significant, Gross and Badger add an important dimension in stating that "the social studies comprise a portion of the school curriculum wherein the content, findings, and *methods* of the social sciences are simplified and reorganized for instructional purposes.

---

[5] The significance of the difference between acquaintance and study and the way in which one depends on the other will be discussed in the next chapter.

(italics added).[6] An essential part of any science is the way in which the scientist gathers and organizes data. Children can acquire increasing skill in applying the general scientific method to the social data they study: raising questions, defining problems, predicting solutions, suspending judgment until data have been gathered that support or cast doubt on the validity of predictions, and so forth.

In addition to using the general method of science, children can become skilled in using some of the specific techniques for gathering and analyzing data appropriate to the kind of social study in which they engage. What children know is limited by their ability to be independent of any authority but their own scrutiny. This independence increases with increasing opportunity to criticize the interpretations of social events made by social scientists. Collingwood describes history as a search and adds that it proceeds by the interpretation of evidence presently existing and available for study.[7] A student has only a very distorted idea of what the data mean unless he has tried to gather similar data himself. Only then can he appreciate the fragmentary evidence upon which hypotheses and judgments must be built. It is in the struggle to gather data that answer a question that one learns the practical limitations of using what he knows for predicting what he does not yet know. Do you think you know what a family is? Try predicting the make-up in people (how many, how old, how related) of a family you have never seen or heard about. Does the history book tell what "really" happened during the Battle of Saratoga, or does it present the best guess that one historian could make, based on his personal way of looking at the incomplete evidence available to him? Instead of separating social studies from the social sciences, it would seem to us that a major teaching problem in the teaching of elementary social studies is extending to children the greatest possible opportunity to behave as social scientists.

Social study, therefore, is the process of learning about variety and change in the actions of people as they arrange to live together in groups. This learning goes on through the gathering and interpreting of social data, as well as through critical examination of the conclusions and generalizations of social scientists.

The Role of Language

The words we use to describe and discuss what we experience are so close to us and seem so right that we sometimes overlook the control they exercise over our thinking. In our everyday vocabularies, some very simple words

---

[6] RICHARD E. GROSS and WILLIAM V. BADGER, "Social Studies," *Encyclopaedia of Educational Research,* ed. Chester W. Harris (New York: Macmillan, 1960), p. 1296.

[7] R. G. COLLINGWOOD, *The Idea of History,* in Part IV of this volume.

dangerously distort the meanings of social data. Words like "always" or "never" rarely describe human interactions with precision. Sentences beginning "The Germans are . . ." or "Negroes feel . . ." or "The Romans believed . . ." will very likely present inaccurate generalizations that obscure important differences in behavior, feelings, or beliefs. It is important that children learn language habits and usages that guard against overgeneralizing and stereotyping. "Some," "sometimes," and "many" are examples of qualifying words that very young children can learn to use. Older children can become sensitive to the fact that one person's "many" may be another person's "some," or even "few." They can learn to strive for increasingly greater precision in their descriptions of social events.

When one tries to capture social behavior in a word, the word can become as slippery as a wet fish. Loyalty is a noble quality when it refers to sacrificing comforts to protect your country; if it refers to refusing to identify a criminal, you become "accessory after the fact." Democracy in our context suggests respect for the dignity of the individual; it may suggest something else in "Chinese People's Democracy." Social events and ideas are often ambiguous; they develop in a changing environment and are themselves continually changing. If the quest for precision depends on defining something "once and for all," it will probably end in distortion or confusion. Helping children to tolerate ambiguity in social situations is another difficult teaching problem in social studies.

Finally, language may affect social understanding in still another way.

Every language is also a special way of looking at the world and interpreting experience. Concealed in the structure of each different language are a whole set of unconscious assumptions about the world and life in it. . . . From the anthropological point of view there are as many different worlds as there are languages. Each language is an instrument which guides people in observing, in reacting, in expressing themselves in a special way.[8]

Language reinforces the special ways of thinking, of feeling, of organizing experience, that each of us begins to learn as soon as he is born into a culture. It is difficult to know anything about another person; it is even more difficult to know something about him if he is indifferent to behavior that we fear or value, while valuing or fearing behavior to which we are indifferent. Ruth Benedict suggests the figure, "the eyeglasses of culture."[9] What we see through a pair of eyeglasses may be quite different from what we see without them. We are rarely conscious of the glass, however, as we perceive through it the reality which it has in part created.

[8] CLYDE KLUCKHOHN, *Mirror For Man* (Greenwich: Premier Books, Fawcett, 1959), p. 12.
[9] RUTH BENEDICT, *Patterns of Culture* (Boston: Houghton Mifflin, 1934).

A graduate student from India, brought up in a vegetarian tradition based on a philosophical reverence for all animal life, tells about his first Thanksgiving in the United States.

Mr. and Mrs. ———— very kindly invited me to dinner. I knew they would have meat but I thought that since I am here, I should at least experiment with the way you live and the things you eat. When it was time for dinner, Mrs. ———— brought in the turkey triumphantly. It lay helpless on a plate surrounded by little potatoes. I had thought it would be all cut up, so it was a shock to see it looking like itself only featherless. Mr. ———— smiled and stabbed it with a fork. Juices ran out through the holes. My stomach gave a little jump, but I was still in control even as he sliced pieces of the flesh away from the body. But when he reached inside with a long spoon and dragged out the "stuffing," I began to perspire and I could only play with the food on my plate.

Definition of *Social Study*

Although it is not likely that we can free ourselves of our cultural eyeglasses, it is possible to become conscious of some of the ways in which they direct our perceptions. Approaching the ability to see the people of another culture from their own point of view, leads to the greater possibility that we can understand them. We may reject what we discover, but we should not be prevented from knowing.

By *social study*, then, we mean:
1. The process of learning about variety and change in the actions of people as they arrange to live together in groups. This learning goes on through the gathering and interpreting of social data, as well as through critical examination of the conclusions and generalizations of social scientists.
2. The development of intellectual skill appropriate to this study.
   a. Acquiring a language whose content and structure are capable of patterning, ordering, and communicating social realities.
   b. Acquiring the "suppleness of mind" that permits the examination of alien individual and cultural forms.

This kind of abstract description of social study takes on a more precise meaning as it leads to description of things that children do and say as they engage in social study. Returning to the questions we asked about Mrs. Claridge and Miss Shelton, we would conclude that the children in Mrs. Claridge's room (studying Community Helpers like The Policeman, The Fireman, but *not* The Snowplow Man) have given no evidence of being involved in a social study. What we saw of their activity did not deal with people at all, but with idealized types. The sense of human variety is lost in the term "The Policeman," suggesting that policemen are all alike and exist only in their institutional roles. An attempt by one child to test the category "Community Helpers" against his own experience is gently, though somewhat illogically, suppressed. Instead, children are directed to accept pre-established, rigid "concepts" on the strength of their being preferred by authorities such as the teacher and the textbook. If Mrs. Claridge were to encourage the children to challenge the stereotypes after they have become acquainted with them, to gather data themselves by visiting and talking to "helpers," to examine and construct meanings for "community" and "helper" that allow them to decide for themselves what individuals belong and who, if anyone, does not, then their activity would become more like a social study.

Miss Shelton might have been directing social study. Certainly, children were being challenged to think carefully about the words they used to describe social events ("work or play?") and encouraged to gather data at first hand. How these data were used and focused would determine the effectiveness of their study.

The whole of Part III of this book (Chapters Ten through Fourteen) will present descriptions of children and teachers doing and discussing social studies.

The Term *Social Studies*

Objections to the Term

Though used more frequently than any other term to describe its area of study, *social studies* is not universally accepted either within or outside of the teaching profession. Objections to the use of the term come from several sources and for many reasons. Some people worry about any term with the word *social* in it, believing that *social* is a nasty word, if not downright subversive. At best, it seems to them to smack of politics and controversy and should on those grounds be excluded as a description of a curriculum area. A few concede that it is all right to study *about* controversy and politics in school, as long as you do not take part in it, and as long as careful guidance prevents children from making unfortunate or "immature" choices. Others maintain that controversy has no place in an elementary-school curriculum. This latter position would be easier to act upon if only there were broad areas of agreement that could be taught. Disagreement seems to be as common among social scientists as among ordinary men of affairs; they are as little able to agree about what happened in history as about what causes juvenile delinquency. Sincere and intelligent men disagree about the propriety of referring to the United States as a republic or as a democracy, or whether it can properly be called both. Take everything controversial out of the curriculum, and very little social content would remain.

Rejection of the term *social studies* also comes from those who believe that blending together material from several disciplines produces a hodge-podge that is possibly social but offers little opportunity for study. From this point of view, every discipline or "subject" is a specialized way of looking at specific kinds of problems. The record of accomplishment of a discipline such as history or economics is its content. This content includes both reports of inventions and discoveries within the specialized area and the history of the intellectual struggles, successes, and failures of its specialists. "Abuses" of school time have produced a shift from emphasis on intellectual development, through acquainting children with these specialized contents, to a concern for producing correct social or group behavior. In advocating a return to the study in elementary schools of history, geography, and civics as separate subjects, critics of social studies raise the specter of the erosion of standards of intellectual excellence and the encouragement of a deadening conformity to group norms of behavior. Intellectual excellence suffers when study is merely a sharing of opinions, free of the rigors of citation of substantiating data. Learning demands committing large amounts of material to memory. This is tedious and difficult, requiring self-control that becomes a habit and leads to intellectual excellence. Conformity is the result of pressing children to become agreeable members of a group, submerging personal interests in the interest of group harmony.

The several strands of argument presented above frequently appear together, although they are not always consistent with one another or with an understanding of the meaning of social studies. As already suggested, social studies need not be a blending of disciplines at all. What is labeled "history" or "geography" may or *may not* be a social study in terms of the definition that has been proposed. If it consisted of opinion-sharing without the support of data, it would be considerably less than a social study. Memorizing or accepting blindly the judgments of authorities is also less than study. It is debatable whether memorizing, though more tedious, demands as much intellectual toughness as the risk and effort involved in combining facts into a testable hypothesis or prediction. The kind of challenge, thought, and second thought that we believe social studies demand, depends on encouraging and rewarding difference, debate, and individuality. While the concern for doing is present, it exists as one of the possible tests of thinking, or as another form of thinking.

Although social studies can refer to collections of studies within separate disciplines, it is interesting to notice the attractiveness of interdisciplinary study for contemporary social scientists. An anthropologist comments:

I venture to predict that increasingly education will be phrased in terms of problems and theories rather than in terms of areas or disciplines like Southeast Asia and anthropology.[10]

[10]CORA DUBOIS, *Social Forces in Southeast Asia* (Cambridge, Massachusetts: The Harvard University Press, 1959), p. 11.

Regions and areas like fields of academic learning are artificial boundaries which we erect around our curiosity. They do not represent limits of integrated reality, but defenses built to encompass the frailties of human comprehension.[11]

An economist writes:

. . . it must be confessed that we know very little about the forces that cause the process of (social) change and govern its course. . . . In part the inadequacy of our understanding is due to the fact that until very recently the three major social sciences have gone their separate ways. (It is also true that they have gone their separate ways partly because of the inadequacy of our understanding.) The study of culture and of primitive societies by anthropologists, of the social structure of societies by sociologists, and of personality formation by psychologists have been largely separate disciplines. They have reached a point at which they should be brought into interaction to form a theory of societies and social change.[12]

That these notions are not new to social scientists is demonstrated in this statement, made by a sociologist in the early part of this century: ". . . the main function of the social sciences is to make out the meaning of human experience.[13] . . . there must be team-work between the social sciences, if they are to advance from the ranks of boys' play and constitute serious social science."[14] There may be singular value in an interdisciplinary approach to social study in the elementary school.

Value of the Term

For our part, we have chosen to reaffirm in our definition the value of the term social studies for describing that part of the elementary curriculum with which we are concerned in this book. Social content is an essential part of the elementary curriculum. As children become better able to predict and understand their own behavior and the behavior of other people, social institutions, and social forces with which they have some experience, they come to know more about the meaning of the participation of citizens of a democratic community.

Social content can be distorted or infused with intellectual vitality, depending on what it is that children are encouraged to do in the name of study. It is to the meaning of "study" in the term "social studies" that we turn next.

---

[11] *Ibid.,* p. 27.

[12] EVERETT E. HAGEN, *On the Theory of Social Change* (Homewood: Dorsey, 1962), pp. 3–4.

[13] ALBION W. SMALL, *The Meaning of Social Science* (Chicago: The University of Chicago Press, 1910), p. 19.

[14] *Ibid.,* p. 21.

II

What Is *Study?*

What is social *study?* What can one *do* to seek to understand the various people who have lived and are living on this planet? Within the context of elementary school, what social *study* is possible? In this chapter, we will begin to discuss what we see as social *study*.

We think social *study* is an activity; we use the word "study" as a verb. The task of teaching is to induce children to engage in the activity *study*. Usually people think of study in terms of the objects of study: one studies history or geography, Pueblo Indians or Brazilians. But if study is an activity, then one must learn how to do it by engaging in the activity. Just as one learns to swim or ride a bicycle by getting into water or on a bike, one learns to study by studying. One must know what study is and how to do it if he is to engage in teaching social *study*.

The main concern of curricular guides is the designation of topics which should be taught in the various grades. Much attention is given to describing what should be studied, but little attention is given to a description of study. The result of this lack of attention is that teachers, in their preoccupation with topics, engage their children in activities, in the name of social studies, which have nothing to do with *social study*.

Study: Thinking and Observing

The word *study* is used in many different ways. Children are said to study such things as history and arithmetic. Scientists and scholars also study. Physicists may seek to invent conceptions that will represent "spin systems"; historians, to determine the purpose of Caesar's voyages to Britain; anthropologists, to devise conceptual tools that help account for the stability or the progressive change of selected societies; literary critics, to assess the significance of the poetry of Mallarmé.

The study of scholars and scientists has much in common. Although children in elementary school do many things that are labeled "study," they seldom engage in an activity that a scientist or a scholar might recognize as study.

17

We think that study is an important and worthy human vocation. A person who studies learns how to recognize what he knows and what he does not know. He engages in a uniquely human activity. Study is the means by which men seek truth, and no person can learn too soon the sense of excitement and power that comes from the discovery of those tentative truths to which human beings can aspire.

How do scholars and scientists study? What is fundamentally characteristic of their kind of study? It involves three discernible elements: thought, observation, and things. If a person wishes to study, he may think, and he may observe things around him. These two *actions* are all that any person can do who wishes to study. One who studies must gain experience with these two possibilities.

This statement is very general; it makes use of three important words. These words have familiar, common-sense meanings. But as used above, they have an uncommon sense.

The Role of Thought

Thinking refers to the formulation of questions, the invention or use of notions that help explain some aspects of the observable world. There is no routine way in which to devise possibilities or construct interesting questions. A student in school or in a professional laboratory, when he confronts a problem, *may only hope to come up* with useful ideas; such ideas are: ". . . always the product of an ability of the human mind; this process may be called induction, inductive guessing, imagination. In any case it is not logical derivation."[1]

A fundamental feature of study as scholars engage in it is simply to confront this demand for thought.

The Role of Observation

Observation may involve any of our senses and a large variety of instruments to extend them. In addition, events may be induced to occur and may then be observed: questions may be asked; experiments may be performed. Whatever a scientist or a scholar may be said to know is directly or indirectly related to what he can observe in the things around him. It is the appeal to things that differentiates study from other kinds of mental activity. The student knows, not on the basis of authority, but on the basis of the testimony of things as his sense reports this testimony to him. The student of Greek drama must refer to the relics of Greek antiquity; the student of the cosmos must refer to his photographic plates; the student of delinquency must refer to court records of delinquent acts.

---

[1] PHILIPP FRANK, *Philosophy of Science* (Englewood Cliffs: Prentice-Hall, 1957), p. 22.

The Role of "Things"

Things are simply existing "objects" about which one can think. A "thing" may be a poem for a literary scholar, answers to a series of questions for a psychologist, a painting for an art historian, a sound for a linguist, or a liver for a biologist. Although historians and scientists are interested in events and processes, it is only the residue of events and the effects of processes which may be observed. If something happened in a town square fifty years ago, a student of that event can only consult the witnesses who are still alive and physical residue: photographs, newspaper accounts, diaries, memoirs, and interpretations of the event that other scholars may have proposed. A "thing," for a student, is any person or poem, painting or proclamation about which one can wonder.

Important Characteristics of Study

If the above paragraphs present an accurate, though general, description of study, then one may examine this description and seek to gain some additional insight into the character of study. The description itself is an existing "thing" about which one can think.

Perhaps the first observation that might be made is this: study is an active quest or search. The person who studies must decide what he wants to know. He must formulate what he wants to know in a question. Finally, he must seek means to answer the question that he poses. For one who studies, an answer to a question is not to be found in authorities, whoever or whatever they may be. Answers to questions come as a result of a student's thought about some existing things. Perhaps these things may be sentences in a book or statements of living people. However, for a student, the answers to questions rest in his thinking about "things" and not in authorities. A person who is engaged in study directs his *questions* to himself. He answers his questions on the basis of what he can observe.

Before one can study a problem or situation, an event or an institution, one must have some acquaintance with it. It is convenient to distinguish between becoming acquainted with a situation and studying it. One can become acquainted with a situation by reading about it, by listening to what people have to say about it, and perhaps by observing some aspect of it. It is impossible to study problems with which one is unfamiliar. Thus, an important prerequisite to study is familiarity with things connected with the problem. For example, it is impossible to ask and answer a question about the poetry of Mallarmé if one is completely unfamiliar with this poetry. One problem of teaching is developing sufficient familiarity with a problem so that it may be studied.

Some teachers expect children to acquaint themselves with information simply by reading textbooks, but textbooks usually present only a succession of generalized statements and conclusions presumably based on someone's assessment of information. Who studied the information and created the generalizations is usually unclear, although children often get the impression that the textbook authors are responsible. Most textbooks and most examinations are concerned with developing and measuring the degree to which students are familiar with the conclusions of others, although they do not see the data from which those conclusions are derived or they see them only in a form which makes alternative conclusions highly unlikely.

Preoccupation with topics leads to the belief that becoming acquainted with topics is studying. Developing familiarity with a situation is absolutely prerequisite to studying it, but if students only become acquainted with ideas they do not engage in *study*.

Preparation for study is simply contact with appropriate "things"—poetry books or people, newspapers or cloud chambers, textbooks, or novels, or datelines. After one becomes acquainted with some relevant things, he may begin to inquire, to formulate questions, and thus begin to study.

No doubt, one of the most important "things" connected with a problem is a report of previous studies. To a large extent, both science and scholarship are progressive. An initial task of a student is to become acquainted with the work of other students, but mere contact with the work of other students is not study. Acquaintance is preparation; it is not study.

It is possible to force a person to become acquainted or familiar with the contents of a book or a lecture, but it is impossible to force him to study. Study is a voluntary, more or less spontaneous, activity that may occur when people come into contact with things around them. No one can be compelled to be curious; without curiosity, one cannot study. The circumstances of contact may encourage study or make study difficult or impossible.

If students are taught to satisfy their curiosity by appealing to the author of a book for answers to their questions, then the capacity to study is being discouraged. One studies when he answers questions on his own authority as a result of confronting things. Of course, one such thing may be a book. But a book, for a student, is testimony to be examined and analyzed rather than read and believed.

In the classroom, the expressed curiosity of children may impede a rapid, easy flow of activity toward a predetermined goal. If the coverage of topics is the paramount value, then study is discouraged. For study often begins with the formulation of tangential, troublesome, even unanswerable questions. Unanswerable questions, of course, have to be reformulated, but if one does not ask them, and discover their unanswerability, he is deprived of contact with the problem of study.

Study is a dialogue with "things." It consists of formulating and answering a series of questions that are not directed toward authorities but toward oneself. The student answers his own question by contemplating the "things" around him.

Thus, the central task of teaching students how to study lies in the problem of teaching students what questions are, how to formulate them, how to order them into a productive series, and how to answer them through the scrutiny of things.[2]

An important aspect of learning how to study is simply learning how to ask questions, because the questions one asks limit what he can discover. To ask, "How do the Ceylonese worship God?" makes it difficult to discover a type of religious experience that does not include any idea at all like the Western notion of God.

One who studies limits what he knows by the objects he examines. If he systematically ignores items that are important for his study, the fruits of his investigation may have serious flaws. A rather famous anecdote illustrating this problem concerns the investigation of the Navaho Indians by American anthropologists. Intensive studies of the Navaho were made during the time of the year when anthropologists were free for ethnological investigations—during the summer. One of the most important rituals in the Navaho calendar occurs during the winter. Thus, years of investigation of the Navaho failed to discover this ritual.

The problem of "things" is variety. The scholar must depend upon himself to guarantee the integrity of his findings. The student, however, is dependent upon his teacher to guarantee the integrity of his investigations: the teacher must bring his student into contact with sufficient variety in "things." Without variety, the dialogue may become trivial.

As has been suggested above, study may be fruitful or fruitless. A student may be curious, may formulate questions, may seek to force his circumstances to answer the questions that he poses and still he may make little progress toward truth or understanding. His line of questioning may take him in useless directions: the questions may be poorly conceived. The concepts that he develops, although plausible, may fail to order or explain the circumstances which interest him. The concepts may be too much a part of the common world, insufficiently criticized and clarified. The "things" that he examined may not have reflected adequately the variety that exists in the situation. These are the various dangers that the teacher of study must help his students avoid, and to which he must aid them to become sensitive.

A Description of Social Study

In the previous discussion, study was defined as thought in confrontation with "things." What is unique to *social study* is the repertoire of "things" that

[2] It may be instructive to compare this statement with that of R. G. Collingwood, in "The Question," in Part IV.

one may confront. Remarkably few kinds of "things" are of interest to one who is engaged in social study. Briefly, social study can be regarded as inquiry that confronts the residue of social events.

The Residue of Social Events

1. There are "things" such as pots, flags, boats, butter churns, plows, and postage stamps.

   That is, there are things that people make with their hands and with the machines that they design and operate.

2. There are "things" such as letters, newspapers, plays, poems, travel accounts, journals, magazines, ships' logs, records of inquests, pamphlets, novels, philosophical discussions, comic books.

   That is, there are written things that are produced by, or are written about, the situation and the people of interest.

3. There are, in addition to the above sorts of writings, two additional kinds that deserve special mention:

   a. There are scientific or academic reports. For example, there are ethnological reports on many literate and preliterate societies. In addition, there are books and articles written by historians, or economists, or political scientists.

   These writings have a special place in the activity of study: they are writings which report the study of others.

   b. There are social-studies textbooks. Most of these books are not reports of research. Sometimes they are quite inaccurate, and often they consist of bland overgeneralizations. At best, they provide an oversimplified account that may become the object of fruitful study as they lead to questions and a search for evidence that supports or contradicts conclusions drawn by the authors.

4. There are "things", such as people, to whom one can talk. Some of the talk that one can listen to may result from the questions one asks. An inquirer can tape-record the talk; he can remember what was said as best he can; he can take notes partially recording what was said.

   The existing "things" about which one can think and to which one has continuous access is the memory or the record of the past event.

5. There are "things" such as artistic portrayals of people, events, and situations. There are paintings, statues, possibly films and dramatizations.

   These are interpretations of events growing out of the artistic vision of sensitive observers within or outside of the situation of interest.

6. There are "things" such as mechanical records of various kinds: documentary films, photographs, and recordings that provide records of past events.

7. There are responses that people write to formal questions, such as those in a questionnaire or a letter. This record of response can become an existing "thing" about which one can think.

8. There are "things", such as records, notes, and memories, that can be obtained from watching people behave. As a neutral nonparticipant observer, one can note behavior. Playground behavior, behavior at dances, and behavior on busy streets can be watched. The records, memories, and notes are the existing "things" about which one can think.

9. There are records, notes, and memories that can be obtained through participant observation. One can join a group with the intent to observe and understand the character of the group. The records and memories of this kind of participation are the "things" about which one can think.

Each of these "things" represents something "left over" from the actions and interactions of people. A student can only observe something that exists "now." An ancient tool, a letter from Columbus to the Spanish court, or an eyewitness account of an accident is a carrier of information about an event that has already occurred. The event is gone (even if it is only a few hours or a few minutes past) and can never be repeated or even described completely. The residue of the event must obviously be available to a student if he is to invent a reconstruction or a meaning from the little that remains of the past event for him to observe.

Social Studies in the Classroom

The social-studies program should nurture in children the desire to seek to understand themselves and the world in which they live—the urge to study the human condition. We regard the fundamental task of social studies to be to help children appraise and evaluate the mass of information they encounter that tells them about themselves and their world.

Whatever men may know of themselves is, in a sense, historical, that is, it is inferred from the residue of their previous activities. The essential obligation of the social-studies program is to teach children how to engage in critical dialogue with this residue. Each relic may have many meanings if we can only learn what they are and can formulate the insightful questions which close scrutiny may answer. Thus, the art of teaching lies in nurturing the fruitful question.

Useful Categories of People

Social study is concerned with people and with the manner in which they react to one another. It is concerned with the customs they invent and with the various ways in which they kill and cooperate. It is the residue of this activity that students must confront with their thought. People produce the residue. If people are categorized according to the kind of residue that has been produced and is being produced, then the following categories may be identified.

Categories of People

People who are nearby	People who are living	People who are past
People who are far away	Living and nearby	Past and nearby
	Living and far away	Past and far away

These different kinds of people cannot be studied in the same way. You cannot study the ancient Greeks in the same way in which you can study postmen. A limited number of "things" exists that one can confront to study the Greeks, while a large number of "things" exists that one can confront to study the postman. The structural or fundamental differences associated with studying the above-mentioned categories of people do not become apparent until study is initiated. For study requires confrontation with a variety of "things."

Before looking, briefly, at each of the four categories, an examination of two types of residue may be helpful.

NATURAL AND INDUCED RESIDUE

Most of the "things" available for children to observe are objects, photographs, movies, and written materials of various types that they have been lucky enough to find in museums or attics, in libraries or classrooms. We use the term "natural residue" to refer to "things" that exist and can be observed if they are discovered.

Another kind of residue exists only because a student asks a question; we call it "induced residue." How does a part of a main street look early in the morning, at noon, in mid-afternoon? A student in Nebraska can ask a correspondent in Seattle, Washington; or Melbourne, Australia; or Lagos, Nigeria, to describe the scene in writing or to send photographs. Why do eighth-graders think some children commit delinquent acts? What do they think should be done about delinquency? What explanations for delinquency do the parents of eighth-graders give? What do these parents think we should do about the problem? Even though it was the student's initiative that brought them into being, the collected answers to these questions are as "real" as the diary of a famous general or a photo of "Main Street in 1910" discovered in a family album. The answers to the questions about delinquents, for example, are used as "things" when they are manipulated and observed from different angles. Do eighth-grade girls answer differently from eighth-grade boys? Do children differ in their answers from parents? Under what general headings do answers fall: Do Nothing; Punish; Educate; Help Get Jobs; Punish Parents; others? Children, in this instance, "get at" the problem of delinquency by examining variety in the way that different groups of people think and talk about it.

Studying contemporary people, whether nearby or far away, permits the use of both natural and induced residue.

LIVING AND NEARBY PEOPLE

In studying people who are nearby, one can make use of most or all of the nine sorts of residue previously mentioned. By studying the nearby community, one can nurture the whole range of social-studies skills. Both natural and induced types of residue are available.

LIVING AND FAR-AWAY PEOPLE

Although one can examine "things" that may be produced by people who live far away, fewer of them are available. The obligation upon teachers is to acquire a sufficient number of such "things" as newspapers, magazines, and other writings. There is little, although there may be some, opportunity to talk or interact with representative members of a far-away group. This deficiency imposes serious limitations on those who wish to study them.

PAST AND NEARBY PEOPLE

The study of people who are no longer living is even more difficult than studying people who live far away. All that remains of the lives and affairs of previously existing people are their buildings, their writings, their art, and other products of hands and machines. There may be a fair supply of these remains if one confines his investigations to the past affairs of his own country, state, or community. The various Historical Societies do a great deal to preserve the records of the past, and much of this is available with little effort.

PAST AND FAR-AWAY PEOPLE

These people, for example, the ancient Egyptians, are difficult to study. It is not hard to become acquainted with the many accounts of their lives and fortunes, but to study the people themselves depends on confronting those remains that are available. Children in elementary school cannot read Egyptian hieroglyphics, but they can read translations; they cannot visit the pyramids, but they can look at photographs; they themselves cannot search for ancient relics, but they can make use of the findings of others. The basic problem of instruction is to discover source material.

Ideas and Notions

Social studies concern people. We have, for convenience, divided people into various sorts, depending upon the residue one can examine in the pursuit of study. But in addition to the people who are living and have lived on this earth, there is at least one other focus of interest for social study.

Great ideas have moved men at various times in history, and one important aspect of social study is the scrutiny of such ideas. These might be important for social study in the elementary school: democracy, nation, state, honor, loyalty, communism, capitalism, socialism.

What does one confront when he seeks to study ideas? Basically, two kinds of "things": one is variety in writings concerning the idea. In addition, perhaps, one could confront the physical consequences resulting from the actions of men holding certain interesting ideas. A second kind of "thing" is the personal experience of children with the ideas: children's statements about them and the physical and emotional consequences of children's behavior, as these are observed, recalled, and thought about. In this case, as in all others, study will involve confronting some social residue to confirm, sustain, or refute the speculative accounts that are produced.

In Part III, we will deal with the various categories of people and with ideas and notions as aspects of a social-studies program.

III

Social Study and the Social Sciences

Chapter Two suggests that *social study* is a dialogue with the residue of social activity: study is something one does that involves thought, observation, and "things." Little attention was paid to the various social scientific disciplines. The documents one can examine and cross-examine, the people one can observe and interview, and the confusion of human tragedy, delight, and despair exist quite independently of the activities of social scientists.

Each of the different social sciences may best be thought of as a dialect, that is, as a way of talking about what any one of us could see. One can speak of human affairs in French or in Urdu, in the sociological dialect or in the anthropological dialect. It may be possible to pose questions and make statements in Urdu that are very difficult to translate into French. But whether spoken or written in Urdu, or in the economic dialect, the sound of talk or the pages of a historical account comprise a human symbolic comment on the world of men.

A single social science is a limited conversation about a narrow range of social residue. Human problems come whole: they do not sort themselves into university departmental structures or styles of discourse. The study of human problems is necessarily interdisciplinary: no one perspective and no one dialect can exhaust the ways in which men can regard and talk about their own circumstances.

A student who seeks some understanding of the world must learn to distinguish between a way in which to talk and the people and events he may observe: "En suma, tenemos que aprender a disintelectualizar lo real a fin de serle fieles."[1]

Study, as we have conceived it, is a way in which to talk, to form questions and to answer them. Study is a dialogue with the residue of human happenings. The more "languages" a student speaks, the more questions he can ask. We think that children should confront, perhaps in "little league"

---

[1] JOSÉ ORTEGA Y GASSET, *Historia Como Sistema* (Madrid: Revista de Occidente [Cuarta Edición en Castellano], 1962), pp. 31–32: "In short, we must learn to disintellectualize reality if we are to be faithful to it."

27

fashion, a wide range of human happenings from a variety of viewpoints in a variety of "languages." Problems of men and society can be only trivially understood in the dialect of a single social science. Variety of perspective and variety of encounter with "things" should be provided to help students to develop some understanding of the character, method, and limitations of social inquiry.

Study and the Sense of the Verb

There is a real advantage to the elementary-school notion of social study. The virtue of the words "social study" is that in the structure of our language the verb sense is prominent. One can say, "I study," or, "We study." There is no oddity in this usage. It is interesting to observe, however, that the sense of action, the sense of the verb, is missing in English when one refers to any of the traditional disciplines. It would be odd to say, "I history," or "we anthropologize." The structure of our language makes it difficult for us to notice that the word "history" has both the sense of the noun and the sense of the verb—history is both something to do and something said. Each of the social-science disciplines has this quality. The use of a single word with a muted sense of the verb obscures fundamental aspects of social investigation.

History—An Example of the Muted Sense of the Verb

As an illustration of the problem of the muted sense of the verb, take the discipline of history. Because all knowledge is, in a sense, historical, that is, inferred from a residue of past events, a discussion of history will illustrate some basic problems of any social study.

One simple confusion involving the notion of history is a lack of distinction between *history* and *past events*. Colloquially, we often refer to the past as history. In one sense, history is an account, that is, talk, about past events; in another sense, history is an investigation, that is, posing and answering questions regarding the past; in neither sense is it the past itself. Many people regard the study of history as the scrutiny of some more or less ultimate written record of events of the past. History is thought of as the account that some omniscient observer might have written as he sat on Mount Olympus watching the affairs of men. In a sense, this account has become identical with the past. But there is no such record of the affairs of men.

History is a human product. Many accounts can be written of a single past event. Northern and Southern historians say rather different things about the causes and conflicts of the Civil War. English and American historians have somewhat contrasting things to say about the American colonial episode. What a historian has to say is often deeply influenced by the society and times in which he lived and worked.

Not only do historians differ in their interpretations of civil conflicts and international affairs, they differ on the worth of possible topics. Politics and military affairs capture the imagination of many. Much has been said about kings, generals, battles, and conquest. Much less has been said about poets, scientists, the social affairs of ordinary men, and the problems and achievements of minority groups. Negroes, for example, are largely ignored in American historical writings. The American Indians have received attention only in fairly recent years.[2] Holidays and marriage customs have not been thought to be fit subjects for serious scholars. The result is that few of us know, for example, anything about the origin of Christmas as a Christian holiday. We think of Christmas in religious terms, and the interesting historical question does not arise: When and under what circumstances was Christmas first celebrated as a Christian holiday? The preoccupation with politics and economics has impoverished our understandings of our social heritage. Historians are human beings with particular interests and understandings, who write about selected events that have occurred in the past in the light of that understanding. It is essential that students become aware of this quality of all historical writings. All that one can expect from any historian is some accounts of things that happened in the past that were of interest to him. The past is infinite and to some extent unknowable. History, in the sense of writing and talk about the happenings of the past, deals with a small sample of the human drama.

History is not only something said about the past, it has the sense of the verb; history is something to do. Like swimming or baseball, it makes use of skills that are learned only with practice. No amount of reading about history, or swimming, or baseball can substitute for engaging in the real activity. Of course, just as the little- or minor-league baseball player is not a major leaguer, a student is not a professional historian. But if students are to understand what history is, they must engage in it. They are going to have to learn how to play the game, for only in so doing will they encounter the drama, the adventure, and the spirit of it.

Lack of sensitivity to this verbal sense of the word "history" makes it difficult to understand the nature of history. A person who is unaware of the verbal sense of history does not know that history is made by men; he does not know how men make history; and he does not know the private concern and passion that may influence the making of history. Without

---

[2] See John Collier, "The Cherokees," in Part IV. There, a brief interesting account of some of the problems that Cherokee Indians faced may be found. The article is taken from Collier's *The Indians of the Americas.*

this understanding, he is ignorant of the ways in which men know about themselves.[3]

Conceptions of Social Inquiry

A teacher of social study must have an intellectual conception of what he is about. In order to teach, say, history, one must be able to say what history is. We have suggested that history is something to do. What is the purpose of this doing? Social scientists have struggled with this question for many, many years. Even today there is some conflict regarding what the proper purpose of social inquiry may be.

Work of the Historian

What Have Historians Thought They Were Doing?

Historians have thought many different things about their craft. The contemporary view is that the problem of history is to try to find out what has happened in the past. This is a simple statement. Its significance becomes apparent only when it is compared with other possible responsibilities of historical inquiry. In medieval times, the study of history was regarded as the effort to detect the plan of God in the affairs of man. The philosopher-historians of the eighteenth century were preoccupied with discovering social customs that were in harmony with nature, so that they could be recommended to people who were obviously living in a depraved and savage condition. Marxist historians have believed that all human events may be explained in terms of economic ideas. In this view, economic circumstances solely or primarily determine the ideas men hold and the conflicts and enterprises in which they engage. The problem for Marxist historians is to search for and to discover these economic forces, so that the past is explored and the future foretold. Some historians have seen an analogy between the movements of stars and galaxies and the affairs of men. These historians think the problem of doing history is to formulate laws that describe how societies progress and decline. Such historians as Toynbee see human affairs as illustrations of limited numbers of great principles; the writing of history is the ordering of illustrations of these "laws" and foretelling what will be. Most often, this sort of writing is a somber statement of despair. Collingwood, the famous British historian, made this comment on efforts to make of history a godlike judgment on the affairs of men: "The historian's business

[3] See R. G. Collingwood, "The Nature, Object, Method, and Value of History," in Part IV. His discussion may usefully be compared to the one found here.

is to know the past, not to know the future; and whenever historians claim to be able to determine the future in advance of its happening, we may know with certainty that something has gone wrong with their fundamental conception of history."[4]

The contemporary view of history is that it is the historians' task to create coherent pictures of episodes in the human drama that help us understand certain events and conflicts that happened in the past. This self-assigned responsibility imposes three important obligations upon historical study:

1. Historical accounts must be localized in space and time. The historian deals with what actual people have done, believed, and suffered.
2. Historical accounts must have chronological and topological order. Human dramas take place at some place and at some time.
3. Historical accounts must be justified by evidence. Evidence, for historians, is some building, painting, papal bull, ship's log, fingerprint, or letter that exists here and now, perceptible to the investigator. This evidence is mute until an investigator can pose a question to himself and answer his question by examining the particular thing that is available. For historians, anything can be evidence if it can be put to the question.

Paradigmatic Tasks of Historians

An examination of history, thought of as a verb, will disclose a number of paradigmatic, that is, exemplary or typical, historical tasks. These tasks may be divided into two types: tasks related to the clarification of the purpose of inquiry, and tasks related to the conduct of inquiry.

CLARIFYING THE PURPOSE OF INQUIRY

Three basic tasks of clarification are these:
1. Examine with great care the questions that are to be asked.
2. Evaluate the key words that will be used in the construction of questions and explanations.
3. Make explicit the notions of cause in human affairs that are presupposed in anticipated explanations of human actions.

Questions–Because the questions that historians ask limit what they will discover, it is a fundamental task of historical scholarship to seek variety in the questions asked and to make explicit the presuppositions that characterize the questions to be posed:
1. Questions that appear to presuppose universal laws and transcendental designs should be avoided.

[4] R. G. COLLINGWOOD, *The Idea of History* (New York: Galaxy Books, The Oxford University Press, 1956), p. 54.

2. Questions that relate to "origins" should be stated so that they call for historical answers and not mythical ones.
3. Questions should not be phrased so that they presuppose what is to be found out.
4. Questions should be historical, that is, they should be related to the convictions and actions of people involved in the drama of life.

Words–Words must be recognized as convenient symbolic devices. Words may be logically related, but the drama of life may have a different "logic." The historian must be careful to avoid reifying and attributing causative effect to the ideas that exist only as thoughts.

An important task of scholarship is to distinguish between words and the things to which they may conveniently refer. When historians fail to keep this distinction in mind, they undermine the possibility of historical understanding.

Explanations–Vague notions of "influence" and simplified notions of human motivation should be avoided in historical explanations. The world is not made up of "good guys" and "bad guys" in a conspiracy of competition. One can explain a happening to some extent when one can understand how those involved saw themselves in that particular episode. That sort of explanation is the one for which historians search.

CONDUCTING INQUIRY

Three basic tasks involved in the conduct of historical inquiry:
1. The invention of an initial, motivating heuristic question.
2. The search for and the cross-examination of the "tracks" of human happenings.
3. The construction of an account of the human drama that is being investigated.

The Heuristic Question–Until a heuristic question, one that stimulates investigation, is posed, there is no historical inquiry. Typically, heuristic questions arise in one of three ways: general questions are focused on *commonplace features of life, artifacts,* or *situations.*

General questions are focused on commonplace features of life in the following fashion. We are all familiar with our own customs of dress, speech mannerisms, food preferences, and sex roles. The question of how these various things came to be might initiate the invention of a heuristic, historical question. Just such inquiries regarding the historical origins and changing character of food preferences or sex roles inspired Trevelyan's work.[5]

Inquiries regarding the circumstances of production of artifacts, such as

---

[5] GEORGE MACAULAY TREVELYAN, *English Social History: A Survey of Six Centuries— Chaucer to Queen Victoria* (3rd ed.; London, New York: Longmans, Green, 1946).

coins, paintings, or papal bulls may initiate the construction of heuristic questions that may motivate study. Huizinga, for example, began his famous investigations as a result of curiosity about the paintings of the Van Eycks.[6]

Another approach to the invention of heuristic questions is to pose questions regarding situations that are said to have occurred in the past. One question is simple to ask: Did the actions occur as they are said to have occurred? Did Richard III murder his nephews? Did Europeans migrate to the New World in pre-Columbian times? Did Lee Oswald conspire with others in the assassination of President John F. Kennedy?

Situations can evoke heuristic questions in another way. We know that the Spartans were warlike, that the Germans gassed the Jews, that the American government has broken most of its treaties with the Indians. Some of these situations may be puzzling and disturbing. A historian might seek to understand any of these happenings by asking why and then seeking to uncover the motives of the men who were involved.

Cross-Examination–Once the heuristic question has been invented, then evidence of one kind or another becomes historically relevant. The tasks of historical cross-examination involve the interrogation of narrative documents, such as textbooks and the Gospel of John; private messages, such as letters and personal memoranda; legal documents, such as trial records and inquest reports; and artifacts, such as paintings, guns, coins, and buildings.

A preliminary to cross-examination is the establishment of the date and location where the "track" was found. A constant problem of inquiry is the detection of fraud. A historian has to decide that the document is what it appears to be and that it was produced at some specified time and place.

In the light of the established relevance of the document, a historian is then obliged to discover the human meaning that may be concealed within it. This is done by posing questions about the significance of detailed characteristics of the historical "track."

Writing–Every historian faces the task of writing an account of the human drama that he has investigated. He faces the responsibility of ordering his thoughts and of sharing them with others. Historians must be writers.

Work of the Anthropologist

What Have Anthropologists Thought They Were Doing?

Anthropologists, like historians, have struggled to come to an understanding of the nature of their discipline. An understanding of contemporary

---

[6] JOHAN HUIZINGA, *The Waning of the Middle Ages* (Garden City: Doubleday Anchor Books, Doubleday, 1954).

anthropology may best be understood in the light of a history of anthropological thought.

When the discipline began about one hundred years ago, anthropologists were very excited about the findings of Darwin. They devised evolutionary conceptions to guide their questioning activity and formulated a basic vocabulary to express their fundamental attitude. Prominent in nineteenth-century anthropological writings are the terms "natural law," "simple and complex societies," "savagery," "barbarism," "civilization," and "reason." The anthropology of the time was an effort to talk and write about social organization making use of these basic words.

Presuppositions of this anthropology could be expressed in this way:

1. All men are essentially alike.
2. Men are reasoning beings.
3. Men strive to improve themselves by means of their intellect.
4. Unchanging natural laws regulate the development of complex societies from simple societies.
5. Anthropology is the search for these laws.

All societies occupy some position on a scale between unreasoning savagery and reasoned civilization. Within civilized societies, one could expect to find some remnants of savagery; within savage society, one could expect to find anticipations of civilization. In the study of modern primitive society, early anthropologists believed, by analogy, they could study the origins of present-day civilized societies. They sought to identify cultural epochs analogous to the geologic epochs in the evolution of complexity from simplicity.

The preconceptions of nineteenth-century anthropology have been largely abandoned, but the notion of "simple societies" persists. It is not unusual to hear or to read about "simple Indian societies." In the following suggestion to teachers, this nineteenth-century notion is clearly stated:

A unit of work on Mexican village life is an appropriate one for children of fourth grade level since it represents a simple culture in which the processes of community life are understandable to young children.[7]

The notions of simplicity, savagery, and barbarism imposed several limitations on the kinds of questions that men asked and on the observations that they were inclined to make. Around the beginning of the twentieth century, anthropologists began to criticize conceptions with which they had been working. They found the notion of "simple" societies a useless scientific concept; all societies are complicated.

Anthropologists eventually abandoned their interest in the search for general laws and began to study unique, concrete events; they wanted to

---

[7] LAVONNE HANNA, GLADYS L. POTTER, and NEVA HAGAMAN, *Unit Teaching in the Elementary School* (New York: Henry Holt, 1956), p. 438.

investigate specific societies and discover the nature of the specific environmental adaptations that were being made. A new vocabulary was formulated which expressed the ideas of the new brand of anthropology: "diffusion," "adaptation," "interaction," "accidental processes," "historical processes." These conceptions excited anthropologists in the beginning of the twentieth century.

The presuppositions of anthropologists in the early part of the twentieth century could be expressed in this way:

1. All men are born essentially alike.
2. A culture is a complicated accumulation of traits and interactions.
3. Individuals are habituated products of a cultural process.
4. Cultures are primarily influenced by the accidents of geography and contacts with other cultures.
5. Anthropological inquiry is largely concerned with a search for the antecedents and the accidents that have led to the present organization of society; anthropology is essentially historical inquiry.

These conceptions and vocabulary influenced anthropological thinking for about thirty years. Anthropologists eventually lost interest in the notion that "culture" is an accumulation of traits, habits, and interactions that are historically determined. A new vocabulary developed, and anthropologists again changed their conception of their discipline.

The basic notion of the new mode of anthropological thinking was that any culture should be thought of as a complex "system"; the task for anthropologists was to discover how the system maintains itself. How and why do cultures persist? The anthropology of the 1930's was written in the new vocabulary; the key words in this vocabulary revealed the new interests: "functionalism," "biological needs," "institutions," "role expectancy," "sentiment," "integration," "holistic," and "breast feeding."

The presuppositions of the anthropologists of the 1930's could be expressed in this way:

1. All men are born essentially alike.
2. A culture is a complex system with basic maintenance requirements.
3. These anthropologists differ on the nature of culture.
   a. To some of them, a culture is a vast instrument for the meeting of man's biological needs. The imperatives of man's needs determine the systems of interaction that men invent.
   b. To others, culture is a pattern of institutions; it is this unity, the ordered relationship among institutions, that is the fundamental cultural reality. It is not man's needs that shape culture; it is culture that shapes the manner in which men gratify their needs.
4. Man is a product of his culture: both his conforming and his deviation are determined by his milieu. Each man is an illustration of a type.
5. Anthropology is largely concerned with describing cultures thought of

as unified systems and with identifying the variety of types that each produces.

What most of us think of as anthropology is a result of inquiry which makes use of this notion of "system." Ruth Benedict and Margaret Mead are two of the most famous names that are associated with this mode of inquiry.

Contemporary anthropology can best be regarded as historical inquiry. The "tracks," the residue that anthropologists examine and cross-examine, are people and their artifacts. The usual intent of the inquiry is to develop a portrait of the life, community values, hopes, anxieties, and delights of a particular group of people. Historians cross-examine letters, coins, photographs. Anthropologists cross-examine people and whatever artifacts they produce. Both historians and anthropologists seek to formulate vivid descriptions of the ways in which people live or have lived. Neither discipline is concerned with formulating general laws regarding human affairs. Both disciplines may borrow from psychology, economics, political science, and philosophy in order to develop explanations of the people and events that are their primary interest.

These are some important presuppositions of contemporary anthropology; ten years from now, it may be much easier to suggest some such list as this:

1. All men are born essentially alike.
2. A culture is a configuration of loosely-interacting "themes" with recurrent consistencies *and* inconsistencies; the inconsistencies may be essential for the maintenance of the society. A "theme" may be regarded as an implicit or expressed postulate regarding the nature of man and his world.
3. An individual is a complex rational-irrational process; he is not a habituated social unit, nor is he a mirror copy of a cultural type.
4. The study of men must be interdisciplinary; no one conceptual approach to understanding the human situation will be satisfactory. Psychology, anthropology, history, economics, and political science must contribute to the science of men.
5. Anthropology is an attempt to identify the values men hold and the manner of life they lead.

There have been three significant contributions of anthropological inquiry. Two of them are important findings about human culture and society; one of them is an identification of an important mode of social inquiry.

The two findings of anthropology relate to human variety and language. Anthropologists have documented an amazingly wide range of human social arrangements. We know, as a result of their efforts, that there are many ways to organize families, raise young children, order societies, and engage in ceremonies that cope with the mystery of human existence. Anthropologists have done this *without recourse to extensive theory,* in the fashion of any historical investigation. In addition, they have "discovered" language; this may be their greatest achievement: "It is difficult to see adequately the functions of language because it is so deeply rooted in the whole of human behavior."[8]

Anthropologists have found that languages have properties that influence the ways in which people conceive themselves and their world. In spite of the powerful influences of language upon thought, it appears to be without attributes. It is difficult to notice the functions of language because it is such an intrinsic part of our thinking.[9]

Anthropological inquiry not only led to the discovery and analysis of language and the documentation of human variety, it also led to the identification of milieu that is relevant to anthropological investigation. The tasks of inquiry were developed in the study of small nonliterate homogeneous societies. Anthropologists work face-to-face, in intimate social contact, with the people being investigated: "He tries to feel with them, to see things as they see them, to experience some portion of their life with them."[10]

Participant observation, the basic anthropological methodology, compels anthropologists to investigate relatively small groups of people. These groups need not be nonliterate societies. Hospital wards, schools, social clubs, swim teams, or the school office might be investigated through the techniques of participant observation. The anthropological method of inquiry was developed in the study of nonliterate societies, but it has wide application.

Although anthropologists, like historians, have no distinctive theory, they work on the assumption that societies, like languages, have grammars. The grammar of a language is uncovered in the process of learning to speak it; the grammar of a society is learned in the process of living it.

Anthropological inquiry involves posing and answering questions. The questions are directed by the anthropologist to himself. Anthropologists answer their questions by cross-examining people, by observing social happenings, and by developing portraits of the people under investigation based on various observations.

Inquiry is usually initiated by the formation of heuristic questions. A heuristic question is a general curiosity that, hopefully, will lead to fruitful questioning. Anthropologists have, typically, been curious about family life and about social activities, such as parties and civic celebrations. Inquiry often proceeds when an anthropologist forms questions that direct his atten-

---

[8] EDWARD SAPIR, *Culture, Language and Personality: Selected Essays,* ed. David G. Mandelbaum (Berkeley and Los Angeles: The University of California Press, 1958), p. 15.

[9] For a brief discussion of the influence of language on thought, see H. Millard Clements, "Three Observations about Language," in Part IV.

[10] CLYDE KLUCKHOHN, *Mirror for Man* (Greenwich, Conn.: Premier Books, Fawcett, 1957), pp. 251–252.

tion to specific happenings in the lives of those he is investigating. Remember that the questions that an anthropologist may direct to his informants, whoever they may be, are not the anthropological questions that he directs to himself. Questions may be directed to an informant in order to discover what a person in a particular social location may say, believe, and do. The job of the anthropologist is to think about and to cross-examine what has been said and observed in order to develop an answer to his own questions.

Anthropologists usually try to obtain several perspectives on the people under investigation: they may remain neutral observers, become participants in social affairs, and interview members of the community. Using several methods of collecting impressions of a community helps to avoid the distortions that might result from the use of a single mode of observation.[11] Participant observation is the typical mode of inquiry in anthropology; the other perspectives provide an opportunity for corrective observation.

Anthropology, in theory and practice, is a discipline closely parallel to history:

1. Both historians and anthropologists seek to write vivid accounts of the actions, beliefs, and values of a selected group of people.
2. Both examine documents. The documents that historians examine are "tracks" of happenings in the past. The document for the anthropologist is a person, who may be encountered in his own milieu, or alone in an interview situation.
3. Neither historians nor anthropologists formulate theories about the general workings of society.

In the past, anthropologists have conceived of themselves as searching for illustrations of conceptions of progress, or of blind historical process, or of system. Contemporary anthropologists borrow theories where they can, but their job is not to make theories; it is to provide intimate portraits of the ways in which a people live, think, believe, value, and behave.[12]

Paradigmatic Tasks of Anthropologists

A number of paradigmatic anthropological tasks have already been identified. These tasks may be divided into two types: tasks related to the clarification of the purpose and character of anthropological inquiry, and tasks related to the conduct of anthropological inquiry.

CLARIFYING THE PURPOSE OF INQUIRY

Five basic tasks of clarification are these:

---

[11] See Jurgen Ruesch and Gregory Bateson, "A Word About Method," in Part IV, for a discussion of this point.

[12] See Oscar Lewis, "Approaches to Study," in Part IV. In this excerpt, Lewis describes his method of studying what he calls the culture of poverty.

1. Disintellectualization of human happenings.
2. Identification and criticism of conceptions borrowed from philosophy and related social sciences.
3. Identification of curiosity about a suitable milieu.
4. Appraisals of vocabulary and metaphor.
5. Formulation and criticism of questions.

Disintellectualizing Happenings–Anthropologists, like historians, try to contrive vivid portraits of human happenings that they have observed and in which they have participated.

A basic task of anthropological inquiry is to seek to avoid intellectualizations of the functions of anthropology and the character of the human happenings that are being observed. It has already been noted that anthropologists in the past conceived their tasks as the search for cultural epochs, or for historical processes, or for typologies of one kind or another. These intellectualizations presuppose as reality what is only a linguistic perspective. A basic task of anthropology is to treat abstractions and conceptions as linguistic conveniences. They provide ways of talking about human happenings, but ". . . really everything in human life blends into everything else."[13]

Words one talks with may or may not be useful; but the dramatic occasions of life are unregulated by this talk. The problem of anthropology is to penetrate the grammar of human happenings. This linguistic penetration can be done in many interesting ways, with a number of different metaphors and vocabularies. Linguistic vocabularies, however, must be distinguished from experiences of living. For man ". . . no es cosa ninguna, sino un drama—su vida, un puro y universal acontecimiento que acontece a cada cual y en que cada cual no es, a su vez, sino acontecimiento."[14]

Identifying and Criticizing Borrowed Conceptions–Anthropologists borrow theories and conceptions where they can. If such conceptions as "circular," "causal system," or "teleology" are borrowed from communication theory and philosophy, then: (a) they should be recognized as possibly convenient ways of talking; and (b) they should not be regarded as the only way to talk.

The use of one or another conception of learning or of personality dynamics may lead to the formation of interesting questions, but any such conception provides only perspective on behavior. An anthropologist must

[13] CLYDE KLUCKHOHN and DOROTHY LEIGHTON, *The Navaho* (rev. ed. Garden City: Doubleday Anchor Books, published in cooperation with the American Museum of Natural History, 1962), p. 179.

[14] JOSÉ ORTEGA Y GASSET, *Historia Como Sistema*, p. 36: ". . . is nothing but a drama— his life [is] a pure and universal event that happens to everyone and in which everyone, in turn, is nothing but event."

decide what, if any, use the conception might have for him when he is engaged in contriving his account of human happenings.

Identifying a Curiosity–Inquiry begins with a discovered curiosity about a particular milieu. Regardless of the array of available conceptions or the status of disintellectualization, particular curiosities have to be expressed before inquiry can begin. The variety of subcultures in our own society that might fruitfully be investigated is almost infinite. Interest could be focused upon:

   a. suburban family life
   b. school dances
   c. Boy Scout clubs
   d. athletic groups
   e. playground society
   f. social cliques
   g. the slot car set
   h. hot rod society
   i. elementary-school society

Each of these groups is relatively small and could be investigated by a participant-observer, with corrective supplemental observation.

A paradigmatic task of anthropology is to conceptualize a society that is small enough to be investigated in the face-to-face style of anthropological inquiry. Anthropologists frequently identify nonliterate societies, such as the Hopi or Nuer. In recent years, extensive anthropological investigation has been done in the villages of India among semiliterate, technologically underdeveloped communities. But any relatively small community might be investigated in the anthropological mode.

Appraising Vocabulary and Metaphor–Once a curiosity about a milieu has been identified or experienced, then statements will be made about the milieu, and questions will be formulated. The key words in these statements and questions must be carefully appraised. One paradigmatic anthropological task is to assess the meaning of important words in the context in which they will be used. Another is to identify and to choose metaphors that may be used in the description and explanations of social happenings.

Formulating and Criticizing Questions–Questions are the persistent concern of all social investigators. A paradigmatic task of anthropological inquiry is to identify and appraise the presuppositions upon which the proposed questions are based. As all social inquirers, anthropologists must seek to avoid presupposing what they wish to discover. To ask, for example, What is the Navaho view of religion? presupposes that the Navahos *have* a view of religion. An anthropologist must decide whether or not this is a warranted assumption.

CONDUCTING INQUIRY

Among the basic tasks in the conduct of inquiry are:
1. The establishment of rapport with the people being investigated.
2. The invention of a heuristic question.
3. The formulation of general and specific questions.
4. The observation and cross-examination of people and events.
5. The construction of descriptions of the human happenings observed.

Rapport–All anthropologists mention the necessity of becoming acceptable to the people being investigated. One technique for accomplishing this may be to try to learn the language of the group being investigated. An interest in the language often encourages the friendly feelings that lead to rapport. If the investigator speaks the language of the people he is investigating, then he must, in his social actions, demonstrate that he is a trustworthy person. A paradigmatic task of anthropologists is to create a climate of opinion that will encourage people to talk to them and share their honest thoughts.

Heuristic Question–The basic heuristic question of anthropology is simply: How does this group of people think and behave toward each other and toward the outside world? Heuristic questions can be focused on particular ceremonies, festivals, or incidents. But the basic concern is always with the ways in which these people act, believe, and regulate their affairs. A paradigmatic task of anthropology is to formulate a basic heuristic question that will focus attention upon some milieu.

General and Specific Questions–Once a heuristic question is formulated, the task of anthropology is to compose related questions that may, if answered, lead to an answer to the heuristic question. The posing of questions is to some extent an art and to some extent a skill. The art is to invent a question; the skill is to examine and appraise it for the purposes of the investigation. There is no routine way of generating interesting questions. It is an act of imagination that is, apparently, cultivated with practice. If the questions lead to some understanding, then they are good ones; if they do not, then new questions have to be formed. The skill of questioning is learned only with practice. The practice is the search for answers to heuristic questions.

Observation and Cross-Examination of People–Observation typically involves these activities:
1. One can talk to population members who make generalizations about

their own culture. Religious, political, and ceremonial leaders do this almost professionally.

2. One can observe from a neutral position the interaction of group members.
3. One can talk to population members who can report their own experience, beliefs, and concerns.
4. One can become a participant and observe and personally interact with population members during the course of community affairs.

Skill at these modes is developed with practice. Whatever anthropologists discover about men, their beliefs, and their fears is based on making these four kinds of observations. Astonishingly enough, there is little else one can do to learn about the human situation.

Writing–Anthropologists must be writers: one job is to construct written descriptions of the events they have seen and in which they have participated.

Work of the Sociologist

What Have Sociologists Thought They Were Doing?

Sociology, unlike history and anthropology, is an abstract or theoretical intellectual enterprise. We have seen that the history of anthropology and the history of history is an account of abandoned conceptions. The classic tradition of sociology is different. Little was abandoned in the development of sociology; each innovation became a new, complementary perspective on the human condition.

The "classic tradition" of sociology involves a set of customs and attitudes towards social inquiry and the human situation. The customs relate to the convenient fictions that sociologists have developed and used in the study of human societies. The attitudes predispose sociologists to be empirical and skeptical.

Three words represent the three basic fictions of sociology: "prison," "puppet," and "drama." Each of the three "fictions" may be regarded as stages in the development of sociology. Sociology began in the use of prison fiction, was eventually extended by the use of puppet metaphors, and, with the work of Weber, confronted human drama involving intentionality. These "fictions" did not succeed each other in the development of sociology; they provided alternative, additional perspectives from which human events might be viewed. In a sense, they are all true and all false: they are *fictions*.

To think of men as either caught up in a prison, dangling from puppet strings, or on stage involved in a drama is to affirm the basic sociological attitude: things are not what they seem. "We would contend, then, that there is a debunking motif inherent in sociological consciousness. The sociologist will be driven time and again, by the very logic of his discipline, to debunk the social systems he is studying."[15]

This debunking attitude can be seen in the sociological studies of Émile Durkheim. He affirmed, according to Berger, the autonomous character of social processes:

. . . to live in society means to exist under the domination of society's logic. Very often men act by this logic without knowing it. To discover this inner dynamic of society, therefore, the sociologist must frequently disregard the answers that the social actors themselves would give to his questions and look for explanations that are hidden from their own awareness.[16]

Max Weber expressed a similar skepticism with his phrase, "the irony of history." A constant theme of Weber's work that Berger mentions is ". . . the unintended, unforeseen consequences of human actions in society."[17]

Robert Merton's distinction between "manifest" and "latent" social functions is identified by Berger as an elaboration of Weber's concept of the irony of history:

. . . the "manifest" function of anti-gambling legislation may be to suppress gambling, its "latent" function to create an illegal empire for the gambling syndicates. Or Christian missions in parts of Africa "manifestly" tried to convert Africans to Christianity, "latently" helped to destroy the indigenous tribal cultures and thus provided an important impetus towards rapid social transformation. Or the control of the Communist Party over all sectors of social life in Russia "manifestly" was to assure the continued dominance of the revolutionary ethos, "latently" created a new class of comfortable bureaucrats uncannily bourgeois in its aspirations and increasingly disinclined toward the self-denial of Bolshevik dedication. Or the "manifest" function of many voluntary associations in America is sociability and public service, the "latent" function to attach status indices to those permitted to belong to such associations.[18]

The task of sociology is to look beyond, as well as behind, official interpretations and the taken-for-granted points of view: "We will not be far off if we see sociological thought as part of what Nietzsche called 'the art of mistrust'."[19]

The questions that sociologists raise are expressions of this skeptical mistrust. The basic fictions of the classic tradition of sociology are the tools that sociologists use to help them penetrate the social facade.

---

[15] PETER L. BERGER, *Invitation to Sociology: A Humanistic Perspective* (Garden City: Doubleday Anchor Books, Doubleday, 1963), p. 38.
[16] *Ibid.*, p. 40.
[17] *Ibid.*
[18] *Ibid.*, pp. 40–41.
[19] *Ibid.*, p. 30.

PRISON

This view of the human condition presupposes that men are thrust by chance into organized social systems. Each person at birth is located in the center of a circle of social forces. The most distant system of commands upon the individual are the established laws of a society. Nearer to the individual are the demands of custom regarding dress, tastes, and beliefs. Impinging also are specific customs of various occupation groups. Closest to the individual are human beings and their immediate personal demands. Every man is:

. . . an individual located at the center of a set of concentric circles, each one representing a system of social control, . . . location in society means to locate oneself with regard to many forces that constrain and coerce one. The individual who, thinking consecutively of all the people he is in a position to have to please, from the Collector of Internal Revenue to his mother-in-law, gets the idea that all of society sits right on top of him had better not dismiss that idea as a momentary neurotic derangement.[20]

This is the prison to which Berger refers.

The problem for sociology is, then, conceived to be an analysis of this system. How does the prison work? An essential concept for "prison sociology" is "stratification." Clearly society has many locations, many ranks. What are the life chances or life styles that may be associated with the various ranks? Each location may be thought to yield probabilities with regard to the fate of an individual:

An upper-middle-class person of, say twenty-five years of age has a much better chance of owning a suburban home, two cars and a cottage on the Cape ten years hence than his contemporary occupying a lower-middle-class position. This does not mean that the latter has no chance at all of achieving these things, but simply that he is operating under a statistical handicap.[21]

The force of the ranking system may be overt and explicit:

. . . the corporation executive who has the "wrong" address and the "wrong" wife will be subjected to considerable pressures to change both. The working-class individual who wants to join an upper-middle-class church will be made to understand in unmistakable terms that he "would be happier elsewhere." Or the lower-middle-class child with a taste for chamber music will come up against strong pressures to change this aberration to musical interests more in accord with those of his family and friends.[22]

---

20 *Ibid.*, p. 78.
21 *Ibid.*, pp. 79–80.
22 *Ibid.*, p. 81.

The study of ranks and associated life chances is one facet of sociological inquiry.

The second task in "prison sociology" is to discover how the influence of rank works. According to Berger, the concept of "institution" provides the means of carrying out this analysis. Not only do the forces imposed by our contemporaries dictate the styles of life associated with the various locations, our ancestors weigh upon us as well:

> Our lives are not only dominated by the inanities of our contemporaries, but also by those of men who have been dead for generations. What is more, each inanity gains credence and reverence with each decade that passes after its original promulgation. As Alfred Schuetz has pointed out, this means that each social situation in which we find ourselves is not only defined by our contemporaries but predefined by our predecessors. Since one cannot possibly talk back to one's ancestors, their ill-conceived constructions are commonly more difficult to get rid of than those built in our own lifetime. This fact is caught in Fontenelle's aphorism that the dead are more powerful than the living.[23]

An institution is usually thought of as a complex of social actions. Thus, marriage, religion, and law are historically determined institutions. According to Berger, one way to think of an institution is to say that it is:

> . . . a regulatory agency channeling human actions in much the same way as instincts channel animal behavior. In other words, institutions provide procedures through which human conduct is patterned, compelled to go, in grooves deemed desirable by society. And this trick is performed by making these grooves appear to the individual as the only possible ones.[24]

Berger compares the imperatives of institutions to the imperatives of constitutional tendencies. Cats, he suggests, do not have to be taught to chase mice. When a cat sees a mouse, there is something in the cat that says, "Eat! Eat! Eat!" The cat does not choose to eat, he simply follows the impulses of his innermost being. Young men, in their interactions with young women, feel analogously the imperative, "Marry! Marry! Marry!" But men were not born with this imperative: marriage is an institution, not an instinct.

> This becomes obvious if we try to imagine what our young man would do in the absence of the institutional imperative. He could . . . do an almost infinite number of things. He could have sexual relations with the girl, leave her and never see her again. Or he could wait until her first child is born and then ask her maternal uncle to raise it. Or he could get together with three buddies of his and ask them whether they would jointly acquire the girl as their common wife. Or he could incorporate her in his harem along with the twenty-three females already living in it. In other words, given his sex drive and his interests in that

[23] *Ibid.*, p. 85.
[24] *Ibid.*, p. 87.

particular girl, he would be in quite a quandary. Even assuming that he has studied anthropology and knows that all the above-mentioned options are the normal thing to do in some human culture, he would still have a difficult time deciding which one would be the most desirable one to follow in this case. Now we can see what the institutional imperative does for him. It protects him from his quandary. It shuts out all other options in favor of the one that his society has predefined for him. It even bars these other options from his consciousness. It presents him with a formula—to desire is to love is to marry.[25]

Institutions provide predefined courses of action that appear to be inevitable. But this apparent inevitability is a deception: ". . . every institutional structure must depend on deception and all existence in society carries with it an element of bad faith."[26]

"Prison sociology" discovers an omnipresent external reality that predetermines and predefines what people do and believe, fear, and are willing to die for:

Society, as objective and external fact, confronts us especially in the form of coercion. Its institutions pattern our actions and even shape our expectations. They reward us to the extent that we stay within our assigned performances. If we step out of these assignments, society has at its disposal an almost infinite variety of controlling and coercing agencies. The sanctions of society are able, at each moment of existence, to isolate us among our fellowmen, to subject us to ridicule, to deprive us of our sustenance and our liberty, and in the last resort to deprive us of life itself. The law and the morality of society can produce elaborate justifications for each one of these sanctions, and most of our fellow men will approve if they are used against us in punishment for our deviance. Finally, we are located in society not only in space but in time. Our society is a historical entity that extends temporally beyond any individual biography. Society antedates us and it will survive us. It was there before we were born and it will be there after we are dead. Our lives are but episodes in its majestic march through time. In sum, society is the walls of our imprisonment in history.[27]

PUPPETS

"Prison sociology" is not sufficient:

If this picture were left unmodified, one would obtain a quite erroneous impression of the actual relationship, namely, an impression of masses of men constantly straining at their leashes, surrendering to the controlling authorities with gnashing teeth, constantly driven to obedience by fear of what may happen to them otherwise. Both common-sense knowledge of society and sociological analysis proper tell us that this is not so. For most of us the yoke of society seems easy to bear.[28]

[25] *Ibid.*, pp. 88–89.
[26] *Ibid.*, p. 90.
[27] *Ibid.*, pp. 91–92.
[28] *Ibid.*, p. 93.

Each of us comes to desire what society expects of us. We want to obey rules. We want to become whatever roles our society assigns to us. The prison metaphor is defective because it does not reveal the full power of social control: "Society not only determines what we do but also what we are. In other words, social location involves our being as well as our conduct."[29]

The task of "puppet sociology" is to discover how it is that men come to love their chains. What are the dynamics of the puppet stage? Two basic notions have been used in "puppet sociology": "role" and "ideology." Role investigations provide some insight into how men come to *love* their own circumstance. Studies of ideology reveal how men seek to make their loves appear *reasonable*.

One can think of the biography of an individual as an account of the sequence of situations that he encounters during the course of each day, year, and decade:

From the viewpoint of the individual participant this means that each situation he enters confronts him with specific expectations and demands of him specific responses to these expectations. As we have already seen, powerful pressures exist in just about any social situation to ensure that the proper responses are indeed forthcoming. Society can exist by virtue of the fact that most of the time most people's definitions of the most important situations at least coincide approximately.[30]

A student in a university has expectations about his own behavior in university classes; his professors, most likely, share these expectations. A man may act like a student in a university class; like a father with his own children; like a boss, should he support himself in business; and like a teacher, should he on other occasions have this responsibility.

A role, then, may be defined as a typified response to a typified expectation. Society has predefined the fundamental typology. To use the language of the theater, from which the concept of role is derived, we can say that society provides the script for all the *dramatis personae*. The individual actors, . . . need but slip into the roles already assigned to them before the curtain goes up. As long as they play their roles as provided for in this script, the social play can proceed as planned.[31]

Roles are patterns of response appropriate to specific situations. Associated with each role is an identity or label that is socially bestowed:

Every role in society has attached to it a certain identity. . . . Some of these identities are trivial and temporary ones, as in some occupations that demand

[29] *Ibid.*, pp. 93–94.
[30] *Ibid.*, p. 94.
[31] *Ibid.*, p. 95.

little modification in the being of their practitioners. It is not difficult to change
from garbage collector to night watchman. It is considerably more difficult to
change from clergyman to officer. It is very, very difficult to change from Negro
to white. And it is almost impossible to change from man to woman. These differences in the ease of role changing ought not to blind us to the fact that even
identities that we consider to be our essential selves have been socially assigned.
Just as there are racial roles to be acquired and identified with, so there are sexual
roles. To say "I am a man" is just as much a proclamation of role as to say "I
am a colonel in the U. S. Army." We are well aware of the fact that one is born
a male, while not even the most humorless marine imagines himself to have been
born with a golden eagle sitting on his umbilical cord. But to be biologically male
is a far cry from the specific socially defined (and, . . . socially relative) role that
goes with the statement "I am a man."[32]

Playing a role is not a conscious, deliberate act; it is an interaction with
other people in a socially defined situation.

. . . the exception is the man who reflects on his roles and his role changes . . .
Even very intelligent people, when faced with doubt about their roles in society,
will involve themselves even more in the doubled activity rather than withdraw
into reflection. The theologian who doubts his faith will pray more and increase
his church attendance, the businessman beset by qualms about his rat-race activities starts going to the office on Sundays . . . , and the terrorist who suffers
from nightmares volunteers for nocturnal executions . . . . they are perfectly correct in this course of action. Each role has its inner discipline, what Catholic mo-
nastics would call its "formation." The role forms, shapes, patterns both action
and actor. It is very difficult to pretend in this world. Normally, one becomes what
one plays at.[33]

The "puppet sociology" view is that the individual is not a substantial
entity who moves from place to place in society; rather, the individual is a
process of interactions in a range of social situations. The individual *is* the
various roles he plays. People who are regarded as normal must have, or
appear to have, a consistent repertoire of roles.

Thus society will allow an individual to be an emperor at work and a serf
at home, but it will not permit him to impersonate a police officer or to wear the
costume assigned to the other sex. . . . to stay within the limits set to his mas-
querades, the individual may have to resort to complicated maneuvers to make
sure that one role remains segregated from the other.[34]

The sociologist whose interest is exploring the puppet theater seeks to
answer such questions as these:
1. What roles does a society offer?

[32] *Ibid.*, p. 98.
[33] *Ibid.*, pp. 97–98.
[34] *Ibid.*, p. 107.

2. What alterations in roles are occurring? With what social effect?
3. What are the ceremonies of role support?

The "prison" metaphor focused attention upon the structures and institutions that determine human behavior. The "puppet" metaphor directs attention to the means by which men come to love the roles that social structures create. "Every social structure selects those persons that it needs for its functioning and eliminates in one way or another those that do not fit. If no persons are available to be selected, they will have to be invented—or rather, they will be produced in accordance with the required specifications."[35]

Not only must men love their chains; the chains must be thought to be wise.

Let us construct a simple illustration. Let us assume that in a primitive society some needed foodstuff can be obtained only by traveling to where it grows through treacherous, shark-infested waters. Twice every year the men of the tribe set out in their precarious canoes to get this food. Now, let us assume that the religious beliefs of this society contain an article of faith that says that every man who fails to go on this voyage will lose his virility, except for the priests, whose virility is sustained by their daily sacrifices to the gods. This belief provides a motivation for those who expose themselves to the dangerous journey and simultaneously a legitimation for the priests who regularly stay at home. Needless to add, we will suspect . . . that it was the priests who cooked up the theory in the first place. . . . We will assume that we have here a priestly ideology. But this does not mean that the latter is not functional for the society as a whole —after all, somebody must go or there will be starvation.[36]

An "ideology" is a set of ideas that support and make rational the vested interest of certain groups within a society. When it is necessary, ideologies distort reality to make a particular social structure appear rational:

. . . the racial mythology of the American South serves to legitimate a social system practiced by millions . . . The ideology of "free enterprise" serves to camouflage the monopolistic practices of large American corporations whose only common characteristic with the old-style entrepreneur is a steadfast readiness to defraud the public. The Marxist ideology, . . . serves to legitimate the tyranny practiced by the Communist Party apparatus whose interests have about as much in common with Karl Marx's as those of Elmer Gantry had with the Apostle Paul's. In each case, the ideology both justifies what is done by the group whose vested interest is served and interprets social reality in such a way that the justification is made plausible. This interpretation often appears bizarre to an outsider who "does not understand the problem" (that is, who does not share the vested interest). The Southern racist must simultaneously maintain that white women have a profound revulsion at the very thought of sexual rela-

35 *Ibid.,* pp. 109–110.
36 *Ibid.,* p. 111.

tions with a Negro and that the slightest interracial sociability will straightway lead to such sexual relations. And the corporation executive will maintain that his activities to fix prices are undertaken in defense of a free market. And the Communist Party official will have a way of explaining that the limitation of electoral choice to candidates approved by the party is an expression of true democracy.[37]

Ideologies serve two primary functions:
1. They legitimate existing social structures.
2. They assuage suffering.
Structures are legitimated by the language and ideas that order experience:

. . . society supplies our values, our logic and the store of information (or, . . . misinformation) that constitutes our "knowledge." Very few people, . . . are in a position to reevaluate what has been imposed on them. They actually feel no need for reappraisal because the world view into which they have been socialized appears self-evident to them. Since it is also so regarded by almost everyone they are likely to deal with in their own society, the world view is self-validating. Its "proof" lies in the reiterated experience of other men who take it for granted also. To put this perspective of the sociology of knowledge into one succinct proposition: Reality is socially constructed.[38]

Suffering is alleviated by the affirmation of a mythology that makes its endurance intelligible. Religions often explain suffering as the means to redemption and salvation. Political ideologies justify present suffering for the accomplishment of future Utopias. Social ideologies may interpret social difficulties as the price for adhering to the traditional and established social ways. If people are to suffer, and if they are not to revolt against outrageous circumstances, then they must conceive purpose and meaning in their own distress. Ideologies provide the myths for such assuagements.

The study of ideology leads to the investigation of the social location of ideas. All ideas are examined to identify the social location of those who thought them. The study of ideology:

. . . more clearly than any other branch of sociology, makes clear what is meant by saying that the sociologist is the guy who keeps asking "Says who?" It rejects the pretense that thought occurs in isolation from the social context within which particular men think about particular things. Even in . . . very abstract ideas that seemingly have little social connection, the sociology of knowledge attempts to draw the line from the thought of the thinker to his social world. This can be seen most easily in those instances when thought serves to legitimate a particular social situation, . . . when it explains, justifies and sanctifies it.[39]

The investigation of ideology involves asking such questions as these:

[37] *Ibid.,* p. 112.
[38] *Ibid.,* pp. 117–118.
[39] *Ibid.,* p. 111.

1. How do people in the various locations of the society explain and interpret their own social reality?
2. What are the distortions in the perception of reality?
3. What ideas are under greatest threat?
4. What are the most self-evident, the most taken-for-granted features of
   the ideology of the society?

The sociologist raises such questions because he conceives each individual
as one who:

> . . . derives his world view socially in very much the same way that he derives
> his roles and his identity. In other words, his emotions and his self-interpretation
> like his actions are predefined for him by society, and so is his cognitive approach
> to the universe that surrounds him. This fact Alfred Schuetz has caught in his
> phrase "world-taken-for-granted"—the system of . . . self-evident and self-
> validating assumptions about the world that each society engenders in the course
> of its history.[40]

Human beings are not imprisoned in a social milieu:

> A more adequate representation of social reality . . . would be the puppet
> theater, with the curtain rising on the little puppets jumping about on the ends of
> their invisible strings, cheerfully acting out the little parts that have been assigned
> to them in the tragi-comedy to be enacted. The analogy, however, does not go
> far enough. The Pierrot of the puppet theater has neither will nor consciousness.
> But the Pierrot of the social stage wants nothing more than the fate awaiting
> him in the scenario—and he has a whole system of philosophy to prove it.[41]

DRAMA

The fictions of "prison" and "puppet" illuminate social reality and, undoubtedly, have a degree of useful validity. Even taken together, however,
they are defective.

> It is clear, . . . that in a situation whose meaning is strongly established by
> tradition and common consent a single individual cannot accomplish very much
> by proffering a deviant definition. At the very least, . . . he can bring about his
> alienation from the situation. The possibility of marginal existence in society is
> already an indication that the commonly agreed-upon meanings are not omnip-
> otent in their capacity to coerce. But more interesting are those cases where
> individuals succeed in capturing enough of a following to make their deviant
> interpretations of the world stick, at least within the circle of this following.[42]

"Anomie," an idea first used by Durkheim, is a symptom of both the success and the failure of society. With the anomic, society has failed to work

---

[40] *Ibid.,* p. 117.
[41] *Ibid.,* p. 121.
[42] *Ibid.,* p. 126.

its will; and the anomic demonstrate, at the same time, the minimal success of resisting the blandishments of "prison" and "puppet theater."

"Drama sociology" introduces "intentionality" as the legitimate concern of the sociologist:

Part of the inexorable impression conveyed by the Durkheimian and related views of society comes from their not paying sufficient attention to the historical process itself. No social structure, however massive it may appear in the present, existed in this massivity from the dawn of time. Somewhere . . . each one of its salient features was concocted by human beings, whether they were charismatic visionaries, clever crooks, conquering heroes or just individuals in . . . power who hit on what seemed to them a better way of running the show. Since all social systems were created by men, it follows that men can also change them. Indeed, one of the limitations of the aforementioned views of society (which, . . . give us a valid perspective on social reality) is that it is difficult to account for change within their frame of reference.[43]

"Drama sociology" confronts the fundamental social paradox: ". . . society defines us, but is in turn defined by us. . . . As soon as we view society in this way, . . . it appears very much more fragile than it did from the other vantage point. . . . it is not only ourselves but society that exists by virtue of definition."[44]

Just as there is no total power in society, there is no total impotence. Control systems are in constant need of confirmation and re-confirmation, just as is individual identity.

"Drama sociology" is primarily concerned with the task of exploring the paradox of mutual definition between societies and individuals. Berger suggests that prosaic insight into the artifice of society may be obtained by deliberately altering a role in an established situation:

. . . pretend to be a tolerant but firm abstainer at a New York cocktail party, or an initiate of some mystic cult at a Methodist church picnic, or a psychoanalyst at a businessmen's luncheon—in each case, . . . the introduction of a dramatic character that does not fit into the scenario of the particular play seriously threatens the role-playing of those who do fit. Experiences such as these may lead to a sudden reversal in one's view of society—from an awe-inspiring vision of an edifice made of massive granite to the picture of a toy-house precariously put together with *papier mâché*. While such metamorphosis may be disturbing to people who have hitherto had great confidence in the stability and rightness of society, it can also have a very liberating effect on those more inclined to look upon the latter as a giant sitting on top of them, and not necessarily a friendly giant at that.[45]

[43] *Ibid.,* p. 128.
[44] *Ibid.,* p. 129.
[45] *Ibid.,* p. 131.

In the effort to explore the social paradox, sociologists may raise such questions as these:

1. What techniques for resisting the will of society are being used?
2. How does the redefinition of society occur?
3. What dramatic roles are being threatened?
4. What new dramatic roles are coming into being?
5. What ideologies are dying? What are competing alternatives?
6. What are the carriers of innovation? Men and ideas? Structural changes in society?

"Drama sociology" focuses upon social change. Society is a process. To understand it, one must uncover what is happening in the lives of men.

We thus arrive at a third picture of society, . . . society as a stage populated with living actors. This third picture does not obliterate the previous two, but it is more adequate in terms of the additional social phenomena we have considered. . . . the dramatic model of society . . . does not deny that the actors on the stage are constrained by all the external controls set up by the impresario and the internal ones of the role itself. All the same, they have options—of playing their parts enthusiastically or sullenly, of playing with inner conviction or with "distance" and, sometimes, of refusing to play at all. Looking at society through the medium of this dramatic model greatly changes our general sociological perspective. Social reality now seems to be precariously perched on the cooperation of many individuals—or . . . acrobats engaged in perilous balancing acts, holding up between them the swaying structure of the social world.[46]

PRISON, PUPPET, AND DRAMA

The social utility of uncovering the three perspectives of "classic sociology" is that it confronts each of us with the possibility of examining his own human drama.

The animal, if it reflected on the matter of following its instincts, would say, "I have no choice." Men, explaining why they obey their institutional imperatives, say the same. The difference is that the animal would be saying the truth; the men are deceiving themselves. Why? Because, in fact, they *can* say "no" to society, and often have done so. There may be very unpleasant consequences if they take this course. They can not even think about it as a possibility, because they take their own obedience for granted. Their institutional character may be the only identity they can imagine having, with the alternative seeming to them as a jump into madness. This does not change the fact that the statement "I must" is a deceptive one in almost every social situation.[47]

Berger borrows the concept of "bad faith" from Jean-Paul Sartre to refer to the human tendency to say "I must" when there is no real imperative.

[46] *Ibid.*, p. 138.
[47] *Ibid.*, p. 142.

. . . "bad faith" is to pretend something is necessary that in fact is voluntary.
"Bad faith" is thus a flight from freedom, a dishonest evasion of the "agony of
choice." "Bad faith" expresses itself in innumerable human situations from the
most commonplace to the most catastrophic. . . . The terrorist who kills and
excuses himself by saying that he had no choice because the party ordered him
to kill is in "bad faith," because he pretends that his existence is necessarily linked
with the party, while in fact this linkage is the consequence of his own choice. . . .
"bad faith" covers society like a film of flies. The very possibility of "bad faith,"
however, shows us the reality of freedom. Man can be in "bad faith" only because
he is free and does not wish to face his freedom. . . . attempt to escape that
liberty is doomed to defeat. . . . as Sartre has famously put it, we are "condemned
to freedom."[48]

The study of sociology in the "classic tradition" uncovers the fact that
society is an immense apparatus of "bad faith."

Each role carries with it the possibility of "bad faith." Every man who says
"I have no choice" in referring to what his social role demands of him is engaged
in "bad faith." . . . this confession will be true to the extent that there is no choice
within that particular role. Nevertheless, the individual has the choice of stepping
outside the role. . . . given certain circumstances, a businessman has "no choice"
but brutally to destroy a competitor, unless he is to go bankrupt himself, but
it is he who chooses brutality over bankruptcy. . . . It is true that in some cases
a judge has "no choice" but to sentence a man to death, but in doing so he chooses
to remain a judge, an occupation chosen by him in the knowledge that it
might lead to this, and he chooses not to resign instead when faced with the
prospect of this duty. Men are responsible for their actions. They are in "bad
faith" when they attribute to iron necessity what they themselves are choosing
to do.[49]

Society may be thought of as a network of roles, each one of which may
be an excuse for failure and an opportunity for freedom.

We are social beings and our existence is bound to specific social locations. The
same social situations that can become traps of "bad faith" can also be occasions
for freedom. Every social role can be played knowingly or blindly. And insofar
as it is played knowingly, it can become a vehicle of our own decisions. Every
social institution can be an alibi, an instrument of alienation from our freedom.
But at least some institutions can become protective shields for the actions of
free men. In this way, an understanding of "bad faith" does not necessarily lead
us to a view of society as the universal realm of illusion, but rather illuminates
more clearly the paradoxical and infinitely precarious character of social existence.[50]

[48] *Ibid.,* p. 143.
[49] *Ibid.,* pp. 143–144.
[50] *Ibid.,* p. 145.

The study of society is one way in which an individual may begin to construct his own identity, rather than to take on whatever roles may happen to be assigned to him by the accidents of birth and circumstance. "Society provides us with warm, reasonably comfortable caves, in which we can huddle with our fellows, beating on the drums that drown out the howling hyenas of the surrounding darkness. 'Ecstasy' is the act of stepping outside the caves, alone, to face the night."[51]

The social world we experience is infinitely complex. Any effort to say anything about it involves an element of irony. The sociologist's general intellectual stance is ironical because he seeks for underlying reasons for the actions and beliefs of men. His method of inquiry is ironical because he constructs heuristic fictions and then seeks to examine what people do in the light of his fiction.

Three metaphors have had a prominent place in the development of sociology: "prison," "puppet," and "drama." To view the social world as a prison focuses attention on social locations and typical behavior patterns that are associated with the various locations. To think of the human condition as a puppet state directs attention to the fact that men do not seek to escape their prisons. The concepts of role and ideology help illuminate the way in which both behavior and thought may be related to social location. An awareness of the paradox that men and society mutually define each other leads to the construction of the drama metaphor and the study of intentionality in human affairs.

In general, sociology proceeds by posing and answering questions. Sociological questions have a distinctive character:

1. They are related to heuristic fictions regarding human societies.
2. They involve the key concepts of location, institution, role, ideology, and intentionality.
3. They must be formulated so that eventually they focus attention upon specific happenings in selected milieux.

Questions are answered as a result of the examination and cross-examination of the "tracks" of human happenings that are made to occur. Specific people are selected and interviewed. Particular meetings, social gatherings, or ceremonial occasions are observed. Statistical data relating to the incidence of crime, the volume of business, or the percentage of voters who elect officials may be scrutinized.

An essential part of sociological activity is writing. As specific questions are answered, arguments that lead to the solution of more general questions must be formulated. This can only be done with care in writing. Writing permits the objectification of thought. It permits criticism, evaluation, analy-

[51] *Ibid.*, p. 150.

sis, and revision. The effort to write with clarity, for a specific audience, is a constant demand upon sociologists.

Paradigmatic Tasks of Sociologists

Based on our analysis of sociological thought, a number of paradigmatic sociological tasks have been identified. These tasks may be conveniently divided into four types: tasks related to the identification of basic sociological problems; tasks involved in the development of general questions that direct attention to various aspects of social happenings; tasks related to confronting people and documents; tasks related to writing reports based on the experience of inquiry.

IDENTIFYING AND CLARIFYING SOCIOLOGICAL PROBLEMS

1. Identify the major issue upon which attention is to be focused.
2. Identify explicitly the value conflicts that are involved with the issue.
3. Think about the issue in its largest context.
4. Examine relevant literature.
5. Resist sociological imperialism.
6. Formulate the issue into general questions that direct attention to a specific milieu or range of milieux.

Issues–An issue is a crisis of institutional arrangements. It may involve such things as unemployment, anomie, marriage, nationalism, the uses of political power, and the distortions of ideology that are implicit in religious, economic, or political views. A task of sociologists is to identify the issue or issues that influence the way in which men live.

Values–A defining task of sociologists is to seek to avoid the uncritical presuppositions of any particular value system in the formulation of sociological problems. What moralists, businessmen, military leaders, or policemen think of as "social problems" are not "sociological problems." The problem of sociology is not to discover what has gone wrong from the point of view of management, moralists, or military men; the problem is to discover, as concretely as possible, how society works. Attention can be focused on institutions, social locations, or social change. The concern is with the institution of marriage and not the problem of divorce. Divorce, for example, may turn out to be a highly desirable custom from certain viewpoints. Sociologists must seek to form their questions so that they will not presuppose, uncritically, the value system of a social class or of a bureaucratic elite.

Sociological inquiry is inescapably involved with the values of the investigator and of the society within which he is working. These values must be specifically encountered.

Context of the Problem–Horowitz[52] has suggested that the problems of sociology can only be understood in an international context. Mills[53] has suggested that the nation is the smallest unit within which meaningful sociological problems can be formulated. An important sociological task is to formulate problems in a national or international context.

Relevant Literature–Science is a cumulative enterprise. To pose new questions, one must know what others have done. To avoid uneconomical, empirical investigation, one must discover ideas that actually require empirical investigation. Sociologists seek to make the literature serve the interests of the investigation. The inquirer can learn: (a) what the status of information regarding the problem is; (b) what conflicts in the interpretation of the information may exist; and (c) what possible avenues may be empirically investigated.

Imperialism–Professional sociologists or students in school should remember, as they formulate their problems, that their perspective on human events is one among many.

Milieu or Milieux–The most difficult task for the sociologist is, finally, to transform a general interest, such as the crisis of cities, underdeveloped regions, or work, into a set of questions about a relatively limited range of human happenings.

DEVELOPING GENERAL QUESTIONS

The general questions that arise in sociological investigations are related to the three basic sociological fictions: "prison," "puppet," and "drama." There are tasks associated with each of the fictions.

Prison–The sociologist using the prison idea poses questions that relate to locations and institutions that metaphorically regulate society.

Puppet–The sociologist using the puppet fiction raises questions about the variety of roles and the techniques of role support that are to be found within a particular society. He seeks distortions of ideology and identifies threats to prevailing value systems.

[52] IRVING L. HOROWITZ, ed., *The New Sociology, Essays in Social Science and Social Theory in Honor of C. Wright Mills* (New York: The Oxford University Press, 1964).
[53] C. WRIGHT MILLS, *The Sociological Imagination* (New York: Grove, 1961).

Drama–The sociologist concerned with drama sociology tries to discover techniques that are used to resist the metaphoric will of society, focusing his attention upon the alternatives and innovations in social organization.

CONFRONTING PEOPLE AND DOCUMENTS

Unlike historians, sociologists induce "tracks." They interview selected people, observe social gatherings and political meetings, and participate in community affairs.

Sociologists pose their general questions to themselves. They then devise the questions they direct to other people. The people to whom sociologists talk could not answer directly the general questions that interest sociologists. The sociologists can only answer their own questions on the basis of a scrutiny of the "tracks" of their various personal experiences with people and events.

Basic tasks of sociology are to induce the "tracks," and, then, to interpret them. Sociological tracks are the records of interviews, descriptions of observed social situations, and autobiographical reports that an investigator may be able to collect and assemble. Once these tracks have been obtained, the investigator must cross-examine them in the hope that he can develop answers to his general questions about the society that he is investigating.

WRITING

In order to find out what he has really discovered, a sociologist must write down what he has found out about the way in which society works in the particular milieu that he has investigated.

Sociologists write so that they may examine and criticize their own ideas, so that other sociologists may appraise and judge what has been written, and so that generally interested people may understand what has been done and discovered.

The task of writing is to put ideas into communicable form. Mills[54] suggests that a writer should think of what he writes as speech. He must then think of the audience that is to listen to his speech and adopt a style of writing likely to be understood by that audience.

Teaching Social Study

A major problem of teaching social study is to help students become sensitive to the human source of all human knowledge.

Each social science has a sense of the noun and a sense of the verb: a teacher's obligation is to help students engage in the activity of *history* or

[54] *Ibid.*

sociology, appraise the findings produced by such disciplines, and distinguish between the events and situations studied and the accounts of those events that men propose.

Social studying should be the fundamental activity nurtured by the elementary social-studies program. The plural of "study" denotes the range of residue that the student of social events must confront and the various modes of inquiry in which students should learn to engage.

Teachers who are concerned with sensitizing their students to the cultural influences on historians can easily obtain histories produced in Great Britain that reflect the English view of our American adventure. Similarly, the Southern and the Northern accounts of the Civil War are not hard to find. The purpose of using a variety of historical writings dealing with one significant event is to help children understand the limitations that men impose upon themselves in the ways in which they know about each other. Students should learn to be critical. They should expect conflicts of opinion in historical writing.

In a similar fashion, elementary-school teachers should seek to help students practice the mode of inquiry that is engaged in by sociologists and anthropologists.[55] Students can observe school functions, athletic contests, playground behavior, and other similar activities as participants. They can interview and observe professional people, businessmen, teachers, homemakers, and so on, to pursue lines of inquiry regarding their own social reality.

The study of the Now and Here provides some of the most exciting possibilities of the entire social-studies curriculum. Social study in the elementary school can lead students to study problems and issues rather than to memorize information related to topics. A person can only study, as we have defined it, when he confronts a problem. A student can become acquainted with the context of a book, but this may not involve him in the study of history or contemporary affairs. We have said that students in school should study problems. But what is a problem? It has taken us many pages to elaborate upon our notion of study; associated with this notion is our conception of a problem.

There are two kinds of problems with which you may be familiar: problems of choice, and problems of knowledge. Problems of choice are problems of everyday life:

1. What should the United Nations do about the Gaza Strip?
2. What should a city council do about the problem of delinquency?

[55] This book focuses attention upon the social sciences that are often associated with the elementary-school curriculum. We give little explicit attention to geography. But see Richard Hartshorne, "What Is Meant by Geography?" in Part IV, where the author gives an account of geography that might be compared with the text's discussion of history, sociology, and anthropology.

3. What should the United States Senate do about foreign aid?
4. What should a parent do about his daughter's coming home late?
5. What should a teacher do about sharing responsibility for curricular planning with his students?

Problems of knowledge are problems of understanding:
1. Why have the Seneca Indians been dispossessed of their treaty-protected tribal lands?
2. Why is delinquency a chronic social problem?
3. Why do so many children not like school?
4. Why are some of our cities so ugly?
5. Why are so many fish dying in our rivers?

The solution to a problem of choice is a rule of practice implicitly or explicitly based on notions of value. The solution to a problem of knowledge is a set of true sentences that together are an answer to the problem.

We think that students in school do not usually confront problems of choice that are concerned with major social problems, but every student confronts the responsibility to understand the human condition as best he can. To work with a problem of knowledge is to engage in an honest task; we feel that the adventure of inquiry should become the primary motive for learning.

Perhaps this discussion could be clarified with an illustration. You are, no doubt, familiar with the ways of life that are commonly attributed to the ancient Athenians and the Spartans. You may not, however, be familiar with an interesting problem connected with the Spartans. The Spartans were not always warlike. At one time in their history, Herodotus mentions, they were thought to be the most poorly governed people in Greece. They were an affluent, luxury-loving, effete people. Archaeological remains suggest that this is the case. The problem is this: Why or under what circumstances did the Spartans change from a pleasure-loving, artistic people into a society devoted exclusively to the cause of war? To pose the question and to seek an answer to it is to engage in history.

We suggest that you seek to answer this question. Any answer you may formulate will depend on your judgment regarding the presently existing residue of that long-past event. No one can tell you the answer. History is the business of writing answers to questions for which there are no answers in the back of the book. Each man must be responsible for his own judgment regarding this event. The obligation upon the historian is that he must deal intelligently with the residue of that time. He must not ignore inconvenient residue; he must be an honest craftsman.

IV

The Discipline of Inquiry

The Discipline of Study

The discipline of study is to submit one's ideas and hunches to the *test of things,* the use of experience or observation to confirm or deny the usefulness of ideas. A hard discipline, it is one with which few of us have had much experience. We learn, most of our lives, from authorities. To some extent, the process of public education duplicates the process of family education; teachers and books become criteria of truth, just as father and mother were criteria of goodness.

The responsibility of teachers is to help children become *students.* One definition of a pupil is a person who learns what he knows on the basis of what an authority tells him. A student, however, may be defined as a person who learns on the basis of self-directed inquiry, disciplined by the test of things.

Probably no study is more difficult than social study; the test of things is not always obviously relevant. Each of us is born into a society that instructs us regarding the natural order of civilized life. Other societies are regarded as quaint, primitive, debauched, or slovenly. The Eskimos of Greenland, for example, thought that white ethnographers who studied Eskimo society were searching for a model of good manners and morals that their own lands desperately needed.

In the study of physical phenomena, examination of actual occurrences is obviously relevant. The authority of custom at one time affirmed that heavy weights fall toward the earth much faster than light weights, but the observation that heavy and light weights fall at the same speed transformed the traditional view. The criterion of things was relevant.

Our understanding of the physical world has been profoundly modified by inquiry that is disciplined by the criterion of things. There has been no comparable modification of our understanding of our social world. Today, as in the past, our understanding of social events and processes is influenced more by faith and custom than by inquiry.

The purpose of social inquiry is not to destroy the tribal view of the world that we all possess. Each of us can participate in and enjoy the ritual, customs, and language of his own society. The purpose of social inquiry and of social study in the elementary school is to help men and students in school develop a view that is independent of tribal traditions and considerations, of themselves, their circumstances, and the circumstances of others. The purpose of study is to encourage general understanding of the human condition. General understanding is nurtured by inquiry disciplined by the test of things.

Replacing Authority as a Basis of Knowledge

The quest for an alternative to authority as a basis of knowledge is ancient. In early Egypt, there were few alternatives to authority as a criterion of truth. Wise men decided, on their own authority, the amount of grain that a granary contained. Important interpersonal problems were resolved by the magical intuition of a professional knower. Much later, in ancient Greece, oracles determined the movements of armies. In a similar way, modern oracles pronounce support or opposition to "medicare" or federal aid to education, the effort to reorganize the judicial system, or the "look and say" method of teaching reading. Oracular knowledge is always mystical; it makes use of simple idealization of very complex situations, and its answers are always complete. Wherever the authority of wise men is the primary criterion of truth and knowledge, however, controversy is widespread.

Customary Procedures

Public procedures for estimating the amount of grain in a granary or the area of a piece of land were the first alternatives to the criterion of authority which men devised. The ancient Egyptians developed procedures, or rules of thumb, or mathematical formulae that became standard or customary fashions of estimating volume or area. Some of these rules of thumb were rather inaccurate. But a standard, customary, public procedure, even though wrong, was socially useful. The Egyptians did not invent a systematic way of developing these formulae or rules of thumb, but they did initiate the use of a public, customary procedure to confront certain problematic situations.

Such a customary procedure for determining truth was a revolutionary change. Although the criterion of authority remained undisputed in most aspects of human life, in one phase of human intercourse, at least, a public procedure became a standard method of resolving interpersonal disagreements.

Logic

A second great effort to replace the criterion of authority in determining truth or knowledge was the invention of logic. What we know as logic was invented in ancient Greece. The Greeks sought to curtail the influence of the authoritative "wise men" and to discover a means of identifying truths to which all reasonable men could give assent. They found in logic an instrument for the discovery of truth or knowledge.

The Greek invention had two aspects. The first concerned self-evident truths, also called axioms. Obvious features of human experience, these truths could not be proven. One such famous truth concerned parallel lines. No logician or mathematician can prove that these lines do not meet. It is a self-evident truth of the real world. The second aspect of the invention concerned the existence of fundamental rules of logical or correct thinking, which the Greeks identified and clearly formulated.

The essence of the Greek invention was that argument from self-evident truths, following the rules of logic, would produce *truth*. Thus truth could be publicly ascertained.

Whatever statements could be derived by logical means from the self-evident truths of nature were true, and had to be true, regardless of the passions and the self-interests of the men involved in this pursuit. Here was a clear alternative to the criterion of authority as a basis of truth and knowledge.

This way of truth-seeking persisted in Western culture for over a thousand years. Eventually, however, it created as many difficulties as it solved. A major problem of the use of logic to identify what men may know is that men may differ about the "self-evidence" of certain "truths." A second problem is that men may disagree about the nature of logical or correct thinking.

What are the self-evident truths of nature? Since no man can prove these truths, some person, on his own authority, must say what they may be. Who is going to have the right to say? The criterion of authority has not been abandoned; it is merely disguised.

Consider an example of the problem of self-evident truths. If it were self-evidently true that the universe is perfect, and, say, that the number seven is perfect, then it must follow that there are seven planets in our solar system. This is one dilemma: logical thinking alone cannot yield any knowledge of the empirical world.

The Test of Things

At one time in Europe, the accepted view was that our earth was the center of the solar system, and that the number of planets was a perfect number. Men were burned at the stake for proposing anything so contrary, so traitorous, as systematic observation to determine the empirical validity of customary views. Science, inquiry disciplined by the test of things, began when Galileo looked through his telescope, dropped weights from his tower, and carefully watched the movement of a pendulum. Since Galileo, the test of things has been relevant to the study of the natural world.

The study of our natural world was impeded for many centuries by conceptions of logic and the natural order that made observation unnecessary or seditious. Similar conceptions impeded the development of social science. Anthropologists who seek illustrations of a theory of stages of civilization will certainly find them—and little else. Historians who seek to find analogies between the growth and decay in organic life and human societies will certainly find them—and, again, little else. The preconceptions of social scientists have not made observation irrelevant, but they often have made observation narrowly selective and unrepresentative. The preconceptions of social science have appeared to be self-evident and natural, just as the preconceptions of the Greeks appeared to them to be natural and apparent.

Self-evident truths of logic or social reality are no longer as incontrovertible as they once appeared to be. The Greek laws of logic are not as correct as logicians imagined for many hundreds of years. Modern logicians have discovered several sorts of logic, each with its own advantage. Some person must still say when one or another sort of logic is appropriate. The decision to accept one or another set of self-evident notions regarding man and the world or to accept one or another system of logic is a human choice; logic provides no escape from the criterion of authority as a basis of knowing.

Disaffection with Greek logic led men to begin to use telescopes; that is, they sought to test their ideas by observing the things around them. Centuries of such scientific investigation have brought us many insights into the nature of the physical world. We have barely begun to be scientific or empirical in our approach to understanding our social world, however; observation has often been a means of illustrating our conceptions rather than of testing them.

Some things about themselves, their circumstances, and their effects upon each other, men can know by "looking" around them. Such empirically tested knowledge is not based on the authority of wise men, nor on the authority of self-evident truths. It is based on the variety of questions that men can learn to ask and to answer by confronting "things."

On many occasions, believing an authority is the only intelligent action one can take. When a student is in school, however, his obligation is not to believe authorities, but to learn how to become one. A student becomes his own authority when he learns how to test empirically the ideas that he encounters. The task of instruction in social studies is to help pupils who read, listen to, and believe a multitude of wise men become students who can put their own ideas and the ideas of others to appropriate tests.

Social study is a dialogue with "things," involving both a *method* and an *art*. The art is concerned with the invention of questions and concepts; the method is to confront things. The problem of teaching social study is to nurture the art and to implement the demand to confront "things."

The art of inquiry may be demonstrated. Teachers can publicly formulate questions, can express curiosity, can order their questions in some productive series. Although it may be publicly displayed, only the results of the art can be observed. Invention is always a personal activity, always hidden from public view. Instruction relating to the art of inquiry must always proceed indirectly; no recipe exists for producing inventive, curious, inquiring students.

The discipline of study may be imposed. A teacher can systematically challenge students with the primary obligation of study: Make use of the Criterion of Things. In addition, a teacher can provide students with opportunities to practice the art of inquiry and to communicate what they discover, thus facing the task of transforming an ineffable human experience with sights, sounds, and thoughts into language. A teacher of social study must help his students to make use of the criterion of things and to seek clarity in their efforts to write or communicate their thoughts.

The Criterion of Things and Social Study

One who studies must formulate his questions in such fashion that they may be answered through observation rather than through appeal to authority. The problem involves the transformation of rather large, more or less unanswerable, questions—the Big Questions—into a series of small, more or less answerable, questions. These small questions must lead somewhere, and they must be answerable through observation.

The Mystery Model

The above paragraph is easy to write, but the discipline that it affirms is not easy to practice. A crude model of this discipline, however, is familiar. Television, films, and numbers of books have presented murder mysteries. Essentially, in such a mystery, someone gets killed; a historian-detective seeks to discover the murderer. The large, unanswerable question is simply, "Who did it?" The historian-hero-detective seeks to answer this Big Question by formulating a series of productive, smaller questions, which can be answered by the close observation of some of the following:

1. The place where the event occurred.
2. The testimony of the various people involved in the event.
3. Relevant documents, such as wills and contracts.
4. Personal and business records: letters, travel reports, expense reports.
5. The testimony of other relevant people.

The historian-hero-detective is limited in what he will discover by the questions he has the wisdom or the good fortune to ask. If enough small questions are asked, and if they lead in the right direction, the culprit is eventually caught. Usually, a number of false leads are pursued. The crude model of inquiry which mystery fiction follows involves these features:

1. A Big Question is identified: Who did it?
2. Small questions are formulated: Who was the deceased? Who was present at the time? Who gave lying testimony? Who stood to benefit by the death?
3. These questions are answered by observations or by scrutiny of reports of observations.
4. An argument is formulated, involving hunches or hypotheses that can be tested by further observations, which leads to the identification of the probable murderer.

There are significant differences between this crude model of inquiry and the procedures that social investigators follow; in its essential features, however, the *mystery model* is the method of social inquiry.

The Big Question

Study begins with the formation of interesting Big Questions. Knowledge of one's ignorance makes study possible; skill at inquiry makes knowledge possible.

Some Big Questions are the result of noticing one's ignorance of certain aspects of his own cultural milieu. An art of inquiry is the ability to select a commonplace aspect of one's everyday life and convert it into a "thing," an object of contemplation and curiosity. Words, customs, institutions, beliefs, and people can become things, simply by noticing them and formulating a Big Question about them. Here are a few examples:

1. When, and under what circumstances, did "OK" come into our language?
2. When, and under what circumstances, was Christmas first celebrated on December 25?
3. When, and under what circumstances, was the jury system with which we are familiar first developed?
4. Every city has many streets. Some of them have distinctive names, for example, Detroit's "Woodward Avenue" and "John R" street. Where, how, and when did these streets get their names?

Some Big Questions develop from acquaintance with information regarding past or contemporary affairs. The art of inquiry here is to convert the information into an object of curiosity and to invent a Big Question concerning it. Here are a few examples:

1. If one learns that the Romans built a great wall in England, then one can ask:

   Why did they build it?

2. If one reads the accounts affirming the devotion of the ancient Spartans to war, then one can ask:

   Why were the Spartans so warlike?

3. If one encounters descriptions of the voyage of Hoei-Shin to the Western Hemisphere in the fifth century A.D., then one can ask:

   How well-established are the facts confirming the accounts of this voyage?

   If he came, then why did he come?

   What effect, if any, did this contact with Chinese culture have on the Indian civilization of Mexico and Central America?

4. If one reads of the migration of Irish monks to the New World in the tenth century, then one can ask:

   How well-established are the facts confirming the accounts of this migration?

   If they came, then why did they come?

   If they came, then why has their adventure here been ignored by historians until now?

5. If one encounters statistics and discussions of the delinquency problem in the United States and the other technologically advanced countries, then one can ask:

   What is the cause of delinquency?

6. If one learns that a Minnesota farmer found, in 1898, a rectangular stone, on which was to be found writing in the runic alphabet, then one can ask:

   How did the stone get there?

These are questions that a class might formulate and seek to answer. Students would have to use the reported findings of others in their search, but they could assign their own interpretations to these findings, and they could confront such original documents as were available and relevant.

An important difference between these questions and the murder-mystery question is that the student must create his own mystery by his questions. The hero-detective is given his mystery. The student must determine his ignorance in formulating his own question.

There is another important difference between the murder-mystery and social inquiry. The murder-mystery usually has a unique solution; with the identification of a murderer, the mystery terminates. No unique solutions can be found to the mysteries with which social scientists work; there may be fifty different ways to write about the cause of war, a migration, or delinquency. The social scientist seeks understanding. New understanding or fresh conception may always provide new ways of thinking about old problems.

Using the Mystery Model

Let us recall the features of social inquiry that are based upon the murder-mystery model:

1. Identify a Big Question that is interesting and may initiate inquiry. It is always possible, of course, to identify questions that will turn out to be fruitless or silly.
2. Translate this Big Question into a variety of smaller questions that, hopefully, may lead you somewhere. Develop the *skill of inquiry* by formulating some of the small questions, so that they may be answered by simple observation.
3. Develop the *art* and *skill* of close observation. Seek to answer the small questions on the basis of observations or the reports of observations.
4. Invent or select concepts and ideas that help order the answers to the small questions, so that an answer to the Big Question may be formulated.

The Search for Clarity

All that we know about human history and the contemporary world is stated in some language. No facet of human knowing is divorced from language. The teacher of social study must thus help his students to develop sensitivity to the powers and limitations of their language.

The power of language lies in its ability to represent, symbolically, ideas and things. But confusion arises when words representing ideas are used as if they represent things. The words "democracy" and "love" represent ideas; the words "cat" and "couch" represent things. One can expect more agreement about the use of the word "cat" than the word "democracy." In either case, the representation is somewhat arbitrary: language only approximately represents the world of ideas and things experienced. No way has been found to represent the difference in taste between red and white wine. The distinctions which are commonplace in one language may be unknown in another. In any case, there are no words or concepts to represent much of everyday experience.

The effort to transform a living experience into the arbitrary symbols of language is always, for all men, difficult. The art and discipline of writing can only be learned by practicing the expression, in language, of one's own thoughts about one's own experience. The report of a scientist and the report of a student in school confront the same challenge.

Good social-scientific work is almost always good literature; Freud, for example, will be a significant literary figure long after his psychology becomes obsolete. Margaret Mead, Ruth Benedict, and David Riesman have influenced American thought as much by their command of English and their use of fresh metaphor as by the substance of their research findings.

A great disservice is done to students in school by sending them off to encyclopedias and other such books, with the assignment to write a report. The student is compelled to read other men's thoughts, steal their sentences, and, at times, their paragraphs. If the theft is done neatly, the reward is often a good grade. The student is rewarded for doing something that undermines his writing capacity. He learns how to use scissors and paste in the construction of what is to pass for his own thoughts; he fails to meet the challenge of writing.

That challenge is simply to select some aspect of ephemeral human experience and to seek to represent the experience, to the extent possible, in language. The experience may result from contact with a person, a newspaper, a photograph, a letter, a crowded street, or a series of such experiences. The chief task of the writer is to decide upon the meaning of his experience in relation to the inquiry in which he is engaged. Most men discover what they know by trying to represent this knowledge in language; the discipline of writing one's thoughts down on paper affords the opportunity to order those thoughts and to criticize them. Writing, criticizing, and rewriting are essential features of scientific work and should be prominent features of a social-studies program.

There are two basic purposes in nurturing the writing capacity of young people in school. First, writing about one's personal experiences provides practice at an important skill that is learned only with practice. Second, as children seek to transform their experiences into language, they will objectify and criticize their own knowledge. They will be compelled to acknowledge the limitations in what they know, and they may be compelled to seek further knowledge and other ideas, as a result of the clarification that expression provides.

Two Illustrations of Inquiry

The preceding sections of this chapter have discussed discipline, inquiry, the appeal to experience, and the formulation of questions in the conduct of inquiry. By way of illustration, let us explore two of the Big Questions that we have formulated.

Juvenile Delinquency

Delinquency is a popular subject these days. A local incident, or an awareness of the general adult concern with the subject, may arouse interest among young people. How would they go about starting an inquiry into delinquent behavior?

1. Identify a Big Question that is interesting and may set the class off in a desirable direction. This question may be suggested by students, or it may be one that a sensitive teacher expects will intrigue his students. Probably the most obvious question will turn up:

    What is the cause of delinquency?

2. Identify some small questions that will start them off, hopefully, in a fruitful direction. Encourage the *skill of inquiry* by stating some of the small questions so that they may be answered through observations, or the appeal to experience, or the *criterion of things*. Again, students may develop these with their teacher's guidance, or a teacher may offer the first few as models of the type of question that can be answered through observing "things." Here are some possibilities:

    a. When do delinquent acts occur? Winter? Summer?
    b. Is there any regularity in the performance of delinquent acts?
    c. Is there a standard conception of a delinquent act?
    d. How are delinquent acts recorded?
    e. What do some selected delinquents have to say about their own behavior?
    f. What do clergymen think about the problem of delinquency?
    g. What do policemen think about the problem of delinquency?

3. Seek to answer the small questions through observations. Social scientists and children in school can make relevant observations regarding each of these questions. Let us consider some possibilities:

    a. There are statistical records which may be obtained from city and state officials. A social scientist or a child may write to juvenile officials and ask for documentary reports.

       For example, an examination of the documents concerning juvenile crime in Detroit will show that delinquency occurs primarily during the time of the year when the public schools are in session. During three-day holidays and during the spring vacation, juvenile crime[1] declines sharply.

       The first small question regarding juvenile crime can be answered. The cause of delinquency, however, is still unknown. But formulating the small questions provides information about which the class can think. Why does the juvenile crime rate rise sharply in Detroit when school starts? What question should be asked next in this series?

    b. What do delinquents say about their own behavior? Social scientists may do their own investigation to answer this small question; school-

---

[1] "Delinquency" and "juvenile crime" refer, in this sentence, to children's being "booked" as offenders by the police.

children will probably have to make use of the reported investigations of others. All scientists make use of the findings of others: science is a cumulative, cooperative enterprise. The problem for teachers and students is to find records of interviews and autobiographical statements that have been made by delinquents. When this material is made available, then it may become the subject of study, and small questions may be formulated regarding the interview material.

c. What views do people hold regarding the character of delinquency? A phase of the study of delinquency may involve an exploration of various personal views. Children in school can sample the views held by members of their own community. Comparisons can be made between the findings of the students and the reported findings of similar studies made by social investigators. Existing views regarding delinquency may turn up ideas that would be useful subjects of further investigation.

4. Invent or choose concepts and notions that will direct further inquiry, and that may help to explain the social behavior or situation that is being studied.

The formation of useful concepts and hunches is a matter of art and judgment. Here are some concepts that are frequently used by investigators into delinquency:

broken homes	overprotection	lack of affection
family stability	growing up absurd	adventure
competence	poverty	life chances

Which of them, if any, may be found useful in the classroom? What others are possible? Perhaps there are many kinds of delinquents, and more than one kind of explanation may have to be invented. The formulation of a hypothesis is always an imaginative act; no methods exist that will always lead to the production of interesting hypotheses. A child in school, like a social scientist, can contemplate the available information and, on the basis of intuition or imagination or judgment, formulate ideas concerning delinquency. These ideas may be tested to see if they account for the available facts, and if they provide any useful means of accounting for problems of delinquency. Delinquency will probably never be finally understood, but some disciplined understanding is possible. The tentative answer to the Big Question will be some kind of argument based on the hunches and the ideas that have been formulated.

5. Encourage the art and discipline of communication. Scientific investigation always ends in a report, sometimes in great literature. Some reports are formulated in a vocabulary only experts can understand, but others may be simple, clear, interesting statements.

All reports of social investigation reveal as much about the investigator as about the subject he is investigating. Consider this brief statement by

Paul Goodman concerning delinquency, and the remedy for it that he believes to be intelligent. After posing the Big Question under discussion, he formulated many small questions and speculated about the answers he found to those questions. His answer is an argument—all answers to Big Questions are arguments. Different men will formulate different arguments because they hold differing beliefs and values. Goodman argues:

Positively, the delinquent behavior seems to speak clearly enough. It asks for what we can't give, but it is in this direction we must go. It asks for manly opportunities to work, make a little money, and have self-esteem; to have some space to bang around in, that is not always somebody's property; to have better schools to open for them horizons of interest; to have more and better sex without fear or shame; to share somehow in the symbolic goods (like the cars) that are made so much of; to have a community and a country to be loyal to; to claim attention and have a voice. These are not outlandish demands. Certainly they cannot be satisfied directly in our present system; they are baffling. That is why the problem is baffling, and the final recourse is to a curfew, to ordinances against carrying knives, to threatening the parents, to reformatories with newfangled names, and to 1,100 more police on the street.[2]

The Spartans

Another Big Question proposed earlier was:
   Why were the Spartans a warlike people?
Inquiry begins with the formulation of Big Questions that are interesting. It is impossible to formulate a Big Question that will initiate study unless the class is acquainted with relevant information and conjecture. Big Questions regarding the ancient Greeks cannot arise if the class knows nothing about the ancient Greeks. A simple preliminary to inquiry is to have the students read the available text materials. The students will discover that the Spartans were warlike, but that the Athenians were democratic, culturally productive, and, although expansionistic, not "Spartan" in their social organization.

All these affirmations about the ancient Greeks are inferences; only the relics of that ancient culture exist today. What we know are the conjectures developed by men who have confronted these relics. Students can begin study by becoming acquainted with the ideas and conjectures.
1. As before, identify a Big Question.
   We believe that the Spartans were warlike because many books tell us so. Some of these books report archaeological discoveries to support this belief. Indeed, the word "spartan" has become an adjective in our language. Why did such a remarkable civilization develop? What plaus-

2 PAUL GOODMAN, *Growing Up Absurd* (New York: Random House, 1956), pp. 50–51.

ible conjectures can be invented and checked that might help to explain or to account for that remarkable society?

2. Formulate small questions to set the class off in a fruitful direction.

   a. Were the Spartans always "spartan"? Is there any evidence of a "non-Spartan" culture among the Spartans? Are there any written reports of any such non-Spartan cultures? Are there any archaeological remains of any such culture?

   b. Who were the Spartans? Were they native to the region? Is there any evidence of invasion or migration?

   c. What was the geography of the region? Were there any unusual or distinctive features of the land or the area?

   The important obligation of a teacher of social inquiry is to insure that some of the smaller questions formulated must be answerable through direct observation of a primary source or document or through the report of some responsible person who has made an observation of a primary document.

   The question, "Were the Spartans always 'spartan'?" is still a Big Question; it calls for an inference or an argument. The question, "Are there any existing documents or reports which affirm that the Spartans were not always 'spartan'?" is a small question. The answer to this question does not call for an inference.

   On the basis of small questions that call for observations, larger questions that call for inferences can be answered. A pattern or set of inferences can be arranged by a social scientist or a student in school to provide an argument that may be regarded as an answer to the Big Question; such an argument may be one of many possible arguments.

3. Seek answers to the small questions through observations.

   On such a question, how might a teacher help his students to observe primary documents or observe the reports of men who themselves have examined primary sources?

   a. Consider the first question: "Were the Spartans always 'spartan'?" The report of a Greek historian who was contemporary with the Spartans and whose work is extant could be considered a primary source. What does Herodotus say?

   Herodotus affirms that the Spartans were recently the most poorly governed people in Greece. He reports that they had been a pleasure-loving, artistic people. This is certainly not "spartan." If the Spartans were not "spartan" shortly before the time of Herodotus, what made them change?

   Note that a tentative answer to the first question has led to a new Big Question: Why did they change? Social inquiry proceeds in this fashion from question to question. Some small questions may turn out to be fruitful, and others may lead into dead ends.

   b. Who were the Spartans? Were they native to the region? Archaeological remains suggest that the people we know as Spartans migrated to the Laconian region before 1200 B.C. They brought techniques for using iron to Greece, and their superior weapons helped them to subdue a native population.

   c. What was the geography of the region? Laconia, one of the richest areas of ancient Greece, was near the major trade routes. It was invaded frequently, the last time by the Spartans.

4. Invent or select concepts that will help to order the available information and lead to the formation of an answer to the Big Question.

   An answer to the Big Question will be some kind of argument, one of several answers possible. A *geographical* answer might be: Sparta was one of the richest agricultural regions of Greece. Much invaded, it produced enormous per capita wealth. There was a large resident population of noncitizens whom the Spartans maintained as serfs or slaves. This line of observation will lead to the formulation of a theory accounting for the Spartan transformation.

   Any effort to explain the Spartan character will be conjecture, and the explanation can be labeled and evaluated as conjecture. It is up to the teacher to help his students to formulate and evaluate any conjectures that purport to answer a Big Question.

   Social-scientific accounts are plausible explanations and descriptions of events and situations that are of interest to social investigators. One who fails to understand the human source of all social-scientific knowledge is fundamentally ignorant of social science. While still in school, however, a student can engage in this disciplined but human activity. He can have some experience at forming his own impression about past events or present situations, and he can seek to test his conjectures with whatever facts are available. To a large extent, the *art* of social inquiry is based on the ability to invent small, answerable questions that will lead to the solution of big, unanswerable questions. The *science* of social inquiry is based upon the ability to test conjectures empirically. Both the art and science can, with the guidance of thoughtful teachers, be practiced in the classroom.

5. Using the information gained from inquiry, write out an answer to the Big Question.

   A student who labors over his own answer is re-enacting the task which every intellectual worker faces. There is, in this responsibility, no need or *possibility* to plagiarize a textbook or an encyclopedia.

   Writing is a part of social inquiry that students must confront. One effort at putting together some ideas about the early Greeks may be found below. This brief essay is an interpretation, an impression, an account of events which took place long ago. Without any sure knowledge regarding those ancient times, we have only such conjectures as these:

Peculiarities of geography and the distribution of racial migrations played an important part in the creation of Athenian and Spartan cultures. Attica is surrounded by mountain barriers; its soil is not rich; only occasional marauders invaded its isolated valleys. Homer does not even mention its existence. The culture that developed in Athens was based on a stable population; refugees were absorbed because they were few in number and posed no threat to the indigenous group. The society that developed had a broad base of hereditary citizenship.

In Laconia, the land was fertile and many times invaded. The Dorian conquerors imposed their will on the existing societies and, in order to preserve the integrity of their race and culture, maintained a narrow base of citizenship—citizenship was restricted to their own caste.

From these sources sprang the remarkable differences between Athens and Sparta.

Sometime before 1200 B.C., Dorian invaders began to move into parts of Greece and Crete and the islands of the Aegean Sea. These invaders were the third of a series of northern invaders. Archaeological remains indicate their presence in strength in the area around Sparta in the year 1200 B.C.

The Dorians brought techniques for using iron to Greece, where iron replaced brass as the common metal. These people, with weapons that would cut as well as thrust, were technologically superior to the inhabitants of Laconia. Only a few city-states were able to resist them; Argos and the Achaeans successfully remained independent in this area.

For many hundreds of years, the early Spartans enjoyed the pleasures and rewards of a conquering people with a vast subject population of slaves and serfs. They extended their empire to the limits of easy conquest and lived on the fruits of their labors. They were an artistic people; pottery, music, and sculpture were important activities, according to the archaeological remains. Contrary to the sometimes popular notion, the men were not warriors, nor were they noted for their bravery. The women of Sparta were famous for their beauty and were desirable as wives or slaves. The "good life" —sensuous, voluptuous, effeminate—was Spartan.

By 600 B.C., the ruling caste of the Spartans was spread very thin. Thucydides and Herodotus agree that the Spartans were the poorest-governed state in Greece. There were many serfs and half-castes with no citizenship status. The Spartans had lost much of their impulse for conquest. The serfs or Helots revolted. One estimate of their numbers gives these figures:

Spartans   12,000
Perioeci (half-caste)   80,000
Helots (serfs)   190,000

It took a supreme effort, and twenty years, for the Spartans to quell this revolt. At its end, the strength and wealth of the Spartans were expended;

although they were the victors, they were outnumbered twenty to one by the defeated Helots.

The ruling Dorian caste confronted its dilemma. The Dorians were outnumbered; they recognized that they would inevitably be absorbed by their slaves. They could restrict their empire and thus maintain effective control. They could broaden the base of citizenship in their society and thus eliminate the hostility of the disenfranchised Laconians. They decided for empire and slaves, thus engaging in one of the most remarkable educational programs in the history of mankind. They deliberately resolved to live solely for war. They completely reorganized their way of life and subsumed all of the amenities of living to this one objective.

The records do not indicate clearly how this transformation took place. The Oracle at Delphi was consulted; Lycurgus effected the change, and he was revered as a god. That Spartan society was transformed was evident to contemporaries. The Spartans became efficient. Thucydides refers to them as well-governed, as does Herodotus. Socrates was impressed with their organization; every oligarch in Athens wanted to mimic their transformation, and some tyrants tried.

Family life disappeared in Sparta. The men lived and ate in barracks; they devoted their lives to training for war, the only occupation for the citizen.

Until the age of seven, the child was cared for by his mother; she taught him to be unafraid and to endure hardship without complaint. This education was continued in the barracks. Here, with his age-mates, he drilled, played, and fought; only the barest rudiments of learning were required of soldiers. As the boys grew older, the severity of the training increased. The last phase of their training was called *crypteia*. At this time, they were thrust from the barracks to forage among the Helots; they might steal their food and pleasures so long as they were not caught. They learned to pillage, murder, and rape; deceit and trickery as methods of war were intrinsic in the Spartan educational program.

The Spartans, in response to the pressure of an indigenous population, transformed themselves from pleasure-seeking plantation-owners into an organized army in a constant state of war. The government was put into the hands of a general staff of five ephors, elected by lot from the eligible members of the army reserve. The sole purpose of this government was to wage war and extend the empire. The purposeful lives of its citizens determined the success of the educational program of Sparta. Without a narrow base of citizenship, without the pressure of a geometrically increasing serf population, the Spartan experiment would have been impossible.

The source of Athenian democracy lay in its largely autochthonous population. Attica is not a fertile area; it was not a trading center; there were no great accumulations of wealth. A frugal and protective nature created the conditions of approximate equality of its citizens. There were rich and there were poor, but the similarities of race and heredity were as important as material differences between rich and poor; nobles and farmers were of one blood. There was continual pressure for equity for all citizens.

This pressure first manifested itself in the publication of Draco's laws in 621 B.C. The citizens forced the publication of the laws, by which they were ruled and judged. The people were horrified by the severity of the punishments. Conflict of interest between noble and citizen endured for many years. The pressure of this autochthonous population was steady, and in 594 B.C., Solon attempted a resolution of the conflict. He transferred sovereignty from a small group of nobles to a large group of the people. The reorganized government thus had a broad base of citizen participation. He also initiated broad economic reforms. He created the condition that developed participating citizens under a rule of law.

The Athenians, in response to autochthonous population pressures, created a system of government involving huge portions of the society; men argued and debated important questions of policy. In juries numbering in the thousands, they adjudicated their disputes. Out of this ferment of thinking and action, out of the debate and inquiry that reached beyond questions of law, came the philosophy, the science, and the mathematics that are the wonders of the world.

Participation was the key to Athenian creation; not until the rise of the universities in Europe, with their largely autonomous, quasi-democratic system of students and faculty was there an approximately equal intellectual outburst of activity. The autonomous student nations were the essential catalysts for intellectual advance in the twelfth century.

V

Language and Study

Language is essential to human thought. One who engages in study must learn to be sensitive to the possibilities and the limitations of language.

Language allows us to represent our thoughts, observations, anxieties, hopes, and dreams symbolically. But a single language is limited in the set of concepts it can provide. Any situation, even the most simple, is far more complex than any description of it can ever be. To describe is to ignore: an infinity of statements can be made about a rose, a ball game, a political speech, or a field of snow. According to some ethnologists, one Eskimo language has fifty different words for snow. These Eskimos can say more about the qualities of snow than one can say in English. So it is with any description: there is more to a personal experience of love, snow, or fear than any set of words can represent.

Study often begins with reading. Students may read textbooks; social scientists may read reports of scholarship found in the journals. The Big Questions that initiate inquiry are often posed as a result of appraising and evaluating ideas that have been formally expressed in writing, but working with the written language is not easy.

Many notions may be expressed in writing:

America wants "free enterprise."

Negroes want "freedom now."

The "Katanga Freedom-Fighters" were sold out.

Asians migrated to the new world 37,000 years ago.

Democracy is better than communism.

Richard III murdered his nephews in the tower.

In addition, many kinds of questions can be posed:

When did you stop cheating on examinations?

What is the major export of Brazil?

Why is Argentina one of the most stable and one of the most progressive countries in South America?

Why should China be admitted to the United Nations?

Should China be admitted to the United Nations?

Why are all white men agents of the devil?

Many sorts of statements are made in print, and many questions are posed. To engage in social study, one must be able to evaluate the language encountered in books, newspapers, letters, and journals.

Aspects of Written Communication

What is to be found in journals? Books and newspapers? A customary answer might be that information, wisdom, or perhaps humor is to be found in print. This is not the answer intended. Books are bound paper on which may be found conventional symbols, arranged into words, sentences, paragraphs, and chapters. Words and sentences are basic units of language; the ability to appraise and evaluate written material depends on the ability to analyze words and sentences. Three aspects of written communication, *words, sentences,* and the *inferences that can be made about the intent of an author,* should be understood before scrutinizing written materials.

Words

Words are familiar to us all. Most of the words we use come more or less automatically. Some are hard to pronounce; others are hard to understand without a dictionary. But word usage deserves the careful attention of students engaged in social study.

For the purposes of elementary-school social study, words can be classified as *pointing* or *nonpointing.*

POINTING WORDS

Words That Point to a Narrow Range of Things–Many words in our language denote common objects; these provide little of the confusion that seems to be inherent in the use of language. Words that denote things can be defined by pointing at some object, for example, "cat," "dog," "goat," "fish," "book," "table," or "chair." Of course, each person has his own set of associations with the many objects denoted.

A Word or Symbol	Thoughts	Things
goat	smelly gives milk eats paper	
cat	sleeps a lot independent affectionate	
pencil	something to write with prefer a pen like a soft lead	

Words That Point to a Narrow Range of Actions or Processes–Many words can be defined fairly clearly by pointing to something or by demonstrating something. Such words as "dig," "run," "jump," "talk," "friendly," "sad," "vote," "buy," "build," and "cry" are examples.

These words, too, have many personal associations.

A Word or Symbol	Thoughts	Actions
hit	home run Mays Maris	
friendly	touching talking walking	
needle	sharp sewing mother	

Pointing words are used extensively in statements of fact, those statements relating what we can observe. Notice that most of the words in the following sentence point to things or actions:

Bob hit Jim on the nose.

NONPOINTING WORDS

Some words are nonpointing, that is, they refer to a wide range of events, actions, or beliefs. No particular thing or activity uniquely illustrates the word. Most of the important words in our language are nonpointing, for example, "love," "justice," "democracy," "children's needs," "communism," "socialism," "conservatism," and "liberalism." It is possible to obscure meaning by pretending that such words are pointing words. Nonpointing words must be defined by talking; they mean what people say they mean, and they mean different things to different people.

Nonpointing words are deeply involved in most controversies and in most statements about the causes of wars, depressions, delinquency, and dropouts. Knowledge of social reality which goes beyond mere description must make use of words and ideas that have relatively unfixed meaning, and, thus, are subject to continuous controversy.

A Word or Symbol	Thoughts	Many Things and Actions But No Specific Thing or Action
democracy	1. People choose leaders. 2. Leaders come from no special class. 3. Leaders are chosen by majority vote.	1. The Queen of England 2. The President of Mexico 3. A ballot box

4. Leaders are to govern for the benefit of the people.
5. Every citizen is to have equal opportunity.
6. Citizens may speak and write freely.
7. Private enterprise should be encouraged, and public enterprise, forbidden or discouraged.
8. Private exploitation should be discouraged, and public enterprise, encouraged.
9. Men and women should have equal opportunity.
10. There should be no abridgement of religious activities.

4. The Canadian Prime Minister
5. The U.S. Constitution
6. The U.N.
7. A strike
8. A picket
9. A criticism of the President of the U.S.
10. A lockout
11. The Magna Carta
12. A Senator (Canadian; American)

learning

1. Organizing experience
2. Changing behavior
3. Adapting to environment
4. Doing what one is told

1. Marks on paper
2. Speech sounds
3. Pictures
4. Smiles
5. Frowns

love

1. Sexual desire
2. Respect
3. Submission

1. A facial expression
2. A glance

"Learning," "democracy," and "love" are words that can be defined only by other words. When a student works with words that point to a narrow range of objects or actions, he can ask himself these questions:

To what object or action does this word point?

Would I know it if I "saw" it?

Could I show it to someone else?

When a student works with nonpointing words, he should ask himself these questions:

How have people used this word?

How is the word being used right now?

How do I want to use this word?

Some of the nonpointing words that interest teachers are concerned with the hopes and aspirations that have excited the minds of men. The task of instruction is to help students discover how such words as "democracy," "freedom," "free enterprise," "free speech," "communism," "socialism," and "justice" have been used. These words have no ultimate meaning, but students can discover the variety of uses to which they have been put.

Some nonpointing words have been developed by social scientists to facilitate their study and analysis of some phase of social activity. Words such as "social class," "latitude," "culture," "enculturation," and "deutero-learning" are explanatory concepts that have been invented and proved useful. They exist only as explanatory devices: they *point* to no particular things, but they may help the inquirer to organize his perceptions in useful ways.

Some words that may be defined by pantomime or pointing in their ordinary senses become nonpointing words when used in metaphor. To *nurture* self-reliance, to *build* concepts, to *meet* children's needs, to *practice* democracy is to engage in metaphor. The metaphor evokes a mood but has obscure cognitive meaning. The obligation of a person who engages in this sort of metaphor is to illustrate the mood with examples that make use of words definable by pointing or pantomime.

For example, two teachers might affirm the following sentence:

We practice democracy in our classrooms.

One teacher might illustrate this by saying, "Once a year we elect class officers; we have a campaign; we have voting booths and official mimeographed ballots. The elected officers are responsible for the class parties and other social affairs." Another teacher might say, "I regularly confer with my students about the curriculum for our grade. I want to involve them in making decisions about the conduct of their own education. I must fulfill what I think of as my obligation to them, but they must participate in determining the pace and character of some of our work. The capacity for self-direction in *education,* in *moral behavior,* and in *politics* is essential for free citizens. I seek to give my students some experience at self-direction. This is what I mean when I say 'practice democracy.'"

Words used in nonpointing senses mean only what particular users say they mean for them. Because most of the words that are used in social study are nonpointing, it is essential for students to discover the basic character of these words and to learn how to seek their meaning in specific uses.

Sentences

The sentence is the fundamental unit of communication: writing is the ordering of words in sentences. The words "the," "trains," "seals," and "man" convey no thought. But when sentences are formed with them, more than one thought can be expressed:

The man trains the seals.

The man seals the trains.

Sentences can be classified in a variety of ways; one convenient way is simply to use the conventional distinctions among sentences: statements, questions, exclamations, and commands (or requests). Exclamations and commands are not frequent in expository writing, but what are questions and what are statements?

STATEMENTS

Working social scientists routinely distinguish between their statements of fact[1] and their statements of hypothesis, interpretation, or conjecture. For the purposes of elementary-school social studies, a simple distinction can be made: statements of fact can be distinguished from statements of inference, conjecture, or judgment. The following are practical definitions to facilitate this distinction:

A factual statement relates an observation that can or has been made.
Examples: Bob hit Jim on the nose.
              The Dead Sea Scrolls contain a verse from the Gospel of John.
              In 1925, a flint point was found near Folsom, New Mexico.
              This flint point is known as the Folsom point.

A statement of inference relates thought, opinion, or conjecture.
Examples: That nasty bully, Jim, finally got what was coming to him: Bob
              hit him on the nose.
              The Gospel of John is of pre-Christian origin.
              The Folsom point was made by a human being about 10,000
              years ago.

If a *student* should affirm the thoughts of another, or if he should put forth his own personal view, he is obligated by his craft, by his status as a student, to ask in the words of the historian Marc Bloch: "How can I know what I am about to say?"[2] To answer this question, a student must have some general ideas about how statements of fact and statements of inference may be evaluated.

Statements of fact relate what can be seen, heard, tasted, and felt. Statements of inference tell about thoughts, opinions, judgments, and conjectures of some person about an event or a situation.

Evaluating a piece of writing involves (1) noticing the factual statements and checking them; and (2) noticing the inferential statements and seeking to determine the extent to which the inferences are supported by evidence. For example, anthropologists infer that men first migrated to the new world about 25,000 years ago. No one now living observed this early migration. What evidence supports this inference? What statements of fact can be

---

[1] See Carl Becker, "What Are Historical Facts?" in Part IV. This famous article points out that the notion of "facts" is not so simple as it might appear at first.

[2] MARC BLOCH, *The Historian's Craft* (New York: Vintage Books, Random House, 1964), p. 71.

made to support it? What small inferences support the big inference about
the age of man in the new world?

Problems of Factual Statements–Many problems are involved in the
evaluation of factual statements. Some important questions are:

1. *Are enough facts presented?*

One of the easiest ways to distort and misrepresent a situation is to omit
relevant facts. Although there is no sure way to decide whether enough facts
have been reported, posing the question may help the decision. A useful
restatement of the question may suggest a way to answer it: are enough
facts presented to justify the opinions that are being presented?

2. *Who reported the facts?*

Different persons may report the facts of a situation in very different ways.
Witnesses in court may often present conflicting testimony; yet, each may
believe he is reporting simply the facts as he saw them. For the student, the
statement of fact is not, for example, what Mr. Jones said. The fact is that
Mr. Jones made a particular statement.

Let us consider, for a moment, the witness, Mr. Jones. Mr. Jones says
that he saw a man in a black coat run away.

We do not know:

a. That it really was a man; it may have been a woman dressed in a man's
   coat.

b. That the coat was really black. It may have appeared to be black. It
   may have been dark brown or dark blue.

c. That Mr. Jones is telling the truth.

We do know:

a. What he said.

b. That he said it.

With a clear understanding of what is known and what is not known, an
investigator may seek to establish the facts regarding the event that Mr.
Jones and others may have observed.

An infinite number of factual statements could be made about any event.
A reporter who decides to report one fact must ignore others; all the facts
can never be reported. Thus, it is important for a student to know who selected the facts he is encountering; without this knowledge, it is difficult
to evaluate what has been reported.

3. *How are the facts reported?*

Statements that are apparently factual sometimes have been systematically
slanted by the reporter. One kind of slant—leaving out some of the facts—

has already been mentioned. Another way of slanting an ostensibly factual account is to use descriptive words that encourage the reader to interpret the facts in a given way. Such words can reveal a writer's biases as they purport to deal with people and events. Consider these illustrations:

> JFK, Harvard intellectual, took over the U.S. government in 1960.

> The left-wing government of Mr. Adoula, with the help of the United Nations, has conquered the Katanga Freedom-Fighters.

In the first example, the term "Harvard intellectual" is a judgment. One can only judge or infer that a man is an intellectual. Among certain American writers, the word "intellectual" is regarded as an insult, implying that a man lacks clear-headedness or even integrity. The words "took over" imply force and impropriety. The sentence could be rewritten, and an entirely different mood will be conveyed:

> John F. Kennedy, Harvard graduate, became President of the United States in 1960.

The second example uses the key words "left-wing" and "Katanga Freedom-Fighters." The message of the sentence is that something bad has taken place. "Left-wing" tells you that Mr. Adoula is "no good," and "Katanga Freedom-Fighters" tells you that these are "good guys." Since the U.N. is for the "bad guy" and against the "good guy," by implication the U.N. is "no good" either. The judgments about the "good guys" and the "bad guys" are based on unstated premises. An alternative formulation of the sentence might be:

> The Congolese government, with the help of the United Nations, has brought peace and stability to the Congo.

Facts and opinions can be united in many seductive ways. An important problem of instruction is to help students to gain insight into the subtle usage of words.

4. *Is the statement of fact true? Are the facts facts?*
Factual statements relate:
a. What the author has seen, done, or experienced.
b. What the author believes, on the basis of what others have seen, done, or experienced.

Such statements are relatively easy to evaluate. A consensus of testimony may establish that Bob hit Jim on the nose. There is often little disagreement concerning the facts, and factual statements can ordinarily be checked and verified with reasonable assurance. When facts appear to be in conflict, however, more investigation is required.

That Jim is a bully and finally got what was coming to him is one person's view of the facts. As with all opinion or inference, there is no routine way of establishing their truth. We may agree upon the facts, but differ regarding their meaning.

In the classroom, acquaintance activities, preliminary to study, should lead to an identification and evaluation of the facts that have been presented.

Problems of Inferential Statements–The evaluation of statements of inference is much more complicated. The following are some important considerations.

1. *Often, inferential statements are confused with factual statements.*

A factual statement relates something that can be directly observed. An inferential statement tells something that cannot be perceived through the senses. We cannot see needs, hopes, and fears; when we talk about them, we are making inferences based on the smiles, scowls, and the noises we can hear. We cannot see or hear democracy, or loyalty, or communism, but we can see Congressmen, constitutions, prime ministers, parliaments, and pamphlets. We cannot see or hear what went on in the market place in ancient Athens, the ritual of initiation that takes place in the Hopi kiva, or the conferences that take place in the Kremlin; but we can make inferences about what took place, based upon the things that we can see. Inferences are impressions of facts formulated by various men. Any account of early America, ancient Greece, or causes of delinquency is an impression, a view which may or may not be consistent with the facts.

2. *Inferences are man-made.*

Inferences are the impressions, explanations, or judgments that some person has made regarding a situation.

What circumstances have led this person to wish to share his impressions with the reader? He may be concerned with persuading the reader to adopt certain beliefs. He may wish to inform the reader of his own thoughts and understanding. Perhaps he wants to share his feelings and passions regarding a particular situation.

Who is the writer? Is he competent to deal with his subject matter? Is he writing as an expert? As an intelligent layman? What are his qualifications? Is he reporting his own thoughts, or is he restating or summarizing the thoughts of others? Much social-studies textbook writing for children is done by writers who paraphrase and summarize the opinions of others.

Examination of such motives and qualifications will aid students in weighing the inferences that they encounter.

3. *Inferences are influenced by the values of the writer.*

Inferences about the causes of war, the character of political leaders, the wisdom of treaty ratification, and the morality of government policies are strongly influenced by the values held by a writer.

The inferences made by honest men are influenced by many factors. Who a man is often determines, in large part, the inferences he will invent regarding contemporary and historical events. American students can read accounts of the American Revolution written by English historians for Englishmen; these will be rather different from American school-textbook accounts. Where the students discover conflict in an opinion, inference, or conjecture, inquiry can be initiated.

Consider, for example, these accounts of an encounter between the British and the Colonialists at Lexington:

a. A book, released by an English publisher, concerning famous battles:
James Grant, *British Battles on Land and Sea* (London, Paris and New York: Cassell, Petter & Galpin, no date), Vol. II. p. 138.

[At the order to disperse] . . . they obeyed, with evident reluctance, but as they did so, several muskets were fired at the troops from neighboring houses and from behind a wall. More than one man was wounded, and Major Pitcairn's horse was shot under him in two places. The troops, naturally initiated by this skulking treachery fired upon the militia, killing (eight) and wounding some others on which the rest fled in an instant.

b. A report of the British commander, taken from Major Pitcairn's report to General Gage, as reported in:
John Richard Alden, *The American Revolution, 1775–1783* (New York: Harper and Brothers, 1954), p. 21.

When I arrived . . . I observed drawn up upon a green near 200 of the rebels; . . . I instantly called to the soldiers not to fire . . . some of the rebels fired four or five shott [sic] at soldiers . . . upon this, without any order or regularity, the light infantry began a scattered fire, and continued . . . contrary to . . . repeated orders. . . .

c. An American historian:
Oliver Perry Chitwood, *A History of Colonial America* (New York: Harper and Brothers, 1948), pp. 647–648.

. . . the British soldiers had reached Lexington on their march. Here a body of armed men was encountered who refused to lay down their arms when ordered to do so. Firing ensued and eight militiamen were killed and ten wounded. The British went on to Concord and destroyed the supplies there. . . .

d. An American historian:
John Richard Alden, in b. above, pp. 22–23.

At cold dawn when six companies of the advanced guard under Pitcairn came to the village they found Captain Jonas Parker and about seventy men lined up on the green in crude battle formation . . . Pitcairn rode toward the three ranks of Americans, telling them, profanely it seems, to lay down their muskets and disperse. . . . shot or shots rang out. Who fired the first will probably never be known, nor whether the man was British or American.

4. *Inferences are not true in the same sense that factual statements are true.*

A factual statement, as already suggested, may be determined to be true or false by looking, checking, and consensus. Probably it would be wise not to use the concept of truth when talking about inferences. Inferences may be consistent with the facts; they may be plausible; they may be tested; but they are not true *in the same sense* that factual statements are true. Of course, many inferences are very well-established indeed.

Is Jim a bully? Did he get what was coming to him? In order to answer these questions, an argument must be made—in most cases, more than one. Jim's girl friend may have a view different from that of his teacher; Jim's coach may differ with Jim's neighbors. It may be agreed that Bob hit Jim on the nose; there may be total disagreement about the cause of the conflict and the virtues of the participants.

5. *Some inferences are extraordinarily obscure.*

Many inferences, or thoughts, or opinions are stated so that they obscure complexities; they are inaccurate, and, thus, they are difficult to assess in any way. Obscure inferences should be restated so that they may be dealt with rationally.

Here are some examples:

Science tells us that drinking alcohol is dangerous. Science cannot talk. The person who writes such a statement means that he thinks drinking is not a good idea. He may be basing his judgment on an interpretation of research findings. He uses the metaphor "science tells us" in order to make his admonition not to drink persuasive.

America wants "free enterprise." There is no entity "America" that can have wants, that can talk, or sing, or desire. A person who writes in this way is seeking to persuade the reader by obscuring reality. It is certainly true that many individual Americans may be in favor of something they think of as "free enterprise." Nevertheless, there are many different notions regarding free enterprise. There are many Americans, probably, who are opposed to it. It may be that a majority of Americans share a common desire for it. The interesting question is: What sort of free enterprise do most Americans favor?

The milkman is a community helper. Elementary-school children are frequently confronted with sentimental obscurities such as this one. *Helping* is a concept that little children understand: they help their mothers and their teachers and their baby sisters. But it is simply confusing to call the highly competitive enterprise of selling milk "helping." It may be that the milk companies sell a convenient service in the home delivery of milk; however, the milk companies engage in extensive, competitive advertising; some of the companies have trouble with state regulations regarding butterfat content—indeed, the ordinary notions associated with "help" are simply inappropriate when attached to milkmen.

Inference and Metaphor

The examination of metaphor is an important aspect of evaluating written information. Metaphors are somewhat like women: "You can't live with 'em and you can't live without 'em." It is probably impossible to think without metaphors; yet, they are often dangerously confusing.

A metaphor is simply a comparison between two relations. In the abstract, a metaphor affirms that A has to X the relation that B has to Y. Whenever the relationship that A has to X is hard to describe, we search around and try to find some other relationship—say, the relationship of B to Y—that is generally understood, and then we seek for some way to say that one relationship is like the other.

President John F. Kennedy, in the 1960 campaign, coined a phrase—a metaphor—to represent what he thought the effect of his leadership on the economy would be: he spoke of "getting the country moving." The invention of metaphor is probably one of the primary obligations of politics and leadership. The world is enormously complex: metaphor appears to make this complexity comprehensible.

Three dangerous uses of metaphor are of particular importance to teachers: the *metaphor of personification, the metaphor of homogeneity,* and the *metaphor of number.*

The Metaphor of Personification. Personification is the comparison between a human being and anything which is not human. When the purpose of the metaphor is to create a mood or evoke feeling, personification is useful. But when the metaphor purports to have an explanatory function, then personification is dangerous because it obscures real processes and complexity.

Mr. Kennedy's admonition to "move ahead" was not advice to economic-policy makers; it was a poetic image, without any cognitive functions.

To personify a state is a dangerous—frequently encountered—confusion:

America is in favor of "free enterprise."

Russia has signed the test ban treaty.

Germany hated the Jews.

China wants war.

The simple fact is that "America" is not a person: it does not like; it does not favor. What is America? What is a country? What sort of sensible things can be said about it?

America might refer to the people who live in the United States (excluding aliens and possibly Indians, and possibly Negroes in the South).

America might refer to all past, present, and future residents in the United States.

America might mean the government, that is, a particular group of men who hold office.

America might mean the land, the rivers, the forests, and lakes that constitute a particular area.

It is clear that none of these collections *is* a person. It does not contribute to understanding to write and talk as if America were a person. To personify any state is to deny the variety and complexity of nations.

Teachers should help students to use language that accurately represents reality. The attribution of human qualities to nonhuman entities seriously undermines social study. The three most common personifications encountered in social study are the personification of the state, the personification of a race, and the personification of nature (as in "Mother Nature gives us robins").

The Metaphor of Homogeneity. The metaphor of homogeneity appears to make singular that which is plural and possibly highly varied. The temptation to homogenize is a serious problem in social study:

Chinese are inscrutable.

Negroes are easygoing.

Indians are placid.

White people are modest.

Frenchmen are lascivious.

Jews have all the money.

Mexicans are lazy.

Foreign nations and peoples demonstrate a wide variety of types and predispositions. What is alien is often thought to be one. For instance, the comment, "I can't tell one from another; they all look alike to me," has been made about whites, Negroes, Mexicans, and Orientals. The homogenization of collections is a serious hazard that a student of social reality must avoid; indeed, one objective of social inquiry is the discovery of variety in the existence of Negroes, Jews, delinquents, suburbs, families, or the middle class.

The Metaphor of Number. The world is full of number; we count people, IQ points, votes, and the number of drinks in a fifth of whisky. It is useful to understand the uses to which numbers are put:

1. *For counting: in this use there is no metaphor.*

There are fifty states in the United States.

Seven people were reported hurt in the fighting.

There are three hundred students in this room.

2. *For measuring: sometimes there is a metaphor and sometimes not.*
Mary weighs 105 pounds.
Sam is 6 feet tall.
It is 80° F. today.
John has an IQ of 162.
3. *In metaphor: deliberately.*
John is twice the man he used to be.
Mary is one hundred per cent improved in her poetry comprehension.

Apples, people, and potatoes can be counted. But the cause of things, the tears of childhood, and the number of social classes cannot be counted; none of these things is clearly separable. To number them may be to engage in dangerous use of metaphor—one can come to believe that there really are three social classes, or seven drinks left in a bottle. Such divisions are arbitrary; there can be as many or as few of them as particular persons may wish to decide. Three social classes may, for another man, be five; seven drinks in a bottle may turn out to be two. No one can determine the "real" number in either case.

What can be measured? All physical measurement can be converted to measurements of length: that is, we measure the length of a column of mercury if we want to know about temperature; the distance (or length) a needle travels along the markings on a scale tells us about weight.

Usually, connotations of physical measurements cling to attempts to measure human qualities and capacities, as in measuring intelligence with metaphors of measuring hamburger. *Human qualities are without measure;* no scale measures kindness, courage, compassion, virtue, wisdom, social concern, creativity, or the capacity for folly or intelligence.

All such uses of number may be dangerously confusing; the more common they are, the more they are unnoticed—the more insidious may be their influence. We remain unaware that we do not understand the reality to which these numbers refer. Test-makers understand this metaphor very well. They have devised an esoteric vocabulary that explicates the special, "un-hamburger" sense in which they propose to measure, but most of us interpret numbers with "hamburger" metaphors. One of the special obligations of social study is to help students to avoid the inappropriate use of numbers in measurements.

Explicit metaphor is usually used for emphasis. The numbers convey a general impression that is seldom confusing. But the danger of this sort of metaphor is that, at times, the numbers can be taken to be precise description rather than general emphatic statements.

Judgment and Comparison

Judgments are statements of inference that directly involve comparison. Students may seek to compare communism and democracy, liberalism and conservatism, capitalism and socialism, France and Italy, men and women, one politician—or baseball player—and another, California and Michigan, Central High and Jefferson High, San Francisco and Birmingham, and my dad with yours. How may rational judgments be made with comparisons such as these? Consider these judgments:

1. Sam is taller than Mary.
2. It is hotter inside than outside.
3. Bob is a better baseball player than Sam.
4. Men are superior to women.
5. France is better than England.
6. Democracy is better than communism.
7. Mary is a good student.

Let us look at each of these seven judgments. The first question to raise regarding judgments is this one: *What is being compared?*

1. The heights of Sam and Mary.
2. The temperature outside and the temperature inside. (If the comparison is not temperature but feelings of comfort and discomfort, then *feelings of comfort* are being compared.)
3. Bob's and Sam's ability to play ball.
4. Don't know.
5. Don't know.
6. Don't know.
7. Not sure: Mary, as compared with others, is good at doing something not stated specifically, but generally indicated with the word "student."

There are standard ways of comparing heights; such comparisons raise few problems *because* of these standard ways of comparing. The judgment regarding the heights of Mary and Sam can be verified, that is, several independent observers can agree.

There are standard ways of comparing temperature. There are few problems about this comparison. If you are talking about the way someone feels, you might have some conflict in judgments.

The comparison of ball players is more difficult. One player may field well and be a weak hitter. Another may be a strong hitter but only a weak fielder. Still, from the point of view of winning games, it is probably possible to make a judgment about the two players.

Because there is no statement of what is being compared, the judgments regarding men and women, France and England, communism and democracy cannot be verified. Each statement affirms a personal taste, about which, it has often been said, there can be no dispute.

The judgment about Mary does not contain a clear statement of what is being compared or judged. Being a student may mean different things to different people. In general, when statements affirm that something is good, they may be usefully examined with the following questions:

1. Good? As compared with what or whom?
2. Good? What is the basis of comparison?
3. Good? For what purpose?

The responsibility of teachers of social study is to help students develop rational understanding of complex notions such as democracy and communism. Consider the judgment, "Communism is bad."

1. To say that communism is bad is to say that it is bad as compared with something else. What should communism be compared to?
2. If you decide upon the ideas with which you wish to compare communism, then can you identify a basis of comparison? What is to be compared? If you are comparing baseball players, then what you are comparing is the ability to play ball. What is a basis of comparison by means of which communism and, say, democracy may be compared?
3. According to the basis of comparison, for what purposes is communism good or bad?

QUESTIONS

Questions are basic tools of inquiry and instruction. An examination of them in some detail may help you to work with them more effectively in the classroom.

Questions and Their Answers–One way in which to think about questions is to identify the kinds of answers they may have:

1. Some questions have one acceptable answer.
2. Some questions have many acceptable answers.
3. Some questions have no acceptable answers.

Often, questions that may be thought to have one acceptable answer will, upon examination, be shown to have many answers. Sometimes questions that have no answers are seriously posed, but such questions can be answered only in fantasy.

Three sorts of questions that have one acceptable answer are important for the conduct of inquiry:

1. Questions that call for the evidence of one's own senses.
   Is Mary in the room?
   Is the stool put together with nails or pegs?
   Is the man's coat dark blue or black?
   Did the textbook say that Panama was a stable, prosperous country?
2. Questions that call for the evidence of the senses of others.
   Who is the mayor of Detroit?
   What did Columbus write to the King and Queen after his second voyage?
   What are the main features of Monte Alban?
3. Questions that call for logical argument from stated premises. In order

to produce an acceptable answer, one must know the logical system and the premises.

If Sam is three times his brother's age and half his sister's age, how old is Sam's sister if Sam's brother is one year old? (Although there may be several ways to express this answer, these ways of expression are equivalent to one another.)

If all white men are agents of the devil, as Black Muslims believe, then should Negroes seek to integrate with the white American society?

If imperialism is the last stage of capitalism, as some communists believe, then can a communist country be imperialistic?

Questions that call upon sense experience are essential features of inquiry. All inquiry into social happenings finally depends on the observations that men can make. Questions that call for argument from stated premises must be carefully examined. Although all three of the above questions have but one acceptable answer that is consistent with the stated premises, the premises themselves may be unacceptable. Students will have to learn which questions they must reject because of their unsatisfactory premises.

Questions which have many acceptable answers, but no one answer, call for statements of judgment, inference, or conjecture. The answers are many because people have many different views about themselves and the world:

What is the cause of the First World War?
Why are many Southerners in favor of segregation?
Is communism a sound political theory?
Why do we have so many delinquents?
Why is the divorce rate so high?
Why is Argentina a stable, progressive country?
Why did Americans move west?

The important thing to notice about questions with many answers is that they are answered with an argument and an appeal to experience. Direct observation of the world around us is possible and relevant to the process of seeking answers to such questions.

Questions with no answers are hazards in social inquiry. Questions can be so phrased that there is no rational way to go about seeking an answer to them; they deal with the inaccessible, the unobservable, the unforeseeable, and the unverifiable. Consider these examples:

What would have happened if Nixon had been elected?
Are women better than men?
What is the best country in the world?
What would happen if an irresistible force met an immovable object?
What is the ultimate order of the universe?

The question about Nixon deals with the unknowable. It should be noted, however, that this question is quite different in form from questions of the very useful type: What will happen if Mr. Blank is elected President? One can speculate intelligently about the future and then carefully observe and record evidence that predictions are being verified or falsified. Teachers who value the stimulus to imaginative use of information given by questions of the "What would have happened if . . ." type, can get similar responses from children by asking them to predict the course of things to come, basing their predictions on what they know now.

The question comparing men and women has no specified basis of comparison. Perhaps women are better than men *as mothers*. The question about the best country does not specify a basis of comparison that would allow a verifiable judgment—perhaps there is a best country in the world for the production of crude oil. The question dealing with immovable objects deals with the unobservable. The question about the ultimate order of the universe also deals with the unobservable and the unverifiable.

Students who are learning how to engage in the art of inquiry will be fashioning questions. One responsibility of instruction is to help them discover whether their questions have one, many, or no answers.

Questions and Presuppositions—There is another aspect of questions which deserves attention. Briefly, it is: What does the question presuppose?

A question may be regarded as a disguised statement of fact. Before a question can be answered, the state of affairs it presupposes must be accepted. Consider these questions:

When did you stop cheating on examinations?

Why are all white men agents of the devil?

Why is Argentina the most stable and the most progressive country in South America?

The question about cheating, if one does not cheat, and, therefore, cannot have stopped, must be rejected. The question about "agents of the devil," since it affirms that white men are "agents of the devil," would probably be rejected by anyone who does not agree with this assertion. The question about Argentina must be rejected because it presupposes something that is not yet known.

Some questions are more subtle; they have presuppositions, but these are less noticeable. A student engaged in social study must carefully guard against them. For example, consider these questions:

What do Indians look like?

How do the Buddhists worship God?

What are the three causes of the American Civil War?

All of these questions should be rejected. The first question presupposes lack of variety in the way Indians look. What do Americans look like? Alien groups are often thought of as all looking alike. A student must guard against insensitivity to variety, and his questions must not prevent its discovery. The second question must be rejected because it presupposes an analogy between Buddhism and Western, Christian religious practices. Buddhist "religious" activities have little to do with what may be referred to as the "worship of God." The third question must be rejected because it affirms that there are three causes of the war. The causes of wars are, in a sense, infinite. They can be proposed in countless numbers.

Each of these questions can be restated so that they may legitimately initiate study. Among many satisfactory restatements are these possibilities:

> What sort of clothes might a Hopi Indian wear when he enters the kiva?
>
> Do the Buddhists have a concept of God which is analogous to the Western notion of God?
>
> What are two or three conjectures about causes of the Civil War?

The questions that students ask will limit and determine what they discover; a student of inquiry must discover the powers and limitations of his questions.

Questions and Instruction–It has been suggested that questions are the fundamental tools of inquiry, and that one who engages in inquiry must learn how to work with them.

Questions are also tools of instruction; teachers who ask appropriate questions in the classroom teach their students what questions are. Let us examine the different styles of questions that teachers can pose in the classroom.

The style of a question determines the intellectual processes that a student must go through if he is to produce an answer. Some questions call upon students to recall little bits of information; some call for the recall of generalizations or arguments. Any question of the "What did the book say" variety calls upon a student to recall, without comment, the thoughts of others.

Some questions require students to make inferences, judgments, and conjectures—to engage in intellectual activity. If a student makes a judgment, he can be asked questions about the basis of the comparison that he has made. If he makes an inference or a conjecture, he can be asked about the evidence that supports his position.

Some questions ask the student to do the impossible—to exercise judgment and engage in conjecture regarding unobservable, unverifiable, or false and misleading situations. This is a useful instructional activity when the teacher is aware of what he is doing and, in time, helps the student see that the questions are unacceptable.

The art of leading a group discussion involves posing many different kinds of questions. It is easy for teachers to get in a rut and pose only "what-did-the-book-say" kinds of questions. Effective instruction uses questions that call upon students to be intellectually active. Questions that call for judgment, inference, conjecture, and opinion lead students into intellectual engagement; questions that induce students to examine their own views, in the light of evidence, sustain the adventure of inquiry.

Posing Questions–Questions can be asked in many different ways. At times, a belligerent, incredulous, contentious manner of posing questions may arouse excitement and involvement in inquiry. At other times, a more detached manner may encourage pursuing the truth wherever it may lead.

Questions are the main business of both teachers and students. Teachers should be concerned with revealing to students the drama and adventure of inquiry by means of the questions they raise in class. Students should be concerned with developing the art and skill of inventing questions.

Inferences About an Author's Intent

Social study brings students into contact with scientific reports, political propaganda, personal letters and diaries, eye-witness reports, opinions, arguments, and conjectures. The following notions may guide the study, evaluation, and analysis of such written material.

VARIETY IN WRITTEN THINGS: THE PERSONAL AND THE AUTONOMOUS

For the purposes of elementary social study, it is convenient to divide the writings usually encountered by students into two types: writings that are designed to *inform,* and secondarily to persuade; and writings that are designed to *persuade,* and secondarily to inform, or even to misinform.

Writings that are designed to persuade must be read with great caution; the author intends to convince the reader to adopt a particular belief. He may use rational or irrational appeals to accomplish this objective; he may be either honest or dishonest with his facts. Nevertheless, a man trying to persuade a reader is not doing anything immoral. It is up to the reader to discover the author's intent and decide whether he wants to adopt the belief.

Writings which are designed to inform must also be read with care, but the danger is entirely different. The author may be totally wrong in his observations, conjectures, and generalizations; but he believes his own testimony and conjectures and is thus only sharing his misinformation.

VARIETY IN WRITTEN THINGS: THE PERSONAL AND THE AUTONOMOUS

Writing, whether intended to inform or persuade, may be thought to be personal or autonomous. C. Wright Mills identifies the mood of a personal writer in this way:

. . . he is a man who may shout, whisper, or chuckle—but who is always there. It is also clear what sort of man he is: whether confident or neurotic, direct or involuted, he *is* a center of experience and reasoning; now he has found out something, and he is telling us about it, and how he found it out. This is the voice behind the best expositions available in the English language.[3]

A personal writer, in many little ways, affirms that there is more than one view, that the facts are not all in agreement, that the situation may be complex but this is how *he* sees it.

Impersonal or autonomous writing has an entirely different mood. Mills suggests, "It is an autonomous sound. It is a prose manufactured by a machine . . . it is not only impersonal; it is pretentiously impersonal."[4] Autonomous writing appears not to have been written by a man engaged in thought, but by an all-wise knower or some perfect electronic machine whose task it is to set down words that simply report established truths.

Much advertising copy, social-studies textbook writings, and political propaganda appears to be written by no one and directed toward everyone. Mills contends, "Government bulletins are sometimes written in this way. Business letters also. And a great deal of social science."[5]

Personal writers make much use of such words as, "I think," "based on the present evidence," "in the light of my experience," and similar locutions. Impersonal or autonomous writing reports views that often appear to be necessary, obvious, and beyond controversy. Personal writers share the status and character of their own intellectual position; autonomous writings deal with situations as if knowledge about them were secure.

VARIETY IN WRITTEN THINGS: REPORTING FACT, INFERENCE, OR EMOTION

These writers handle their materials in characteristic ways. Let us consider three sorts of writings, reporting: (1) observations; (2) thoughts, opinions, or judgments; and (3) attitudes, feelings, or desires.

Personal Reports of Fact, Inference, or Emotion

Factual Writings

The personal writer usually avoids the use of bias words in his reporting. He acknowledges that different people might perceive a situation differently. He reports not "the truth" but what he has seen.

Inferential Writings

A personal writer tends to treat facts as facts and inferences as inferences. He tries to relate facts to inferences. A personal writer presents his inferences as one rational way to think about a situation. He affirms that the views he presents are his own.

---

[3] C. WRIGHT MILLS, *The Sociological Imagination* (New York: Grove, 1959), p. 220.
[4] *Ibid.,* p. 221.
[5] *Ibid.*

Emotionally Expressive Writings

A personal writer tends to label his feelings as his own; he seeks to share the agony or the joy that he has personally experienced. In general, personal writings are tentative in mood; the author affirms that this is the way *he* thinks and feels.

Impersonal or Autonomous Reports of Fact, Inference, or Emotion

Factual Writings

Some impersonal writers make extensive use of bias words in their reporting of facts. They often lose no opportunity to impress upon the reader their own established view. They tend to imply that their own observations are fair and truthful, and they want the reader to believe that these observations are what any man must see. Such a writer wants to make the reader feel compelled to believe what is being reported; therefore, he may sometimes carefully select the facts he presents, omitting any that embarrass his position.

Inferential Writings

The impersonal writer tends to write as if his views and opinions were not opinions, judgments, and conjectures, but facts. He frequently blurs the distinctions between facts and opinions. When he reports inferences, the author may make no effort to share with the reader the manner in which he came to this particular position. He may make little effort to relate inferences to facts. The impersonal writer tends to treat his opinions as "the truth" rather than as one reasonable view of a situation. He tends to treat difficult nonpointing words as unambiguously meaningful and to treat complex situations as if they were simple.

Emotionally Expressive Writings

The impersonal writer seeks, through the use of emotional words and phrases, to arouse feeling in others; he does not try to *reveal* his own personal, emotional experience. He uses fear words, such as "creeping socialism," or enticing words, such as "rich and spacious," to carry an emotional message, designed to arouse the reader. In general, impersonal writings are authoritarian in mood; they show little personal reference: the author affirms, calmly, enticingly, or with fear words, that *this is the way things are.*

Classroom Evaluation of Written Things

Examples of different kinds of writing can be examined in class. Magazines, newspapers, advertisements, political pamphlets, and scientific reports can be evaluated in the light of the ideas suggested, or others that the teacher may devise.

Suppose a newspaper reports that John Doe won an election by "a mere 5,000-vote margin." If we read, further on, that the final vote was Doe, 10,000, Opponent, 5,000, the word "mere" is easy to identify as a bias word, implying something quite different from: DOE WINS BY 2-1 MARGIN.

Most of us would be startled to read an account such as the following in a textbook. "The hard-riding, hard-fighting Tartars easily routed the hordes of knights assembled to stop the growing Tartar empire." It is not the use of bias words that would surprise us. It is just that they are the wrong bias words; we are used to seeing the shoe on the other foot!

Bias words often obscure facts: What were the military tactics of the two sides? How many men were actually engaged in battle? (How many knights—or Tartars—make a horde?) Still, some writers use bias words in order to produce vivid writing. One way to use some types of bias words appropriately is to defend the interpretation they imply at the time that you use them. An example might be, "John Doe won the election by a mere 5,000 votes. (Winners of the three previous elections had victory margins of well over 100,000 votes.)"

Two of the three statements below are almost completely free of bias words, yet to anyone who cares at all about their subjects, they are lively to the point of provoking controversy.

Consider the first of these pieces of writing, an automobile advertisement: "This rich new ——— brings you more pure luxury per dollar than anybody ever brought you before. For example, the rich, spacious interiors are finished with refinements you generally expect to pay more for." Do you want to be persuaded? The writing is not reporting observations. These are opinions or judgments. They are impersonal: you cannot tell whose views these are. The use of ameliorative words carries their message.

Here is another argument:

In English we divide most of our words into two classes, which have different grammatical and logical properties. Class 1 we call nouns, e.g., "house, man"; class 2, verbs, e.g., "hit, run." Many words of one class can act secondarily as of the other class, e.g., "a hit, a run," or "to man (the boat)," but, on the primary level, the division between the classes is absolute. Our language thus gives us a bipolar division of nature. But nature herself is not thus polarized. If it be said that "strike, turn, run," are verbs because they denote temporary or short-lasting events, i.e., actions, why then is "fist" a noun? It also is a temporary event. Why are "lightning, spark, wave, eddy, pulsation, flame, storm, phase, cycle, spasm, noise, emotion" nouns? They are temporary events. If "man" and "house" are nouns because they are long-lasting and stable events, i.e., things, what then are "keep, adhere, extend, project, continue, persist, grow, dwell," and so on doing among the verbs? If it be objected that "possess, adhere" are verbs because they are stable relationships rather than stable percepts, why then should "equilibrium, pressure, current, peace, group, nation, society, tribe, sister," or any kinship term be among the nouns? It will be found that an "event" to us means "what our language classes as a verb" or something analogized therefrom. And it will be found that it is not possible to define "event, thing, object, relationship," and so on, from nature, but that to define them always involves a circuitous return to the grammatical categories of the definer's language.[6]

Here, too, you find opinions! But here you find inferences related to evidence. This is an example of scholarly writing. There is little or no use of bias words.

Finally, consider this example of writing. A home economist reported that she encountered a newly designed jar of chocolate milk additive:

. . . The same product used to come in a can which was 5⅜ inches tall and contained one pound. The new jar is 7 inches tall and holds 15 ounces. Both cost 65¢. From here we set out to see how many such changes appeared on our grocery shelves in one month. We put everyone to work: the night crews, the home economists, the buyers, the people at our wholesale[r]. We know that we missed some but this is what we found:

1. Weight down, price same: seven items.
2. Weight down, price up: one item.
3. Weight down, price down slightly, but price per pound up; four items.

Analysis of the above items showed an average price increase of 9%. There was just one change that could be an advantage to the consumer: a cereal added waxpaper wraps for maintaining freshness.

We also found the following:
4. Weight up, price same: one item (———)
5. Improvement in packaging *without* a price increase: one item. ——— liquid detergent went from glass to plastic.
6. Change to a standard size: four items. These included ——— Oil which has just returned with a quart bottle after abandoning the quart about two years ago.
7. Change to a non-standard size from a standard size: four items. Crackers went from one pound to 13½ ounces, two milk additives went from 16 to 15 ounces, and waxes which used to come in quarts and half gallons appeared in one pint 10 ounce and one quart 14 ounce sizes. This type of change is especially distressing to those of us who have been working for standard sizes.
8. Change in shape (without change in price or weight): five items. All new packages were taller and thinner than old packages. (Many of the reduced-weight items under 1, 2, 3 above managed to look as big or bigger than their heavier counterparts.)[7]

    [6] BENJAMIN LEE WHORF, *Language, Thought and Reality,* ed. John B. Carroll (New York: John Wiley and The Massachusetts Institute of Technology Press, 1956), p. 215.
    [7] BETSY WOOD, "There Once Was a Package . . . ," *Co-op News* (Berkeley: Consumers Cooperative of Berkeley, Inc.), XVII, No. 1 (January 13, 1964).

PERSONAL AND IMPERSONAL WRITING

	Personal	Impersonal
Statement of Fact: Relate observations	1. Tends to acknowledge that observations are personal and that another person may see the same event differently. 2. Tends to be concerned with a "fair" representation of the facts. 3. Tends to seek to persuade with the facts rather than with their artful selection. 4. Tends to acknowledge his own personal biases explicitly. 5. Tends to avoid bias words in reporting observations.	1. May use many bias words in relating observations. 2. Tends to report "the facts": the situation as it "really" is revealed. 3. May seek to persuade by artful selection of facts to be reported.
Statements of Inference: Relate thoughts, judgments, comparisons, explanations	1. Tends to treat statements of thought or opinion as thoughts and opinions. 2. Seeks to show evidence both for and against the opinions and judgments with which he is working. 3. Tends to write in a tentative mood: avoids appearing to have all the answers and a clear claim of virtue. 4. Tends to regard his own view as one of several possible intelligent views. 5. Tends to persuade by logic and evidence but may regard alternative views as possible and virtuous. 6. Tends to identify himself as one person with these thoughts; avoids the impersonal discovery of absolute truth.	1. Tends to treat statements of thoughts and opinions as statements of fact. 2. Tends to treat complex situations as if they were simple: to imply that he has all of the answers needed. 3. May use many bias words. 4. Tends to write in a dogmatic mood: opinions and judgments are presented with a great sense of authority. 5. Relies more on bias words and authoritative mood than logic and evidence to persuade the reader. 6. Tends to imply his view is the only intelligent view.

This writing makes little use of bias words; it is a personal report of observations.

An evaluation of a piece of writing will lead to the development of inferences concerning the author's purpose in writing. The personal writer tries hard to show how he thinks and why he thinks as he does. He is concerned with clarifying for himself and for the reader the character of his own thought. Often writings about cars, deodorants, and political ideas make much use of emotional words. The impersonal writer tries hard to make his view appear to be the only possible view.

The accompanying table, "Personal and Impersonal Writing," presents a summary of the suggested ideas for use in evaluating written materials.

PART TWO

The Challenge of Teaching

Teaching involves both constraint and choice: teachers must choose among possible alternatives that are limited in various ways. Ignorance is perhaps the most persistent constraint. A teacher of social studies confronts an enormous challenge, the effort to acquire information about the world in which we live. That world is full of many things: ideas, such as communism; concepts, such as automation; social change, such as the proliferation of leisure-time activities; passions, such as racial hatreds; and anxieties, often complicated by such "remedies" as the extensive use of tranquilizers and alcohol. The constraint of bureaucracy and custom is a second major problem, regulating school practice in many ways—both obvious and subtle.

An effective teacher of social studies must realistically appraise the constraints that he faces and the choices that are open to him. This section identifies some of the important constraints and attempts to clarify the choice and challenge of teaching social studies.

VI

Choice and Constraint

The Obligation to Choose

Teaching is an occupation of infinite variety and continual excitement. In the interplay of the thirty or so personalities in a classroom, moments of delicately balanced achievement and blundering struggle propel teacher and student toward one goal or another. It is difficult to think of an activity less predictable, yet potentially more rewarding.

Certainty is a stranger to the classroom: a teacher can never predict how a group of children will behave or be sure that he will achieve what he hopes for. Nonetheless, teaching can be and ought to be, a deliberate, purposive endeavor. The teacher is not aimless in his instructional behavior, nor is he indiscriminate in his intended goals. The array of possible classroom activities includes some that are judged more valuable than others and that should be pursued explicitly. The teacher is committed to such goals, but he should be flexible enough to change direction if it is apparent that he is making no headway toward them.

To encourage learning, the teacher: foments discussions; makes assignments; poses a variety of questions; makes materials and information available; elicits and prizes certain behaviors; denies, ignores, and withholds rewards for other behaviors; and fosters independent, cooperative, or competitive settings for learning. Whatever it is that he does, however, he does it at the expense of *not* doing something else. On what basis does he make this choice?

His decision to act in some specific way may be regarded as a prediction, still to be verified, of the likely consequences of his behavior: "*If* I do these things with these children, *then* these learning outcomes should follow." On what basis does he make one prediction rather than another? What sensible outcomes can teachers choose to seek?

A teacher may permit others to decide for him what, how, to whom, and when he ought to teach. In the 1890's a candidate for teacher of a one-room school in southern Illinois was being interviewed by the school board. After some casual conversation, one of the board members suddenly asked, "And tell me, Mr. Smith, how do you teach the world?" Most of the community's residents claimed to find support in the Bible for the view that the earth was flat. The question, therefore, was pointed and important, and the room was quietly tense as the board waited for the candidate's answer. Mr. Smith leaned back confidently, twirled his moustache, and replied, "I can teach her any way you like her." He got the job.

When a teacher allows decisions to be made for him by people in administrative authority, or by textbook writers, or by concern about what next year's teacher might say, or by tradition ("That's the way we've always done it"), or by someone else's consensus ("That's what everyone else is doing"), then he abdicates his responsibility as a professional person. What everyone else is doing, or what was done in the past, or what someone in administrative authority recommends might be excellent practices to follow. It is possible to discover this by analyzing the recommended practices critically. The teacher may test for himself the logic of each idea and measure the consequences of certain practices, comparing them with the consequences of logically promising alternatives. Teachers should become responsible for their actions.

Teachers confront constraint as well as choice as they engage in their professional tasks. The curriculum guide, the citizen's report, school-building design, supply lists, and personnel policy combine and articulate a network of choice-by-others. The pattern of these choices restricts the realm of teacher decision. Part of being a teacher is facility in reckoning with the decisions of others; teachers must accommodate. But, at the same time, they face the necessity for personal choice. They are obligated to organize their classroom in some manner. They must formulate directions, compose assignments, proportion time, and deploy materials. They must decide whether to counsel or to punish, to award or to withhold praise, to choose alone or in consultation with the learners. They must render appropriate evaluative symbols or statements.

Becoming a teacher involves developing competence at two tasks: rendering and effecting personal instructional decisions; and reckoning with the impersonal, controlling decisions of others.

Preparation for Choosing

Piety and faith are evoked abundantly in the preparation of a teacher. Piety converts a job into a calling; faith sustains those called when set upon by doubt. Even the faithful entertain some doubt as they struggle with such pleasant-sounding, but obscure, notions as rapport, creativity, empathy, readiness, democratic attitudes, and intrinsic rewards. No matter how necessary faith and piety may be, however, they are not sufficient counsel for the conduct of instruction. Two important additions are required for adequate preparation. First, the real constraints in teaching can be determined, and a strategy for dealing with them can be formulated; and, second, teachers can be helped to develop a range of proposals in the areas where choice is possible.

Nevertheless, support for the idea that decision-making is a pivotal ingredient in teaching must rest on more than dogma, more than appeals to good feelings. One must deal, moreover, with the decisions teachers do not make and with the decisions they are unaware of making.

Constraints

Origin of Constraints

There appear to be two sources of constraint in classroom teaching: the restraints that originate from without and the restrictions that arise within the teacher himself. "Without" constraints include textbooks, manuals, workbooks, school-board directives, the work of local pressure groups, policy interpretations of the principal, and so on. "Within" constraints include concern that a certain social-studies topic may be controversial, fear that some small fact may be overlooked in the curriculum, or uneasiness lest something be taught too early and thus offend the teacher in the next higher grade. Perhaps the most pertinent "within" constraint is ignorance— the legacy of the uninformed.

In many instances, of course, it is difficult to separate "within" from "without," to appraise whether the restrictions stem from the characteristics of the teacher or from the managerial makeup of the school. Often they are intertwined. Frequently, teachers feel compelled to "cover" the textbook, yet their building principal will confide that he is concerned because so many of his teachers are unimaginative and preoccupied with the text. Wide differences can often be noted in the informal staff organization of elementary-school buildings. Acceptable teacher behavior may vary dramatically from building to building within a given school district. In one school, no culture study is complete unless it is highly decorative; in others, the social-studies program is austere and the decoration lacking. In one building, learning activities are tightly contained within the classroom; in others, class projects and committee work overflow into halls and courtyards, into the gymnasium, and into the supply closet. The point here is not that certain arrangements are preferable to others. It is rather that sometimes only one style of teaching behavior is sanctioned in a given building. Does such a constraint come from without; say, because the principal sets a dominant tone? It is equally plausible to say that such constraints are manufactured by teachers themselves; a consequence, possibly, of strong needs to affiliate with or to defer to others. Determining the source of constraints is a central task of the thoughtful teacher, but he risks a human error in the enterprise. He will prefer to classify most constraints as impinging from "without" when they should properly be labeled constraints from "within."

Varieties of Constraints

A brief listing of the varieties of constraints includes those stemming from *manageable solutions* we invent for the efficient conduct of schools. A second broad category concerns the *expectations for teachers* held by themselves and by others. A final category deals with *teachers and their tasks*.

IN MANAGEABLE SOLUTIONS

Schools are complex operations. Their size, number, logistic support, and personnel require coordination. Classroom instruction is a complex operation. The diversity of learning tasks, the range of talents, and the differing moods and interests of the learners must be incorporated into some instructional solution that the teacher can manage. Both the school administrator and the classroom teacher must fashion solutions to their everyday tasks. But sometimes the solution that is manageable restricts the nature and quality of the social-studies program.

The Standard Supply Unit–School "systems" need operating procedures, command chains, channels, delegated authority, and the like. And these internal, organizational demands mold quite directly the instructional decisions of teachers. For example, classrooms are likely to be treated as interchangeable units provided with interchangeable resources. Hence, fourth-grade teachers throughout a given school system are nearly always supplied with identical social-studies texts, regardless of the patterns of economic and social differences across the district, the individual strengths of teachers, and the possibility that in some schools the children cannot even read the text. Of course, teachers can use books in a variety of ways, or even deliberately ignore them altogether. But the standard textbook must be taken into account somehow. Practically, it is nearly impossible to ignore thirty-six texts stacked on a shelf under the windows. The sight of them, gathering dust, points to the wasting of—at four dollars each—one hundred and forty-four dollars.

Certainly, the standard supply unit (a fourth-grade text for each fourth grader in each fourth-grade classroom) is an eminently manageable solution to the problem of administering schools. It is also a contraint upon teachers. Uniformity may erode the teacher's power of choice. When the accouterments of instruction—films, maps, globes, workbooks, chalkboard, texts, art supplies—are the same everywhere, the probability that many teachers will find a standard use for these supplies is high. The penalty for developing a divergent teaching notion is that one must develop the instructional resources required by the new scheme. Readings within children's ability, current and authentic information, artifacts, knowledgeable resource people, and productive tasks must be gathered before they can be used. The temptation, therefore, is to think within the limits set by the instructional apparatus available in every classroom.

Homogeneity—The diversity of tasks the school performs must be ordered in some fashion. One arrangement for reducing these tasks to manageable proportions is that of neighborhood-alike schools and age-alike classes. Typically, schools do not draw from diverse neighborhoods, and classrooms normally contain children of very similar age. In this way, the principal and his staff need not cope with extreme heterogeneity. This, too, is a manageable solution. But, again, what is feasible and useful for general school operations may be neither helpful nor encouraging in the particular operations of social-studies instruction. In school, children see around them only people like themselves, with homes like theirs and values like their own. A possible consequence of this sort of deprivation is that one comes to know less and less about people who are different. If some understanding of the nearby is necessary in rendering the far-away comprehensible, then children need to confront diversity in the close-at-hand. But the effect of school organization is that of managed sameness. Apparently, we achieve efficient administration at a cost of learning loss. Would managed diversity produce efficiency in learning, even though at an administrative loss?

Habit and Routine—Few people can continually face afresh the tasks of school instruction. Teachers become well practiced. Once teaching becomes a habit, however, learning often appears routine. Walks and bus trips, firehouse and harbor, the farm and post office are as predictable for some teachers as the first hard-backed reader. Little wonder that children develop practiced responses to satisfy our practiced questions:

"Our next study will be about Mexico. Let's think about what we want to learn about our neighbor, Mexico." The teacher writes on the board as the children make suggestions: geography, government, food, clothing, products, natural resources and history, education, cities and sites.

"These are the same ideas we gave for the study of China," the teacher comments.

Paul replies, "You know why, we always have tests on these same things." The others nod in agreement and the study begins.[1]

This teacher's "Let's think about what we want to learn about our neighbor, Mexico" is akin to the rhetorical question. That is, a response from the class is not really required, because it is obvious to everyone what that

[1] ALICE MIEL (ed.), *Creativity in Teaching* (Belmont, Calif.: Wadsworth, 1961), p. 118.

response should be. Asking a particular kind of question can become well-practiced teacher behavior, limiting and constraining the quality of classroom learning.

Beyond individual predilections for the habitual, teachers are preyed upon by the publicized schemes of others. Educationdom is amply populated with method, with plan, with stylized procedures. Ritual, a demanding mistress, appears to have been ardently courted.

IN EXPECTATIONS OF SELF AND OTHERS

The "Next Year" Expectation–Perhaps the earlier, rather dogged assertion of the teacher's obligation to choose suggested a certain naiveté regarding schools and children, classrooms and community. Casting the teacher in the role of decider may appear to ignore the realistic limits in directing school instruction. Teaching, after all, may only consist of doing the expected. For example, how often is today's instruction actively dictated by the content or conduct of some future classroom? Because common fractions must precede decimal ones, because kindergarten must prepare for the demands of first-grade reading tasks, because sixth graders must be prepared to meet the self-reliance demands of junior high school, and, above all, because, "You'll be glad you had this when . . . ," teachers are spared the rigors of decision-making.

The Survey Expectation–Teachers entangle themselves in, or are somehow snared by, the survey expectation. Some sixth graders, for example, are introduced to Europe and the Soviet Union, southern and eastern Asia, Australia, New Zealand, Antarctica, and Africa. Because so much must be surveyed, much of the study appears to be routine. In part, teachers adopt routine in order to be systematic. Afraid of leaving out something important, they choose a level of instruction whose distinctive quality is its unimportance. Under the compulsion to survey, they transform Africa's bewildering variety of languages, peoples, diverse art forms, and histories into a study of "natives, beasts, and jungles." Fortunately, much of this jumble of misinformation is easily forgotten.

Perhaps the fear of overlooking some kernel of knowledge is prompted by loss of purpose. Are the goals of the social studies entirely satisfied by acquisition of information? Or can schools nurture the capacity to formulate and pursue fruitful questions? Can children become inquirers; participate in some primitive fashion, for example, in the intellectual activities historians engage in as they come to know? Or is school history contained entirely in what scholars agree upon as historic knowledge?

The "Tool Subject" Expectation–Teachers in the primary grades are often expected to teach reading skills and little else. The general argument for this position is that of the "tool subject," i.e., that certain subjects are prerequisite to instruction in other fields. The central tasks of the primary grades, in this view, are defined within the language arts—reading, handwriting, spelling, speaking, and so forth. Science, art, music, numbers, and the social studies lie on the periphery of the curriculum. Consequently, a "number" page is freely employed to mark time for those waiting to be called to the reading circle. "Sharing time" passes for social studies, and coloring the illustrations that decorate mimeographed exercises suffices for art instruction. No doubt the "tool subject" expectation actively dictates priorities in the primary classroom.

The force of the "tool subject" argument continues through the grades. If social studies, by design, must be delayed until the child achieves basic mastery of reading, then beginning instruction may be chained to the developing "tool." The study of people may serve as an intermediate exercise in reading. Indeed, the study skills in social education are commonly defined as library and textbook behaviors, e.g., using an index, skimming for information, ferreting out key paragraphs. And teachers must contend with this restricted definition of study: that the path to understanding people lies entirely in what others write about them.

The Opinion of Others–The opinions of others, whether fancied or real, are often coercive. In this, the social studies are particularly vulnerable. The risk of appearing controversial is a severe constraint; better Simon Bolívar than Fidel Castro, better the artifacts of the past than the actualities of the present. Perhaps this is why "bland" is so appropriately applied to social studies.

"Models" for Instruction–Finally, problems of regression often plague the beginning teacher, the tendency to revert to the textbook-recitation-test triad. Possibly, undergraduate courses in the teaching of social studies contribute to this problem by holding up as a model the fully embellished, elegant instructional program. In effect, the message is, "There is no apprenticeship to be served in teaching; expect of yourself this high level of competence immediately." But, for most graduates, the entry year in teaching is forcibly instructive, each week bringing greater awareness of the complexity of the learning process. Unable to achieve the model of instruction held up for him, the new teacher may seek the ego protection found in rejecting as "impractical theory" the mode of instruction discussed in his preparation program.

The point is that administrators rarely look at beginning teachers as anything less than wholly competent and accomplished. Because they are not yet at that state of high skill, the beginners must manage in some fashion to look skillful. They usually "play it safe."

IN TEACHERS AND THEIR TASKS

Selection of Occupation–Teaching appears to be a gentle occupation. Moderate job demands, leisurely vacations, secure salaries, attractive hours, frequent holidays, a brief and not too arduous training period, all these attract people. Father's prudent counsel, *viz.,* "Should anything ever happen you will always be self-supporting," persuades still others. For some, teaching is compatible with marriage and motherhood. That is, the classroom offers opportunity to cultivate useful skills in child-rearing; and, when the offspring become independent, the teaching certificate can be reactivated to augment household income or to provide an occupation for an idle middle age. A few undergraduates find their way into an elementary-education program simply to satisfy a university's demand for a declared major field of study. Contingency, then, appears to be an important factor in electing to become a teacher; entry and persistence in the profession are conditional upon a series of external considerations. Competence in directing an instructional program, however, is central in the teaching role. Possibly, the reasons that encourage entry into teaching may function as constraints in the full realization of that role. Motives arising out of contingency considerations are satisfied by the acquisition of ordinary vocational competence. In most instances, the peripheral advantages, the "fringe benefits" of the profession, are quite independent of, even unrelated to, artistry. Teaching, as any profession, risks becoming precisely what its practitioners believe it to be.

Diversity is not a striking attribute among elementary-school teachers. They often share common social origins, common preparation, common duties, common responsibilities, and common salaries. Moreover, experience in teaching seems to present them with a certain common lesson to be learned. Jackson and Guba, for example, offer the interesting notion of a needs syndrome emerging in teachers of some tenure.[2] Experienced female teachers described in this report recorded much higher needs for deference, for orderliness, and for endurance than did those of lesser experience. Because of latent capacity, the pressures of the role, or other reasons, experienced teachers seem to display an affinity for regularity, perserverance, and docility. And the mechanisms bringing this about may be precisely those that drive the autonomous and the decisive out of the classroom.*

Common Tasks–Every teacher is employed to perform duties much like those of any other teacher. The artistic and the ordinary, the inexperienced

---

[2] PHILLIP W. JACKSON and EGON C. GUBA, "The Need Structure of In-Service Teachers," *School Review* (Summer 1957), pp. 177–192.

* See for example: Kaufman, B. *Up the Down Staircase* (New York: Prentice-Hall, 1965).

and the tenured face comparable responsibilities. In at least two ways, this common definition of teaching tasks may precipitate a very common level of skill in choice-making. Because few distinctions are made between the "journeyman" and the "master" teacher, some practitioners may find this reason enough to develop only moderate teaching proficiency. The novice, the beginning teacher, having to deal with all the complexity teaching can offer, may be forced to devise a manageable, but impoverished, learning setting. In effect, he blinds himself to the subtleties of the instructional problem, enough so that his unpolished skills appear appropriate to the task. Once constructed, even a jerry-built curriculum takes on permanence. If the provisional procedures of the beginning teacher cannot be surrendered, then the increment of experience may be nothing more than a repetition of what is essentially a trial response.

Isolation–A significant deterrent to controlled, consciously examined, instructional acts may reside in the isolation built into the teaching role. Classroom teaching, largely because of school organization, affords little opportunity for analysis or appraisal by other knowledgeable adults. The prevalence of the term "self-contained" for the classroom recognizes this condition. Very rarely can the principal or curriculum staff function directly as a consultant to the teacher. Supervisory personnel are far more likely to be engaged in general support and logistic activity, removed from the focal acts of classroom instruction. Central-office scurry and motion centers on scope and sequence charts, mass achievement data, personnel policy, Business-Education Day, parent-teacher conference handbooks, curriculum construction, textbook purchase, and all the other activities seemingly necessary to schools, but remote from the intimate acts of learning. To a marked degree, teachers must instruct themselves in how to analyze the design and consequence of their own classroom efforts.

The Context of Choice

This opening discussion of constraints may give the impression that all restrictions are bad and that they always result in diminished, or meager, classroom teaching. This is not true, however; some constraints are reasonable and necessary restrictions upon teachers. For example, in order to coordinate the efforts of individual teachers, school districts often empower groups of teachers and administrators to impose constraints in the form of curricular designs or suggested sequences for instructional units of work. Teachers are not often free, nor should they be, to consider any topic whatever in the classroom. Instructional choices are limited so as to fall within a predetermined pattern that promises to tie together the efforts of an entire staff. A variety of other restrictions are also necessary and prudent in the conduct of schools, in order to provide for the safety of children and a balanced school program.

The restrictions encountered in teaching are of several kinds; they may vary in number and source or in their power to constrain, but they exist. It is within the context of constraint that teachers exercise choice.

VII

Winning the Freedom to Choose

Warranted Choice

Chapter Six discusses the variety of constraints teachers face in directing classroom instruction. Some teachers accept these restrictions woodenly, passively obeying the directions in "manuals" and the directives of administrators, occasionally becoming dutifully excited by one glib faddist or another. Other teachers, surprisingly enough, enjoy nothing so much as a good fight. Incessant automatic rejection of constraints, however, sometimes wins freedom but leaves the winner too tired to enjoy it. There is a middle way between passivity and truculence.

Schools cannot condone irresponsible change. The innovations teachers propose must be warranted, that is, choice must be justified by the demands of a particular teaching-learning situation and its potential for increasing the efficiency with which children learn. Warranted choice is that "middle way" between truculence and passivity.

The following discussion presents tactics for dealing with external and internal constraints on classroom teaching, in order to travel this "middle way."

Dealing with External Constraints

Creating Alternatives

Because the business of the schools will proceed, those who fail to act decisively will have their decisions made for them. Freedom is to be used *for* something; it seldom abides with those who have no use for it.

Bruner, in commenting on the enterprise of the mind, recently observed that "The guarantee against limits is the sense of alternatives."[1] This notion is highly relevant to the teacher's struggle to establish his freedom to control

[1] JEROME S. BRUNER, *On Knowing: Essays for the Left Hand* (Cambridge, Mass.: The Harvard University Press, 1962), p. 117.

117

the quality, the direction, and the sequence of his instructional activities. A lively, well-developed "sense of alternatives" is basic to winning and safeguarding freedom of choice.

Obviously, poverty in ideas renders decision-making dry and academic. If he has only one idea concerning the way something might be taught, then the teacher does not choose; he sets about accomplishing his singular task. Only the possession of counterproposals or alternative teaching plans makes possible a choice among them. Before deciding, one must assemble the array of possible decision. Freedom to choose obligates the teacher to formulate ideas, to know well what might be done.

In developing alternative instructional plans, one can turn to at least three sources for ideas. These are (1) children; (2) teachers' thoughts and experiences; and (3) the modes of knowing in the social sciences.

CHILDREN AS A SOURCE OF IDEAS

Children are by far the sprightliest source of instructional schemes in classroom teaching. A child's question, a remark, a certain use of language frequently provide the basis for some important learning sequence. The range of class interests, attempts to interpret events, and earnest as well as playful moments all suggest ideas teachers might use in patterning the development of instruction. Pupils may habitually force problems into the mold of the simple dichotomy, e.g., good or bad, for or against, modern or backward, labor or management, liberal or conservative, red or dead, win or no-win, them or us. They may demonstrate a preference for a range of two in matters of choice. Observing this, a teacher can find quiet ways to make plain the high risks involved in narrowly restricting alternatives when choosing a course of action. One might concoct a healthy sort of game in which the class begins with a taut, two-dimensional situation and strives to unfreeze it by ferreting out the several viewpoints the involved participants have ignored or the potential solutions they have overlooked. A discussion, a timely comment, a passage read to the class might all be useful in demonstrating what happens to the quality of communication when people they know, groups they belong to, and nations they identify with rapidly lock into fixed positions on the questions of the moment. Schools may play some small but urgent role in reducing the number of adults who instantly polarize their everyday social and civic situations. The beginnings of this small role probably lie in the observations teachers make of children and the tasks of instruction.

Knowing something of the texture of children's lives has been the overarching theme for much of Hilda Taba's work. In "diagnosing," "focusing," and gaining "perspective" on human-relations needs, the Taba group developed a number of techniques for assessing the concerns and interpretations children generate in urban communities.[2] One participant in the Intergroup Education Project asked her second graders to respond to the question "What is a community?" Children of another cooperating teacher (also second graders) wrote suggestions on how their community might be improved. The replies were revealing and instructive:

WHAT IS A COMMUNITY?

"A community is our neighborhood. A place where you own property. Where mothers and fathers help boys and girls grow up."

"In our community we learn and live like other people. Our community is a lovely place."

"It is a place where we work together to keep our community beautiful. It is a nice place because we have freedom."

WAYS TO IMPROVE OUR COMMUNITY

"The fences lay down on the walks. The children have to walk over them. It is hard to walk over so much junk on the sidewalks."

"I like my neighborhood because it is the best we can afford. We do not have any rats and our lavatory is not outside."

"Too many beer joints around here. The gully has too much glass. Too many children fight. Too many factories around here."[3]

The statements given by these second graders indicate that for the social-studies teacher the world of privilege poses as many educational problems, perhaps, as does the world of deprivation. Both of these neighborhoods impose distinct and particular limits on experience. A part of the school's role is to free children, gradually, from some of the limitations of immediate neighborhood experience.

Classroom teaching is sometimes harried, however, and teachers are not always in a position to "field" the ideas that come bounding their way. This point is sharply illustrated in the last line of the following excerpt from the classroom:

The teacher remarks, "The picture here shows the man putting in the telephone. Do most houses have telephones?"

PATTY: "Every house should have a telephone."

JILL: "Every house does have a telephone. Who ever heard of one that didn't?"

ARNIE: "Even my maid has a telephone."

ERNIE: "Telephones are put in every house."

[2] See the Intergroup Education series, Hilda Taba (ed.) *Diagnosing Human Relations Needs* (1951), *With Focus on Human Relations* (1952), and *With Perspective on Human Relations* (1952) (Washington: American Council on Education).

[3] HILDA TABA, *Elementary Curriculum in Intergroup Relations* (Washington: American Council on Education, 1950), pp. 9–10.

TEACHER: "Where might one find a house without a telephone?"
PATTY: "That's impossible!"
TEACHER: "No, houses in rural areas don't have telephones sometimes."
ANN: "I know someone who doesn't have a phone because she doesn't have enough money."
PATTY: "Everyone has enough money for a telephone."
TEACHER: "Who puts in the plumbing?"[4]

The teacher in this episode seems to be trying to help children face the shaky base of their absolute judgments. But after awhile she seems to find it necessary to put the line of inquiry aside and to go on to something else. Whether or not these children get to know that some people do not have telephones is not crucial in this learning situation. They should, however, learn to exercise caution in making judgments. It is up to the teacher to devise a way of focusing on this learning problem at some later time.

TEACHERS AS A SOURCE OF IDEAS

Observing children is but one source of alternatives. Teachers also glean ideas from participation in the community of adult events and concerns. A conversation, a traveler, a newspaper column may precipitate some variation in usual classroom procedure. One might observe, in a great inland city, for example, a paradox in technology: alongside the expressway and the massive automotive industry, the ore boats and ocean vessels along a nearby seaway, the steam, diesel, gasoline, and turbine engines of various carriers, and lunar rocketry and supersonic jet-liners, two-wheeled carts operate, drawn laboriously by the junk collectors of the central city. Are there other "living" time lines to be discovered? Could this be the beginning of an approach to the study of the city or the study of technology and transportation?

In reading a passage on Africa's rush toward the center of the world stage, one might be struck by the kaleidoscope of maps picturing the continent's development. From this might develop an approach to investigating with children the mute tale of Africa told in maps—the Africa of the Nile Kingdoms; the Africa of Imperial Rome; the mariner's sketchy, peripheral maps of Africa, with its heartland inhabited by elephants and crocodiles; maps of Africa in 1850 and at the turn of the century; Africa in 1940, 1950, 1960; the maps of Africa predicted for tomorrow.

The sweep of surrounding events may inspire observations of still another order. One might find in population statistics and in the visible development of urban belts the notion that privacy will be a scarce com-

4 MIEL, *Creativity in Teaching,* pp. 122–123.

modity in the near future, cutting down severely the possibility of solitude and repose. With this idea in mind, the teacher might take a somewhat different view of the usual approach to the social studies, an approach that fosters an inordinate amount of practice in the membership skills required of individuals working at group tasks. He may encourage children to find ways to be alone in the midst of a group by discovering the private joys of hobbying or of individual creativity.

Following their own interests, teachers may travel through Canada taking color slides or collect Haida carvings or Indian pottery. One might be made sharply aware of current issues through membership in the League of Women Voters; another might pursue the local history of an area, collecting personal accounts, old photographs, or tall tales. Teachers are individuals, engaging in individual pursuits. Many times this activity can provide ammunition for instruction.

Upon graduation, young teachers cannot be expected to know everything they might need to know. They may not know the way in which wool was carded in pioneer American homes, the effects of tribal structure on governmental forms in Ghana, or the routines and organization underlying the assembly-line production of goods. But there are advantages in making an avocation out of learning about the eras, events, and processes that one deals with regularly in the classroom. There is the advantage of authenticity, especially in sharing with children such artifacts as letters, photographs, and homely objects in the everyday life of far-away people. There is the advantage of liveliness of instruction, based on personal involvement with the material to be learned. There is the advantage of "inside knowledge," when a teacher can go beyond the textbook, either in supplying current data, or in confronting children with information the textbook writers dismissed. What is too complex, unnecessary, or inappropriate for the general textbook market may be quite an important commodity in the market of ideas for a particular classroom.

MODES OF KNOWING AS A SOURCE OF IDEAS

A third source of ideas for classroom instruction may be found in considering the work of the various social scientists. What operations lie behind the findings of the historian, the geographer, the anthropologist? The effect this sort of awareness might have on classroom instruction is nicely illustrated in "School History and the Historical Method."[5] In that text, the writer portrays a classroom discussion concerning Herodotus and the search for the oldest people in the world. The teacher first asks the class what people they know about and what group of people they think might be very old. Individual children reply indicating that they have read about

[5] HENRY JOHNSON, "School History and the Historical Method," in Part IV.

Indians, heard about Germans, seen Orientals, etc. It is interesting here to anticipate the line of questioning the teacher will choose, what direction learning will take at this point. Many teachers would turn to the chalkboard and write a statement equivalent to: "There are these people in the world—Indians, Germans, Chinese . . ." and elicit from the class still other "known" peoples. This particular teacher wrote on the board the statement: "We may know of people by hearing about them." She went on to read from Herodotus and to discuss the manner in which historians "know."

Another teacher might discover again how frequently the scholar pursuing a problem must consult various documents. Such a teacher might locate several telephone books and propound these questions: "What can these tell you about Tacoma and the Pacific Northwest, Beaumont and the Southwest, Montgomery and the industrial South; what can a telephone book reveal about our own city?"[6]

Any human behavior can be regarded in the language of the sociologist, anthropologist, political scientist, historian, or economist. A discipline does not stake out a segment of human activity to study; it stakes out a set of constructs, a mode of questioning, a set of presuppositions. Churches and church-going behavior, for example, can be understood in a variety of ways, depending upon the particular questions posed, the constructs and presuppositions employed. One can understand the economics of churches through the use of that special language. One can understand the sociology of churches and church-going behavior. The church can be understood politically, anthropologically, historically. That is, one can know about churches in a variety of ways. The several social sciences use different modes of interrogation, but they have in common their subjects: human beings behaving as humans. The various social sciences are alternative ways of looking at people; they are not alternative ways in which people behave.

Supporting Alternatives

KNOWING WHY

One should know not only what might be done but why he wants to do it. There are cogent reasons for adopting one alternative over another. What are they? Why is the study advocated particularly relevant to a certain group of youngsters? How will it help them to achieve some worthwhile goal? What are the avowed intentions of the general curriculum for the grade level concerned? Perhaps a proposed scheme offers a likely vehicle for the realization of these commonly-agreed-upon goals. Beyond these may be worthwhile learning goals not yet recognized in statements of general goals for the social studies. Many schools intend that children develop understanding of

[6] See Chapter Eleven.

wider geographic communities, that is, home, school, city, state, nation, etc. Is the proposed study relevant to some of the other communities in which people live: the community of work, the community of values and heritage, the family community, the community of language? What priority does the study have with respect to these?

Does the teacher have some special or unique personal resource? Can he therefore suspend the general and well-anticipated topic for an unanticipated and unique study of some depth and intensity? What are the advantages of personal enthusiasm for a given topic? This is another tactic teachers employ in establishing the prerogative of choice—the tactic of knowing why.

GAUGING EFFECT

But how does one know if the promise of an instructional choice *does not* obtain? Under what conditions might innovative procedures be terminated or altered? Choice involves reasonable preparation for measuring the effects of proposed alternatives. In many instances, this means that one must make preparations well in advance of proposing a change in content or method. If, for example, a teacher would like to choose an alternative to "going through the text" in the social studies, then perhaps he might begin by determining the quality of current learning in his classroom. An attractive text, attentively read and imaginatively recited, produces a learning increment whose nature can be assessed. What increment does the alternative offer? Can it be demonstrated? To be sure, some dimensions to learning can be measured with a degree of exactness and objectivity, and other evaluations will be relatively awkward and impressionistic; but some basis of comparison can be obtained.

From a clear statement of the educational significance of the proposed study, one can usually infer the personal commitment of the teacher to the study, as well as the care with which he has prepared himself to carry it through to a successful conclusion. The ability to support proposed alternatives on the basis of their potential values as learning experiences may win for a teacher the opportunity to try them out.

Dealing with Internal Constraints

The Problem of Elephants

It is said that once an elephant is taught that any tether is powerful enough to contain his strength a rope of grass is sufficient to confine him to a tight little circle. This problem of elephants has a particular relevance in teaching. In a recent example, several teachers expressed the firm opinion that if they seriously questioned certain district instructional policies they should seek work elsewhere. Choice lay between obedient employment and quiet resignation from their positions. Yet each of these teachers was experienced and tenured. Their principal and fellow teachers respected them. Many of them were selected by the curriculum staff to help in making district decisions about textbook selection, the sequence of social-studies topics, and the like. The status of these teachers made it very possible that they could introduce instructional change in their classrooms. But they all regarded change as an "everyone or no-one" proposition. This monolithic attitude was agreed upon in all curricular matters. It was very effectively maintained, maintained, in part, because teachers participated in the fiction of the grass rope.

The notion of constraints from within is somewhat at odds with much of the romantic literature in the field of public education. Until recently, writers in curriculum and school administration were fond of developing long passages extolling the virtues of the autonomous classroom teacher. Each staff member was perceived as a visionary curriculum planner; every teacher was a significant participant in the process of rendering executive decisions. "Dynamic," "democratic," and "creative" became the watchwords of the new administrative efforts to cut away the fetters of the instructional staff. The present discussion, too, at times may appear rose colored; frequently teachers are obedient to constraints of their own making. Not all restraints impinge from without—teachers themselves are directly responsible for some common classroom restrictions.

The Problem of Boundary Testing

Children will find ways of testing what the limits are for appropriate school behavior. This observation leads to various policies. Teachers are advised, for example, to be consistent in what they accept as appropriate behavior. They are urged to adopt the clinical view of child behavior in preference to the overly moralistic one. Teachers themselves can learn to test what the "limits for appropriate school behavior" on their own part might be; as William James observed, possibly teachers "are a mite too docile."[7]

Sometimes teachers feel, quite consciously, "My responsibility is to the children of this class, I can hardly be expected to *experiment*." No matter how minor the hazards of failure might be, teachers such as these feel constrained to abide by well-practiced methods and well-rehearsed content. It is not at all unlikely, though, that a teacher's devotion to the *status quo* may at times be profoundly irresponsible. Comfortably unproductive classroom procedures may create an air of responsible instruction only because they are practiced so widely. A teacher's most responsible act is sometimes that of facing the uncomfortable fact of needed change.

[7] WILLIAM JAMES, *Talks to Teachers* (New York: W. W. Norton, 1958), p. 23.

An experiment would not be one, of course, without the possibility of failure. Whatever a thoughtful teacher might do experimentally, however, will produce some profit. If a trial procedure does not achieve the potential anticipated for it, the failure is only comparative; compared with standard instructional procedures, the innovation was not successful. But the class still learned something, and it may have learned quite a good deal.

Even when it appears that a procedure did not work, the project may have failed only because the teacher was measuring the wrong things. Usually a shift in instructional procedures is accompanied by a shift in what is desired as an outcome of instruction. But teachers are often tied to inflexible measuring devices, appraising new schemes as if a shift in expected outcomes never took place.

Possibly, the willingness to test the boundaries of choice in teaching is related to the ability to view trial procedures with detachment. After all, it is the instructional plan that fails, not the teacher. Schemes that are less than successful can be a source of information and better decisions, rather than a personal defeat.

Frequently, it helps to enlist others, to share the effort, to increase the sample, so that the procedure under consideration may be criticized from a wider base. As a number of minds work over an idea, there is the hazard that the idea may change radically in the hands of the group. Consensus may be reached at the cost of the idea. But if this does not happen, and if the idea remains comparatively intact, once the course of the experiment is run, the satisfactions may be greater in the company of others. And, if the group expectations are not fully realized, there is a built-in cushion to the setback in sharing the failure.

Varying the approach to a standard social-studies topic is one procedure for testing the boundaries of choice. The risks are minimal—the teacher clearly remains within the sequence of studies sanctioned by the school district. If middle-graders are expected to become acquainted with the regional United States, is it mandatory that each area be surveyed state by state? Or might one abandon Iowa, Illinois, and all their sister states, in favor of the topics, water and soil? This latter approach might be justified, partially, because water (as well as a host of other factors, to be sure) is essential to the Midwest in its development into one of the largest urban-industrial belts on the earth's surface. Pertinent questions might include: What is the character of the enormous water needs of city and industry? Why are river cities forced into closer ties with one another without regard for state and county political boundaries? The characteristics of different soils provide another avenue to understanding this region. Population density in the Lower Michigan peninsula and the attendant problems in political representation may be related to the character of soil deposits distributed in the same area. Still another approach to this region might be made through the study of the relationships between car and farm. Perhaps if children investigated these two things—automotive and agricultural production as complex industrial processes—they would understand a great deal about mid-America.

In nearly every upper-elementary-school or junior-high-school classroom, children wrestle with the welter of early political activity on this continent, with particular emphasis on winning and maintaining political independence. One might convert this teaching task to a comparative study in the achievement of political independence. Might not colonial America be viewed in comparison with the key figures, forces, and events of India in the years prior to 1946? Certainly the American struggle for sovereignty is not unique in the records of man, nor even without parallel in the events of the present day.

Many successful innovators in the classroom first establish themselves as journeymen social-studies teachers. They are careful to demonstrate competence within the program and procedures commonly advocated by their school system. For the beginning teacher, this may be a particularly appropriate strategy. As a beginner, one may yet be in the process of developing a stock of pertinent resources for instruction. One may have yet to develop poise and assurance as a director in the activities of thirty or so children. An experimental social-studies program will call into play a full complement of management skills. The trick is to retain the will to depart from routine teaching ways once the apprenticeship has been served. The satisfactions gained through the practices of a particular school may leave one with little appetite for the hazards of the less-than-conventional. But it should be noted that some of the happiest inventions are the work of young and inexperienced teachers. Their verve and energy, and possibly a sureness born of innocence, carry them through complex management solutions to ultimately successful innovations.

The Problem of Being Informed

Topics in the social studies undergo a special hazard—that of being rendered superficial and stereotyped—when teachers fail to become informed. To the extent that teachers are students of the content under their general jurisdiction, the risks of vacuousness are minimized. If one does not keep abreast of the social, economic, and political development of the local community, for example, he may present the image of city government "as if it were a den of cub scouts presided over by a parent figure interpreting the charter."[8]

Acquiring relevant knowledge is a healthy antidote to fearing loss of control in the teaching situation. When one has personally studied the topics

[8] BRUNER, On Knowing, p. 124.

taught, he no longer feels vulnerable—he is less fearful that areas of ignorance will be probed and made public. The informed teacher can control the learning encounter, refute the quick stereotype, emphasize more than the quaint and colorful in culture studies, and emphasize the present as well as the past in studies of the far away.[9]

There is an alternative to being uninformed. Teachers can set about enlarging their grasp of content. The information teachers command remains the basic resource in every classroom. It is our assumption that a certain crispness and clarity in the control of instruction will follow from its development.

[9] See Jack Ellison, "Using Anthropological Materials," and Barbara Ward, "Communism," in Part IV. The first excerpt illustrates the alternatives that are available to teachers who are aware of and have thought about anthropological studies. The second is an introductory discussion of Communist thought. These two excerpts illustrate the kind of reading teachers must do if they are to provide their students with an authentic encounter with men in society.

VIII

Varieties of Control

Choosing What and Where

If one is obligated to choose, then there must exist both a number of possible choices and a setting where choice can be acted upon. For teachers, the range of choice pertains to the conduct of instruction, and the classroom is the matrix in which the consequences of teaching-learning choices are realized. Within this domain, teachers exert four varieties of control: those of dialogue, of resource, of setting, and of development in the program of instruction.

The Dialogue of Instruction

Teachers exert some control in directing and attending to:
1. proportion in talk,
2. pattern in talk, and
3. repertoire in questions.

Proportion in Talk

Talk—teacher talk and pupil talk—is a significant element in any classroom. Dimensions in classroom talk are not hard to tease out. The two difficult tasks are those of identifying the consequences of various patterns in talk, and of helping teachers adopt a style of talk appropriate to the desired learning outcomes.

Teachers retain significant controls in establishing the communication climate within the classroom. They initiate significant messages, and they coax a certain quality of response from the class. They amplify key trans-actions by directing children's attention to comments or questions that might otherwise be overlooked (for example, "That's an interesting idea, Dick! I wonder how many of you have ever thought about that? Would you mind saying it again?"). They may provide models of precise lan-guage and reinforce inventive use of language. They give directions; they signal, "Easy! You're in dangerous waters"; they indicate, "Full sail! There's clear water ahead." Sometimes, they are simply adult targets—grownups responding to the "trial messages" of youngsters feeling their way toward adulthood.

Though teachers are undoubtedly influential communicators, we have very little understanding of the precise effect various patterns of communication have on the process of instruction. Teachers are forced to infer for themselves what seem to be reasonable outcomes of particular interaction patterns. Awareness of the several dimensions in classroom talk, however, may be a step toward their control.

Even the casual visitor to the classroom can notice the proportion of messages initiated by teachers as compared to those initiated by pupils. In many classrooms, children have abundant opportunity to rehearse ideas out loud, to combine and explore notions, to demonstrate simply whether or not the teacher message "came through." One primitive control teachers can effect is that of refraining from heavy domination of classroom talk.

Teachers continually demonstrate compassion and ingenuity in reducing the heavy competition children face in participating in the classroom dialogue. A particularly poignant example of this sensitivity was related in a recent publication examining creativity in the classroom:

I threw a log on the fire by asking if there were any poisonous snakes in New Jersey and, if so, how they could be distinguished from the non-poisonous snakes. Edna's hand shot up but I made sure to recognize the hands of other children; I wanted her to feel her hand up over her head for as long a time as possible, especially since this was her first attempt to be recognized. I had made it a practice to go to Edna's desk to discuss matters with her rather than to expose her to the necessity of speaking to me across the room. But now she wanted to speak and I finally recognized her hand.[1]

Pattern in Talk

Pattern is another easily noticed dimension in classroom talk. Often teachers encourage pupils to respond directly to the statements of classmates. Moreover, in such classrooms, students frequently initiate statements, intending that only another pupil, and not the teacher, respond. This pattern of messages seems to take root in the classroom as a consequence of both the verbal and the nonverbal behavior of the teacher. A quizzical expression, the look across the room inviting rebuttal, the calculated pause, these small though deliberate gestures of teachers often elicit interaction among pupils. A playful comment by the teacher or even a direct request for another pupil's response also promotes such interaction. But with other student

[1] MIEL, *Creativity in Teaching*, p. 126.

groups and other teachers, quite another pattern of interchange is found. Here the narrative of the classroom is channeled to permit, for the most part, only exchanges between teacher and pupil. Each verbal episode is likely to begin with a teacher question, which requires that a child answer; the pupil response, in turn, triggers an evaluative statement on the part of the teacher. In this last type of classroom, each verbal transaction is likely to be self-contained and noncumulative, each episode being initiated and terminated by the teacher. In the pupil-to-pupil instance, very often a chain of messages is built up which culminates variously in smoking out an issue, uncovering a nettlesome sense of doubt, or discovering a previously unnoticed link between ideas. The element of "benediction" or heavy-handed evaluation so prevalent in the teacher-pupil-teacher episode seems to curtail the building of a chain of responses and to make divergent or inventive responses a decided risk for the pupil. A teacher may react to a child's suggestion with, "Very good, John. That's exactly what I was thinking. Don't you think it would be *fun,* class, to write a story about our trip?" The class answers, "Yes!" Fannie Shaftel, of Stanford University, is fond of characterizing this latter situation as the problem of cue-oriented children—children who have been taught to figure out what teachers want and then to give it back to them, even to using the very words teachers prefer.

Repertoire of Questions

Some elements of classroom dialogue are less noticeable. One of these is the repertoire or range of questions teachers employ. In reflecting upon some classroom interlude, it is often productive to attempt to recall the style of question asked by the teacher. Sometimes this identification process turns up but one species: the Discrete Information question, one that can be satisfied by recall of fact without comment. The better tactician has a wide repertoire of questions. In Michener's account, a new teacher seeks to discover how an exciting and somewhat mysterious former teacher worked with children:

"Well, I said, "We've now reached the end of the first unit. I wonder if it wouldn't be a good idea to go back to a discussion of the big ideas of this unit?" I paused.

Not much response, so I added, "The way Mr. Fry used to do. Remember?"

Immediately all the pupils sat up and started to pay attention. Most of them smiled. Two of the girls giggled and some of the boys squirmed. "Tom," I asked, "will you take over?" for I had no idea of Mr. Fry's method.

Tom nodded vigorously and came to the front of the room. "All right," he rasped, "who will dare?"

"I will," said a girl, "I believe that Columbus came to the New World more for religious reasons than for commercial reasons."

"Oh!" groaned a group of pupils snapping their fingers for attention. Tom called on one.

"I think that's very stupid reasoning, Lucille. Spain was only using religion as a mask for imperialism."

Lucille turned in her seat and shot back, "You wouldn't think so if you knew anything about Philip the Second."

And the debate continued until Tom issued his next dare. A pupil accepted and defiantly announced: "I think all that section about Spain's being so poor at colonizing is the malarkey. Everything south of Texas except Brazil is now Spanish. That looks pretty good to me."

I winced at the word "malarkey" and the pupils winced at the idea. The tigers of Anglo-Saxony rose to the defense of the text and the challenging pupil did his best to stand them off.[2]

Possibly then, the "belligerent question" can be productively employed in the classroom. There are still others.[3]

Attending to the questions one asks exerts some control in the direction and fruitfulness of classroom instruction. A basic assumption of the present book is that teachers can cultivate the ability to wield questions adroitly.

The problem of propounding questions is central to the problem of learning. Teachers must be professional "question mongers."

The Resources and Apparatus of Instruction

Teachers exert some control in assembling and deploying:
1. material to be read (stories, documents, texts, and other printed or written material),
2. material to be handled and examined (physical objects and artifacts),
3. material to be viewed (flat pictures and other graphic displays),
4. material to be listened to and/or viewed (films, tapes, and records),
5. people to listen to and interact with (the resources of knowledgeable people), and
6. Material evoking channeled responses (programed learning).

Not all of the problems of instruction are procedural ones. A prior question is often that of obtaining materials to "proceed" upon. One great advantage experienced teachers sometimes enjoy is that of wide acquaintance with provocative "things." Perhaps they possess dramatic photographs or pictures. They may know people who will lend authentic materials, or, pos-

---

[2] JAMES A. MICHENER, "Who Is Virgil T. Fry?", *The Clearing House*, XVI (October 1941), 67–70. By permission of the publisher.

[3] See the passage on "Questions and Instruction," Chapter Five.

sibly, they have collected a small number of artifacts themselves. Those engaged in teaching may be familiar with the particular or potential instructional usefulness of local collections, displays, museums, and industrial plants. In all, the experienced teacher is often in a better position to make influential choices simply because a greater variety of resources are there for her to choose among.

Beginning teachers often fall back on a "safe" style of instruction, a style dominated by the text, the recitation, and the test. This reactionary teaching mode sometimes follows a first but unsuccessful experiment with a somewhat unstructured, rather turbulent, instructional scheme. A possible cause for the failure of this initial approach to teaching (and the comfort found in the refuge of the text) can be found in the beginner's lack of practice in the timely retrieval of "things" to encourage the study of people, places, institutions, and events. If the yeast of instruction lies in the canny use of "things," then without these resources teachers cannot expect that quality of learning excitement to rise in their rooms.

Books and Things

Years of teaching may bring facility in retrieving for use at just the right moment interesting documents, journals, letters, texts, trade books, and stories. In making such a variety of source material available to children, teachers make it possible for the children to gather data about places and people far away in space and time. These data can be used to build generalizations or conclusions that confirm or challenge what a textbook has to say. The same events can be seen from different points of view: a private soldier's letter, a general's autobiographical account, the textbook's summary of a famous Civil War battle; an editorial about the conquest of Goa appearing in the *New York Times* and an editorial statement in the *Times of India* (published in English).

Books and articles written at varying levels of reading difficulty help in meeting the needs of a classroom's usual range of abilities. Where unusually pertinent material is available that is too difficult for anyone in a class to read, the teacher may find it necessary to rewrite the information if he thinks that reading it independently is a necessary experience for certain children.

Reading materials that deal with different facets of a broad study invite some children to follow specific and personal interests at greater depth than will most children. Books on specific aspects of Chinese life—cooking, history, fashions in dress and architecture, art and writing, inventions, religions, and games—are examples of materials which can encourage children to follow their own interests as these are seen within the framework of a larger study—in this instance, of China. The National Council for the Social Studies has published an extensive and annotated bibliography of books related to topics in social studies, as well as a booklet on developing appropriate reading skills.[4] The New York Public Library produces periodic bulletins describing current books for both children and adults on specific topics and areas of the world. Additional bibliographies are published by the Association for Childhood Education, International.

One of the problems teachers face repeatedly is that of bringing children to raise questions that have significance for the social studies and that commit the children to effort. The handling of objects precipitates a number of questions concerning the use, the "biography," and the social importance of that artifact. Instructors frequently ask groups of students who are preparing to teach to arrange and stock a college classroom as if a group of children were about to engage in the study of some topic. One such group, interested in presenting the idea of man's ways of gauging the passing of time, contrived to display the workings of a kitchen clock, the swing of a pendulum, the trickling of sand, the dripping of water, and ancient drawings of the moon. Even for these college students, the objects were too inviting to be ignored. Picking up a clock to get a closer look at its exposed works, swinging the pendulum, and turning the hourglass over led to questions and observations about the variety of time-units man has invented, the presence of movement in many of the devices, and the notion of time itself.

Pictures, Films, and Recordings

Pictures can be arranged to indicate the probable outlines of a major idea. Combining views of desert, grassy plain, jungle, snow-topped mountain, skyscrapers, mud huts, industrial smokestacks, and hoe-culture farming sends an unmistable message about the variety that is contemporary Africa. Arranging pictures of baseball players, children in school, men fishing, and so forth, under the heading *Is This Work or Play?* challenges the conventional meanings children have for each concept.

Films, records, and tape recordings offer children an opportunity to see and hear, as well as read about, the far-away people and places they are studying. Tape recordings, especially, can be used with amazing flexibility to provide a firsthand experience for children. Tape-recorded information about themselves and questions about others can be sent to English-speaking residents of the British Isles, Australia, India, Singapore, and Japan. In addition, one can look at these places and their inhabitants through the eyes of American children who are living abroad because their parents are

---

[4] See Helen Huus, NCSS Bulletin No. 32, "Children's Books to Enrich the Social Studies for the Elementary Grades" (Washington: NCSS, 1961), 196 pp.; and Leo C. Fay, Thomas Horn, and Constance McCullough, NCSS Bulletin No. 33, "Improving Reading in the Elementary Social Studies" (Washington: NCSS, 1961), 72 pp.

members of the armed forces or employees of the United States government, or employed by American businesses with overseas branches. Perhaps even more than films, tape recordings can give children a sense of intimate, immediate contact with people and events many miles away.

People and Machines

Every community possesses a vast store of teaching resources in its citizens. They are the people-who-have-been-there, who-know-how-to, who perform important functions or services related to some study pursued by children. Two problems are frequently encountered in using resource people, however. First, a traveler, a worker, someone who has had a special experience, may, under certain circumstances, unknowingly arrest the development of inquiry in the classroom. He may tell too much, too soon. Secondly, the resource person used as a "teller" may be only a sort of talking book. The information must be comprehended, must be believed.

We have little practice and few skills in converting what people say into data, or things to think about. There is a difference between asking an elderly person what the town was like when he was a boy and interviewing a number of elderly people to help the class decide what the town might have been like, say at the turn of the century. There is a difference between asking a carpenter how houses are built and deciding how a house is built from the testimony of carpenter, lumberman, draftsman, subcontractor, and owner. In securing and examining testimony, children need to develop the skills of sorting among facts for information relevant to their investigation, of developing questions which probe and aid in clarifying important points, and of maintaining alertness for unexpected but relevant information.

Teaching machines presume to help children learn the answers to questions to which the programmers know the answers. Where there are facts of a routine type with which children can profitably become acquainted (how many United States Senators represent each state; how often and by what process a British Prime Minister is selected), a machine can probably get the information to most children more efficiently than a human can. Machines disseminating "routine" facts, however, may ignore nonroutine characteristics, such as the infighting that may precede the selection of a candidate. There is also the "pall effect," in which the tedium and loneliness of interaction with the machine cuts down learning efficiency. Of greatest significance, however, is the nature of the bulk of questions that structure social studies. These are questions for which we either know no answers or for which there are only tentative answers. A whirring of little gears is likely to suggest a certainty that is only a mechanical illusion.

Whatever tenure may follow initiation into teaching, the period can be more than time spent repeating the acceptable responses of the beginner.

Full professional competence is something that must be achieved. One part of the achievement process involves "tooling up," or acquiring a stock of pertinent resources for use in fashioning a persuasive program of instruction.

Instructional Settings

Teachers exert some control in devising and effecting settings that are intended to help children to:

1. find out, become acquainted with, or comprehend information about people and events (facts, concepts, generalizations, etc.);
2. become aware of their own and others' feelings about people and events (attitudes, perceptions, motives, etc);
3. analyze or speculate regarding information and feelings about people and events (making inferences, proposing explanations, examining data, offering hunches, etc.); and
4. develop skills (mapping, planning, reading, cooperating, expressing, and so forth).

Teachers orchestrate materials, pace the development of instruction, and evoke particular communication patterns in order to achieve certain intents or purposes. Thus they exert another control, that of fashioning a focused setting for instruction.

Acquaintanceship

A fundamental enterprise of the social studies is that of helping children "see themselves plain as occupying a wedge of space and a slice of time."[5] So teachers devise settings whereby children may acquire information—information about regions and eras, groups and cultures, wars and governments, institutions and ideologies. Teachers talk to children; they arrange for others to talk about specific topics and experiences. They display objects and pictures for examination or viewing. They exploit a wide range of reading materials. Children relate what they have seen or heard or experienced themselves. They go for walks and other excursions. They interview interesting people. And the object of all this is acquaintanceship—making it possible for children to acquire a fund of useful information.

Triggers for Study

But acquaintanceship is not the whole story in the social studies. Teachers fashion settings, too, that give promise of triggering study. A beginning

[5] MARTIN MAYER, *The Schools* (New York: Harper and Brothers, 1961), p. 340.

might be made when young children face the need to explain—to explain, for example, why a city "needs" small, corner grocery stores as well as big, shiny supermarkets.[6] Inquiry might begin with a kind of analogue to history: "What happened on the schoolground yesterday?"[7] Investigations sometimes begin with common terms like "Ghost Town"[8] and everyday things like pennies.[9] Trolley cars,[10] rivers,[11] freeways,[12] and pieces of sculpture[13] can all be important objects in settings devised to elicit the behavior called study.

The direct actions of teachers are always a significant part of the problem setting. Teachers invite children to spin out hunches. They fasten attention on the hypotheses the class has generated—"Which ideas might be mined profitably?" They play the role of the doubter—"How can you prove it?" "Show us!" Among older children, they call attention to the line of reasoning being pursued. They remind young children of "the Big Question we want to answer." They design the most conducive seating arrangement possible, carefully nudging the hesitant and the timorous in the classroom inward from the periphery. When these children are surrounded with more vigorous classmates, everyone seems to participate, and the process of solution-making appears decidedly contagious.

Sometimes teachers nurture the process of inquiry indirectly. They may find quiet ways of helping children develop a concept of self that says: "I'm an adventurous guy. I'll risk a 'far out' hunch." Other teachers may help their classes to feel: "We've got stick-to-it-iveness, we'll chew and worry a problem until we come up with a good solution. Halfway answers are not our style." Often teachers arrange a sort of "osmotic" process: they support one courageous guesser and thereby make others willing to risk an off-beat hunch; cherish a skeptic and thus help a Pollyanna class member to "try on" the role. Teachers make their most eloquent contribution, however, in personal acts—of speculation, development of data, expressions of wonder, and expressions of delight at finding for oneself a plausible route to discovery. Without contact with models, developing the ability to inquire is a boot-strap operation. If an investigative attitude is to suffuse the social studies, it will originate with teachers.

Attitudes, Perceptions, and Motives

The social-studies program deals, too, with children's attitudes, with the way in which people and events are perceived, and with development of

6 See "Grocery Stores" in Chapter Ten.
7 See Chapter Twelve.
8 *Ibid.*
9 See Chapter Fourteen.
10 See Chapter Ten.
11 *Ibid.*
12 *Ibid.*
13 See Chapter Eleven.

some understanding of the motives people display. Attending to these, teachers engage children in wonder about the "biography" of an event— "What thoughts would compel you to dismiss John Scopes from school teaching?" They may probe gently for a deeper understanding of myth and heroic figures—"Why would Lincoln, the successful lawyer and railroad attorney, a former congressman, a friend of many prominent men, an alto- gether sensitive and urban gentleman, why would such a man be presented in his presidential campaign as Abe, the rail splitter?"[14] Or, "Could some- one have made up a story about an axe, a cherry tree, and young George Washington?" "Why might someone invent such a story?" A teacher may use particular source materials in attempting to link the acts of men to plausible motives for those acts. The widely circulated poster of the land speculator, for example, advertised "good, cheap land" in the West.[15] Why would "good land" hold such appeal, especially for potential buyers who already held "good jobs"? Was the life of the subsistence farmer that attrac- tive? Why the drive for self-sufficiency on the American scene? Does the appeal hold true today?

Teachers devise settings to help children become aware of their own feelings and the feelings of others regarding people and events. These may include poignant stories, drama, and role-playing by the children to promote awareness. Teachers contrive to have children write, to record how they might feel in another time and place, or how they might feel facing another's situation. They teach the children a dance, a song; these, too, convey the mood and tempo of other lives, other places, other times. In staging sets like these, teachers exert choice in directing the drama of learning.

Skill Development

Finally, teachers attend to the development of skills. Because skill de- velopment demands opportunity for practice, they choose settings that make trial efforts possible. Becoming skillful requires wide opportunities to do, to practice, rather than to watch or listen. Teachers should give children the opportunity to render or interpret maps; to read passages for purposes of locating relevant data, discerning key paragraphs, and summarizing the writer's point of view; to engage in reports and discussions so that indi- viduals can practice certain communication skills; to serve in groups and on committees so that they may develop the ability to lead, to formulate plans, and to cooperate. Teachers should provide pictures, documents, and solid objects, so that children can practice examining things closely and developing inferences on the basis of their inspection. Teachers should communicate to

[14] See "An American Sacred Ceremony," in W. Lloyd Warner, *American Life* (Chi- cago: The University of Chicago Press, 1953), Chapter One.
[15] See Vincent R. Rogers, "Using Source Material with Children," *Social Education* (November 1960), pp. 307–308. The excerpt is reprinted in Part IV.

the children some evaluation of the level and quality of their skills. Most importantly, teachers should see to it that children realize that possessing some significant thought to express is fundamental to significant expression of that thought. Then they should encourage the skillful expression of thought—in speech or in writing.

The Development of Instruction

Teachers exert some control in deciding on:
1. pace, time commitments, the priority among activities;
2. the flow and sequence of activities.

On the basis of knowledge about the attention span of the learner, or, perhaps, on the basis of some sense of priority, teachers must make decisions regarding the pace of instruction. They should decide if some of the leads that develop in the learning sequence should be followed up, others not. They may allow certain phases of instruction to proceed in a leisurely manner, with great attention to promising tangents; at other times, they may find it advisable to speed up the rate of instruction and fix the focus of instruction. Decisions such as these influence the behavior of the teacher in the following two incidents.

In MR. BROWN's room, JACK C. is reporting on Burma, "his" country in the unit on Southeast Asia.

JACK: . . . and rice is the main part of their food. They grow so much rice that they sell a lot of it to other countries. They sell a lot of things to Communist China and they buy some things from the Communist Chinese, too.

BILL: (*In a whisper to his seatmate, Albert*) I bet they're Communists in Burma or they wouldn't sell anything to those Chinese Reds.

ALBERT: Oh, that's stupid. Didn't you hear him say they were having a war with the Communists?

BILL: Well, why would they sell anything to the Chinese unless they were Communists?

TEACHER: Look boys, if you have something to say, why don't you raise your hands and then you may get a chance to say it.

(*Bill raises his hand.*)

Well, let's just let Jack finish his report first and then we can take any questions that come up. We don't have much time for Burma. We have to get on to Japan. That's our next country and it will take a lot of time to learn about it.

ANN: Mr. Brown, may I do Japan?

TEACHER: (*smiling*) No, Ann, I'm afraid not. Japan is a pretty important country in Asia. I don't think anyone could do Japan properly all by himself. We'll probably break up into committees and the committees will study different parts of it. You can do a part of Japan.

Now Jack, to get on with your report, what kind of religion did you find that most of the people in Burma have? How did they worship God? . . .

In MR. SMITH's room, JERRY is discussing with his classmates the way Cuba is governed.

JERRY: . . . In 1934, the Cubans got their full independence. Since that time the Cubans have been a republic like most of the other countries in South America—and also North America, I guess.

CINDY: (*Waves her arm frantically, looks at the teacher, finally says*) Oh, Mr. Smith! I don't think that's right. That just can't be right.

TEACHER: Cindy, why don't you tell Jerry.

CINDY: (*Turns to look at Jerry. Her voice softens somewhat from the argumentive, almost angry tone it had when she was objecting to Mr. Smith.*) Jerry, I don't think that's right. How can they have a republic when Castro goes around and shoots people all the time.

JERRY: Well, I don't know. That's what it said in the book.

TEACHER: Well, Jerry. Is it possible that we could know something that the book doesn't know?

JOHN: This book has a copyright date that's about two years old. Most of this Castro thing happened after this book was written.

JIM: They didn't have such a prize democrat in there before Castro either. He was some kind of dictator or something, wasn't he?

CINDY: Well, I don't know, but I don't think Cuba has a republic no matter what they had before.

JERRY: Well, I guess we'll have to take that part out. (*Casually tosses paper over shoulder. It lands on a classmate's desk. Children giggle.*)

TEACHER: Is Cuba *not* a republic then?

CINDY: How can it be with Castro shooting people like that?

TEACHER: Suppose that most of the people in Cuba liked what Castro was doing and even liked the way he was doing it. Would Cuba be a republic then?

JERRY: Well, most of the people in Germany probably liked what Hitler was doing but that didn't make Germany a republic, did it?

TEACHER: Why not?

CINDY: In a republic, it's not just that most people like what the leader is doing. The people who don't agree with the president get to have their say, too.

JULIE: I don't think we know enough about Cuba's government to say what kind it is. I think Jerry and maybe some others ought to look up more about it.

TEACHER: Why do you think we ought to spend more time on this? I mean, is it really that important?

TOM: Well, Cuba is pretty close to us and some people say they are Communists, and if we have Communists that close, we could have a war. So we should find out more about it.

(*Many children nod vigorously, make approving comments.*)

TEACHER: Julie, this was your idea. Would you be willing to join Jerry in finding out more about Cuba's government?

JULIE: O.K.

CINDY: Can I do it too?

TEACHER: Cindy. Any one else? Paul? O.K. Where do you plan to look for information?

JULIE: The library. Encyclopedias and books.

JERRY: Most of them are too old. We better use newspapers and magazines.

TEACHER: You sound ready to make a start. You may go to the library during the work period at eleven and give us a progress report at 11:45 . . .

One can only guess at some of the decisions that each teacher has made, but there would seem to be little time in Mr. Brown's room for the interaction of discussion. Even when two boys become involved enough with the subject matter to want to argue about it, he cuts their exchange off abruptly. He apparently sees such a discussion, not as contributing to understanding, but as interfering with understanding. Certainly, he believes it will interfere with a predetermined and acceptable set of learning experiences. "On to Japan" is the watchword for their study of Burma.

Children in Mr. Smith's room seem to share with him much of the responsibility for deciding what they are going to study, how they are going to go about it, and how much time they will spend looking at one or another facet of the total group's unit. Children's casual comments, however, do not automatically force the class to change direction. Having satisfied himself that children can see value in further study of current happenings in Cuba, and after securing the commitment of specific children's time and effort in his study, Mr. Smith encourages a side excursion that promises to yield worthwhile returns.

Control is exerted in deciding upon the sequence of activities. What precedes what? And what shall follow what? What learning activities are companionable and might therefore be fused or be scheduled at adjacent times during the school day? What activities are largely of the "intake" variety, and how can they be balanced with "expressive" learning tasks?

Precision and the Learning Situation

Four important elements within the teacher's span of control—the elements of dialogue, resource, setting, and development—have been explored above.

In some sense, however, any control of the learning encounter can be only a rudimentary one. Teachers may precipitate what they consider a pointed discussion only to wonder once again at the range of perceptions, of attentiveness, of insight displayed by the members of the class. Materials can be assembled and stringent requirements for their use can be announced, but each child will find his unique way of engaging them; some of these engagements will be zestful and productive, others will be less so. Learning remains a personal, volatile process, not accessible to controls of great precision.

But lack of precision does not mean teachers are impotent. While teaching is a great deal less than mechanical, teachers are a great deal more than ineffectual. The stance and motion of teachers have impact. The problem is determining what that impact is. A portion of what has been called artistry lies in gauging the effects of instruction and devising fitting responses in view of this information. This situation is a source of teaching's greatest interest, as well as its chief despair—before the learning encounter, its consequences can be only generally anticipated; afterward, its effects can be only partially appraised.

The process of teaching is that of acting in anticipation of some outcome. Narrative, setting, resource, and pace are all attended to in the expectation that certain learnings will take place. Only in this sense do teacher's "exert control" in the domain of instruction.

IX

Plans, Responsibilities, and Study

Most active and sizable school districts produce a set of documents known variously as a Curriculum Framework, District Guide, or Course of Study. Central offices of the school district give them particular attention. School principals, too, regard them with care. The documents may or may not appear on teachers' desks, and the teachers may appear to ignore them. Regardless of appearances, though, at any particular grade level most children will consider only the topics named in the district curriculum guide.

Plans for the social studies are a part of the context of teaching. These documents must be discussed, if only because the words "guide," "framework," and "course" euphemistically indicate that they are meant to be persuasive.

Plans

Necessary Bounds

Elementary schooling extends over seven years. Each year of the seven and its teacher follows hard on the heels of another year and another teacher. Presumably, these strung-together years ought to add up to something. It is this "ought" condition—that several years of school with their several teachers ought to add up to something—that gives rise to a set of district decisions. Particular school-wide decisions are made so that teachers may act in concert with one another. Plans are adopted so that teaching programs will not overlap and will have cumulative effect. In short, necessary bounds are imposed on individual teachers so that particular school-wide advantages may be gained. The terms "plans" or "designs" may be used to refer to these "necessary bounds." Districts adopt such designs to govern generally the topics for instruction among the various grades and among the several classes at each grade level.

Teachers are held loosely accountable for a set of topics arranged in some sequence. In the larger and more active school districts, these plans take the form of curriculum guides. Among the less active and smaller districts, what is taught, and when, is identical with the various tables of contents for a state or locally approved set of textbooks. In these smaller districts, a separate curriculum guide is considered superfluous—why duplicate with a mimeograph machine what is already available on every pupil's desk? Regardless of the form the plan takes, however, every district will have one; it will govern generally the range and order of topics presented in the classroom.

Two Typical Plans

Every plan for the social studies represents some person's or some group's idea of the point at which children ought to begin, what learnings they should finally achieve, and in what order the various instructional segments should be joined together. Two designers, Paul Hanna and Florence Stratemeyer, have been important in influencing the thoughts and products of present-day practitioners. In referring to the proposals of these two writers, schoolmen have adopted certain abbreviated statements. The Hanna proposals are summarized in two phrases, "Expanding Communities," and "Basic Activities."[1] The Stratemeyer formulations are anchored in a conception of "Persistent Life Situations."[2] A brief discussion of the Hanna and Stratemeyer proposals follows. The reader will find it useful to seek out those writings wherein these two educators speak for themselves.

Normally, plans for the social studies are aimed at establishing the *sequence* of topics. Hanna, for example, proposes that through the grades children ought to be introduced systematically to the wider and wider communities of which man is a member. The social studies should progress sequentially from the community of home and neighborhood outward to the communities of the Atlantic and Pacific nations.

Other decisions seek to establish the *scope* of instruction at the various levels within the proposed sequence. The Stratemeyer Persistent Life Situations (taking leadership responsibility, making ideas clear, determining responsibility to self and others) can serve to establish the breadth of instruction within successive school years. In the Hanna rationale, the scope of any particular topic, that is, what will be considered with respect to a specific community, is determined by the Basic Activities man characteristically engages in, e.g., "organizing and governing," "producing and distributing."

[1] PAUL R. HANNA, "Society-Child-Curriclum," in Clarence W. Hunnicutt (ed.), *Education 2000 A.D.* (Syracuse: The Syracuse University Press, 1956).

[2] FLORENCE B. STRATEMEYER, *et al., Developing a Curriculum for Modern Living* (New York: Bureau of Publications, Teachers College, Columbia University, 1947).

LINEAR AND SPIRAL DESIGNS

There is a sense of progression or movement in every administrative scheme for the social studies. Sometimes that movement appears to be linear in nature. The Expanding Communities design, for example, seems to move in a direct line from the communities composed of family and neighborhood outward to the communities composed of nations. *Linear schemes* characteristically do not repeat or return to particular topics. Instead, they progress step by step from what is believed to be close at hand and relatively simple to what is regarded as rather remote and complex. Other designs do repeat topics or ideas. These curricular schemes are pulsating, in the sense that the progression of topics includes a systematic return to earlier themes, persistent ideas, and recurring issues. Within these last-named designs for schooling, older children may examine again topics introduced in earlier years; but now instruction is governed by more subtle distinctions, more refined generalizations, and wider sources of information. Designs of this sort seem to proceed in a *spiral* fashion, as controlling ideas receive repeated attention at more sophisticated levels.

COMPLETE AND OPEN DESIGNS

Some designs attempt to be all-inclusive or *complete*. Their completeness may refer to analyses of the social sciences or of human social behavior. Some set of criteria is used to identify a group of ideas or generalizations that are considered of major significance in understanding the content of the social sciences. California, for example, recently completed a state-wide revision of the social studies in which academicians and schoolmen attempted to glean from the several social sciences the major generalizations suitable for the education of elementary-school children.[3] Designers and designs are not infallible, of course, and ideas of major significance may be missing from a design. As these are discovered, they are added in a continual process of making the designed school experiences as complete as possible.

Completeness in design refers to the topics or arenas in which understanding will be developed, as well as to the array of concepts and generalizations extracted from the social sciences. Some designs try to indicate all of the major topics children will study. Complete designs, then, specify both the generalizations with which the social studies will deal and the topics within which these ideas can logically be developed.

Open designs exhibit quite contrasting qualities. Some school-wide patterns represent decisions in which major themes or priority ideas have been

[3] State Curriculum Commission, *Social Studies Framework for the Public Schools of California* (Sacramento: State Department of Education, 1962).

established, but several topics or instructional activities through which children will become familiar with these major themes have not been established in advance. It is up to the teacher to decide what will be a useful vehicle for exploring the ideas that have been decided upon. Topics may be made available to teachers as illustrations of activities that may be appropriate, but they are typically only suggestive.

Generally, Hanna and Stratemeyer aim at completeness. Both, however, attempt to create as much freedom for choice as the demands for completeness will permit. Hanna, for example, states that:

In advance, the school faculty not only design the over-all scope and sequence of learning experiences for all grades, but they sketch in the broad but flexible framework for each grade. . . . The unique personality of each pupil and each class vitally influences the immediate choice of activity. . . . The teacher, always the most important member of the classgroup, guides the pupils in designing in process within the broad, flexible framework of that which was designed by the school staff in advance.[4]

INTERPLAY OF CATEGORIES

The Persistent-Life-Situation design emphasizes spiral development. The Expanding-Communities-of-Man design is linear in its compelling movement from the communities closest to the child to those that are farther away. Re-examining basic human activities in progressively widening geographic settings establishes a counterpattern, in the Hanna design, that is spiral in nature.

It should be evident that the categories "linear-spiral" and "complete-open" are not exclusive of one another. We do not usefully ask of a designer whether it is complete or open, whether it is of a linear or spiral type. Rather, a more useful question asks what the interplay of these categories is within any design. It is in the different emphases and relations between completeness and openness, linearity and spiralness that each design demonstrates its unique character.

Responsibilities

There are two somewhat separate responsibilities in planning for instruction. One responsibility is that of deciding upon the *arena* for instruction. Another responsibility is that of planning for the *mode* of instruction. Curriculum specialists appear to be preoccupied with the first of these responsibilities. This preoccupation may mislead teachers into believing they have little curricular freedom, because the arena for instruction has been decided

[4] Hanna, pp. 174–175.

for them. The following discussion considers the character of these two curricular responsibilities: arena and mode.

The Arena for Instruction

In many public schools, the topics children should encounter are agreed upon at the district level, thereby determining an *arena* for social-studies instruction. The word "arena" suggests boundaries, perimeters, and spheres of action. The decision on the general boundaries of instruction performs an administrative function by insuring that the work of separate teachers is somewhat integrated and cumulative.

Arena decisions make it possible for schoolchildren to have contact with a wide variety of information and topics. No doubt, students should consider their own and foreign nations intermittently during their school years. But there is more to know about ourselves and others than can be learned in several lifetimes. Because there is so much to know, many quite different lists of social-studies topics can be formulated. A number of these lists could be very attractive; each might be quite persuasively defended. Because several appealing and defensible lists are potentially available, adopting any one list is always somewhat arbitrary.

The word "arbitrary" is apt to be misleading because it is so abrasive. The term does not imply that schools adopt lists of social-studies topics capriciously, nor that the selections are indefensible. Any list of topics usually reflects two negotiated agreements: (1) an explicit rationale; (2) a conception of what is most important. That is, the adopted list of social-studies topics must appear schematic, and it must appear to be relevant to the values of some group. In this sense, the word "arbitrary" means only that more than one organized and relevant list of social-studies topics can be formulated for any given community.

The Mode of Instruction

Very few teachers persistently and knowingly conduct instruction outside the bounds of the adopted plan for their district. Most of the instructional acts of teachers are efforts to engage some prescribed set of topics. This effort to engage topics may be referred to as the *mode* of instruction. The word "mode" suggests the companion terms "form," "fashion," or "manner of doing." The manner or form of instruction can be planned for; this is the second curriculum responsibility.

The ideas related to the various topics that children are to consider can be encountered in the "mode of acquaintanceship" and in the "mode of study." Simply to name an idea, such as "democracy," however, does not explain what might be done by teachers when they seek to help students discover the meaning and history of this idea in human society. Consequently, plans must make clear the mode of instruction; they must address the question: What will be the character of an encounter with ideas?

The problem with curriculum guides is not what they do; it is what they do not do. Usually, they fail to be concerned with the second curriculum responsibility at all. They are not concerned with the way in which ideas might be encountered; they are concerned with labels for topics and their orderly arrangement. The problem of instruction, however, is to encounter ideas, not just name and place them.

Unfortunately, we never quite lose our naïveté about schooling: we seem to believe that some sort of magic would take place if we could only correctly arrange the labels for what is to be taught. We seem to believe that if we could only compose the master list of content, and if we could only determine the precise order of labels, then all would be well in educationdom.

Alas, there is little magic in present-day social studies. Much of what we do is ineffectual: it has little impact and even less staying power. Preoccupation with lists and labels may be our very special way of being irrelevant in the lives of children.

Study

Study and the Arena for Instruction

The activity called "study" in this book is independent of any particular list of topics. Certainly, man's various communities, important in the Hanna proposals, harbor study possibilities. Occasions for study may also be found within schemes organized around Persistent Life Situations. Whatever the topic, whatever precedes or follows what in the yearly cycle of topics, instances of inquiry can be fostered.

Big Questions can be developed with respect to firemen, Chicago, constitutions, or the Congo. These Big Questions can give rise to a number of smaller, more directly answerable ones. The arbitrary choice of a topic leaves the teacher relatively free to decide what a proper confrontation of that topic might be.

While no plan will guarantee study, neither will any plan preclude it. Some patterns for schooling, however, do make it difficult to promote inquiry in the classroom. These latter administrative plans are frequently restrictive because they specify that so much content must be covered. Curriculum guides sometimes force the pace of instruction to a level at which time cannot be spared for the process of examining some question thoroughly in an investigative manner. Helping children to understand the grounds upon which they know something requires considerable instructional time. Under some schemes, that time is not easily available.

Other curriculum patterns are restrictive in that they consign the Now and Here topic[5] entirely to the primary grades. These designs restrict study because certain questions and forms of social residue are not considered in the intermediate and upper grades. Under these restrictive designs, the Now and Here topic is exclusively the concern of the very young child.

Unquestioned adherence to a plan for restricting the close at hand to the primary grades works a disadvantage on both the early and the later elementary levels. Under schemes such as these, the problem of the way in which we know about alien cultures is delayed until about the fifth or sixth grade. Then, not only is there the disadvantage of a prolonged parochialism in the primary years, but there is the added deprivation caused when older children are not helped to study events in communities close at hand. No doubt, inquiry about the commonplace is difficult. Propounding questions about the conventional, the comfortable, and the familiar is exceedingly difficult. Perhaps even more than the first-grader, however, the pre-adolescent needs to deal thoughtfully with identity and meaning in things and acts near at hand.

Most plans for the social studies are strongly egocentric. They assume that children must begin with the familiar community and then work their way out to the state, the region, the nation, and the rest of the planet. We would argue that schools might provide an early emancipation from parochial experience rather than encourage a prolonged immersion in it.

It may be that kindergarteners cannot be expected to understand much about the ancient far-away places. But they can be shown a painting or a picture to be interpreted with the class. They can listen to the reading of a folktale or handle an artifact. These things and more can help even very young children to begin to comprehend alien ways—the ways of people who never lived here but lived very far away and long, long, ago.

In the curriculum plan offered in this text the arena for instruction would include, each year and at every level, the Far and the Near, the Past and the Present.[6] Because inquiry varies with the kind of residue that can be confronted, different kinds of people must be studied in different ways. To provide for variety in inquiry, our list of topics would encourage and permit the study of all four categories of people each school year and at every grade level.

Study as a Mode of Instruction

HEURISTICS

Paul Tillich, we understand, once observed that, "The fatal pedagogical error is in throwing answers like stones at the heads of people who have

[5] See Chapter Ten.
[6] See Chapters Eleven, Twelve, and Thirteen.

not asked the questions." However, there is no routine way to avoid the "fatal pedagogical error." But if the teacher engages his students in a confrontation with the various sorts of residue discussed earlier,[7] then the following questions will often prove fruitful:

1. *Variety.* What is the problem of variety?

Variety should be a constant concern to the social-studies teacher. Two kinds of variety are worth considering. There is variety in the situation. With what variety of beliefs and attitudes do Mexicans, suburban dwellers, or Buddhists live? Students can learn to avoid talking about *The* Indians, or *The* Negroes, or *The* Americans. In addition, there is the variety of views regarding any one belief or opinion. Students can anticipate that there is a variety of views regarding communism, socialism, free enterprise, the cause of delinquency. Questions that direct attention to variety are usually fruitful.

2. *History.* What are the antecedents of the situation, custom or belief?

It is usually fruitful to explore what has led up to an existing condition or situation. For example, how did we come by the name, *America?* What are the antecedents of this naming?

3. *The Basis for Knowing.* How can one know that?

It is usually fruitful to explore the basis upon which things are said to be known. How can one know that democracy is better than communism? That Sparta was warlike? That Argentina is a stable, progressive country? That trolley cars are in most large American cities, or that delinquency is caused by broken homes?

A basic task of instruction is to help students discover how social knowledge is acquired. The question, "How can that be known?" is useful for directing students' attention to the statements that they encounter in textbooks or elsewhere.

These three questions suggest how social residue may be examined in the classroom. The use of these questions will be illustrated in Part III.

EVALUATION

An elementary-school teacher who is concerned with the development of social-studies arts and skills will have to devise methods of evaluating the capacity to engage in inquiry. A method of evaluation is a way to inform students about the relative importance of parts of the curriculum.

If it is essential that students learn how to write clear, interesting reports of the experience of being engaged in inquiry, then evaluating this capacity will be an important concern of measurement and the distribution of grades.

If being able to conduct a fruitful interview is an important skill, then the teacher will have to devise ways of assessing the development of this capacity.

What is important in the curriculum must be measured and evaluated. One

[7] See Chapter Two.

purpose that tests serve is to tell students what the teacher thinks is really of value. He should guarantee that his method of testing reflects the values he holds. The appraisal of a student's ability to remember the miscellaneous, unevaluated information that happens to be in a book that he happens to have read will provide little insight into the growth of social-study arts, skills, and understandings. If the teacher bases his grades on the student's abilities at miscellaneous remembering, then he affirms to the student that miscellaneous remembering is what is fundamentally important.

The tests a teacher devises are important communicators. If he prizes the study activity, he should think carefully about the ways in which he appraises achievement in his classroom. First, the tests should clearly communicate that the teacher cherishes the ability to study. This sounds sentimental and simple-minded. It is not. Most test-construction habits and professional training enable teachers to communicate the value of *acquaintanceship,* not study. Second, a child's performance on the tests should provide him with information on the extent of his development in the skills of study. What information do the results of tests feed back to the test-taker? In the realm of evaluation, teachers have a two-fold obligation: (1) to keep pupils informed of their progress in acquiring the skills and abilities of study; and (2) to employ tests that communicate the value placed on inquiry.

Plans for the social studies must make clear what children should learn how to do as they confront sociological, political, or historical questions. What is an encounter with an idea? What are worthy tasks for children? What should study be? These questions must be dealt with so that teachers will know more clearly what their obligations to students are. Deciding what students should learn how to do also enables teachers to gauge when progress has been made. Until the second curriculum responsibility is met, plans for the social studies will remain, for the most part, intellectually impotent.

PART THREE

Tasks of Instruction

Teachers face perplexing problems in moving from a general point of view to specific classroom practice. This difficulty is attested to by three very noticeable conditions in public education. First, certain pedagogical notions seem to remain just that—unpracticed notions for the education of children. These topics are likely to be dealt with in college courses and texts, but the recommended practices are not carried out to any reasonable degree in the classroom. Second, words are sometimes used by school people to fool themselves and their patrons. That is, ordinary teaching procedures are sometimes cloaked in a new jargon and then publicized as educational change. Finally, many innovative ideas in education have been transformed into fixed and heavily prescriptive procedures. Even powerful ideas lose their growth potential when they are rigidly coded in the "Hobgoblin Plan" or the "Terra Cotta Method." These three problems—vagueness in pedagogical notions, educational jargon, and prescriptive procedures—are familiar ones to every practitioner. Maintaining a clear strategy and interpreting productive procedures are demanding tasks for the classroom teacher.

The chapters in this section face the important problem of translating general notions into plausible classroom practices.

X

Now and Here:
Some People Live Nearby

In the elementary school, study centering in the Now and Here will have two important characteristics. First, the source of residue will be living men; the "things" that the class contrives to interrogate or fashion an explanation from will originate with living people. Second, a strong possibility will exist that children can observe, and interact with, these people directly.

The Central Problem

Now and Here study suffers the embarrassment of riches. Living men can talk and respond; of the great number and variety of such men, to whom shall we listen? If we listen to only a few, what are the risks in generalizing about the many? If we listen to many, when can we stop? How can we order the diversity of responses we obtain? What distortion is inherent in any capsule statement we devise? Moreover, living men do many things. They marry, build rockets, make wine, confine children to schools, gather at churches, chase butterflies, and find holes eaten in their stomachs. What to attend to? What to ignore? This is the central problem in studying living men—the problem of specifying the events to be inquired about and calculating the residue with which one will deal.

"Then" Versus "Now"

History, broadly conceived, is concerned with nonrecurrent happenings: there is one Napoleon, one Roman Empire, one American Civil War. An understanding of these never-to-be-again events is based on the questions one can ask of a "natural" residue; the events themselves cannot be run off again to permit fresh observations. Only rarely, such as in the recent discovery of the Dead Sea Scrolls, are additional remnants uncovered. It is possible, however, to devise ways of compelling the available relics to yield more expansive testimony. Recently, the carbon-14 test made possible a more accurate dating of objects; relatively new computer techniques can help to determine the authorship of disputed papers. But, in all, the special genius of the historian is his verve in developing a persuasive answer to a significant question despite a scarcity of source material.

The study of events-in-process, "Now" events, is not subject to the restriction of "natural" residue. In studying the "Now," one can design residue, that is, one can decide what "things" are relevant to the questions being asked, and these relevant "things" can be obtained in some responsible fashion. One can ask people questions; one can go and watch events occur; one can send another observer, at another time, to see if the two observers agree that the event occurs in just that way. In a sense, this residue is "artificial," that is, its manufacture is systematic, deliberate, and not left to chance.

Promoting Study

Because the central notion of this book is study, some forms this activity might take are illustrated below, in this and the following chapters, under varying classroom circumstances. Some of the illustrations from the classroom will not be commented upon; the content and placement of these vignettes should trigger reflective thought. A number of illustrations, however, are speculated upon. In these speculations, it is possible to dissect classroom procedures reported as descriptions of past events. Teachers, unfortunately, seldom enjoy this luxury. Rarely can they retrieve any of the several instant decisions they must make in the course of a school day. But yesterday's decision can be mulled over today as a guide to the many decisions that must certainly be made tomorrow. Perhaps, then, the illustrations and comments here will be of some value in making tomorrow's decisions.

In Texts and Topics

TEXTS

If the notion of study is to have impact in the classroom, the usefulness of textbooks must be demonstrated. Every classroom teacher must make peace with the school textbook. But the conditions of this settlement need not be one-sided and unconditional. Textbooks can be used to initiate and sustain classroom inquiry.

The great problem with textbooks is the customary way in which they are regarded. They are objects of belief. In the schools, their authority is prized very highly. Study, however, begins at the point where the textbook becomes a "thing." The teaching task is that of helping the class to convert the text to an object about which they can think and speculate.

This problem of regarding something in a particular way is shared by the child psychologist. One psychologist, for instance, finds that his graduate students have considerable difficulty in shedding or putting aside their nurturant and sentimental views as they begin to consider the psychology of the child. The psychologist wants his students to develop the "knack" of viewing the child dispassionately. To help bring about this frame of mind, he has formulated a cold, austere definition of the subject in his course. The child, in his terms, is to be regarded as an "ambulatory complex of variables." Perhaps there are occasions in the public schools when the textbook can be regarded just that coldly. Perhaps it need not be believed implicitly; it need not be fondled excessively in pursuit of the multiple choice and the true-false; and perhaps it need not be cherished for its own sake.

In the following illustration, the textbook is viewed coldly. This report is taken from the plans of a teacher beginning her first school year. The textbook referred to in her plans is rather current, attractive in appearance, and widely employed in middle-grade social-studies programs.

TROLLEY CARS: TRUE OR FALSE[1]

The quotation below appears in the social studies text I am supposed to use with my fifth graders next year. I plan to use the statement somewhat as follows:

"There are trolley cars in almost every large city in our country."

Do you think that statement is true? I've never seen a trolley car. Have you? Have you ever ridden on one? What does one look like?

Let's look at this statement very closely. If we want to question it, we must first know exactly what it means. I see two parts of this statement which we will have to make concrete before we can test it. Do you?

First, what are "large" cities? Shall we say cities the size of Lansing are large? Second, how many cities are "*almost* every large city?" The author leaves that up to us to decide, and so we shall.

Shall we think of this statement as meaning seventy-five per cent of all the cities the size of Lansing or larger have trolley cars? Fifty per cent? Ninety per cent? What are trolley cars? Let's think of them as a kind of bus that runs on a track like a train does, only it is powered by electricity. Now that we know what we are after, what can we do to find out if they now have,

[1] By permission of Mrs. Joanne Clock, Lansing, Mich.

or ever have had, trolley cars, and when they did. To whom shall we write in that city?

Let's use Lansing as a trial run. We know Lansing has no trolley cars now. Did it ever? Whom can we ask? (I called the Michigan Historical Commission and they were most helpful. In their archives, they found a book entitled *Electric Railways in Michigan*, published by the Central Electric Railway Association. According to this book "horsecars" were introduced in Lansing in 1886. In August 1890 they were converted to electricity. During succeeding years they changed management several times, and in 1920 there was a dispute about fares. Finally, on April 15, 1933, the electric trolley cars were permanently discontinued in favor of the private automobile. The lady I talked to on the phone said they also have a large collection of photographs which a teacher could borrow. I shall make good use of the Michigan Historical Commission next year for other problems as well as this one.)

I suspect that the answers we receive to the trolley-car query will be mostly negative. However, my husband's uncle does have some excellent slides of cable cars in San Francisco which he took this summer. I'm sure he would be glad to let us use them.

After we can say this statement is probably not true, we might ask why it is in the book at all. Do we know anything about the nature of books which could explain the presence of this statement? Let's look in the front of the book.

I'm sure someone would mention the copyright date. What is a "copyright?" Trip to the dictionary. The book was published in 1951—thirteen years ago. Was the statement true then? Let's go back even further. How long would it take to write a book like this? Maybe five years? Substracting five years from the copyright date would mean preparation for this book might have begun around 1946? Maybe there were trolley cars in most large cities in 1946. However, there were none in Lansing then.

Would there be one good way of finding out what the author had in mind when she wrote this statement? Certainly! We could ask her. Let's compose a class letter and find out!

Before we leave the trolley cars, we should consider one more thing. Sometimes, books are "revised" or brought up to date. Let's revise this section of the book concerning trolley cars on the basis of what we've found.

We can learn from this activity that the time a book was written and published may have some bearing on the truth or falsity of its contents.

Because the illustration above is many-sided, there are several facets that could be discussed. Probably, though, it is necessary to deal first with the question of focus or priority. The truth or falsity of the trolley-car statement is not information of great importance. Nor is the fact that textbooks contain flaws, that are important as a learning consequence. What is worthwhile and important is that children begin early, in whatever primitive fashion possible, to become their own authority for some of what they "know" about people and events around them. This report contains such possibilities. What might be nurtured here is an awareness of our acts of knowing and the skills required to resolve matters of doubt. In setting her plans in motion, this teacher might remind herself of her central objective: developing class skill in formulating and engaging a series of productive questions. The strategic objective is study; the tactic of the moment is that of interrogating a statement from the textbook. Since justification for these instructional plans does not rest on the acquisition of information, the teacher must take care to center her attention and effort on the defensible enterprise, the possibility of study.

Should this interlude take place in the classroom, children might gain something more than a sensitivity to the date of copyright in dealing with books. A more important learning might have to do with words and the role they play in conducting an investigation. The character of the class findings will no doubt hinge on the provisional definitions they assert for "trolley car," "almost," and "large cities." Perhaps with an older group, maybe even with fifth graders, it would be profitable to adjust these provisional definitions in various ways. If one defined "large cities" as only those ranked among the top ten in population, and if "trolley car" meant any public conveyance whose power source was an overhead electric wire, how then might the statement in the textbook be regarded?

Obtaining relevant and useful data when pursuing a question is another study skill. This teacher provides little information about the process she intends to use in obtaining responses from various cities other than Lansing. A number of problems could be considered here. Certainly for any major city there are several fairly current population figures among which to choose. Which one to use—the various census figures, estimated current population, population for the greater metropolitan area? Fifth graders would appreciate, too, the problems in deciding from whom to obtain data: the office of the mayor, the city engineer, the utility companies, chamber of commerce, the transit authority? Might the chamber of commerce, for example, be likely to use the most generous population figure available? Might they also try not to have their city appear old-fashioned in responding to an inquiry about trolley cars? These and other considerations might well sensitive youngsters to the frailty of their revised paragraph on even so simple a question as: Trolley cars, true or false?

Perhaps the most instructive practice described in this illustration is that of converting a book into an object to be regarded coldly. Facility in regarding a textbook as a thing about which one can think and inquire is not easily obtained. Perhaps only one other form of residue poses quite as many problems, the objects one creates himself. The temptation is to neglect turning the skills of inquiry on one's own works. Perhaps teachers should continually be alert for opportunities for the class to subject printed matter and class works to study, to tease out problems in which self-authored "things" must be scrutinized well.

TOPICS

Virtually all of the usual topics dealt with in the primary grades harbor the potential for study. In most social-studies programs, first and second graders explore such topics as the neighborhood, work roles, transportation, farm, and home. In the following illustration, study is promoted within the confines of one of these familiar topics.

GROCERY STORES[2]

In my school I am expected to teach two units: The City and The Farm. Because the curriculum guide is so uninspiring, though, I tried something new this term. We took an economic look at The City.

I have noticed that my classes are almost always self-conscious about their dresses and sweaters, coats and blue jeans, newly purchased for school. Therefore, I began this unit by commenting on the very obvious new apparel in our classroom. I went on to draw attention to the less noticeable purchases that had been made for the beginning of school, i.e., new library books, paper supplies, a new kick ball, and so on.

With the help of some prepared pictures, we next considered the many things families buy (food, furniture, toys, etc.). Controversy arose almost immediately. "What do you buy if you pay rent?" "Is it buying when you trade stuff with a pal or if kids give you a lot of stuff say like at a party?" "Where does the store man get all of those things?" "What do you buy, say, if you put 10¢ in a meter downtown or in a laundromat?" "You get good things by saving Blue Stamps." A number of other questions and statements tumbled out concerning "payments" and "time." We ended by agreeing to write a chart story recording our discussion and "what puzzled us."

In the next few days, our work centered on our chart stories and what families bought. I then approached the question of where things were bought. We compiled an extensive list, ranging from the corner ice-cream stand to the large, downtown department store.

At this point, I summarized where we were. In effect, we knew what things were purchased for families and we were fairly well acquainted with the places in which this activity took place. But we had a collection of puzzles about exactly what adults do when they buy and sell things. I discussed with

---

2 Adapted from the informal reports of a classroom teacher.

the class some ways of finding answers to our puzzle. A lot of answers could
be obtained by simply asking Mommies and Daddies questions and then reporting to the class what had been said. We discussed some of the risks and
profit in this method of finding out. John suggested that kids found out a
lot by "just hanging around [adults] and keeping still." Several children
suggested that we could find out by visiting some businesses around town
but that we couldn't go to all of them. I held back here and teased them
a bit by remarking that they had all been to grocery stores and department
stores many times before. What good would it do to visit a store one more
time? This was most upsetting. I had quite a time surviving the "hubbub"
that followed. I am sure that at this point they didn't really understand my
concern. Most of the class felt I was being rather capricious and unfair. Until
that moment, I don't think I had really thought about the difference between an excursion to a place where most of the class had never been (for
example, the trip first graders take behind the bars of a large, downtown post
office) and a field trip to a common, everyday place in the community. But
I persisted.

After mulling it over for a day, the class was a little more willing to grapple
with the problem again. I had some success now in coaxing from the class
why we didn't know much about buying in a store though we all had been
to stores many times. The class offered these thoughts:

> "Stores are fun: they have lots of things, and kids look
> around while Mommies buy."

> "Sometimes Mommies and Daddies don't like us around
> while they decide."

> "They won't let you go behind the swinging doors [stock
> room]."

> "We have talked to a store man about whether we have got
> enough money for a present or something, but we have
> never talked to him about being a store man."

> "Even though my Mommy works in a store, she doesn't talk
> about it much at home."

I think I did communicate to a fair part of the class the idea that going to
a store to buy is quite different from going to a store to understand stores
and about buying.

By this time, a week end was coming up, and I was able to collect my wits.

On Monday I confronted the class with pictures of several grocery stores.
Among these were pictures of several small, rather old, cluttered neighborhood stores. The large chain store and shopping-center supermarket were
well represented too. At my suggestion, we divided the pictures into two piles
—"new and big" versus "old and small." It was quite apparent that the class
recognized and had some considerable experience with chain stores. But

few of these suburban children were acquainted with corner groceries. I had
located two such stores across town and described them to the class.

No matter how I fished, the just-right question was never asked. So I
finally presented, rather badly, *my* puzzle. "Why does our city need two
kinds of grocery stores?" (I still cringe a bit at the wording of that question.
Lately, I have become aware of how much we invest all sorts of inanimate
objects with animate and human qualities. Letters have faces, arms, and legs
and skip about the post office explaining how they travel to grandmother's
house. If I could reword the question we worked on, I would probably ask
why these two very different grocery stores are found or are just here in this
city. In any event, I didn't ask how the corner grocery store and the supermarket "help" us!)

In the next day or so we considered how to answer "Miss Moore's puzzle."
The one thing I really did deliberately in this whole enterprise was to keep
this "Miss Moore's puzzle." I was more than a little intrigued by what a
comprehensive explanation might contain. If it was my puzzle, then I could
be a little bit "fussy" about what we did to find an answer. They were good
troopers and played along with my game.

So we "fussed" about the just right questions to be asked. We decided
that just now we were not too much concerned with where products came
from, what was a down payment, etc. We wanted to ask only the questions
that might lead to finding out "Why does our city need two kinds of grocery
stores?"

Up until now it had been touch and go, but now they seemed quite
caught up in my game. The class seemed really puzzled as to why a small,
cluttered, somewhat shabby, one-owner store could compete with a big,
rather new and shiny, very clean, well-stocked, busy, bustling, supermarket.

I can close this too-long, too-breezy account quickly now. As the sense
of puzzle really took hold, I caught a few "explanations" being developed
around the room. I was careful to record these, and they were the center of
some heated arguments later when we returned from our field trip.

Our first explanation had to do with prices. Many children felt that a
small, old store was inferior and hence was a "cheap" store. There seemed
to be a feeling, too, that these stores were patronized by some dimly known,
but vaguely distasteful people. Put most bluntly, a city "needs" marginal
stores for marginal people. A second, a benevolent explanation, was developed, too. That is, the storekeeper "sort of gives food to very poor people."
Other children did, as I remember, mention special sales, being friends with
the clerks, proximity, and "just liking to [shop at a particular store]" as reasons why people patronized various stores.

When we finally did go to "look and ask questions," the seriousness and
intensity of my puzzlers couldn't have been greater. The clerks, managers,
and owners we talked to in those two stores were given a real third degree.

Because second graders can be embarrassingly direct, both of these grocers soon began to sell us on their kind of store.

Our brief attempt to find out by "just hanging around and keeping still" was something to behold. Thirty second graders clumped around in a silent, staring group can soon become a subject of considerable curiosity themselves!

But they fairly wiggled themselves out of their seats in the discussion that followed. Our "off-hand" explanations suffered a quick and noisy rejection of considerable modification. Our new "explanation" centered on the real but different customer advantages these stores offered. We set down completeness of stock, variety of brands, the general lower prices, the convenience of one-stop, once-a-week shopping, the efficient check-out service, carts, etc., of the supermarkets alongside the personal attention, service, home delivery, small charge accounts, and specialty items of the small store. We developed such a firm faith in this "answer" that I was almost tempted to remind the class of how taken they had been with their prior "explanations."

As we were tidying up the loose ends of the field trip, it soon became apparent that the two-category classification system we had started with simply would not hold up. We were too aware of stores now. We first had to account for the local supermarket under independent ownership as distinct from the regional chain store. We discovered an almost endless variety of small neighborhood stores, too—the delicatessen, the bakery, the bakery and coffee shop, the butcher shop, the vegetable market. Many of these were clean though small. Many were not old at all. Several stores were highly specialized. The implications of that word occupies our attention now.

I am not sure but what I may have lost the initiative with the present group, but either now or next year I am going to sneak up on the notion of history. As I begin to think about it, the supermarket and the shopping plaza are not unrelated to the development of the automobile. We missed another possibility, too, when we noticed a difference in buying habits among the customers in the two stores—weekly versus daily purchases—and I am sure this is partially related to the development of refrigeration and other means of preserving food.

Later I plan to shift our study to buying things in other sorts of stores. Probably we will visit a downtown department store.

I thought, finally, that with some planning and care on my part we might move from buying things to making things. I know of at least three small manufacturing plants nearby—a furniture factory, a sporting goods and toy producer, and a small supplier to the automotive industry. We are going to see what there is to know about working and producing things.

Present curriculum patterns seem to restrict the Now and Here to the kindergarten, first, and second grades. But many teachers contend this sort of study might profitably be present at all grade levels, because only when dealing with the Now and Here are all forms of residue available. When studying far-away people, it is not possible for children to face the special problem of obtaining and using their own notes as observers (residue categories eight and nine, Chapter Two). When studying people who lived long ago, one cannot, obviously, obtain formal responses from them (residue category seven). Nor can children formulate questions concerning people who lived very long ago using mechanical records, films, recordings, and the like (category six) as sources of data. Only when children deal with the contemporary and the close at hand can they engage in all forms of study—hold dialogue with each of the nine forms of residue.

There is quite another reason why children at every age might engage the Now and Here in study. Among the four categories—Then and There, Now and There, etc.—only this one is unencumbered by residue three-B, social-studies text materials. Text material dominates the field of "things" available for study in the other categories, often stifling inquiry. But, in dealing with the Now and Here, it is somewhat easier to become one's own authority for what one knows, simply because fewer other authorities exist.

In the following illustration, the teacher describes the development of a possible study interlude involving upper-grade children. The description makes little use of the conventional social-studies textbook.

RED CEDAR[3]

In recent years there has been a growing feeling about the Red Cedar River. One often hears it referred to as "that sewer," a "public menace," a "so-called river," and so forth. Off and on I have heard quite a number of imaginative tales from children about the dire things that were sure to happen if you fell in the river or if the river water were to be splashed on you. I'm sure these schoolboy tales about the Red Cedar can be capitalized upon. Even in the "Water Wonderland" there are important water problems; we place exorbitant demands—urban, industrial, agricultural, recreational—on our existing resources. The Red Cedar seems to offer good possibilities for considering the "social side" of a stream.

It seems likely that our study of the Red Cedar will have two phases. Our first problem will be that of determining the status of the river. If the marginal character of the stream is confirmed, then we can begin to examine causes as well as proposals for its rehabilitation.

As a starting point, I talked with an engineer for the city of East Lansing. According to him, the Red Cedar has been "cleaned up a lot in recent years. It's in fairly good shape now." I was able to obtain some specific informa-

[3] Adapted from informal reports of a classroom teacher.

tion about the city sewage plant and the interceptors installed at various points along the north river bank. From the standpoint of the city of East Lansing, everything is under control, except for a few old homes along the river that are discharging raw sewage directly into the stream. The engineer admitted that this was a danger but very decidedly emphasized the positive aspects of the situation. Finally, I learned that the city makes weekly checks at three different points along the river to determine the condition of the water.

This initial encounter seems to offer an opportunity to sensitize the class to problems of communication in interviewing people. What do the phrases "cleaned up a lot," "recent years," and "good shape" mean in the engineer's testimony? This might be a good time, too, to raise the question of self-interest in the replies we hear to our questions. With respect to the engineer, we must deal with the responses of a person employed by the city to do a specific job. In some ways, the answers he gives reflect the effectiveness of his branch of city government, and he will not be unaware of this evaluation.

I decided then to talk with someone not connected with city government. A representative I contacted from the Ingham County Health Department had quite a different opinion of the Red Cedar. In this interview, I was trying to find out if children could take their own samples of water from the river to perform simple tests or to send them to a state or county agency for analysis. The representative I talked to was very discouraging about this idea. He informed me that it was a foregone conclusion that the river was severely contaminated. Personally, he would not risk exposing children even simply to obtain water samples from the river. The same instances of river-bank homes with direct sewage discharge were then cited. But his emphasis was quite different from that of the city engineer. The Health Department representative went on to say, though, that conditions were being improved remarkably; he estimated that in about two years conditions would be "satisfactory."

In helping children develop skill in analyzing the information gained through interviews, it might not be good strategy for the class to confront the speakers directly. If I reconstructed each interview on paper and mimeographed it, or if I tape-recorded these interviews, it might help the class to feel "analytic" rather than "personal" or "destructive." Sometimes the remembered presence of a speaker makes it difficult for children to question what was said. Typed copies and taped recordings of interviews offer the additional advantage of permanency; they can be scanned or listened to again when new issues are raised.

My search uncovered four additional "things"—a report, a letter, a newspaper article, and a name. A 1959 commission report to the governor of our state characterizes the waters flowing by Lansing and East Lansing as "used up." A high university official's letter to the County Health Department requests help with respect to the condition of the Red Cedar as it flows through the campus. A series of three-year-old local-newspaper articles states that the "continued use of the Red Cedar for canoeing and water carnival activities is considered dangerous." My final discovery was that "Cedar" is the true name for the "Red Cedar" river. The descriptive "Red" appears to be a local phenomenon. Although it certainly describes the coloration of the water, the coloration is not an important index of pollution. But discoloration does prejudice people and property owners in the recreational uses they make of streams.

In all, I discovered a great number of "things" to provide a basis for helping the class to come to a defensible judgment about the status of the river.

Through a discussion of the river as portrayed on the map, I should be able to raise one of the elements in the causes of current conditions on the river. I'm sure the children would readily note and understand the plight of down-river cities and property owners along polluted waterways. Minimal searching is sure to turn up some documents concerning riparian rights to waters "undiminished in quantity and unimpaired in quality." Now every school district, I understand, retains legal counsel in the conduct of its affairs. Perhaps that firm or some other legal counsel in the community would be willing to discuss with me or with the class some of the legal and political arrangements involving water resources. I'm sure my sixth graders will be able to understand, for example, the need to show cause or prove damages in the court of law. We'll consider how difficult it must be to determine "unreasonable" use of water rights. Apparently the riparian status of municipalities and their legal right to use streams for waste disposal is not at all clearly defined. Consequently, we have such situations arising as that involved in designing and building a combined storm-drainage and sewer system. During storms, such systems will discharge raw sewage directly into nearby rivers and streams. The Michigan Water Resources Commission and the Tri-County Regional Planning Commission will be two agencies of great help in resolving some of our questions of law and politics in stream uses.

The physical characteristics of the watershed, as well as the legal and political arrangements of men, determine the status of a stream. From the map, I'm sure the class will be quick to notice that the Cedar is part of the Grand River watershed. Probably they will soon sense the importance of land formation, soil characteristics, elevation, precipitation, and all the physical elements that go to make up the character of a stream. I'm not sure they will be quick to give equal attention to the cultural characteristics of the watershed and the effects these have on the character of the rivers and streams.

Throughout our investigation, the class will have abundant opportunity to develop skills in utilizing technical reports. One publication I found ("Drought Flow of Michigan Streams") contains information on "low flow" conditions expected for the Cedar. One table, for example, shows the low runoff expectancy (cubic feet per second) for various cycles (once in five years, once in ten years, etc.) of particular duration (five days, thirty days, etc.). These "low flow" characteristics of the Cedar are consequential. That is, the volume of water in a stream and the available free oxygen are related to that stream's ability to absorb waste products effectively. "Low flow" conditions, therefore, are likely to mean a turgid and dangerously polluted stream, because it has neither the water volume nor the available oxygen to meet the sewage demands placed upon it.

One way of stabilizing stream flow and preventing "low flow" conditions, of course, is to develop upstream reservoirs to store excess runoff and release it as needed. Our second report ("Water Resource Conditions and Uses in the Upper Grand River Basin") contains criteria for selecting storage sites as well as descriptions and analyses for potential catchment areas. Many of these are close enough for on-site inspection by the class. Examining these reservoirs and considering the possibilities of stabilizing stream flow will be one alternative we'll examine in proposing a program for rehabilitating the "Red" Cedar.

In Spontaneous and Contrived Study Situations

Study will probably be somewhat infrequent in most public school classrooms. Generally, the activities of schoolchildren will be concerned with acquaintanceship matters—acquiring information, organizing and conveying facts, using maps. Matters pertaining to attitudes, to zeal and patriotism, will command time and attention, too. These worthwhile concerns will occupy a large block of time in any social-studies program.

There are other reasons why inquiry, the act of study, will not be an everyday event in the classroom. One of the most difficult phases of any investigation is that of framing a powerful question, and powerful questions do not emerge ready-made. They must be solicited with a certain flair and cunning. Many questions a teacher might coax into the open will not snare the imagination of the class. Others may seem to command earnest class attention, but earnestness will not be enough. If study is to proceed, it must be possible for the questions to be resolved by the children themselves. Many questions will suggest immediate appeal to the authority of others for their answer. But some questions are powerful because they entice children to develop answers on their own authority.

In the vignette below, the teacher responds to a spontaneous situation; she helps the children to decide what it is they want to know, to arrange their questions in careful order, and to consider means whereby they can fashion answers to their questions. This illustration demonstrates why study might be an infrequent thing—time must be committed, a special classroom tone or atmosphere is required, and the teacher must have high skills in listening, probing, and focusing.

A FLOWERING PLUM TREE[4]

At the present time we are working on a unit about trees in a third grade classroom. Recently one of my slower students brought in a leaf from a tree he called the "Flowering Plum." Some of the other students immediately discounted his discovery.

PUPIL: "There's no Flowering Plum Tree."

PUPIL: "Yes, there is. The lady said the tree is a Flowering Plum."

PUPIL: "Well, I never saw one."

TEACHER: "Because you have never seen one, you're sure there isn't one."

PUPIL: "Well, I never heard of one either."

PUPIL: "Did you ever see a Redwood?"

PUPIL: "Well, no, but I've seen pictures of them, and I've read about them."

TEACHER: "Barry, tell us more about the tree."

PUPIL: "It's about as big as you."

TEACHER: "Anything else?"

PUPIL: "It has pink flowers."

TEACHER: "Now?"

PUPIL: "No, just in the spring. It's just got leaves now."

PUPIL: "It doesn't have flowers, it has blossoms."

PUPIL: "What's a blossom?"

PUPIL: "It's just a flower that grows on a tree."

TEACHER: "Then is a blossom the same as a flower?"

PUPIL: "Sure."

PUPIL: "How do you know? Flowers can't grow on trees."

PUPIL: "I've seen flowers on apple trees."

PUPIL: "They're blossoms. Flowers can't grow on trees."

TEACHER: "I think we have some questions to answer. Can anyone tell me what they are?"

PUPIL: "Is there really a Flowering Plum tree?"

PUPIL: "What's a blossom?"

PUPIL: "Are flowers and blossoms the same?"

PUPIL: "Can flowers grow on trees?"

TEACHER: "How can we answer these questions?"

PUPIL: "Well, I'll go over and see if that tree is really a Flowering Plum. I can be like a witness. I'll tell you tomorrow what it looks like."

[4] By permission of Miss Carol La Rose, Saint Claire Shores School District, Mich.

TEACHER: "What else can we do?"

PUPIL: "I think Barry means it's a plum tree."

TEACHER: "Why?"

PUPIL: "That's what it sounds like."

PUPIL: "It's not a plum tree, it's a Flowering Plum."

TEACHER: "Ask your neighbor again to be sure."

PUPIL: "I'd like to see it."

TEACHER: "Ask her if we can come and see it."

PUPIL: "I'll have her write the name, and if we can come to see it."

PUPIL: "I'm going to ask my mother. We have lots of trees."

PUPIL: "I'm going to the library and look for a book."

TEACHER: "Those are good ideas. What about our other questions?"

PUPIL: "We can find out what a flower is."

PUPIL: "Yes, and we can find out what a blossom is."

TEACHER: "Will that answer our question?"

PUPIL: "Sure, then we can tell if they're the same or not."

TEACHER: "What about our other questions?"

PUPIL: "That's a hard one."

PUPIL: "Not if we find out what flowers and blossoms are."

TEACHER: "Why did you say that?"

PUPIL: "Well, if flowers and blossoms are the same, then flowers grow on trees."

TEACHER: "But what if they're not the same?"

PUPIL: "Then we better look in books."

TEACHER: "What books?"

PUPIL: "Books with flowers."

PUPIL: "Books with blossoms."

"A Flowering Plum Tree" portrays well how a teacher might respond to a situation so that children might pursue their own questions strenuously. This study sequence revolves about a tree and its name, but people are the special concern of social studies. With regard to social studies then, powerful classroom questions focus attention upon variety among men and groups of men, the sources of man's behavior, and man's intellectual tools for understanding social events.

There is another, rather homely reason, why social study will not be common in the schools—it takes time. Many areas and concerns compete for instructional time, and the competition grows more fierce each year. Social study is expensive in its use of school time; if and when social study takes place, it will likely dominate the available instructional time. Therefore, teachers will be hard-pressed to balance time for social study against acquaintanceship tasks and against the various other curricular demands of the school program.

Acquaintanceship is preparation for study. Under the direction of teachers, children will become acquainted with the work of others who have studied and with the information and interpretations these students have derived in the process of examining "things." Understanding of this order will occupy a significant part of class attention. But within the normal topics and activities of the social studies, some study is possible.

Classroom study customarily originates in two ways. One of these is the spontaneous situation; the other, a contrived circumstance. The "Flowering Plum Tree" study sequence seemed to arise out of a spontaneous situation. The teacher was able to begin her work when members of the class took exception to a fellow student's assertion. Study may frequently begin in just this fashion. A question asked by a child, something overheard, a story read, or a warm argument between two students might trigger some study segment. But at other times, perhaps most often, a teacher must seek to precipitate study through situations of his own making.

The teacher might contrive to focus class attention on a word, a custom, a holiday, or a behavior ordinary and common to all. He might bring a person, recording, diary, poem, poster, or political cartoon to the classroom. He might seek special ways in which to help children notice a puzzle, a contradiction, a peculiar fact, an unusual statement, a bald generalization, or an anachronism appearing in printed material. He would hope that one of these might arouse questions; that these questions might be refined, recast, or criticized; and that students might weigh carefully the procedures and processes upon which they based their findings and the "answers" of their own manufacture.

The study interlude below illustrates the contrived circumstance. In it, the teacher contrives a special use for the preliminary conclusions drawn up by a committee of students concerned with an aspect of city transportation. The teacher helps the children to plan to engage in certain activities and to record the results of this involvement. These records then join memories as residue of the involvement about which the class can think, propose meanings, and suggest further questions.

FREEWAYS[5]

Eighth graders in one of our larger cities are studying the metropolitan community in which they live. They have discovered that transportation poses difficult problems for large cities. The complexities of arranging for huge groups of people to move freely and safely into and around the city seem to fascinate these youngsters. They decide that the characteristics of

[5] Adapted from informal reports of a classroom teacher.

transporting people and goods in the city are worthy of intensive investigation.

There is an auto in each family represented in the class; ten families have two cars. These children live in a middle-class neighborhood that was once considered pretty far out of the city but is now well within the city's outer limits. About half of these children live in rented, and half live in individually owned, homes. Of the renters, slightly more than half live in multiple-family dwellings housing from two to four families.

Mr. O'Toole is working with six children as they think about the way in which limited-access highways meet or create transportation problems. Every child has driven on the city freeways and is familiar with them. In telling him about their progress, they show him a list of "how freeways are better than regular streets." The list states that speeds are higher on freeways than on ordinary streets; the flow of traffic is smoother because it is not interrupted by stop lights; and that rarely, if ever, does a driver have to worry about avoiding pedestrians on the road.

MR. O'TOOLE: How do you know the freeway is faster?

CHILD: The speed limit is 45 on the freeway in the city limits and only 25 on the streets.

CHILD: Yeah, but if there's an accident, you can get stuck in a long line. My father always picks the wrong lane.

MR. O'TOOLE: Bob thinks the freeway is faster because the speed limit is higher. How do you know the limit is higher, Bob?

CHILD: I've seen the signs maybe a hundred times.

MR. O'TOOLE: You *know* about the speed limits because you've *seen* the signs. Do you know *how much* faster the freeway is?

Mr. O'Toole is working toward two kinds of objectives. He wants these children to learn something about the significance of the freeway system to their community. He is also concerned that they become sensitive to the way in which they know. Knowing may demand different kinds of observations as the question changes. Three of the children have visited the natural history museum. They drove on the freeway and remember it as about a half-hour drive. They are pretty sure it would take longer to drive through the city, but they don't know how much longer. One child suggests that they can compare the time it takes to drive there on the freeway with the time it takes them to return through the city. Mr. O'Toole offers to drive them on Saturday morning if their parents will permit the trip.

Later, during the time when small groups report to the whole class their plans for finding information that will help answer their questions, this group tells about their proposed experiment. Although most children think it is a good idea, some children object. It may be an unfair comparison because the traffic going in one direction is heavier than the traffic going in the other. Also, they will be returning slightly later in the morning than when they made the trip down town. The group decides to change its plan by enlisting the help of one of the children's parents, so that two cars can go and return by different routes at the same approximate times.

In response to the teacher's question about the kinds of differences they expect to observe between travel on the freeway and travel on the streets, they predict the conditions on their list (smoother flow on the freeway, etc.) and anticipate that a greater variety of vehicles will use the streets than use the freeway. Children are detailed to keep track of the total distance, average speed, total time from start to arrival, the number of stops that must be made, and the number of different vehicles they see. The committee is quick to notice that they can't "keep track" of "average speed" directly. Finally, it is suggested that a reading be taken from the speedometer at three-minute intervals.

When they took the trip, children in one car started counting the number of cars that passed them as they traveled as close to the speed limit as possible without exceeding it. They were surprised at the number of cars they counted that traveled faster than the speed limit on the freeway. They noticed that only when they drove along a four-lane divided boulevard did any cars pass them on their way through the city.

In the discussion that followed their report to the class, the experimenters were disappointed that the freeway trip had not been as much faster as they had predicted. Children discussed the limited-access characteristic of the freeway and the time needed to drive to and from the freeway from the start and finish points. The same children who had objected to the "unfair" comparison, suggested again that a similar test made during a weekday might give different results, especially at certain hours of peak travel. Children suggested that the advantage in time might increase as the distance of the trip increased.

Recognizing their inability to sample traffic comprehensively, the class began to wonder if any public agency had comparative figures they could use. One child volunteered to call the local offices of the State Highway Commission; another thought of calling the City Planning Commission. The experience with "speeders" led to a concern for accident prevention and the suggestion that someone examine accident records and safety programs.

Mr. O'Toole brought the class back to the title of the committee's list, "How Freeways are Better Than Streets," by referring to an article he had read recently. The writer claimed that freeways were not better but worse! In his opinion they were often ugly, added to the downtown congestion, and increased air pollution. He presented statistics to support some of his opinions. Mr. O'Toole asked how they could know if freeways were "better." In the resulting discussions, children began to understand that "faster" could be determined by an observation of standard units of time and speed, but that "bctter" dcpcndcd on nonstandard units of valuc and attitudc. For someone who valued speed more than beauty, freeways might be "better"; for someone who thought overhead roads contributed to a dark and dingy city, freeways might be "worse." They also learned that some freeways manage to be both efficient and beautiful.

The freeway committee broadened its task to include a survey of attitudes toward driving and the value of freeways, using their parents as a source of data.

Traveling on the freeway and through the city presented members of the class described above with an opportunity to study their own participation in an event. It stimulated awareness of problems and suggested new questions and sources of information. It allowed them not only to use their own perceptions as a basis for forming conclusions, but dramatized the practical limits of personal observation, and pointed up the necessity for consulting expert testimony and scientific reports.

Study Demands on the Teacher

Whether study begins with a spontaneous event or is initiated through a contrived circumstance, the demands placed on the teacher are great. His ability to "size up" or to appraise the developing situation is at a high premium. He must see among the everyday events of the schoolroom the possibilities of study. He must be able to carve some problem of workable dimensions out of a broad topic. When the class can isolate and fasten on something unknown, something problematic, then study is possible. A teacher must develop the ability to recognize worthwhile social questions, particularly those questions upon which children can be helped to impose the criterion of "things."

He must also exercise restraint as he seeks to foster study. It is sometimes very difficult to decide how much information to feed into a discussion. Without certain information, it may be difficult to help children develop a clear awareness of what they do not know. But, if there is a common pattern in teaching errors, it is probably that of dispensing information so freely as to blunt a developing curiosity. The teacher who seeks to nurture study must learn to calculate the effect of information on the process of inquiry. Used calculatingly, information might yield up a sense of mystery, an urge to know. It might provide a seedbed in which questions are likely to germinate. It might help children to reconsider their questions and the means they propose for seeking solutions. And it might help them to appraise their findings and the limits to their knowing.

Although restraint is sometimes required in initiating classroom social study, at other times exuberance may be required. When a teacher is urging the class to try out a new idea, to foresee a certain consequence, to view common matters a bit starkly, he may need a certain intellectual zest or playfulness.

No doubt, too, a teacher must have a special ear for the narrative of the classroom. The brief spark for kindling inquiry may originate in some student's use of an idea, in an erroneous impression shared by the class, or in the way in which the children regard certain people or political events.

A teacher who strives to help children practice the art of study must be skillful in sensing areas of profitable investigation. He must collect support for these promising studies. He must be skillful in his use of information to feed and shape the developing inquiry. He must be able to quicken the tempo of the classroom when necessary. He must be capable of appraising and responding to the flow of talk in the classroom. And he will need all of these teaching talents, and others, as well, whether study begins with a spontaneous or a contrived circumstance.

XI

Now and There:
Some People Live Far Away

Where is There?

Studying people at a distance presents a teacher with several interesting problems. One of these is simply knowing when he has moved out beyond the everyday experience of his class. Children living in the decaying center of a large city may never have seen the rural countryside that helps to feed them. For them, trees may grow only in the park, cows live in the children's zoo. The farms and villages thirty miles away are far away from their experience. Merely another part of the city may be "there"—a place where each house contains only one family, and the clamor of everyday life is compounded of the sounds of people and animals muted by distance.

Similarly, many rural children still thrill to a ride in an elevator, wonder at the rush and saunter of crowds of strangers, puzzle over arid fields of concrete, marble, and macadam, and toy with the idea of coming "home" to one of the honeycomb units of an apartment building.

If it is easy to assume mistakenly that certain experiences are commonplace in the lives of children, it is at least as easy to underestimate their breadth of experience with life in other places. It is a truism that ours is an extremely mobile population. In states like New York, Ohio, Michigan, Illinois, Texas, and California, in which population has increased dramatically in the last decade, it is not unusual to find that the children in a fourth grade were born in a dozen or more different states. A Negro child who knows little about the way in which people live in the suburbs surrounding his own city may know a great deal about life on a tenant farm in Mississippi. Some of the children attending a country consolidated school may have spent some of their preschool years at an army post in Germany or a naval base in Japan. National and state parks serve increasing numbers of vacationers every year and attract visitors from every corner of the country, as the family camping trip gains in popularity. Although television's purpose is entertainment, it sometimes manages to be instructive as well.

In its more lucid moments, it floats children down Thai rivers, lifts them into Swiss pastures. Often, it provides simple amusement in its incongruous transformation of history's delinquents into self-righteous moralists remaking the Old West, or its motivation of medieval despots with the congenial ideas of twentieth-century American Style democracy.

Any experience can be valuable or shallow. A year in Germany insulated from any real contact with Germans or a television glimpse into the tent of a Lapp or a desert nomad or down the unerring sight of a sheriff's six-shooter frequently provide only the illusion of knowing. Nevertheless, as experiences, they exist. They can be converted into take-off points for genuine study.

Studying distant people begins with the recognition by teachers that "there" is a relative concept. Some people may be fairly close to children in absolute distance, yet far removed, in the things they commonly do and value, from the children's everyday models of behavior. They are separated from the children not only by space, but also by difference in language, social tradition, and spiritual experience.

Values and Valuing

As they investigate the people and social institutions of far-away places, children will inevitably encounter customs and appearances that seem strange and "illogical," whose novelty may lead to feelings of rejection or to an acceptance based on appreciating what is quaint. Different behaviors may be based on beliefs and values that either do not exist in our culture or that we deliberately reject. A culture is a complicated network of relations between certain patterned ways of behaving and believing, feeling and knowing. The separate parts of a culture, its artifacts or beliefs or practices, take on meaning through their existence in the cultural context in which they have developed and in which they are functional. Arranged with care and skill, flowering weeds can acquire a special aesthetic appeal for someone who would view them with distaste in his lawn. Another observer will value the same weed only if he finds it growing and thriving in its natural habitat. The weed's "meaning" changes as the context in which it is found changes. An old Japanese teacup in an American home or classroom may evoke feelings of aesthetic appreciation or even remind its owner of the intricately symbolic ceremony in which it once functioned. It is unlikely to mean to an American what it would mean to a Japanese owner, whom it linked in an intimate way with past owners and for whom it signified either that he maintained a tradition that was fast disappearing, or that he, too, had abandoned a tradition that had in the past ennobled the teacup and its users.

Americans share with most European, and some Oriental, cultures, the placing of value on aggressive, striving, achievement-oriented behavior.[1] Some cultures, however, value a type of apparent passivity that emphasizes self-control, rather than control or manipulation of others or of one's environment. A small group of Menomônie Indian men, for instance, dedicated to preserving traditional Menomonie beliefs, were gathered in a circle to perform a religious ceremony, chanting to the accompaniment of drums. An Indian who had become converted to Christianity and was now a missionary to the Indians, came near to the circle. As he approached, he raised a trumpet and began to play hymns. The men continued their chanting and drumming, without looking up, as the missionary delivered a ringing sermon, exhorting them to change their ways. No one appeared to notice the intruder, and, defeated, he gave up and went away.[2] Had an Indian interrupted the service at one of the churches in town by blowing loudly on a trumpet, he would have been hustled into the street, and probably none too gently, by members of the congregation. Whether the Indians' reaction was "passive," or nonhostile, or represented a variant of hostile behavior that is strange to us in such a situation, is difficult to decide. Whatever their behavior means, it has that meaning within, and in terms of, their own culture, not of ours.

Can even older elementary-school children understand the subtle determinants of the different value systems and behavior patterns of different cultures? Some educators would answer, "No." According to Preston: "Children lack the background and maturity to study human customs around the world with a view to discovering differences in standards."[3] Preston is a vigorous supporter of the study of people of other countries and of minority subcultures (racial, religious, and nationality groups) within our own country. He believes firmly in the necessity of increasing international understanding through teaching children, beginning in the elementary grades, about the different peoples who inhabit the earth.[4]

He also believes that children should be guided away from a close examination of ethical principles that differ from ours. Such a position is based on his feeling that children can only be confused and hurt by study that suggests that standards may be the result of local circumstances, or that people in some cultures reject some of our values and accept ethical principles which we reject.[5] This implies that teachers should try to prevent

[1] DAVID C. MCCLELLAND, *The Achieving Society* (Princeton: D. Van Nostrand, 1961).

[2] We are indebted to Professor George Spindler for this anecdote.

[3] RALPH C. PRESTON, *Teaching Social Studies in the Elementary School* (New York: Holt, Rinehart and Winston, 1962), p. 211.

[4] *Ibid.,* Chapter Eight.

[5] *Ibid.,* pp. 211–212.

children from discovering that Spartan boys were rewarded for stealing without being caught, or that the Siriono in the Bolivian forest "abandon their dying kinsmen without a word."[6]

There is no evidence to suggest that children are unable to understand values unlike those accepted by their own cultures, or that such an understanding is in any way damaging to them, and there is some question whether an absolutist view of values is essential to children's psychological or moral well-being.

It is at least logically possible that a commitment to principles may be too weak to stand up under pressure if that commitment has been carefully protected from the challenge of alternatives and has never been toughened on the necessity to defend itself against opposition. (The inability of "hot-house-grown" principles to withstand stress is the theme of Mark Twain's amusingly satiric story, *The Man That Corrupted Hadleyburg*. It may also have been a factor in one of the tragic chapters in United States history, the "brain-washing" of some American soldiers by Chinese Communists during the Korean war.)

In avoiding the discovery and examination of values different from ours, a teacher risks studying other cultures in a superficial way. In her extensive analysis of "culture units," Robertson discovered five characteristics that appeared to work against the achievement of such stated goals as "to appreciate all people of the world." These were: (1) a tendency to picture foreign people in terms of stereotypes (Holland, Land of Wooden Shoes; Japan, Land of Cherry Blossoms); (2) the use of a sentimental approach; (3) the practice of judging others in relation to our own standards ("the impression is left . . . that peoples of non-industrialized cultures are to be liked but pitied because they are ignorant, lazy, and incapable of governing themselves . . ."); (4) an emphasis on the quaint and picturesque; and (5) a stress on the past at the expense of the present.[7] It is at least logically possible that a search for the values that give meaning to the practices of a people may produce learning of greater significance than that decried by Robertson. Professor Fannie Shaftel points up the difference in commenting:

Human arrangements are a complex built around a system of values. You can't study the Hopi, for instance, by saying, "They eat corn." You must understand how intimately the corn cycle is bound up with their whole concept of the universe, with the rhythms of the year, with the rituals by which they live spiritually. If we do not understand [ideas such as this], we do not help children to understand what holds a good many American Indians of Hopi ancestry in a very

[6] ROBERT REDFIELD, *The Primitive World and Its Transformation* (Ithaca: The Cornell University Press, 1953), p. 140.

[7] WANDA ROBERTSON, *An Evaluation of the Culture Unit Method for Social Education* (New York: Bureau of Publications, Teachers College, Columbia University, 1950).

traditional way of life in the midst of technology, and that has caused for many of them extreme trauma.[8]

Children can also be helped to make inferences (*cautiously*) about values, based upon records of human interaction and descriptions of such social institutions as arranged marriages, extended families (those including aunts, uncles, cousins, grandparents, etc., in addition to mother, father, and their children), village ownership of land, and private ownership of land.

Learning what different peoples value, the way in which values shape behavior, and the characteristics of valuing are important facets of social study that are intellectually accessible to elementary-school children. Although major attention will be given to helping children understand values and valuing in Chapter Fourteen, at least one of the illustrations in this chapter will show a teacher and class attempting to infer values from a few facts that they have collected about a group of people.

"Things" From Far Away

In an earlier chapter,[9] it was suggested that study was compounded of "things," observation, and thought. Suppose the "things" to be American and British textbooks, each of which describes certain events preceding the American Revolutionary War. If observation of these books discovers that different emphases or different treatments are given to these descriptions of events, then the thinking that follows can result in questions about these observed differences. It can guess about reasons for them, directing a search for more "things" that might cause the guesses to be supported or modified—descriptions of *modern* British and American societies; comments of historians about the way in which history is written; or an analysis of the feelings of national pride and identification experienced by children in the class.

If the "things" are maps, showing the suspected or discovered distribution of natural resources in Brazil, and written accounts, describing the limited exploitation of these resources, observation of these "things" can stimulate thinking that raises questions about the reasons such conditions exist and guesses about why they exist. This might necessitate a search for more "things" that are relevant to the questions and guesses—the statements of American businessmen or Brazilian officials; accounts of Brazilian history; and possibly more maps, containing information about roads, railroads, pipelines, and land surface.

[8] Speech at Wayne State University, Detroit, Mich. Quoted with Professor Shaftel's permission.
[9] Chapter Two.

Something must be observed before thinking conducive to study can take place, even if the "something" is a child's comment or a teacher's question. As noted earlier, acquaintance with "things" is a prerequisite to study; it is also a constant companion to study, although study demands more than mere acquaintanceship.

In Chapter Two, nine types of "things" were listed. They were:

1. Objects: autos, shawls, chopsticks, etc.
2. Written materials: letters, journals, novels
3. Special writing: scientific reports, textbooks
4. Special objects of a highly symbolic type: art objects such as paintings, statues
5. People (to watch, to talk with)
6. Mechanical records of events: films, recordings, photographs
7. Responses to formally prepared questions
8. Memories of "neutral" observers
9. Memories of participants in some event or bit of social interaction.

Even a quick look at this list reveals that the term "thing" is being used in an uncommon way. Most of the types of things in the list are messages of one sort or another. If one were to rearrange the list so that things that are messages are separated from things that are objects, he might have two lists that looked like this:

Message-Things

2. Written materials: letters, journals, novels
3. Special writing: scientific reports, textbooks
5. People (to talk with)
6. Mechanical records of events: recordings, sound movies
7. Responses to formal questions
8. Memories of "neutral" observers
9. Memories of participants in some event

Object-Things

1. Objects: autos, shawls, etc.
4. Art objects: paintings, statues
5. People (to watch)
6. Mechanical records of events: photos, silent movies

Some types of things appear in both lists—they have both message characteristics and object characteristics. If one watches people doing things he can guess about the meaning of their action. Such guesses tend to be in terms of one's own experiences, that is, putting oneself in the other person's place and asking what the actions would mean if one had performed them himself. An American theatergoer, observing a Russian performer respond to the repeated applause of the audience by beginning to applaud, too, might conclude that the performer was an egotist who was delighted with himself. If he had an opportunity to ask the performer why he applauded, he might discover that this applause expressed appreciation to the audience rather than for the performer. By asking a question and interpreting an answer, the theatergoer used the message-characteristic of a person; by merely observing the performer, he used the object-characteristic of a person.

Types seven and eight, memories of "neutral" and participant observers, are separated slightly from the other message types of things because the messages are intra-personal rather than inter-personal; they are sent by an individual to himself.[10]

In dealing with an object-thing, a student tries to get near enough to observe it closely, so that he can raise questions about the object itself and about this object compared to others that serve the same function in the culture in which it is found, or in other cultures. Such questions are: How is it made? Who uses it? When? How? Why? Object-things may tell a story that answers questions, too. Kenworthy suggests that:

. . . one can stand on the side of a major highway and learn much about a nation. In Pakistan, for example, the writer saw twelve different modes of transportation on one street corner, ranging from rubber-tired camel carts carrying cotton bales to the modern limousine of the Pakistan Airways.

A view of hats of a country can help one to understand it, for they represent history, position, religion, rank, economics, and politics. A count, for example, of the number of old men wearing the fez in Morocco as opposed to the number of young men wearing them reveals the cleavage between generations in their acceptance of innovations, for the fez is still a symbol there of the old regime.[11]

Kenworthy also describes the experience of savoring a previously unknown place by listening to the sounds that billow around the visitor.

Even children in a classroom have each of these experiences available to them. By watching a film that shows the daily living of the people of some far-off place, they can count for themselves the variety of modes of transportation or headgear. They may have to see a film several times, or slow down its speed by running a sound film at silent speed, or stop the film for a few seconds,[12] to be able to look searchingly enough to answer some of the questions they have raised.

[10] For a discussion of the dynamics of intra-personal communications, see Jurgen Ruesch and Gregory Bateson, *Communication* (New York: W. W. Norton, 1951), pp. 273–289.

[11] L. S. KENWORTHY, "Studying Other Countries," *Social Education* (April 1959), pp. 159–162.

[12] Usually, it is only a film projector with a clutch knob that can be stopped in this way. As the clutch stops the film, a fire screen drops into place. This makes it possible to observe a single frame for two or three minutes without danger, but it cuts the intensity of light considerably and the room must be quite dark to see the picture clearly. Teachers should check with the manufacturer of the projector to learn how to use the equipment in this way safely and efficiently.

The first several viewings of such a film might have the sound deliberately turned off, so that children can see with their own eyes, making their own judgments and categories in the same way that an adult student does when he enters another culture. After they have made their own selections, judgments, and guesses about what is important, they can listen to the organization of the narrator. The film-maker's interpretation of what is happening is not necessarily "correct," but it may be different; and those differences are worth thinking about. It is much more difficult to see with the open eyes of the researcher after an authority has told you what you should be seeing than if you must be your own authority first. These first formulations, too, though they can and should be tentative, are more readily defended against alternatives if an "authority" has not spoken first. The search for evidence that settles the competing claims of alternatives is at the very heart of study.

It is important to remember that the film itself represents a selection from the total of what could be seen by an observer who was on the spot. There may be no way for children to see anything other than the selection made by the cameraman, but the silent viewing may lead to questions about facets of living that the film has ignored. Other sources of information (other things, such as people from that country, textbooks, or answers to questions sent by mail to children in the country being studied) may answer the remaining questions.

Message-things, like messages of any sort, must be received and decoded if they are to be usable. It is easier to do this if someone who is a member of your culture group speaks to you in your language. Studies of distant parts of the United States can take easy advantage of the opportunity to have children confront "things," especially message-things, directly. Such "things" as books, diaries, letters, and tape recordings are obviously easiest to understand when they are produced by fellow Americans.

It is possible that in any of the English-speaking parts of the world, message-things may be produced through similar interchange. A little caution is necessary, however, to understand the distortion that may result from translating British English into American English. Margaret Mead illustrates this distortion with the example of the idea of "compromise" as it exists in Great Britain and in the United States. In her analysis, the British use carries the connotation of a battle won, a problem of conflict resolved; the United States use connotes a battle lost, an ideal partially destroyed. One cannot always assume that an English word has the same meaning wherever it is used.

Direct experiences with message-things become dramatically few once a foreign language intervenes. Letters and tape recordings from French or Mexican or German children and adults are "available" to American schoolchildren only through the medium of a translator. Still, there are enough similarities in outlook and language structure between those countries that share in the broader "Western" culture to make translation possible with a minimum of distortion. So far as investigations of non-Western cultures of Asia and Africa are concerned, translation is more difficult and the availability of translators less likely.

Because it is unreasonable to expect elementary-school children to learn the languages of the many peoples they will study, and because it is quite reasonable to insist that they should learn something about the people of Asia and Africa as well as those of Europe and Latin America, it is necessary, in studying the former, to settle mainly for a careful use of second- and third-hand material (such as textbooks), fictional accounts ("story" books about children living in other countries), or translations of primary sources. The problem is to provide message-things that children can understand; these must be in English before they are useful.

Publishers have made great progress in producing materials about peoples and places around the world. Some of the more significant publications have abandoned the encyclopedic, one-big-textbook format for more flexible collections of inexpensive volumes, each focusing on a single country or a single people.[13] These newer books represent not only careful scholarship, but an attempt to remedy some of the imbalances of many past accounts. They give attention to the lives of ordinary, and even poor, people (not only the wealthy ranch-owner and his family) and to countries of the Near East, Africa, and Asia. Educational groups such as the North Central Association of colleges and secondary schools are producing materials about countries around the world, including some behind the Iron Curtain, and about United States foreign policy. These are produced for use with high-school youngsters, but they might provide valuable sources of information for teachers of elementary-school children, providing accounts that could be rewritten in language easily handled by children.[14]

Putting children directly in touch with people of other places depends upon language and culture as much as upon distance. Children in Alabama are much nearer to Vera Cruz, Mexico, than to Tacoma, Wash.; but letters from schoolchildren in Tacoma are much easier to get and to interpret than those of schoolchildren in Vera Cruz. It is easiest to get message-things for study from distant parts of the United States. It is somewhat more difficult (because of distance and the time it takes for messages to travel), but relatively easy, to set up an interchange with English-speaking Europeans of other countries (Canada, Great Britain, Ireland, Australia, New Zealand). In those countries that were once part of the British empire, English is still widely spoken. In Nigeria, English was continued, after independence,

[13] An example of these is the "Understanding Your World" series, in which some ten titles are available (published by Laidlaw Bros., River Forest, Ill.).

[14] For information, write to: Foreign Relations Project, 57 West Grand Avenue, Chicago, Ill.

as the language of instruction, and it should be possible to establish correspondence and an exchange of information in English with schoolchildren there. Some schools in India, Malayasia, and other British Commonwealth countries are still taught in English, and similar interchange ought to be possible with children in these schools.

Although these peoples are non-Westerners, their use of English makes it not too difficult to get in touch with them directly. Non-English speakers of (generally) Western countries are next most difficult for children to reach. Non-English-speaking non-Westerners are the most difficult of all for interchange of messages.

Although study of non-English-speaking Westerners and non-Westerners will of necessity be based upon textbook and trade-book accounts and news reports, it is possible to get a bit closer to these cultures by exploiting a curious circumstance. In almost every country in the non-Communist world, some newspapers are published in English. The *Editor & Publisher International Yearbook*[15] is a reference source listing all newspapers published around the world and their language of publication. The political slant of these papers is likely to be pro-Western or neutralist, though there is the slight possibility that they may be anti-Western. Information about editorial policy can only be gained by examining individual papers.

By arrangement with the United States Department of State, the Soviet Union is permitted to sell copies of the English-language magazine *USSR,* and Communist Poland distributes the magazine *Poland.* These describe cultural and scientific events in the country of publication. A recent issue of *Poland,* for example, described the country's small but vigorous Moslem community. The part which Moslems have played in Poland's history, especially as soldiers and farmers, is rarely studied in the West. In exchange, the United States government is permitted to sell the Slavic-language magazine *Amerika* in Poland and Russia. It might be of value if children could compare all three magazines, *USSR, Poland,* and *Amerika,* to see what each country considers of greatest importance to tell about itself.

When one classroom in California was studying about peoples of Peru, the teacher discovered a monograph about an isolated Peruvian village and wrote to the anthropologist who had produced it.[16] He became interested in her wish to help her children to an understanding of some facets of life in Peru more authentic than that they could get from the usual textbook or trade-book sources. Not only did he send her some of his original data,

[15] *Editor & Publisher International Yearbook* (New York: Editor & Publisher Annual).

[16] The name of the anthropologist and the village have been deliberately withheld. There are dozens of such monographs. It would be unfortunate to burden one source needlessly.

but he also put her in touch with the priest in the village. She wrote a letter to the priest, in English, that the high-school Spanish teacher translated into Spanish. With the priest's help, her class went on to exchange letters, drawings, and stories with schoolchildren in the village.

In each of the states of the United States, scholars in universities and colleges are collecting data about peoples and places. Throughout the country, the number of "area studies" departments (e.g., African Studies, Indian Studies, etc.) is increasing. Professors and students in these departments, while possibly not able to visit a class themselves, might provide valuable help to a teacher or to her pupils by indicating sources of information, or even by loaning an object—a bowl, or a shawl, or a statuette, perhaps— from a private collection. The request to "Please send me information about India" is really unanswerable. Describing a specific teaching-learning problem, such as the need for "things from far away," defining the type of objects needed and the way in which they will be used, may be more likely to get results. Showing that the writer (teacher or child) has taken the trouble to learn something before asking for help, that he is more than an empty bag waiting to be filled by someone else's effort, will be more likely to excite respect and a willingness to help.

Getting Started in the Now and There

It was suggested earlier that studies may begin spontaneously or as the result of teacher-contrived learning opportunities.

Using the Spontaneous Incident

Spontaneous studies grow out of incidents that could not have been anticipated by a teacher or a group of curriculum builders, incidents that, nevertheless, a teacher recognizes as having value in the development of concepts, skills, or attitudes that are, in his judgment, especially relevant for his particular group of children. Similar incidents may occur again with another year's class, or they may not. Though they occur again, they may not be as relevant to the learning of the second group of children. The decision then might be to deal with them in a more superficial way, in order to focus on learning opportunities that are judged to have greater relevance to the new group.

The spontaneous incident is more likely to be related to an immediate interest of the children concerned. Or it may help the teacher to identify a crucial "need to know" or "need to be able to do," of which the children themselves are not yet clearly aware. In the following incident, both children's interests and teacher-discovered needs of children generated a valuable study out of an unpredictable incident.

During recess Miss Newbury watched and listened as some of her second graders played at chasing and shooting a bunch of "dirty greasers." As the breathless youngsters settled into their seats after recess, Miss Newbury decided to get at the background of what she had seen and heard.* Why were some people called "dirty greasers"? . . . Oh, because they get greasy food. They're bandits, and they live in Mexico, and they steal horses and shoot people. They'll cheat you, and you can't trust them. The best thing to do is to shoot 'em. . . . Well, Miss Newbury had gotten what she asked for, and it didn't sit very well.

When the outpour had died down, she moved in again with a quiet, half-to-herself comment. . . . This is all very strange. I have an aunt who lives in Mexico. . . . A gasp, a whistle, a skeptical snort, and then: You do? I'll bet she has a whole stack of guns. How many Mexicans has she killed? Does she have a big ranch? Has she seen any rustlers? Is it safe there? . . . Yes, it's just as safe as it is here. She doesn't live on a ranch. Her husband is an engineer. They live in very much the same way as we do. I've visited them in Mexico. . . . You have? . . . Eyes and mouths wide open now, and Miss Newbury has undivided attention.

We Make Plans

Where do we go from here? This was the thought that momentarily troubled Miss Newbury. . . . Perhaps you would like to find out some more things about Mexico. Perhaps you would like to write my aunt. . . . Couldn't we visit her? . . . Yes, we could pretend. But we couldn't actually visit because it's too far. . . . As far as Rich's (a large store in Atlanta)? . . . Laughter from the group and a voice: Lots farther, silly, a hundred times, a million times, a million, million times. . . . No, not that far, Tommy, but it would take your daddy several days to drive there in his new car. Now, what are some of the things you would like to know about people who live in Mexico? . . .

As fast as the questions came, the teacher listed them on the blackboard:
1. What do Mexican people look like?
2. How do they talk?
3. What do they eat?

---

* Actual phrasing and events are presented; however, space limitations necessitate condensation and abbreviation. Some readers may prefer the term "Spanish-American" to "Mexican." This will be the case particularly in the southwest portions of the country. However, the latter, rather than the former, was used by the group described here.

4. How do they dress?
5. Do they fly kites?
6. What do they do in school?
7. How do they get places?
8. What kinds of work do they do?
9. What kinds of stores do they have?
10. How do they play? What do they play?
11. What are their towns like?
12. How can we be friends?
13. Do they go to Sunday school and church?
14. What can we do to help each other?

Miss Newbury's next question was not so productive . . . How might we discover some of this information by ourselves? . . . Five ideas came forth.
1. "Play like" we take a trip to Mexico.
2. Write letters to people in Mexico.
3. Read stories about Mexican childen.
4. Look at pictures of Mexican life.
5. Enjoy seeing things that came from Mexico.

The Teacher Makes Plans

The children were still eager, even though the entire process had taken three times as long as those activities usually engaged in by the group. But Miss Newbury wanted both to maintain this enthusiasm and to take stock of the series of events that had occurred in such rapid succession. That afternoon and evening she did some thinking and some planning. She reviewed in her mind her over-all purposes and wrote the following for the proposed study of Mexico:
1. To help the children begin to build a broader conception of the world.
2. To help straighten out the children's misconceptions about the Mexicans.
3. To help them discover the many ways in which Mexican children are like themselves.
4. To help the boys and girls find answers to their questions through their reading and other experiences.
5. To help them develop the ability to plan and select and to attack new activities in a spirit of research.
6. To lay a foundation for further study and research in which they will find rich experiences.

She knew that the proposed activity would fail unless materials suitable for the children were available. Much of this would be brought forth by the children themselves, but some things were needed immediately. Her research brought forth authentic Mexican objects as well as books and pamphlets.

Books for Children—*Pancho* (Hader), *Manuela's Birthday* (Bannon), *Pepe and the Parrot* (Credle), *Pablo's Pipe* (Eliot), *Pancho and His Burro* (Gay).

Film Strip—*Children of Mexico* (Encyclopaedia Britannica.)

Records—"Let's Fly to Mexico" and several recordings of Mexican music.

Other Printed Material—Travel folders and guides, maps, globe, *National Geographic* magazines, pictures, newspapers, UN and UNESCO materials.

Exhibits—Wool rug, pottery, woven mats and baskets, ancient Aztec money, modern money, straw toys, schoolbooks, stamps, picture cards, silver jewelry, Mexican flag.

Then she went to her file of pictures that had been collected through the years. How many times this file had saved the day! Appropriate Mexican pictures were mounted, and words and phrases that might be used in writing stories about them were printed on charts. Next, reading cards were made and filed according to subjects. Stories were printed in anticipation of the needs of slow readers. It was hard work, spread over several days, but it resulted in a rich supply of resources to be used when needed.[17]

Clearly, the decision to capitalize on an unanticipated incident does not free a teacher from responsibilities for planning. Indeed, Miss Newbury's planning load was far heavier than usual because it had to be accomplished quickly without any loss in thoroughness. It was helpful to her to be able to use the collection of pictures, objects, and ideas that experienced teachers added to constantly, but finding books for the variety of reading abilities in her class meant some quick research. To learn something of the content children may study often makes additional work for the teacher.

Seldom do studies blossom spontaneously. Usually an unanticipated incident seems so obviously related to ideas, concepts, or relationships that a teacher had planned to have children study at some time during the year, that he simply switches his timetable so as to develop them sooner. Often, an incident pushes an on-going study into new directions, as when children's observations of "speeders" on the freeway[18] led to an unexpected study of safety and traffic control.

[17] From Virgil E. Herrick, Frank J. Estvan, Paul W. Eberman, John I. Goodlad, *The Elementary School*, pp. 204–207. © 1956, by permission of Prentice-Hall, Inc., Englewood Cliffs, New Jersey.

[18] See Chapter Ten.

Contriving a Beginning

Teacher-contrived beginnings for studies are far more common than spontaneous beginnings. While remaining alert to the power of certain unexpected events, and flexible in being ready to exploit them, teachers can hardly defend building a program of social studies upon chance occurrences. And the contrived beginning has advantages. It can be planned to point toward the major ideas with which the study will deal, and it can fulfill certain specific functions.

1. *Beginning or initiating experiences should pique children's interests.*
Mr. Taylor walked into his classroom one morning and dumped a Navaho saddle blanket on a back table for the class to discover. When they did, and asked him about it, he looked up and remarked a bit sternly, "Yes, that's a pretty interesting thing. Please don't touch it though, it's quite valuable. Let's go on with what we are doing." The next day, the children found a Mexican sombrero on the table on top of the crumpled blanket. When they asked about it, he said, "It is pretty, isn't it? You may look at it, but please remember not to touch it. Now, let's get on with reading." On the following day, a saddle stood on the table beside the unrolled blanket and the sombrero. The children were pretty excited. One boy cocked his head, looked at Mr. Taylor and asked, "Mr. Taylor, are we going to study about cowboys or something?" Mr. Taylor grinned and the study was off!

One way in which to involve children and to stimulate their interest is to encourage controversy and differing judgments. Objects, pictures, displays, and comments and questions by the teacher can puzzle children and start them thinking in divergent directions, as they try to resolve apparent contradictions or to guess about (and to justify guesses about) things about which they know little. This type of controversy is not one of dispute and hostility. The wonder and delight of the teacher should cue children to the interest, excitement, and value of divergence. The teacher's purpose is to make the children feel a direct and obvious need to know which of several alternatives can be confirmed by evidence of some kind as having the greatest value as a solution to a problem.

2. *Beginning experiences can reveal the quality or depth of understanding that children bring to a study.*
Children must have the opportunity to say, or write, or draw, or otherwise do something that the teacher and children in the class can observe, record, and use as a basis for planning future learning opportunities. During a discussion such as that described by Miss Newbury, a teacher learns about the level of thinking of those children who participate. He does not know

about those who did not say anything—usually half the class or more. If Mr. Taylor asks his class to write a short essay about who used the articles on the back table, and why they used them, he will have a measure of what each child *can write* about what he knows. Some children he will know are unable to write well enough to tell about what they know, and he will need to think of other ways to assess their understanding. When a kindergarten teacher asks her class to draw their families, some children will include each family member, others will leave out the younger brother or sister or one parent (even though both parents may be present in the home), and still others will include dogs, cats, and turtles. Both Mr. Taylor, in analyzing the essays produced by his class, and the kindergarten teacher, in analyzing the drawings produced by hers, will discover differences among children in the amount and quality of understanding they bring to each study. Subsequent planning should take these differences into account by providing opportunities for certain children to elaborate or add to their first statements, by making different materials and tasks available to the children particularly suited to them, and by expecting different levels of performance or different kinds of productivity from children whose abilities and interests differ markedly.

3. *The beginnings of a study should lead students and teachers to sketch loosely the range, significance, and possibilities of a problem.*

4. *The beginning steps of a study can stimulate thinking about the variety of ways in which to organize for study, a variety of ways in which to look at the problem, a variety of facets contributing to understanding the problem.*

Children can be helped to refer to concepts and generalizations gained from previous studies, and to sources and methods of producing relevant data that were discovered to be useful in the past. They can assess the need for new ways of gathering data. Most important, they can discover that the range and scope of the study has something in it of significance, of interest, and of value for them.

ARRANGED ENVIRONMENT

One teacher used the device of an arranged classroom environment to achieve these goals of a beginning to a study. When children arrived on Monday morning, the classroom had changed completely. The back bulletin board was covered with bright yellow construction paper, and brown cut-out letters formed the title, "Man Conquers the Air." Suspended by threads against the yellow background were models of trail-blazing planes, from that of the Wright brothers to a modern jet airliner. A small side bulletin board had pictures of cargo planes in various stages of overhaul. On a narrow table in front of this display were some mechanic's tools and a welder's mask, obtained at the local airport. The title declared that more than a pilot and fuel were needed to keep a plane in the air. The table at the back displayed weather instruments and weather maps, as well as maps showing approach patterns to the local field. In addition, a tape recording that the teacher had acquired at the airport contained a transcript of the instructions given by an operator in the control tower to a pilot in foggy weather to bring him in for a landing. A small bulletin board over a bookshelf displayed questions about the dynamics of flight. On the bookshelf were books, at a variety of reading levels, dealing with the science of flight. From a junkyard near the local airfield, the teacher had recovered a light aluminum skeleton of part of a tail section of a small airplane and the small instrument panel from another, as well as some gauges and light instruments. The display that excited the most ooh's and ah's was one placed at one of the front corners of the room. There, attached to the small corner bulletin board, was a Navy pilot's flight suit. The trousers were brought across the small table so that the suit, with the legs dangling down, appeared to be sitting on the table. On the table, too, was an arrangement of training manuals and a pair of flight boots, over which was the question, "What Does It Take To Fill These Shoes?" (The suit, manuals, and boots were acquired from a nearby naval air training station, together with a survival kit, helmet, and a parachute.)

Each of these exhibits and displays was planned to be easily dismantled and replaced by children's later work. The model airplanes at the back would each be surrounded by drawings of the scenes of their triumphs and written historical accounts of each occurrence. The questions about the dynamics of flight would be replaced by answers worked out by the children, and so on around the room. The arranged environment was a beginning, not an end.

The teacher had made a special effort to find something that might interest each child in the room, and something that would be appropriate to each child's ability level. Although there was no reason why girls could not become interested in the dynamics of flight or in the training specifications for pilots, she carefully included a replica of one of Amelia Earhart's airplanes among the models at the back, as well as applications and information about being an air hostess that she had acquired from two of the major airlines. The books which accompanied each of the exhibits were carefully selected to represent a wide range in reading ability.

5. *Beginning experiences should create an appropriate emotional tone.*

Children should be helped to anticipate their own feelings of strangeness or rejection, making it easier for them to create a more open attitude toward some of the more exotic cultures they might study. Professor Hilda Taba describes one classroom in which children were asked to write about anything they thought might make them uncomfortable if they were to visit Mexico. Some mentioned the strange language and the inability to talk with people. Some discussed strange foods and ways of behaving that were different from their own.[19] In another instance, Taba describes the comments of a boy who is permitted to be honest about his feelings of hatred toward policemen. In his experiences with police, he has perceived them to be needlessly "rough," frightening, and punishing. In contrast, children in an upper-class community describe police as "nice men" who are helpful guardians. While recognizing the slum child's need for "new experiences with policemen to extend their meanings of and to change their feelings about what policemen are and do," Taba goes on to describe the severely limited concept of poverty held by children in an upper-class community. Assured that a story in which a family saves pennies to buy a child a pair of shoes is not a fairy tale, but could be a true story, they can only conclude that the father who "would not" buy his child a pair of shoes was somehow inadequate.

The perception of the circumstances of poverty was totally lacking and so was any sensitivity to the values and feelings of those who did not have all the necessities. Their social learning, confined to the swank side of the economic street, created an orientation that was as remote from reality as was the orientation of the slum children toward the policemen.[20]

Children also display understanding when the teacher reads stories and shows films and encourages responses to these and to problems or open-ended questions or sentences (e.g., I think policemen are ————. How do children learn things? Nigeria is a place where ————.). Writing and discussion based on these provide useful information for the teacher in measuring the depth of understanding children bring to a study. The same sort of response is useful in creating a learning climate in which feelings can be examined and greater readiness developed for continuing study of peoples and practices that are alien to, and therefore possibly right for rejection by, a specific group of children.

Beginnings scatter themselves throughout a study. They function not only in introducing children to a large study, but also in preparing them for learning specific concepts, or attitudes, or study skills as the study develops.

Contrive as he will, however, a teacher cannot control what a child will learn. Children may share the same apparent experience (e.g., watching a film or being present at a discussion) and, though gaining concepts that have

[19] Personal communication to the author.

[20] HILDA TABA, *Curriculum Development: Theory into Practice* (New York: Harcourt, Brace, 1962), pp. 142–143.

much in common, carry away quite different impressions of the experience.

The students [in a sixth grade] were working on a unit on India. The teacher invited a university student from India to speak to the children and to describe his country for them. After the talk, the teacher asked the children to write down their impressions of India. During the talk the speaker had illustrated his points with slides, showing various scenes of India. In this situation the child was exposed to a wide variety of events relating to "India" in a fairly unsystematic fashion. He responded in terms of the concepts that he had already developed. Here are some of the impressions of "India" reported by the children after the visitor's remarks:

WAYNE: I'm thinking of the sleeping beauty of the temple, its semi-precious stones gleaming in the morning mist, remains of a ruined Buddha in the age-old temple, the creeping vines growing up through the crack in the ancient rock, its huge boat a monument to the ancient ones who built it.

RUTH: A village home with oxen screeching and stamping up and down the walks.

SANDY: The Taj Mahal with its beauty and luster. The Black Pagoda, cold, black and sinister. The Red Forts worn with battle but still beautiful. The palaces and the temples all symbolize the want for beauty of the Indian people.

LAYNE: The people on the boardwalk seemed so natural, the way they were just sitting there, thinking and talking, with children playing. Everything they did was just so natural.

SCOTT: Drinking water where the cows take a bath seems like eating mud.

BRYAN: It was interesting how the man put a cobra and a mongoose together and let them fight. It seemed sort of stupid because he sat with his legs crossed and let the two fight right in front of him: If the cobra struck at the mongoose and missed he would be bit. Also, the cobra might turn on him.

This rich variety of impressions is all the more striking when we recall that each of these children heard the same words and saw the same pictures. The children had essentially the same stimulus experience, but each child interpreted and selected from the stimuli in terms of his own conceptual system and his attitudes and feelings. One child responds to the beauty of the temples; another, to the awesome sight of a cobra and a mongoose fighting. Another child sees the personal habits of the people as repulsive; still another sees the people as natural and as human as the people he knows.

These children will probably develop concepts about India which have common characteristics. They will remember the Taj Mahal and the large, white, beautiful building, they will know the details of dress and the personal habits of the people of India. In these respects, their concepts will be fundamentally alike, but each concept will still have a different meaning for each child. The total system of concepts of each child will be unique because common concepts will have different associations, that is, meanings, feelings, and emotions associated with them.

These variations in the conceptual systems among children influence the learning of any given concept. Too frequently we assume that the mere presentation of a learning experience guarantees that each child will learn concepts in identically the same fashion. The child who sees the habits of the people as repulsive and the child who sees them as "natural and human" will make different interpretations about the significance of life in India.[21]

Moving Study Along

The preceding text has constantly referred to primary sources as among the most valuable of "things," insisting upon the value of putting children in direct touch with informants and data. How can one find the time to follow such advice? It takes time for a letter to travel to New Zealand and for an answer to return. It takes time to discover with whom letters or tape recordings can profitably be exchanged. However, a study does not grind to a stop while children wait for answers to their messages. It continues through the use of text materials, trade books, maps and globes, scientific reports of investigators (anthropologists, geographers, historians, etc.), films and film strips, and interviews with persons from the countries in question. If there is to be a second or a third exchange of messages, a six- or eight-week period, or longer, may be required for a thorough study. The demands of some curriculums make an extended study of this type difficult, if not impossible. In the earlier discussion of constraints, the survey expectation was described as a block to thorough studies.[22] At the time this book is being written, there are 110 members of the United Nations. (By the time it is read, that number may be different.) In a forty-week school year, a teacher would have to "cover" about three nations a week to get all of these in—a pretty thin cover! What could an Italian child or a Ghanaian child learn about the United States of America in two or three days of "study"? What could he learn in two or three weeks? How important is it that he know more than that? How important is it that our schoolchildren get more than a passing notion about the major areas of the world in which they live?

Some alternatives to the attempt at all-inclusive "study" are helpful in overcoming the time pressures that make such techniques as a direct interchange of messages difficult. One of these is an area-studies approach. Countries of West Africa or of Southeast Asia or of Central America can be studied simultaneously. Small groups of children can compare selected social arrangements and economic, geographic, historical, and cultural

[21] From *Educational Psychology* by Frederick J. MacDonald, pp. 141–143. © 1959 by Wadsworth Publishing Company, Inc., Belmont, Calif. By permission of the publisher.

[22] See Chapter Six.

characteristics across these countries. Or else each group can study an agreed-upon set of such characteristics in an intact culture so that a comparison can be made between groups.

Or a teacher can guide a group of children to select representative countries after they decide what characteristics ought to be represented. These countries may represent a part of the geographical or political world (north temperate, equatorial, far eastern, etc.). They may represent high, moderate, or low levels of technology or industrialization. They may have recently emerged into political independence or occupy long-time positions as world powers. They may be politically aligned with communism, anti-communism, or neutralism. The countries selected may represent more than one characteristic. Japan may represent a highly industrialized, long-time Far Eastern world power, generally pro-Western in outlook. Algeria may represent a newly independent nation and the region of North Africa, etc.

With these decisions made, messages can be composed and sent off while the children turn their attention to understanding how our own country may be characterized in terms of the categories (social arrangements, cultural, geographical, and economic characteristics) that they plan to investigate in other countries. To minimize waiting time and unproductive leads, teachers can gather (in advance) the names and addresses of United States attachés abroad, or even get from these sources the names and addresses of English-language schools or English-speaking teachers who might care to participate in such an interchange. This permits children to learn how to compose questions that will produce the information they need and reserves for them the excitement of sending for and receiving data.

In the following incident, the teacher's purposes for the year include the study of countries around the world, emphasizing culture, economics, geography, and politics. She has chosen to begin with a study of parts of the United States that are at a distance from her class. She expects to help the children review some of what they have learned about their state (as fourth graders) and about their country (as fifth graders), and in the process to develop an understanding of social institutions and geographic concepts that will serve as reference points for later studies. These later studies will provide an opportunity for children to project and test (or use or transfer) in new contexts the generalizations that relate facts and concepts. She is also planning to develop social-study skills to which children will be able to refer and which they will be able to use in a variety of contexts.

Miss Granec[23] teaches a sixth grade in Madison, Wis., a city of approximately 125,000 people. It is the state capital and home of the main campus

---

[23] There is no real Miss Granec. The accounts that follow were compiled from several teachers' reports of studies they carried on with children.

of the state university. Although there are some large industries, it is not an industrial city. Miss Granec's school serves an area of the city that is largely middle and upper-middle class. The parents of children in her room are professional people, salesmen, store owners, managers, and civil servants. Most own their own homes.

One of Miss Granec's purposes was to develop children's awareness of the promise of "things" by helping them wring an unexpected harvest of information and ideas from an authentic but homely source.

On the previous Monday, Miss Granec had asked children to bring a telephone directory from home. By Wednesday each child had one in class. Miss Granec had brought to the class the telephone directories of cities selected from the state of Wisconsin: Milwaukee, Beloit, River Falls, Pulaski, Viroqua, New Glarus, Darlington. She divided the class into random groups, with four or five children in each group. She gave each of these groups the telephone book of some Wisconsin city other than Madison. She asked them to think about what they might learn from each of these books. To the comment that they could tell or discover the phone numbers of the people who lived there she asked, "Is that all?" Children remembered that the phone book gave addresses, too. Miss Granec asked them to think a while and take the time to look carefully, comparing the Madison phone directory with that of the other city which each group had. "Remember," she said, "each book was made for the people in each city. These books might have many stories to tell about the people and the place if only we could find the right questions to ask of them."

After about ten minutes of looking and comparing, groups began to tell what they had discovered in the way of differences. Some books were much different in size from the Madison directory. Milwaukee's was quite a bit bigger. Pulaski's was about half the size. Darlington's was a slim book not much bigger than their copy notebooks. One child (with a Polish surname) was quick to discover the number of Polish names in the Pulaski telephone book. This sent children in other groups to look at their book for similar concentrations of nationality names (German and Swiss in the New Glarus book), or to find a range and variety in some of the larger telephone books. One boy noticed that in Darlington there were only three elementary schools listed; two of them seemed to be out of town while only one seemed to be in Darlington itself. Madison had more than thirty elementary schools listed for addresses in the city. One boy had been unable to resist looking up the address of the Milwaukee Braves and commented that there was no such address in the Madison phone book.

TEACHER: "Have you been looking through the whole book?"
CHILD: "Yep, from A to Z."
TEACHER: "Does the phone book stop at Z?"

CHILD: "Oh, we forgot about the yellow pages."

CHILD: "But that's just advertising about things to buy."

TEACHER: "It may be that the questions you ask will make a difference in what you discover. Brenda found Polish names in Pulaski and asked, "How do Pulaski and Madison compare in the number of certain Polish names?" Tommy found "Schools" and wondered if Darlington had as many elementary schools as Madison? As you look through the yellow pages, can each child in each group think of one question to ask that compares Madison's telephone directory with the one your group is using?"

The reports which followed another ten minutes of looking showed that children were discovering and using the telephone book as an "object-thing." Mainly their questions were questions of number. Were there as many automobile repair places in one city as in another? How many items were listed under F in one book as compared to another? How many *different* items were listed under F? These comparisons led to a discussion about whether if all those F things were important enough to people in Milwaukee to put in the yellow pages, how could people in Madison manage to get along without them? The number of items listed under F in Darlington's book were far fewer than those in Madison. This led to some ideas about the way in which availability of services and goods is related to size.

Miss Granec had helped the children in her class to move from thinking about the telephone directory as a message-thing (a thing that tries to tell you what someone's telephone number is or where he lives; tries to tell you that, if you want to have your car repaired, John Smith's Repair Shop is one place to have it done) to thinking about it as an object-thing. The children had begun to look at it in order to notice differences in size, in numbers of entries under selected headings, in variety of entries under selected headings, in variety of entries. The teacher's next concern was to help the children become a bit more aware of the consequences of comparison. She pointed out that, in order to compare things, one must know in what dimensions they are being compared. If they are alike in some way, a comparison that reveals differences is more dramatic and possibly more revealing.

After collecting the telephone directories from Wisconsin cities, Miss Granec arranged them on a table at the front of the room so that they were in a compact group. She arranged another set of telephone directories on the same table. On the board she wrote the names of the cities whose directories she was placing there. (These were: New Bedford, Mass.; Utica, N.Y.; Torrance, Calif.; Montgomery, Ala.; Pueblo, Colo.; Springfield, Mo.; Tacoma,

Wash.; Beaumont, Texas; Madison, Wis.) All of these cities had between 90,000 and 150,000 residents.

In thinking about the ways in which these two groups of directories were different from one another, children were able to see that in one group each of the books was about as large as another, whereas in the other group there was quite a difference in size, from very thick to very slim. Someone suggested that all of the books in one group were of Wisconsin cities; the other group contained the books of cities from different states. As they talked about what they had been comparing, these children were able to understand that they had been comparing differences in Wisconsin cities that were essentially differences between big and little cities. While they found that there were similarities (for example, every phone book had the entry "Schools"), they found dissimilarity in the *number* of items listed under any one title. In comparing Wisconsin cities, they had said that the differences they discovered were the result mainly of differences in size. Miss Granec now asked them to think about what they might discover if the cities whose directories they investigated were pretty much alike in size. Could there be any differences caused by other factors than size?

At this point someone asked why Miss Granec had chosen the cities whose names she had written on the board. She had been planning to ask that question herself. In locating each city on a map of the United States, the children discovered that they were scattered across the country in such a way as to represent different parts of the United States, with different climates and terrain; some were coastal cities, some, inland cities, and some, lowland or mountain cities.

Using cues from their previous study of Wisconsin cities, the children were quick to discover and wonder about pages of entries of fishing supplies and wholesale and retail fish outlets in New Bedford, compared with the very few entries of that kind under "Fish" in Madison. Those children who were using the Springfield, Mo., book reported even fewer entries there. Someone remarked that there wasn't a single snow-removal entry in the yellow pages in Torrance, Calif., although there were 16 in the Madison book. They began to wonder what it was like to live in each of these cities and realized quickly that as a direct source of information the telephone book was beginning to show its limitations. Before their study concluded, however, the telephone book provided them with other sources. Children who wanted to know something about the way each city had begun and developed looked, for historical information, to the public library in each town. Children who were interested in what was going on in each city right at the time, wrote to the newspapers whose addresses were listed in the directory. And children who wanted to know about the way in which other children lived in these cities, composed a letter to the principal of one of the schools whose addresses were listed.

The children's use of the telephone book had gone full circle. They began by considering it as a message-thing. Miss Granec helped them to see it as an object-thing. They ended by using it in its message-thing capacity to reach the sources of the information they felt they needed in order to understand each of the places they planned to study.

The second incident in this study began with the telephone book, but as the children's questions, with Miss Granec's guidance, became sharper and more incisive, the book became inadequate as a data source. It was Miss Granec's job to move them to other more precise, more powerful sources. In the process, she expected to help them learn how to use the other sources, and she hoped to build feelings of confidence in their own ability to interpret scientific reports.

A few days after their first introduction to telephone directories, one of the children announced to his classmates, "I was telling my dad about studying the Springfield telephone book, and he said his company had a branch office there. We might even go there some day." This created a good deal of interest, and children went back to the telephone books looking enthusiastically for evidence of work that their parents might do in cities other than Madison. Miss Granec asked them to think about how they could decide whether or not there would be a good chance of finding work in any particular city. The suggestion that bigger places would have more jobs than smaller places was of some relevance—there was a range in size of 50,000 in population among the ten cities. The idea that different cities had different kinds of jobs available was even more profitable. "If your daddy is a snow-plow salesman," remarked one girl, "he better not look for work in Torrance, Calif." Some jobs—teaching, doctoring, etc.—were available no matter where the city was located.

Miss Granec recognized that children might profitably use some new information at this point. She told them about noticing a number of houses for sale when she visited her sister in Cincinnati. Her sister had told her that one of the largest companies in the United States had closed one of its factories in Cincinnati. Five thousand men had to find new jobs. Some of them went to other cities to work in other factories owned by the company. Some of them found jobs with other companies in Cincinnati. Many of them decided to go to other cities and find jobs with other companies. She told the class that people who cannot find the kind of work which they are trained to do, even though they may want to find jobs very much, are called "unemployed." Some cities seem to have more jobs for people than do other cities. The number of unemployed people in a city will often tell you how easy it is to find work there.

Could the telephone book tell them anything about how many jobs were available for people in a city? It didn't seem as though the telephone book was an appropriate source. Some children thought that the employment section of the want ads in the newspapers from each city might give some clues about the number of jobs available. They proposed to send for copies of newspapers from each city. Miss Granec offered to check at the public library to see if unemployment figures could be obtained for the cities in which they were interested.

The next day Miss Granec appeared with a real "find." She showed them a book which she explained the library usually did not allow to circulate. The librarian had made an exception when Miss Granec explained their need for it and promised to return it by the next day. The children were to handle it *very* carefully. The book was entitled *The County and City Data Book, 1962.*[24] She told them that the book told a lot of things that the government had discovered about cities during the census of 1960.

After a brief discussion of census-taking, she used the opaque projector to show one of the book's pages. Children noticed what appeared to be a confusion of columns and numbers. Miss Granec helped them focus on the problem they were trying to solve, a problem dealing with work and the number of people who were employed. Children soon selected those columns that seemed to be relevant to their questions. These were columns which detailed the per cent of increase in population, and the per cent of unemployed. Miss Granec wondered if the people who had more schooling would have an easier time finding a job than people who had fewer years of school, and suggested that they include figures in the columns which listed the average number of years of schooling of people who were over 25 years of age.

It seemed reasonable to these children that a town where there were lots of people, and that was growing rapidly, would have fewer jobs available for the people who lived there. A town that was growing slowly would probably, it seemed to them, have more jobs available. They listed, in order of growth, the ten cities for which they had telephone directories. Then they listed each of the cities in order of how large the percentage of unemployed in that city was. Their hypothesis seemed to have been proved completely wrong (See Fig. 1).

[24] United States Bureau of Census, *County and City Data Book, 1962* (*A Statistical Abstract Supplement*), (Washington 25, D.C.: Government Printing Office, 1962). This book may be purchased for $5.25. It contains statistics based on the 1960 Census of Population and other censuses and deals with counties, regions, divisions, states, standard metropolitan statistical areas, urbanized areas, cities and urban places, detailing economic and population statistics as well as data about weather and climate.

Per Cent Increase in Population		Per Cent Unemployed	
1. Torrance	354.1	1. Utica	7.7
2. Springfield	43.7	2. Tacoma	7.0
3. Pueblo	43.0	3. New Bedford	6.5
4. Madison	31.9	4. Beaumont	5.2
5. Beaumont	26.8	5. Pueblo	5.1
6. Montgomery	26.0	6. Montgomery	4.7
7. Pasadena	11.3	7. Torrance	4.5
8. Tacoma	3.0	8. Pasadena	4.0
9. Utica	−1.1	9. Springfield	3.7
10. New Bedford	−6.1	10. Madison	1.9

Figure 1

They noted that three of the four cities that had the largest increase in population by percentage (Torrance, Springfield, Madison) were also three of the four cities that had the least percentage of unemployed people. The three cities that had the smallest percentage of population increase, (Tacoma, Utica, New Bedford; two of these lost population) were the three cities that had the *highest* percentage of unemployed. This led them to ask a new question. Why is it that a city that is growing in population seems to have the most jobs for people, or at least fewer people out of work, than towns that have not been growing so fast? They made some tentative guesses: (1) Towns grow because there are jobs; new factories may be opening up; (2) Other towns may lose people when factories close.

Clearly the data book, while a valuable source, did not seem to be able to answer a question that began with the word "why." They would have to find people in each town to whom they could write and who might care to answer their questions, or else they would have to find people in Madison who knew enough about one or more of these towns to be able to think with them about the reason "why."

This second illustration demonstrates that one "thing" (a telephone directory) leads to another (a scientific report of census data), that leads to still others (responses to "questionnaires" sent to businessmen, newspaper editors, newspapers themselves, a labor economist from the economics department at the University of Wisconsin). The children were gaining experience in associating relevant "things" with particular questions and in seeing themselves as competent users of scientific reports.

In a study sequence, "movement" or development depends upon questions, a sense of doubt, the discovery of some inconsistency, a disequilibrium. When everything is balanced, nothing moves. In the "telephone book" illustration, the children uncovered such problems as: (1) What information is hidden within the covers of a book? (2) How do you decide whether your dad could get a job in another city?

The "Heads at Ife" (following), challenged children's stereotypes of West African art. It also challenged the notions that African history began with the advent of Europeans and that "civilization" was Europe's gift to Africa.

THE HEADS AT IFE

In their study of the way in which people live in Nigeria, children in Mrs. Brown's classroom have had the opportunity to examine a few carvings that are characteristic of this part of Africa. She read them parts of an article in the magazine *Nigeria*[25] dealing with this kind of art and some of the religious meanings represented by its style and subject-matter. Mrs. Brown brought in the pamphlet, *The Art of Ife*,[26] in which there is a discussion (with many illustrations) of the brass and terra cotta heads that have been discovered at Ife. These have an almost classical Greek style. The relatively recent[27] discoveries of Ife sculpture are totally unlike, in mood and form, the art which is typically associated with West Africa. As children wonder about these heads, Mrs. Brown asks:

TEACHER: What do you think about the people who made these heads? What do you think they valued; what did they think was important?

CHILD: They must have thought beauty was pretty important.

TEACHER: Why do you think that, Elaine?

CHILD: Well, they could have been out hunting or getting food. Instead, they took the time to make these beautiful heads.

CHILD: Maybe some rich man or king just wanted to show off.

TEACHER: If that were true, what would it show?

CHILD: I guess that it would show that they thought being rich was pretty important.

CHILD: Well, they didn't know how to write . . .

CHILD: How do you know they didn't know how to write?

CHILD: Well, if they did, they didn't write on anything that lasted and people in Ife weren't writing when the first Europeans came there.

TEACHER: Although it is possible that the writing of these early Nigerians has all been destroyed, it seems likely that they did not know how to write. Go on, Charlie.

[25] *Nigeria* is published monthly by the Government Printing Office, Lagos.
[26] The Nigerian Museum, *The Art of Ife* (Lagos, 1955).
[27] Two of the earliest important finds were made in 1918 and in 1938.

CHILD: Okay, it's pretty likely they couldn't write so maybe the statues were like a record, to help them remember their relatives or a great king or maybe it was part of their religion if they worshipped their ancestors.

At this point Mrs. Brown interrupted their speculating in order to help them focus upon what they knew as facts. The facts as they had them were (1) the heads existed; (2) they were probably done about 500 to 1,000 years ago, though they were discovered only fairly recently; (3) this form or style of sculpture was quite unlike anything that Europeans found when they first arrived in Nigeria. It is only recently that Nigerians are beginning again to sculpt in this way, and this is largely the result of European influence.

Then she helped them to look at what they had been able to guess about values from just these few facts. The existence of these heads *might* mean that these people valued beauty enough to devote time to creating it. (The distorted wood carvings might also indicate a value placed on beauty— enough of a value to allow devoting time to creating *them*.) The existence of the heads *might* show that wealth, power, or status were valued by these early people. The existence of the heads might show that they respected or revered the memory of their ancestors or of great kings. There was no way in which, from the existing evidence, they could be sure that any one of these was correct, or that indeed all of these notions were not correct.

During the discussion which followed, Mrs. Brown tried to help these children understand the way in which what people valued shaped the way in which they behaved. She helped them also to have some idea that a few facts could generate a lot of guesses, but that little confidence could be placed in such guesses. Finally, she helped them to see that a guess attained some stature if the guesser was able to justify it by relating it logically to the facts that he had. This did not mean that, without further evidence, he could consider even logical guesses in any but a tentative way.

Articulating and Developing Study

This chapter has considered "study" in both its noun sense and its verb sense. It has referred to "*a* study" as a set of problems and a body of information centering around a major idea, a region, or a country (for example, in such phrases as "A *study* of South America might include . . . ," or "In their *study* of the way in which people live in Nigeria . . ."). "Study" becomes a verb when it refers (as it does in most of the descriptions of teachers and children in classrooms) to the process of discovering a thing, observing it, and thinking about it, in order to test its value for solving a problem.

This distinction is important in calling attention to two different problems in "moving study along." In dealing with any given topic (e.g., South America, Nigeria, or the Community), a teacher faces the problem of articulation, or smooth movement from one phase of that topic to another. Thus, a teacher considers the problem of moving from learning about industrial Brazil to learning about the politics of Brazil.

But teachers face a second problem. That is, within a broad topic there will be only moments of inquiry, interludes of study. Study may be spasmodic; it may occur only now and again, while children learn about one topic or another.

However spasmodic, there is a rhythm in the development of inquiry. The rhythm of these bits of study involves "things," observation, and thinking about what has been observed. This section has attended to study in the verb sense, to the bits of inquiry related to learning about one topic or another, and the movement or development that takes place *within* one of these study interludes.

The End of Study

Thinking must have some observable product in order for children or their teacher to make judgments about the value of a study interlude or to plan what ought to come next. The action that study produces may be a statement of relationships. This statement can be in the words of a written or oral report; or it can be an organization of facts and ideas through some nonverbal medium, such as a drawing, a diorama, or a mural.

One purpose of the model of the medieval castle or Nigerian marketplace, as of the short essay or oral report, is to permit children to demonstrate to themselves and to their teacher what they have learned and how well they can use what they have learned. Another purpose of these statements of relationship (verbal and nonverbal) is to provide an opportunity for children to create at least one total pattern out of the results of acquaintance activities (such as learning important dates or other bits of information) and study interludes.

Study can produce questions. When thinking, in the sequence of "things"-observation-thought, produces an organization of facts so that they answer a question (e.g., "Cities that are growing fast tend to have a lower percentage of unemployed people than cities that are not growing so fast"), study stops momentarily. If thinking produces answers and questions ("Why do the faster-growing cities have fewer unemployed people than the slower-growing cities?"), these questions may lead to further study. The tendency of one study interlude to stimulate another determines in part how much of children's learning will be the result of study and how much will be the result of mere acquaintance with information.

Action, the product of thought, punctuates the rhythm of study. This action typically takes the form of statements of relationship among concepts and questions. As a class addresses itself to these new questions, it can be moved again into the process of study. If one end of study is increased understanding, another end of study seems to be—more study.

XII

Then and Here: The History of Here

The general concerns of this chapter are with the nearby place, with yesterday's people, and with the events that happened at a past time in that place.

There is within the Then and Here the promise of information. There are men and movements, causes and calamities to become informed about. A lifetime of absorption, however, is probably not sufficient to soak up all the information there is to know about the nearby but long ago.

However, *information* about the people and places of yesterday is not the special concern of this chapter. It is, rather, the process of "historying," of school children practicing the craft of the historian. There is within the Then and Here the promise of study. Study is the prime concern of this chapter.

Town, State, or Nation?

An earlier chapter introduced briefly the notion that school topics are settings for potential investigations. Study takes place within a context, perhaps in the context of a topic such as "Our Community," "The Westward Movement," "Michigan Indians," or "State and Local Government." The Then and Here topic is commonly defined in American public schools as the town, the state, or the nation. Schoolchildren are somewhat systematically introduced to the past of their town, the past of their state or region, and the past of the nation.

This chapter, then, should deal with the study possibilities within the three topics ever present in schools: town, state, and nation. And it shall. But unequal priority will be given to the topic of town or community. Unfortunately, development in some detail of the local study possibilities for children makes it necessary to forego an extended discussion of inquiry within the state or nation topic. A number of reasons recommend this decision.

When children study the "long ago" of their community, it is possible for them to participate in the discovery of source material; they may even unearth an authentic document. The value of such a document can be assessed. As children come to realize the hole it would leave in their narrative had it not been searched out, they begin to understand that their history might have read very differently and might have told quite another story without certain discoveries.

When studying the local community, it is often possible to gather considerable primary material, but few secondary sources are likely to be available. School texts, for example, seldom discuss anything but the main towns of a state. They give attention to the capital and the industrial centers of a state, but they seldom go further; thus, lack of text material is a common reason why some topics are not included in the curriculum. Whenever publishers fail to produce graded textbooks for a given topic, that topic is frequently considered unteachable.

The absence of text material is not always a liability. The absence of the textbook summary makes it possible for teachers and schoolchildren to depend upon their own intellect and to render their own account of whatever it is that seems important from the long ago.

Investigations centering on the past of a community are likely to reveal a scarcity in "things" of a particular type. Children will experience paucity, paucity in text and secondary source materials. This is not the case, however, with study associated with nation or state topics. The amount of secondary material that exists for the Civil War is awesome. Any teacher would find it comparatively easy to swamp a class of thirty children with even a first wave of Lincoln or Jackson or Jefferson materials. One finds it easy to "say uncle" in the face of an ordinary card-catalogue listing for the topics "Westward Movement," "Indians," and "Colonial United States."

Inquiry within state and nation topics thus frequently confronts the question, "What sources can safely be ignored?" But quite another kind of problem is posed in the study of some past, local event. Here, one often confronts the question, "What source material is there that is relevant to the questions we ask?" "What possibility is there that such material, if it exists, can be located and used by a class of thirty children?"

Because children may profit more from learning the process of ferreting out their own documents, because so little text material exists to tempt one to be content with acquaintanceship, and because children can attempt to be resourceful in the face of scarcity, it seems well to concentrate on the Here as a local, a community, place in this chapter.

When Here is defined as the local community, moreover, children have perhaps a wider opportunity than they might otherwise have to learn to deal with the "object-thing." The previous chapter differentiated among the things of study, designating some as "message-things," in contrast to "object-things," such as machines, shawls, statues, and photographs. An overwhelming amount of material pertinent to questions about our nation and about states or regions must be classified as message-things. When studying the nearby, however, it is easier to develop the special skills needed to support inferences by referring to artifacts and sites. For example, children can observe abandoned railroad tracks and nearby potato cellars and relate these observations to the changed agricultural pattern of their area.[1] A building can be examined closely, and the results of that scrutiny can be used in some plausible manner.[2] Sites, monuments, and architecture can be surveyed; tools and machinery can be examined; dresses, trousers, and bonnets can be looked over. In all, the skills associated with rendering objects less mute might better proceed in local studies, simply because these skills may be in particular demand and the artifacts that yield to these skills may be in greater abundance.

Investigating questions pertinent to nation or state topics will likely depend on reading resources. That is, questions about a nation or state frequently demand that one consult message-things, in the form of textbooks, diaries, statistics, chronicles, and so forth. The skillful examination of written records can become well-practiced. But the skill of examining closely spoken words in the records and memories of an interview is nurtured only as one has opportunity to listen, to question, and to recall answers to prepared questions. Listening experiences are more likely developed when the speakers of interest to you are nearby.

Every advantage just discussed can be viewed as a disadvantage. Some teachers feel it a great liability to have to develop their own source material. When a textbook chapter is not available on White Water Falls, U.S.A., they consider it a severe constraint upon instruction. The absence of words and sounds in object-things must be considered a disadvantage by those used to dealing solely with printed material when pursuing questions about the past. And people who have to be interviewed because they neglect to write down what they know can also be considered a liability. The ensuing discussion, however, views each of these "liabilities" as an asset.

Studying the Local Community

If it were possible to publish a handbook for the study of the past of each city, town, and village, that publication could be very explicit. Particular investigations, particular sources, and particular teaching tactics could all be specified. This chapter, however, must address itself to the study of every community's past. It must confine itself to general guides in four categories: questions, sources, skill development, and teaching method.

First, there are certain fruitful questions that might be pursued whatever the town. These are the ever-present questions about the past and about

[1] See "Ghost Town," later in this chapter.
[2] See "The Charters Building," later in this chapter.

towns in general. Some may be irrelevant as far as an individual locale is concerned, and whatever the list, it will likely omit some study possibilities. With all these shortcomings, though, this list could suggest overlooked inquiry possibilities or could be a catalyst in the chemistry of question construction.

Second, where does one begin? How can one set about with a group of children to assemble the "things" necessary for a study of the past of a town? Some source materials can be found for almost all localities.

Third, study is a skilled enterprise, requiring certain techniques and abilities. Their development is probably best not left to "happenstance" and should be detailed at some length.

Finally, teachers are not without method. Study in the classroom is very dependent upon the teacher and his instructional talents, and much of the following discussion will be devoted to developing the wide array of teaching tactics demanded in the study situation.

Questions About Every Town

TOWN LOCATION

Questions that can be asked of almost any town are: "Why is a town here?" "What favored the location of a town here?" "Is there an acknowledged founding group or person for this city?" "Who were the town fathers?" "What impressed the founders about this locale, and were those impressions and expectations fully warranted in light of subsequent developments?" Natural features, such as water, minerals, soil, harbors, timber, and terrain, have all played a role in the placement of a town. Cultural features, such as trading posts, forts, stage lines, and wood and coal depots for steamboats, have played their role, too. One can pose this question for any town: "Why here? Why not across the river, at another rapids down river, at another bend in the pike? Why not out on the trace just five miles further?"

One class examined just such questions and worked its way back to a certain family that had played a particularly prominent role in the founding and early development of its city. Through the state historical society, the class was able to locate a genealogy written and privately published by a later family member. The children were intrigued to find that earlier members of the family had participated in the founding of another town, a New England town, in the early part of the seventeenth century. They found it novel that their town, thought to be unique, should share with another American town a direct family link, and they gave some time to the family generations that marked the period between the settlement of New England and the later settlement of the old Northwest Territory (in which their own town was located). The teacher also noticed in the genealogy a note of pride in the genealogist's satisfaction that his ancestors appeared not to have participated in the seventeenth-century witchcraft trials, though it was acknowledged that one woman had been sentenced to hang in the ancestral New England village. Witchcraft interested these ten-year-olds mightily, and the teacher obtained primary source material and read selections from it to the class.[3] Soon the children confronted the question of how free any villager could be said to be at the time of these trials, considering the likelihood of hysteria. Going back to the genealogy, they were quick to notice that one of the forebears of the founder of their town had been designated by the "selectmen" to watch after the piety and faith of his neighbors. This appointment came near the time of the witchcraft trials. The class ended this particular interlude by examining how comfortable the inference was that because the family name did not appear on the documents extant for the trials, the family could be presumed to be free of guilt or implication.

TOWN STREETS

A Wisconsin city exhibited these street names in the civic section of a telephone directory: Charity, Judgement, Truth, Goodness, Pious, Mercy, Wisdom, Faith, Happy, Virtue, and Friendship. The list is sufficiently distinctive to elicit certain speculations. Moreover, the unadorned map in the telephone book clustered these streets in a certain area near the river and near what is labeled "abandoned railroad." What appear to be later developments or suburbs carry more usual street names, such as Harrison, Water, Park, and Main. The character and growth of this community may be very much reflected in the naming of its streets.

Not far from the city containing "Charity, Judgement, Truth, and Goodness," etc., is another incorporated area having about thirty or so streets. One-third of these streets (all those running east and west) carry feminine designations—Lucy, Minerva, Catherine, Alice, Louisa, Ann, Mary, and Harriet streets. Legend has it that one of the early developers of the town had nine daughters! That legend should be interesting and not too difficult to investigate.

Path, trail, pike, trace, and highway all acquire names. Those names and how they came to be are often interesting, and inquiry about them might prove to be very profitable.

TOWN GROWTH

At some point in its development, probably every village has looked upon a fair horizon and a promising tomorrow. Many a cluster of houses has been reasonably convinced that it was destined to become the regional mining

---

[3] This teacher used selections from the first volume of Albert B. Hart, *American History Told by Contemporaries* (New York: Macmillan, 1897-1929).

center, the county seat, or the foremost city "clean the length of the river." The citizens of nearby cities are not without their aspirations, too. And, therefore, the observations of a rival city are frequently a uniquely titillating source. An editor of the *Leavenworth Commercial,* for example, once referred to Kansas City as "that blustering, impotent Sodom at the mouth of the Kaw, that over-grown village whose every foot of territory is carpeted with three-ply mortgages, that night-old fungus whose whole life is bound up in moneyed exhalations of an Eastern dung-hill, and which . . . is rapidly passing into that decay which presages death."[4]

No matter what the town, it is frequently useful to pursue the question, "What has been the nature of its development?" The growth curve for any village, town, or city will describe a unique trajectory. Events, resources, developments of one sort or another have worked change in the path and acceleration rate marking the growth of cities. What were those long-ago forces making for change?

GHOST TOWN[5]

Nearly every year some one or a group of my fifth graders gets very giggly over the term "ghost town." This term of course occurs frequently as we study the Western states. Usually I quiet the snickers by discussing and answering questions about abandoned mines and towns of the desert and mountain areas in the West.

Next year I believe I can help the children do some "historying" when this yearly merriment is upon us. In fact I will do some conniving to see that there is the question, "What is a ghost town?"

First, through ordinary text materials and minimal discussion, we can establish that under certain circumstances a once active community can become deserted.

To make the question even more meaningful I will introduce the problem, "Could Vale become a ghost town?" Probably I'll ask the additional question, "Did the people of the West believe that their town and homes would be abandoned?" Altogether, I will probably try to provoke and needle the class to consider finding out what their town was like fifty years ago.

In discussing ways to find out, I can imagine that the class will suggest asking questions of some of the older members of the community. Some of the people I know have pictures, newspapers, scrapbooks, and old letters

---

[4] Quoted in Donald Dean Parker, *Local History: How to Gather It, Write It, and Publish It* (New York: Social Science Research Council, 1944), p. 5.

[5] Adapted from a paper by Mrs. Nona Smith, a masters degree student at Michigan State University. The word "Vale" has been substituted for the true name of the village referred to in this illustration.

that give a partial picture of an active village. This first round of collecting material will reveal that Vale once had two railroads making a combined four passenger stops a day; once our village had a bank, a creamery, a hotel, high school, doctor's office, post office, and the usual stores of a prospering agricultural center.

In an extended jaunt around the village I plan to show them the bank (now a brick residence); the railroad grade with its tracks torn up and potato cellars abandoned along the right of way; the creamery building with its signs still legible; the site where the hotel once stood (before it burned down); the weathered building by the park, partly filled with empty oil drums, clearly labeled "town hall." We will then turn back to see the old high school. And, I'll walk the class straight to the building they call "our elementary school."

If my knowledge of fifth graders holds true, I'm sure to get questions like: "How come?" "What happened?" "Why?"

In thinking through the reasons for losing our high school, the class would probably have to investigate population change due, partly, to mechanized operations and the larger and larger farms which resulted in a sharp decrease in the number of farm families in our area. This, coupled with the greater services demanded of schools and the increasing costs of educational facilities, probably made for the closing of the high school. Census records, parents, neighbors, former members of the board of education, the county courthouse, and the county and state departments of education are all likely sources of records and information. From these, I'm sure we could fashion explanations of our own.

With mechanized farm equipment came the change from general to specialized agriculture. In our area, we came to specialize in potatoes. The creamery closed its doors. Competition from trucks directly to the field may have played a role in the disuse of potato cellars along the railroad. This problem may become quite involved, however, because obviously Vale did not provide the only freight revenue for the railroad. Discontinuing the railroad probably was a symptom of changing economic, population, and transport requirements throughout this entire region of the state.

Our county agricultural agent might be of some help to us here. I think that the records kept for some farm would be another productive source reflecting the changes in agricultural patterns of the area. Equipment dealers and the manufacturers they represent could be of help in tracing changes in farm mechanization.

Sooner or later, the class is sure to discover that Vale once had another name—the name Stumptown. Such a name, of course, will suggest a logging past for the town. The origins of our former town name will seem very much self-evident. Logging means stumps on the cut-over land. Their certainty, however, will be a bit shaken when I present them with a picture of an old sawmill showing clearly the sign, "Williams and Stump Co." However, I've recently learned that timber was purchased for a specified amount of money, say, fifty cents, "at the stump" or "on the stump." Could these phrases "at the stump" or "on the stump" have referred to the area where our town developed? Might the phrase have been shortened to "Stump" or "Stumptown"?

Where did the new name, "Vale," come from?

Perhaps the foregoing illustration appears too pat, too evident. The village history is so obviously engaging that anyone with a grain of sense would be sure to recognize its potential were he to teach there. Two items cast some doubt for an experienced teacher upon how easy and self-evident "historying" might appear as an activity for children and teachers to engage in. First, Vale appears to be no different from a hundred other villages in that Midwestern state. It is very easy to take the village for exactly what it appears to be—an unpromising collection of twenty-five or so homes and a crossroads store all situated nearly five miles from a busy trans-state highway. Secondly, while working with the teacher in the development of these plans, her professors undertook to describe Vale as an anonymous village of fifty or one hundred years ago. This description was presented rather informally to a group of fifteen experienced teachers living and working within a twenty-mile radius of that village. One young active teacher working and making her home in Vale was present in the group. In the presentation, that teacher was fully as interested but just as unknowing as the rest of the members of that particular inservice extension course. Vale's past was little known.

Villages growing into towns, towns growing into cities, cities growing into metropolitan areas often undergo change in identity, mood, and temper. Cow towns become commercial centers. Once-neighboring towns with distinct and separate identities merge into the urban sprawl around industrial and financial centers. Was this town always a stolid, blue-collar industrial town? Could it once have been a rowdy, swashbuckling river, lumber, oil, defense-plant, or mining town? Could it have been a summer tourist center with appropriate architecture for that purpose and that period?

Neighborhoods undergo change. What was Quality Row yesterday may be Poverty Row today.[6] Man-made structures—roads, bridges, electric lines, industrial zoning, parks, and so forth—have been of great importance in dividing a community into cultural and economic areas. The children one works with, of course, reveal these divisions. A teacher knows the neighborhood he comes from and knows (or thinks he knows) the child. The emerging divisions within a city and the process of neighborhood change can

6 Parker, p. 19.

be historied. Certainly, urban-renewal projects call attention to the opportunity for study attendant in the flux and change that neighborhoods undergo.

What has been the tempo of change near home? An early visitor from
Virginia is supposed to have observed that Pittsburgh was "inhabited almost
entirely by Scots and Irish, who live in paltry log-houses . . . There are in
the town four attorneys, two doctors, and not a priest of any persuasion, nor
church, nor chapel; so that they are likely to be damned without the benefit
of clergy. The place, I believe, will never be considerable."[7] It piques interest
to know how wrong that Virginian was. But what was a warranted prediction for a Pittsburgh of 1783? It could also pique interest to know what
took place to prove that the Virginian was such a poor predictor.

TOWN LORE

Every locale has its stock of lore and legend, much of which lends itself
to study. It might be water-witching, or it might be the rock gulch where
the highwayman was supposed to have hidden. It could be the flood, tornado,
fire, blizzard, or drought of '57. It could be people making a living.

People at work are frequent subjects of legend and lore. Whether it is
garment-making or steel fabrication, oil drilling or automobile manufacture,
shipbuilding, meat packing or the electronics industry, there is the possibility
of a pioneering or legendary workman, foreman, or owner-manager. There
was the year a new "line" hit the market, the year the shop was unionized,
the year the strike failed. There were the layoffs or the good years. Even
relatively recent events will sometimes move rapidly to become near-legends
in the world of jobs and work.

Whatever the line of work in a community, the lore of special language
exists. That language undergoes change, and it can be inquired about. Language will reflect changes in the industry: changes in tools, work conditions,
product, and production. Today's "chain saw" lumberjack operating in the
redwood of the Humboldt, for example, might not be able to talk intelligently to his counterpart of just twenty years before. It is likely that the
new logger or lumberjack would not know the "dogs" from the "blade" on
a common "drag saw." He might not know a "shim" from a "buckling
wedge." He might not know whether a "whistle punk" was to be smoked,
joked, or poked. And it could be he could not tell a "school marm" from a
"widow maker."[8]

---

[7] Quoted in Parker, p. 31.

[8] Shortly after World War II, in the redwood regions of Northern California, the
chain saw (a high-speed gasoline-powered mechanical saw having cutting edges linked
together much like a bicycle chain) supplanted the drag saw (a low-speed gasoline-
powered mechanical saw having a long, flat, cutting blade pulled back and forth in a
movement much like that of the shafts driving the wheels of a steam locomotive). With
this change in cutting tools came a change in techniques for felling timber. Some terms

TOWN BUSINESS

What industries or businesses have flourished in the local area? Certainly the development of any city is closely linked to the economic growth of an area. Corporations, companies, and small businesses can be objects of study.

Histories can be developed for enterprises that were once a part of the business life of a community. The streetcar company may no longer be in operation, but some local resident is likely to remember its years of service, some of the tokens used as fares on the line may still exist, and its tracks may still be traced along certain streets. The end of the trolley tracks might once have been a distant suburb. A zoo or a park might have stood at the end of the line. The history of that distant suburb, zoo, or park will augment the past of the streetcar.

Local historical societies will frequently have material pertaining to past industries of a community. Many business firms will compile their own sketchy histories. State historical societies and colleges and universities are likely to have material on major area and regional industries.

Changes in products and services can be traced for long-standing local firms. The effect of certain innovations and of changes in production arrangements and procedures can be examined. Some businesses undergo a long, slow demise. Explanations for that attrition might be fashioned from the "things" available to children and teachers. These might be old mail-order catalogues, price lists, advertisements, and products. Study might

---

fell into disuse immediately, others were heard less frequently as the last generation of drag-saw men left the woods.

"Dogs." The steel bar and spike attachment used to fasten the drag saw against the tree.

"Shims." Thin rectangular pieces of metal inserted in the cut before the long, narrow wedges are pounded in to lift or "wedge" the tree over. Without the gain in lifting area the shims provide, the wedges might sink into the soft wood without providing the lift necessary to fell the tree.

"Bucking Wedge." A flat, short blade of metal used to keep a cut open in sawing or "bucking" a log in two. Without the cut wedge open, a saw blade might become pinched or caught as the log shifts.

"School Marm." A tree having a large "sucker" or limb growing out and upward from the trunk some distance above the ground. The two crowns to the tree give the appearance of a school teacher with a pointer or switch upraised.

"Whistle Punk." Young boy who stands in sight of both the "hook tender" and the "donkey" relaying messages by whistles between them. The "hook tender" is a man in charge of placing steel cables and hooks on the log to be pulled out of the woods. The "donkey" is a large steam engine with a drum attached to reel in the steel cable and pull the log out of the woods. Frequently the hand signals of the "hook tender" could not be seen at the "donkey" and so a "whistle punk" was needed to transmit these signals.

"Widow Maker." Any sizeable limb breaking off and hanging high overhead among the branches of the redwood.

proceed by examining an old factory site, a company history, a union hall, shop rules, outdated machinery, apprenticeship regulations, an editorial about a strike, a production citation during war years, or an announcement of bankruptcy.

Questions can be formulated and pursued that have to do with the business and industry of a town. In many instances, teachers already participate in "Business Day" tours and meetings. Frequently, these are little more than public-relation efforts of minimal value to either the business or the school community. But Business Day might be used by teachers to cast about for those prerequisites to study: provocative questions and pertinent "things."

TOWN BUILDINGS

What have been the fortunes of a building in this town? What events could have been witnessed from this building on the avenue, on the square, at the waterfront, uptown, on the hill, or in the Mission district?

Buildings can be "historied." Buildings house people and their concerns; the things that matter, the work and the occupations of people, are associated with buildings. Change takes place around and within buildings. What was the city like on the day a building opened; what was it like when the building was just half as old as it now is? What difference did that building make when it was built? Who noticed and what note did they take? One building, in a town with a present population of some 125,000, was welcomed in 1930 as the "third and largest skyscraper" to appear in the central business district. That "skyscraper" was a ten-story building. But it dwarfed the "skyscraper" hotel of five stories and the seven-story Bank and Trust Building "skyscraper."

Nearly every town will have an ordinary office building, buildings with stores at ground level, professional offices upstairs, and a third-floor Odd-fellows, Eagles, Masonic, Moose, or Pythian Sister's Hall. In part, one can know about the past of the town and the townspeople by knowing the past of that building and the participants in the life of that building.

THE CHARTERS BUILDING[9]

Frankly, the class was somewhat at sea after I sprang on them the notion that a building could be studied historically. It seemed both improbable and unprofitable to consider the history of an office building, especially an ordinary one in their town. Our discussions of the project at first were uninspiring. Most of the events the class suggested might have taken place were of the dramatic and sensational variety, i.e., fire, robbery, suicide, lightning

---

[9] Adapted from informal reports of a classroom teacher.

damage. Parents, newspapers, and the Charters Building itself exhausted their suggestions as to where information might be located. So that is what we started with: a short list of possible happenings and three sources to be investigated.

Often the beginning stages of study are exasperating. Because the class knows of so few possibilities, the use of sources may be uninspired, routine, or aimless. But without consulting some source material, children are likely to remain blind to what some of the possibilities might be. There is a kind of reciprocity between questions and "things" in the beginning stages of inquiry. Naïve and unrefined questions may lead to a perfunctory gathering and using of source material. Yet, the perfunctory may be necessary and useful. Awkward first attempts to collect and examine material frequently result in abandoning, refining, or inventing the questions that direct search. New or reworked questions may demand that additional remnants be located or that the existing source material be searched in a unique way. When this is the case, teachers will feel the inertia of classroom study give way to the momentum of "things" and questions, questions and "things." But until momentum is gained, study is likely to be an exasperating, halting matter.

In this particular project I had the class take two steps before we rushed out to engulf parents, publishers, and building. First, two children were appointed to phone the Charters Building and two to do the same for the newspapers. Their instructions were to explain our project, to gain any general information possible, and to inquire about visitations. Secondly, we gave some time to considering what specific questions we might ask of parents.

The next day's account of what parents know about our building was both discouraging and revealing. Several parents were relatively new to the community and could supply little information. A few remembered shopping in the street-level stores or going to dental or medical offices in the building. But even the parents born here were of little help. Apparently, the building was active and open as far back as these parents could remember (the majority of parents for these children were born in the late 1920's). Furthermore, a quick check of the class revealed that grandparents were not a very likely source in this suburban neighborhood.

Telephoning resulted in quite different information. The two boys who had phoned the Charters Building told of how various telephone operators and secretaries had misinterpreted their requests. Before reaching the building manager's office, they had talked to clerks in the City County Building (building permits) and clerks in the City Parks Office (Charters park). Excitement mounted a bit when it was revealed that both historic pictures of the building and a scrapbook were available in the manager's office. The secretary in the office had worked in the building for quite a long time, and she volunteered a number of dates, stories, and facts.

The report from the newspaper office was noticeably sprinkled with the term "morgue," which the two committee members had discovered was the name for the newspaper library. In the morgue, it was reported, was a small file of clippings relating to both the old and the new Charters Building. That this building that their parents knew so little about should be referred to as the "new" building interested the class.

Before this, the teacher had worried over involving the class in the frustrations and rewards of tracking down promising sources. Obviously, any school district is not too happy to have a teacher request a bus for a field trip every other day, or send batches of children around town willy-nilly. For this teacher, talking it over with her principal proved helpful. He agreed to a "quota" of four two-hour, small-group research trips for the project. On the afternoons these research parties went afield, he agreed to supervise the work of the remainder of the class. Hence, the teacher was able to spend four two-hour periods in the field with seven to nine students. This arrangement had an unexpected payoff. It did not take the class long to decide that because their time afield was limited they had to plan carefully where and how they would collect data.

The entire class helped prepare the first field party. We gave thought to the problem of how to interview the building manager and his secretary, how to examine the building, and how to record the contents of the scrapbook.

Our next two field parties were sent to the newspaper offices and to the City County Building. Altogether, the yield was marvelous. For instance, when the newspaper-morgue research group reported several articles suggesting bankruptcy, the students that had examined the Charters Building office scrapbook were taken by surprise—not one item had appeared pertaining to bankruptcy. The scrapbook had, however, contained a ten-year city-tax review appearing in 1940. In that circular had appeared an item indicating disbursement of $270,000 in "relief" funds during the 1930's. I remembered that *Wright's City Directory* showed the tenants (and, therefore, maybe the vacancies) for office buildings. A quick check for 1931 revealed a great number of offices listed as "vacant" for the Charters Building. At that point we pretty well recognized that we wouldn't know much about the building if we knew only a very little about the 1930's in Daley City.

We even encountered some interesting problems in our early questions about when the building had opened and who its owners were. In the 1920's, we found out, there were no building inspectors for the city. Pictures, newspaper items, and on-site inspection seemed to confirm that the building was erected in two stages. On every level, for example, the halls of one section were much wider than for another. Heating, lighting, and plumbing permits were dated as early as 1927, but these might have been for the old Charters Building on the same site, or for the construction offices put up prior to erecting the new building. The secretary for the building said she could find tax records for as early as 1930. But newspaper accounts used both 1928 and 1929 to date the present building. Our most substantial lead turned out to be a newspaper photograph on which was penciled the date November, 1928. The story underneath the photograph contained a prediction by the construction engineer that the building would be completed by May of the next year.

Our project did have its doldrum periods and vexations. We were excited to discover that radio station WABA had moved its studios to the Charters Building in 1939 and that Bronson's had leased ground-level store space in both the "old" and the "new" building. Unfortunately, neither of these leads seemed to develop for us. People are sometimes very busy. Records are considered confidential, some are lost, some are never retained, and so forth.

TOWN PLACES

The park, the airport, the harbor, and the town square are all places that can be inquired about. Histories can be developed for civic places.

Stations, tunnels, bridges, subways, and canals have not always been there. Some important events are linked to them, and the building of structures and the events associated with them can be historied. Rallies, riots, celebrations, elections, displays, mobs, speeches, and other singular events took place on civic grounds or in civic buildings. Sufficient residue may survive to permit some understanding of that long-ago event associated with a civic place.

TOWN TIMES

What was the city like when Grandpa was a boy? When Daddy was a boy? Did things happen here at the time of the Civil War? What was it like to live here during territorial days? During the Revolutionary War? What were the heydays like for this city?

Teachers can help children pursue questions related to the Here place at a given period in times past.

Assembling Sources

The "study" of the past begins with questions. Perhaps in any town some questions can be formulated about the origins, street names, growth, legends, businesses, buildings, civic places, and eras of that community. To resolve such questions, one must engage in thought and observation about "things." How does one locate the residue of some long-ago local event?

There are a number of affiliated agencies within a state and perhaps even within a community whose interest is to promote historical inquiry of a local nature. They are likely to be a direct and most important help to teachers. A national directory for these agencies can be obtained for two dollars.[10] This directory will list each active organization by state and by city. A brief summary of the listings for two states, Missouri and California, suggests the number and variety of agencies a teacher might expect to find for his state. Missouri, for instance, lists fifty historical societies or agencies within the state. A number of these indicate that they regularly publish bulletins, quarterlies, brochures, or newsletters. The Missouri list indicates societies organized predominantly at the county level. Many of the eighty-six listings under the California heading, by comparison, are for city and town historical societies. The latter state also lists a number of specialized agencies: Railway and Locomotive Historical Society, Barlow Society for the History of Medicine, Southern California Jewish Historical Society, and others.

School-services divisions are actively maintained by the historical societies for a few states. These divisions regularly publish student magazines encouraging student participation in the activity called history. In some cases, school-service bureaus make available reproductions of various important documents, photographs, and artifacts.

In nearly every town someone can be located who has a particular interest in local history—perhaps a businessman, or a newspaper writer, or someone in the office of the county clerk. Such a person can frequently be asked for help as a teacher plans for, or is already immersed in, some form of study with a group of children. The problem is to identify and get in touch with that person. The local newspaper office, the library, the county historical society, some fraternal or patriotic organization, or any one of these, might be a good place to begin.

To a great many people, historical material is anything which appears to be very old. To many of us, the path to better history must lead through dusty tomes and faded ink on yellowed leaves of paper—better cobwebs make better history. But a number of the questions children pursue will probably concern the very recent past of a community, neighborhood, or subdivision. Therefore, much of the material children might work with will be available through the past and continuing records of various governmental and quasi-governmental agencies, *viz.,* the redevelopment authority, the county assessor's office, the planning commission, the housing authority,

---

[10] Write: American Association for State and Local History, 132 Ninth Avenue West, Nashville, Tenn., 37203.

or the health, fire, and police departments. Particular people may have the professional preparation or tasks to equip them to advise a teacher in his search for particular "things." Local lawyers, librarians, and newspaper employees, for example, can often be of brief but knowledgeable assistance. Clerks in various city and county offices, too, can make it easier to locate the needed data.

Parker's *Local History*[11] is a standard handbook in the gathering of artifacts and literary fragments near home. Parker discusses in some detail each of 21 separate sources of information of use to local historians:

1. Published histories of one's locality and nearby localities.
2. Family histories.
3. Military records.
4. Directories, whether county, city, telephone, commercial, or fraternal.
5. Maps.
6. Atlases and gazetteers.
7. Accounts of travelers.
8. Anniversary addresses and sermons.
9. Photographs.
10. Stories and reminiscences of old residents.
11. Private letters, diaries, account books.
12. Keepsakes, heirlooms, relics.
13. Local newspapers and periodicals.
14. Census reports.
15. Abstracts and title deeds.
16. Surveyors' notes.
17. School records.
18. Public records.
19. Business records.
20. Church records.
21. Cemetery inscriptions.

Back copies of newspapers will be a very valuable resource in most communities. Some newspapers employ a librarian to oversee the files and microfilms they maintain. Ordinary tact and forethought will usually pave the way to reasonable use of whatever material is available. Sometimes it may be difficult to obtain access to the material a teacher needs because, like any employees in enterprise, a newspaper staff must "attend to business." Basement floods, fire, and other damaging agents take their toll of newspaper files, too. If particular files have been damaged, have not been preserved, or if the newspaper is no longer in operation, it may be possible to obtain copies at the local library or the county historical society.

Advertisements, legal notices, comic strips, political cartoons, and other features may sometimes be of more use than the standard news articles. Clothing styles, cost, and material may be described or pictured in various paid advertisements. Amusements and diversions for the community can be

[11] Paperback editions of this book (Donald Dean Parker, *Local History: How to Gather It, Write It, and Publish It* [New York: Social Science Research Council, 1944]) can be obtained through the American Association for State and Local History, 132 Ninth Avenue West, Nashville, Tenn., 37203. The Bureau of Publications of Teachers College, Columbia University, New York City, is producing a "Localized History Series," under the editorship of Clifford L. Long.

catalogued through a variety of newspaper features. Employment, sales, and realty advertisements may be of use to a class pursuing economic questions. Editorials and letters to the editor, of course, are revealing commentaries on what was political, what was offensive, what was moral, and what was manly in the eyes of the townspeople in times past.

"Study" Skills

This text has made much of the word "study." "Study," and synonymous notions, have received persistent, even dogged, attention. Because we treat these words with such special interest and regard them with such obvious care, it is sensible to consider other words and other counsel. Relief from our terminology is in order.

History and "Historying"

One professional educator very recently admonished his readers to develop early a sense of history. This early development is, of course, a most attractive goal; the route to its achievement is worth speculating about. According to the same writer, developing the sense of history is a problem in organizing the mind, beginning with the proper placement of dates. He recommends that students cultivate the practice of locating new dates on a time-line, in association with dates already known. Second, he observes that the events of man are located in place as well as in time. Therefore, he recommends that children sketch maps from memory to promote the organized, history-minded intellect. And, third, he says that the development of a history sense is favored when children dramatize past events in their minds, and he recommends that they practice picturing and visualizing events. To him, history sense consists of (1) conceptions of time, (2) conceptions of place, and (3) images of a dramatic and forceful nature.

These three ideas reflect reasonably well the usual view of history and the usual view of the likely strategy required to develop a sense of history. Perhaps it is well to make very clear the differences between the views of the present book and this usual view of history instruction. In the usual view, history is the aggregate of things found out, things known about the past. In our view, history—or "historying"—is a way of finding out; history is the ways in which man believes himself to be the knower in things past. In the usual view, history students are to be active in the sense of recalling, ordering, visualizing, and becoming informed about past events. In our view, history students are to be active in the sense of asking, refining, and even abandoning questions; fashioning plausible hunches and explanations; locating things of relevance to their questions and hunches; remaining skeptical, or at least aware, of the bases upon which even the most attractive and cherished findings must rest. In the usual view, there is likely to be a single best or most authoritative account of the past, and *that* history is to be understood well. In our view, historians are craftsmen in record-making. The assumptions, operations, and point of view of the craftsman will be reflected in his works. There is variety even among good craftsmen, and *that* is to be understood well. In the usual view, the history program is challenged to sustain interest and productivity by helping children to sense the liveliness, drama, and portent of the important long ago. In our view, the history program is challenged to sustain interest and productivity by helping children to sense the process whereby men seek to know about the important long ago.

There will be readers who will level at us the charge of fashioning strawmen for purposes of making our viewpoints attractive by comparison. This is not the case at all. We have enormous respect for the conventional outlook in history teaching. Our experience tells us that the view of history as the unalterable past presents the established view of the public schools. Elementary schools have long practiced a history teaching in which locating events in time and space, and dramatizing those events in the mind's eye, are useful and sensible suggestions. If placing dates on timelines, locating events on map sketches, and visualizing past events is a strawman in the social studies of the public schools, it will require a sturdy goat to crunch it up. Nor will any small stray spark cause it to disappear from the classroom in a puff of smoke.

In the preceding paragraphs, the historian's *record,* the *what* one knows, and the historian's *craft,* the *how* one knows, were cast as alternatives. This was necessary to remind the reader again of what is meant by the use of the word "study." Knowing what study is, is partially a function of knowing what it is not. But the notion of alternative positions is misleading. It suggests that teachers can adopt only one of the two positions—they must be concerned with either the *what* dimension or the *how* dimension of the discipline of history. The discussion so far suggests that to choose one concern is necessarily to exclude the other. In reality, of course, teachers must be concerned with both. They must be interested in history both as a fund of acquired information and as a specialized method of inquiry. Acquaintanceship concerns and study concerns both exist in school curriculums. If in this book great attention seems to be given to the notion of study, it is only because study is not a staple commodity in the normal diet of school history. The history fare for schoolchildren appears one-sided.

Sometimes the word "able" is used to refer to workmen of various sorts— "he's an able seaman," for example. To work at the craft of study also requires that one be "able" in certain ways. Several abilities can be developed when dealing with the Then and Here topic. Children can learn to be tenacious. They can become skillful in locating and employing "things." They can learn how to deal with testimony. And they can practice establishing the authenticity of the records and objects with which they deal.

Tenacity

Study frequently requires perseverance. A great deal of persistent pick-and-shovel work may be necessary to produce even a small, infrequent nugget in the form of a generalization, a conclusion, or a plausible account. One study skill may be simply that of tenacity.

Sometimes, children have to learn to be tenacious in the face of irrelevant, low-yield sources. The initial exuberance of a class and the kind intentions of parents, librarians, and neighbors sometimes bring into a classroom a number of mementos, letters, photographs, and objects of only tangential value in resolving the historical questions confronting a group of children. A certain persistence will be required to ferret out those materials that appear relevant to a particular quest. Teachers, too, confound the development of tenacity in their understandable desire to make their schoolroom attractive, interesting, and decorative. Objects are sometimes collected primarily for their display value. But study is not simply visualizing or capturing the mood of past times. Study is the careful stalking of a question. Some material is useful in pursuing a particular question; other material is not. Tenacity is the ability to persist in seeking out the sources bearing on a particular question.

In doing history, children will confront uninterested, busy, or uncooperative townspeople. Newspaper workers, businessmen, town officials, housewives, librarians, and historical society officers can often be expected to be busy. Accommodating schoolchildren can be time-consuming, a costly nuisance, or both. Therefore, a part of the skill of being tenacious is forethought: through practice, children can develop skill in anticipating and coping with blocks to the collection of the data they need. Preparation for collecting data efficiently and for dealing with likely contingencies can be undertaken in the classroom. Frequently, this preparation means that brute, unreasoned persistence will become less and less a requirement of inquiry.

Sometimes, study demands perseverance of still another nature. In searching for things relevant to questions, lengthy documents are sometimes uncovered—statistics, business records, reports, letters, biographies, family genealogies, secondary writings, and so forth. A certain tenacity is required in the face of these. But with the help of the teacher, the children can plan various methods or tactics for using these documents efficiently. It is one thing to read a lengthy town-meeting report hoping that something important will reveal itself. It is quite another thing to read the same report intending only to chart the issues before the townspeople, or to determine what groups were in conflict, or to notice the role and influence represented by a particular man or position. It is one thing to read extracts from the writings of soldiers and civilians "to appreciate how people felt about the Civil War." It is another to read these same accounts to notice only the hopes people held (or otherwise revealed) for when the fighting was done. In both cases, no doubt, one needs to be persistent and tenacious. But perhaps the designed persistence, the focused tenacity, is a skill with greater rewards in the study sequence.

Acquiring "Things"

Then and Here topics lend themselves to the development of another skill. Because source material may be scarce, children may have to be resourceful. Because text material will be insufficient, the class and the teacher will have to locate pertinent things for themselves. In all, the imaginative development of resources may be a study skill of particular demand in the Then and Here context.

Acquiring the pertinent things of study is sometimes a function of knowing the staying power of certain social residue. What records are likely to be kept by what people? What records does a town keep, for example? Study skills can begin their development at this level. Commercial enterprises normally are not in business to maintain a certain tonnage in records. Yet a great many commercial records are preserved at some expense. Knowing what material is likely to persist and what use can be made of it is knowledge frequently called upon by people concerned with past events.

The development of source material is partially a function of knowing how to exploit traditional repositories. Study interludes might be balanced or sequential in the sense of systematically acquainting the children with various libraries, historical societies, museums, monuments, patriotic organizations, newspaper records, state universities, and other well-used places. But skill in the development of source material must go beyond a knowledge of the expected record and the expected housing for that record. Imagination in exploiting source materials sometimes takes the form of using quite ordinary or orthodox materials in a somewhat extraordinary or unorthodox manner. For example, plans for investigating the "schoolground yesterday" will involve looking at school regulations, class newspapers, and playground surfaces in an unusual manner.

In the illustration that follows, the teacher gives particular attention to cultivating a sense of the possible range of residue to be confronted. Imaginative development of source material is partially a function of understanding well the nature of the question being asked. This teacher will spend some time considering various elements in the Big Question facing the class. And this preliminary discussion should help the children to develop avenues into the problem.

THE SCHOOLGROUND YESTERDAY

Fifth graders in our district spend most of the year studying the history of the United States. The curriculum guide deals with all the usual events, dates, and personalities. But nowhere in the guide is the question raised of how the history we read gets written. What do historians do when they set out to write a history? Perhaps understanding of the *product* of historians— texts, accounts, and other writings—would be greater if eleven-year-olds were introduced to the *process* of writing history.

These are the plans I have developed for introducing my class to the notion of history as process. They are organized around possible initiating, sustaining, and culminating activities.

Initiating Activities

What happened on the schoolground yesterday? You were all there. You all participated. Tell me what happened.

It is very likely that the class will respond to my opening questions in at least three ways. Some children will remember yesterday as very normal and undistinguished. Other children, I suspect, will believe they know exactly what happened because they were there. Surely, too, there will be some disagreements as to what happened on the schoolground yesterday.

Nothing Unusual. If yesterday is remembered as perfectly ordinary, I plan to respond with questions of the following sort:

—No one made a new friend?
—It was no one's first day at our school?
—There were no quarrels?
—No one won a game?
—No one was teased?
—No one was hurt?

We Were There. Some students might see themselves as wide-angle cameras and high-fidelity sound recorders. They may say, in effect, "We know exactly what happened!" And I plan to respond:

—What happened to second and third graders?
—The eighth graders, would they remember different things?
—The yard-duty teacher?
—The school nurse?
—Mrs. Marian, from her porch across the street?

If Mrs. Marian remembers only the baseballs that came into her yard, does that mean only baseball was played yesterday? What does it mean if the nurse's report of yesterday mentions only bloody noses and skinned knees?

Conflict. Hopefully, there will be some disagreements: "Yesterday John's team quit!" "No, we did not!" This sort of conflict should heighten interest as well as provide a series of problems to be decided upon. In this circumstance, I'll have a good opening to discuss our task. The question can be raised, "Are we to *describe* or *summarize* what happened on the schoolground yesterday, or, is our task more like *puzzling* and *investigating* the schoolground and yesterday?"

In this beginning exchange between the class and me, the problems practicing historians deal with and the question of what happened on the schoolground yesterday should emerge as very similar in nature. I will likely have an opportunity to underscore the nature of testimony. Different participants—fifth graders, adults, eighth graders—will remember and report different things. We will have to develop skills in sifting and examining differing and conflicting testimonial accounts.

Sustaining Activities

At about this point I'm planning to have each student write his "record" or memory of the playground yesterday. Several of these will be mimeographed for the class. We can then practice examining these "records." Certain of these entries might suggest the various kinds of things that happen on playgrounds. We might build a preliminary list of what to look for or what to pursue. For example, who was there—adults, first graders, eighth graders? Or, what took place—games, teasing, chasing one another, quarrels, talk, friendships, gangs?

Considering the question "Who was there?" should suggest a variety of witnesses as sources of information. Thinking about what might have taken place will be useful in developing questions to ask of these witnesses.

We will probably add the memories of eighth graders, the school nurse, a school neighbor, the principal's secretary, third graders, etc., to our "recods." A curator might even be selected to house, order, and arrange for the circulation of our documents about the class historians.

I'm sure the class will raise the question of written records as sources. With some maneuvering we might develop a list something like this:
—School rules for the playground and the lunch hour;
—Notes from parents to the school or notes from the school to parents;
—The school calendar of events;
—Official reports of the school nurse, yard-duty teacher, and the principal;
—Class newspapers;
—The weekly plans of teachers (some room activities spill over onto the playground).

I think the written regulations for the schoolground and the lunch hour will provide our most immediate information. Because rules deal with regulating behavior, the list of rules should suggest a number of behaviors the class will want to investigate. For example, the school rules state that "all children will remain outdoors during the lunch hour unless it is raining or cold." With a few hints, the phrase "unless it is raining or cold" will suggest weather as a partial control over schoolground happenings. Furthermore, the rules state that marbles, tops, and yo-yos are not to be brought to school. These playthings might suggest that "yesterday" occurred at a certain time during the year (kite, marble, baseball, or kickball "season"). How can we verify weather and seasonal influences?

The next activity I have in mind might be difficult for fifth graders to handle. What I would like to do is to introduce the class to the notion of examining the site, the *where* of the events we're interested in. I plan to introduce this with pictures or descriptions of various school grounds, equipment, space, and surfaces (macadam, gravel, dirt, and turf). I hope to create a discussion of how such things as surface can control playground activity. We'll go out to examine the nature of our schoolground and observe where equipment is located, the designated areas for various grades, kickball fields, and so on. We'll try our hand at examining buildings, equipment, and terrain for the effect they might have on where children gather and what they do. Cool spots, hidden spots, the eighth-grade wing of the building, dust, trees, and lawn may have been factors in yesterday's schoolground happenings. A certain amount of map building skill may grow out of this.

The idea of facilities and equipment as a key to knowing something about the schoolground yesterday might suggest still another possibility. Our room, as well as other classrooms in the school, has its own equipment box for physical education. Therefore we can raise these questions:

—Could room equipment be related to schoolground activity?

—Do first graders have baseball bats and volley balls in their equipment box? What equipment do they have?

—How many different games can be played with a kickball?

—Can boys jump rope? Do they? Who uses what things?

Culminating Activities

Finally, I plan to have the class consider a way to organize their account of the schoolground yesterday. I want to bring home the point that the framework one builds for reporting, shapes and molds the history one writes. A chronological outline seems very likely to emerge early in the class discussion. Then, if the class does not respond, I will suggest an alternative outline, emphasizing *where* the events took place on the playground yesterday. Thus, we might have two competing outlines for our history—one emphasizing time and sequence and the other emphasizing location and space.

The Schoolground Yesterday	The Schoolground Yesterday
—12:00 to 12:15	—At the big ball diamond
—12:15 to 12:30	—At the little ball diamond
—12:30 to 12:45	—Near the tetherball court and the swings
—12:45 to 1:00	—By the eighth-grade wing

If we wanted to emphasize the various participants (big kids, adults, us, and little kids) how might we build an outline for our history? What if we wanted the several kinds of events and happenings (teasing and chasing, talk, quarrels, games, competition, accidents) to stand out? How might we then organize our account? Discussing and responding to these questions would underscore the influence our framework will have on the history we write.

Eventually we'll put together an outline that suits our purposes. Then we'll set about organizing groups to compose and edit various sections.

Using Skills

When we near the completion of our class account of the schoolground yesterday I intend to set pupils to work on individual tasks. The results of these projects and the way in which the children go about them should give me a good idea of the progress we've made. These are some of the tasks I have in mind for the children to choose to work on individually.

1. There are several toys and interesting things you may never have heard of. How could you find out about one of them? What records could you find and use? Could you write its history?

    tops   hula hoops   big-little books   mumbly-peg

2. What was happening on the day you were born? Are you sure you were born that exact day? How did you get your name? How do you know? What other questions could you ask? How could you seek answers to these questions?

3. How do fashions and styles in clothing begin and disappear? Here are four pieces of clothing you may or may not have heard of. Could you write the story for one of them? What are the different ways you could use to find out?

    dusters   pedal pushers   knickers   shifts

4. Schools change, too. Has the school pledge always been said the way we say it now? What is an inkwell? Could you find out about changes in schools? Try one of these?

    slates   ciphering   the pledge of allegiance   inkwells

    I've located a book—*The Lincoln Nobody Knows* by Richard N. Current

—which should provide a fine device for closing the schoolground yesterday project and to bridge back to the history of this nation. An early portion of this book raises the question of Lincoln's appearance. Was his face a lively, smiling one, or was it more typically sad, gaunt, and melancholic? The author suggests that the tedious wet-plate photography of the times made it difficult to capture an animated, spontaneous likeness of any subject. In some respects, the many photographs we have of Lincoln do not square with other testimony we have about his features.

I plan to read further passages from *The Lincoln Nobody Knows* to highlight the uses of sources in resolving questions about the past. I might, for example, raise the question of whether Lincoln was awkward and uneasy with women in formal social situations. Certain accounts suggest this to be the case. But there is evidence that Lincoln at one time helped to organize what must have been a very important social event—a cotillion at the state capital. What case could we build for the courtly and assured Lincoln?

There are several contradictions in the literature on Lincoln. Reading to children about these puzzles, tracing the evidence for one opinion or another, should help to reinforce and clarify the main outcomes expected for this entire project. I hope that these fifth graders will better understand that the historian's work begins with puzzling questions, doubts, and unknowns; that he devises resourceful ways to obtain, examine, and use material to satisfy these questions; that written history rests both on sources and on the manner in which these sources are used and interpreted.

Authenticity

In pursuing questions developing within the Then and Here topic, children can also practice the skill of verifying the records and objects with which they deal. A historian imposes upon the artifacts and records of interest to him an important set of preliminary questions: How old are you? Are you what you purport to be? What people and what culture lay claim to you?

THE ANTIQUARIAN[12]

My class has just completed a study of our community. Much of our time was spent considering the historic development of our area. As we were beginning the unit I thought of contacting a local antique dealer. Possibly he would possess material or know about the early history of our town and valley.

[12] Adapted from the informal reports of a classroom teacher.

As it turned out, he was quite unwilling to have my thirty-five students troop through his shop. But he did seem very proud of, and very willing to talk about, his small collection of early furniture. This shopowner turned out to be something of a scholar in his field. I was soon hearing about the subtleties of furniture design and the problems of determining age and authenticity. For at least forty-five minutes, I peered at the undersides of various pieces of furniture, examining dovetailing, feeling texture of hand-dressed wood, and noting various details of construction.

Nearly a week later, it occurred to me that the problems of the antiquarian in authenticating furniture were very similar to, or at least analogous to, a set of problems encountered by the historian. To write the history of our town or any town, one would have to examine musty old things—newspapers, diaries, maps, etc. Determining whether these sources are genuine or not is an important first problem.

My antique dealer agreed to come to our classroom bringing with him some of his technical books, various bits of hardware, two chairs, and a small table. We spent a very profitable hour or so considering furniture construction, tool marks, and hardware as evidence of age and authenticity in early American furniture. We learned, for example, of the development of the common nail: the developments from the early hand-forged nail, the later stamped nail, to the comparatively recently developed modern wire nail. We learned to look for vertical saw marks and the shallow gouge of the handplane as evidence that the wood might have been prepared by an individual craftsman before the development of factories with their circular saws and planing mills. We were introduced to calipers and learned how to apply them to the turnings in furniture to tell whether or not they were perfectly round (very old turnings will become slightly elliptical due to the uneven shrinking as the wood ages). By the end of the hour, we could identify hand-forged screws and the diamond-shaped wooden pins characteristic of early furniture.

When the lesson closed, our resource person left with us a chair to authenticate. Later, and after some heated discussion, a committee was commissioned to write the dealer expressing our doubts as to the genuineness of the "antique" chair. The letter discussed the evidence we used in arriving at our conclusion.

In the days that followed, I was able to capitalize on the furniture situation in two ways. First, the children began to bring quite a few "old" objects to the classroom. Each time this happened, someone would raise the question, "How do you know for sure how old it is?" On one of these occasions, I was able to focus attention on the ways in which we were authenticating or dating items. For example, we frequently relied entirely on the word of someone we trusted. For example, a grandmother had verified the probable age of a butterchurn. At other times we relied on what we considered *expert opinion* to date objects (a mechanic had identified old cars in an early photograph). We used one artifact to gauge the age of another. That is, we dated some articles of clothing and styles of dress by either seeing them in advertisements in old newspapers or by seeing them in pictures reputed to portray early scenes. The age of some objects seemed self-evident to us: newspapers, for example. Gradually, we developed and discussed several other procedures for authenticating the objects we were interested in.

Still later, I was able to make the point that as historians of our town we not only had to find and authenticate sources, but we had to use them somehow. We could, for example, ask two questions about our churn: (1) was it genuine—an artifact of a certain era, and (2) was it useful in writing our history? These two questions about the churn set in motion a chain of events. A churn is used in butter-making. Butter-making raised the question of food preparation and manufacture in the home. Household tasks eventually led to comparisons in home life "now" and home life "then." At this point, one group of students splintered off and set about reconstructing what a day might have been like in the kitchen of a home in our town at the time of the Civil War and at about the time of World War I. Later, the class found this useful in attempting to generalize about the tempo of change in our town.

Testimony

Maintaining the initiative is a skill required in dealing with records of some antiquity. It is easy to adopt the passive posture, the posture of respectful attention. That is, one can act as if in understanding some past event a reader need only be receptive to the chronicle of some narrator who witnessed the event in question, participated in the event, or arranged a privileged conversation with someone who did take part in that long-ago event. By attending respectfully to an authoritative account, the story of the past can be understood.

The active mode, in contrast, is the practice of using, employing, wielding, or otherwise exploiting a given account to satisfy a question in some thoughtful manner. The would-be-historian gains the initiative as he propounds questions and reworks those questions in such a manner that a plausible response can be fashioned from the documents assembled or to be assembled.

History in the passive mode requires that the reader be skillful in deciding whom to believe and to be prudent in believing only that which is attested to by the accepted account. History in the active manner requires that one be skillful in deciding upon questions, and that one be prudent in believing only the logic of his use of sources to render an answer to the question posed.

Robert W. Wells[13] illustrates another skill in the use of records and testimony. This series of articles on Wisconsin's role in the Civil War recounts the hospital-organization work of Mrs. Cordelia Harvey. A part of the account concerns an interview with Lincoln. In that interview, the experience, persistence, and careful reasoning of Mrs. Harvey carried the day. She responded surely and adroitly to every reservation or protest offered by the President or the Secretary of War. Later, a hospital for the wounded was ordered to be opened in Wisconsin, seemingly as a consequence of her shrewd handling of this interview with the President. The newspaper writer closed the Presidential interview with the observation, "All this conversation is the way Mrs. Harvey recorded it sometime after the fact. Lincoln, if he had bothered to write down his side, might have given himself better lines." That wry comment points up another skill in dealing with records. Using testimony in resolving questions of one's interest proceeds in part by knowing something about the nature of whoever it is that testifies and under what conditions the record at hand was set down.

In the vignette that follows, a teacher plans for the development of those understandings associated with the skillful use of records and the testimony they contain.

BYLINE: MY SELF[14]

In our fifth-grade social-studies textbook there are many examples of record-keeping. In fact, the whole first part of the book is liberally sprinkled with excerpts from one or another's diary as it tells the history of our country. When we reach the Louisiana Purchase and the Lewis and Clark Expedition we reach a climax in record-keeping, that of Sacajawea's jump into the river to save the Lewis and Clark records.

After reading about the Lewis and Clark expedition, I'd ask the students if they would like to hear some of their actual entries. *The Journals of Lewis and Clark* edited by Bernard DeVoto (Houghton Mifflin, and Co., Boston, 1953) contains these. Even though this book "edits" the records, what the author says in the introduction about his motives for doing so leads me to believe he has not sacrificed authenticity.

The students would realize that if Sacajawea jumped into the river to save the records they must be very important. Next we would talk about records. In our talk, we could make a list of questions we have about records. It might look something like this:

[13] ROBERT W. WELLS, *Wisconsin in the Civil War* (Milwaukee: Milwaukee Journal, 1962), p. 47.
[14] Adapted from informal reports of a classroom teacher.

What is a Record?

1. What is written in a record?
2. When does a person write a record?
3. Who writes it?
4. Why does he write it?
5. How is it used?

To answer the first question, we would discuss the existence of many kinds of records, but emphasize that the kind we are interested in concerns a log of events and how they affect people. The second question can be answered in the following manner: I would have the students write a record of what they did a week ago today. Then they could write what they have done so far today. This comparison, I think, would illustrate the importance of writing records immediately.

To answer the third question, the students can conclude that anyone can write a record. For the time being, I will not mention how each person's record is his own interpretation. Questions four and five are related, in that records are often used to write history later on, and perhaps the record-keeper realizes this. Where did much of the material in history books on Lewis and Clark come from? Their records?

In order to make records more meaningful to the students, to give them experience in keeping records, and to tie all our questions together, they can keep records of their own. I would present the following situation to the children: "Let's imagine each one of us is responsible for telling the people of the year 5000 what being a fifth grader was like in 1965. At the end of the week, we'll read part of our records to the class and discuss the impression of our lives people in 5000 will get from them."

During that week, I would read many good stories, we might have the student council election of officers, and we would visit the television studio of the "World Understanding" program (a field trip visit that can be made anytime) among others.

Then, at the end of the week, we'd read and discuss our records. After discussing and comparing these records, I think we will be able to see that a record is more than a list of events. What is written and how it is written is stamped with the personality of the writer. One person thinks a certain thing is important; another doesn't. However, this "Byline: My Self" makes the record more interesting than a machinelike chronicle of events would be. The personality of the writer gives it life. Some people are very skilled in fathoming the makeup of the man from his records.

I hope from the exercise the children can see that history is based on fact but is to a great extent the *interpretation* of fact by human beings—including historians.

State and Nation

The foregoing text has argued persistently for "study" experiences centering in the local community. Five reasons were offered for that persistent focus. When Here is a community place, (1) children can participate directly in the process of ferreting out source material; (2) they can render their own account of events independent of a textbook; (3) they can, because of a scarcity of "things," develop resourcefulness; (4) they can scrutinize "object-things"; and (5) they can undertake interviews.

When Here is defined as state, region, or nation, study possibilities of another variety exist. Abundant source material will have been developed by others. Interviews will probably be neither pertinent nor possible. Much of the study sequence will be directly related to examining textbooks and other "message-things." But study is possible.

The following classroom incident illustrates one form that inquiry might take when the topic is nation and the question at hand concerns the renowned truthfulness of George Washington.

THE CHERRY TREE CAPER[15]

An intriguing problem-solving experience could be initiated by asking my students if they have ever heard of the story of George Washington and the cherry tree. Probably they have heard it; but, if not, I will tell it to them. It seems that when George was a little boy he chopped down one of his father's favorite cherry trees, and when asked about it, he said, "I cannot tell a lie. I did it."

With this groundwork laid, we can ask ourselves if this story is really true. Did George W. chop down a cherry tree when he was young? How could we find out? To answer this question, we could consult biographies of Washington and encyclopedias and ask historians.

In an effort to know how best to help the children answer this question, I went through the searching process myself, beginning with a look at juvenile biographies to see how they handled the incident. *Hello, George Washington,* by Janice Holland, contained no mention of cherry trees but did relate an episode dealing with veracity. According to her, when George was a boy he was determined to ride a certain colt of his mother's until it was broken to the saddle. He rode, and the colt fell dead! At supper his mother asked about her favorite colt, whereupon her son, George, replied,

[15] Adapted from informal reports of a classroom teacher.

"The sorrel is dead." His mother responded that she was sorry it was dead but was "glad to have a son who always speaks the truth."

George Washington, by Clara Ingram Judson, is another children's biography dealing with Washington's early years. This book contains no mention of never telling a lie. However, the foreword and preface contain some comments pertinent to my quest. In using this book with my students, the comments in the prefatory remarks would provide a perfect opportunity to teach the wisdom of reading the introductory material in a book.

Mrs. Judson says that early biographies required the hero to be perfect—almost a "prig." Later on, "debunkers failed to acquaint us with the man in the opposite direction." Much of the early biographies consisted of "folklore moralizing of the 19th Century by men like Weems of cherry tree fame." Here is my first key to the mystery. A person named "Weems" is connected with the incident.

Next I consulted several encyclopedias. Incidentally, I'm beginning to think encyclopedias are indispensable in a classroom. The *American Peoples' Encyclopedia* said that little is known about Washington's early life. ". . . adventures with a cherry tree are entirely apocryphal and have become part of the general fund of legend and misinformation perpetuated by the early biography by Weems." Weems again! A glance at the "Weems" entry in this same volume explained that Mason Locke Weems wrote his *Life of Washington* in 1800. In 1806 a greatly expanded fifth edition of the book appeared in which "the cherry tree anecdote and others equally apocryphal" first appeared.

The *World Book* says, "So far as we know, he did not chop down his father's cherry tree and then confess." *Compton's Pictured Encyclopedia* says, "Whether he performed such feats or not, he did live the normal life of a country boy." Also, this book presented a charming painting by Grant Wood entitled "Parson Weems' Fable." In it, a person is shown drawing back a curtain behind which stands a small George Washington holding an ax in front of a bent cherry tree while a reprimanding father stands by. The *Encyclopaedia Britannica* says, "Mason L. Weems' stories of hatchet and cherry tree and of young Washington's repugnance to fighting are apocryphal efforts to fill a manifest gap."

By now I was curious to see The Incident in its original form. The closest I could come was *Weems' George Washington* by Mark Van Doren. There, on pages 23 to 25, appeared The Incident just as we all remember it, along with others just as apocryphal. It is supposed to have occurred when George Washington was *six* years old. It must have been a small tree!

The final phase of my search consisted of looking at adult history books to see whether or not they included The Incident, and, if so, how they treated it. *Life of George Washington,* by Washington Irving, scorns it. *George Washington Himself,* by John C. Fitzpatrick, refers to them as "nonsensical stories." Marcus Cunliffe, in his *George Washington—Man and Monument*, says Weems was a "Victorian before the Victorian era." The incidents he coined were put into McGuffy's readers (none of which I could locate) and a book by Morris Heady. I found no book that treated the incident seriously.

I'm satisfied that George Washington did not chop down his father's cherry tree when he was six years old and then confess he "could not tell a lie." In their search, my students would likely conclude the same. We could then discuss what purpose this story served. For what reasons would people believe it?

Another interesting point to discuss would be how they (the class) felt about George before finding out The Incident isn't true, and how they felt about him afterward. What do you think of a boy who never told a lie? Is that possible? Personally, I dislike the goody-goody George presented to me when I was a child. Until I began this small investigation, I had never thought of him as a person. George Washington the "Man," and not the "Monument," interests me very much. So, I hope, will he interest my students.

For the most part, "study" within the nation-topic will be instituted through and nurtured by the use of firsthand historical literature. The few resources listed in the following short bibliography should be helpful to teachers in locating the kind of source material they might require either to spark questions or to support and sustain the process of resolving interesting questions and matters of doubt about the past. It is a brief, representative list of available primary source material in American history.

ANGLE, PAUL M. *The American Reader*. Greenwich, Conn.: Premier Books, Fawcett, 1958. (Paperback, five volumes: I—*New Continent and New Nation;* II—*The New Nation Grows;* III—*The Nation Divided;* IV—*Making of a World Power;* and V—*Uneasy World.*)

BOTKIN, B. A. *Lay My Burden Down: A Folk History of Slavery*. Chicago: The University of Chicago Press, 1961. (Paperback).

BROWN, RICHARD C. *The Human Side of American History*. Boston: Ginn, 1962. (Paperback).

COMMAGER, HENRY S. *America in Perspective*. New York: New American Library, 1947. (Paperback).

———— and MORRIS, RICHARD B. *The Spirit of 'Seventy-Six*. Indianapolis: Bobbs-Merrill, 1958.

———— and NEVINS, ALLAN. *The Heritage of America*. Boston: Little, Brown, 1949.

CROCKETT, DAVID. *Adventures of Davy Crockett, Told Mostly by Himself*. New York: Scribner's, 1955.

EISENSCHIML, OTTO and NEWMAN, RALPH. *Eyewitness: The Civil War as We Lived It.* New York: Universal Library, Grosset & Dunlap. (Paperback), 1960.

HAMILTON, CHARLES. *Cry of the Thunderbird: The American Indians' Own Story.* New York: Macmillan, 1950.

HESSELTINE, WILLIAM B., ed. *Three Against Lincoln: Mural Halstead Reports the Caucuses of 1860.* Baton Rouge: The Louisiana State University Press, 1960.

HART, ALBERT B. *American History Told by Contemporaries.* 5 vols. New York: Macmillan, 1897–1929.

JONES, KATHARINE M. *Heroines of Dixie.* Indianapolis: Bobbs-Merrill, 1955.

SHANNON, DAVID A. *The Great Depression.* Englewood Cliffs: Spectrum Books, Prentice-Hall, 1960. (Paperback).

WESTERMEIER, CLIFFORD P. *Trailing the Cowboy: His Life and Lore as Told by Frontier Journalists.* Caldwell, Ida.: Caxton Printers, 1955.

XIII

Then and There:
The History of the Far-Away

Why Study History?

The study of the Then and There is of particular importance for Americans: their past is *then and there*. As a former colony, America owes manners, morals, laws, language, literature, arts, and science to other times and places, and to understand these origins of American civilization, one must study the history of the far-away.

Not only is the past to be found *then and there,* the future for Americans and for all inhabitants of this planet may also depend on the ability to understand this history. Modern technology has made neighbors of Buddhists and Moslems, Christians and Hindus, Socialists and capitalists, Asians and Europeans, Africans and Polynesians. It is probably a vain hope to expect that all men will become Buddhists, Communists, or capitalists. They must learn to understand themselves and each other, to the extent that it is possible, if they are to survive and live together. The study of Then and There, Caere and Nineveh, Asoka and Baber, Paris and Bologna, Abu Bekr and St. Peter, Vishnu and Allah, Bacon and Galileo, Eric the Red and Cabeza de Vaca, provides some clues to understanding the variety of passions and beliefs to be found among the people of our planet.

One message of history is that neither progress nor survival is essential to human civilization. The study of history may not make men wise, but it makes freedom possible; an awareness of what men have been extends the possibility for choice regarding what men shall be. The study of Then and There is not primarily a moral enterprise that may lead to neighborliness; it is an intellectual adventure that may lead men to understand themselves and the possibilities of human destiny. For reasons of expediency and adventure, the study of Then and There is an essential aspect of social study in the elementary school.

This book is based on the notion that the acts of inquiry, search, and discovery provide some of the most authentic human adventures to which

237

men may aspire. History offers even more than the adventure of inquiry; it offers a view of other times that may be exciting in itself.

Historical inquiry, for example, may turn up poignant documents of another age, inducing a smile, wonder, or sadness. Consider the photographs in figures 1–4 of the trade book of the *Snow Venus*. (See insert following p. 240.)

In 1756 the *Snow Venus* set off from the West Indies for Africa and slaves. On April 7, 1756, the first slave was purchased. Designated man-boy, he was five feet tall and cost sixty gallons of rum. He may have died of the flux on October 12, 1756, or he may have been sold for forty-seven pounds, cash, on August 6, 1757. His fate is unknown—three pages of the trade book of the *Snow Venus* contain what information still exists. Similar relics of slavery carry many messages if one can learn to read them. The mortality log shows that one out of four slaves died on the trip. Why do you suppose so many died?

The *Aramaic Papyri of the Fifth Century* B.C., edited with translations and notes by A. Cowley, contains a contract between two neighbors regarding an addition to a house that one of the men wanted to construct. In this document, the men carefully stated the rights of each regarding the new structure. Many such contracts may be found in this interesting book; the men of that time followed the admonition to "put it in writing." Contracts, agreements, and disputes are fascinating clues to an ancient time.

Napoleon led a "romantic" life, full of triumph and disaster; many books tell about his victories and his Waterloo. What moved men to fight and die for "the little corporal"? The *Notebooks of Captain Coignet* contain intimate details of the life of the soldiers in the army of Napoleon. Coignet was in Russia, and he was at Waterloo. In books such as these, one can find records of the prosaic events that are essential to historic inquiry. They are of vital interest as human documents.

Probably the richest source of journals and records of great historical interest lies in the many works issued by the Hakluyt Society, an organization devoted to the translation and publication of documents of travel and discovery. Teachers can find in their publications the journals of Columbus, Cabot, and Vespucci, to mention only three. A good library will reserve thirty or forty feet of shelves for the works of the Hakluyt Society, with adventure, human interest, and historical significance in every volume.

Historical inquiry does more than bring students into contact with documents reporting day-to-day experience; ideas, conjecture, and debate are fascinating features of historical scholarship. Textbooks say that Columbus "discovered" America. But was he the first European to visit the Western Hemisphere? Considerable evidence indicates that the "Northmen," or the Vikings, explored New England, penetrating, possibly, to the Midwest. The Kensington Stone is an alleged document of that exploration. Regarded by some men as a hoax, and by others as an authentic record, it carries this message:

8 Swedes and 22 Norwegians on an exploration journey from Vinland westward. We had our camp by 2 rocky islets one day's journey north of this stone. We were out fishing one day. When we came home we found 10 men red with blood and dead. AVM [Ave Maria] save us from evil. We have 10 men by the sea to look after our ships, 14 days' journey from this island. Year 1362.[1]

This stone was found near Kensington, Minn., on November 8, 1898, and has been the subject of debate ever since. H. R. Holland, in his *The Kensington Stone,* contends that the stone is authentic; Erik Wahlgren, in his *The Kensington Stone: A Mystery Solved,* denies its authenticity. A class might find the practice of evaluating the merits of the two arguments useful experience in historical inquiry. There is no answer at the back of any book: the authenticity of the stone is still a matter of dispute.

The study of Then and There may bring a student into contact with interesting personal documents, exciting controversy, and a variety of stories, myths, legends, and epics that disclose something of the way of life, the fears, and the aspirations of bygone cultures. *King Arthur, Roland, The Arabian Nights,* and *The Iliad* are not historical writings, but indirectly, in the details of the stories, one can discover clues to the characters of their protagonists. *The Epic of Gilgamesh* is one such tale of men and God; it was written about 5,000 years ago on cuneiform tablets. Here is a portion of the story:

You know the city Shurrupak, it stands on the banks of Euphrates? That city grew old and the gods that were in it were old. There was Anu, lord of the firmament, their father, and warrior Enlil their counsellor, Ninurta the helper, and Ennugi watcher over canals; and with them also was Ea. In those days the world teemed, the people multiplied, the world bellowed like a wild bull, and the great god was aroused by the clamour. Enlil heard the clamour and he said to the gods in council, "The uproar of mankind is intolerable and sleep is no longer possible by reason of the babel." So the gods in their hearts were moved to let loose the deluge; but my lord Ea warned me in a dream. He whispered their words to my house of reeds, "Reed-house, reed-house! Wall, O wall, hearken reed-house, wall reflect; O man of Shurrupak, son of Ubara-Tutu; tear down your house and build a boat, abandon possessions and look for life, despise worldly goods and save your soul alive. Tear down your house, I say, and build a boat. These are the measurements of the barque as you shall build her: let her beam equal her length, let her deck be roofed like the vault that covers the abyss; then take up into the boat the seed of all living creatures."

[1] From Erik Wahlgren, *The Kensington Stone, A Mystery Solved* (Madison: The University of Wisconsin Press, 1958), p. 3.

When I had understood I said to my Lord, "Behold, what you have commanded I will honour and perform, but how shall I answer the people, the
city, the elders?" Then Ea opened his mouth and said to me, his servant, "Tell
them this: I have learnt that Enlil is wrathful against me, I dare no longer walk
in his land nor live in his city; I will go down to the Gulf to dwell with Ea my
lord. But on you he will rain down abundance, rare fish and shy wildfowl, a rich
harvest-tide. In the evening the rider of the storm will bring you wheat in tor-
rents."

In the first light of dawn all my household gathered round me, the children
brought pitch and the men whatever was necessary. On the fifth day I laid the
keel and the ribs, then I made fast the planking. The ground-space was one acre,
each side of the deck measured one hundred and twenty cubits, making a square.
I built six decks below, seven in all, I divided them into nine sections with bulk-
heads between. I drove in wedges where needed, I saw to the punt-poles, and
laid in supplies. The carriers brought oil in baskets, I poured pitch into the furnace
and asphalt and oil; more oil was consumed in caulking, and more again the
master of the boat took into his stores. I slaughtered bullocks for the people and
every day I killed sheep. I gave the ship-wrights wine to drink as though it were
river water, raw wine and red wine and oil and white wine. There was feasting
then as there is at any time of the New Year's festival; I myself anointed my head.
On the seventh day the boat was complete.

Then was the launching full of difficulty; there was shifting of ballast above
and below till two thirds was submerged. I loaded into her all that I had of gold
and of living things, my family, my kin, the beasts of the field both wild and
tame, and all the craftsmen. I sent them on board, for the time that Shamash had
ordained was already fulfilled when he said, "In the evening, when the rider of
the storm sends down the destroying rain, enter the boat and batten her down."
The time was fulfilled, the evening came, the rider of the storm sent down the
rain. I looked out at the weather and it was terrible, so I too boarded the boat
and battened her down. All was now complete, the battening and the caulking;
so I handed the tiller to Puzur-Amurri the steersman, with the navigation and the
care of the whole boat.

With the first light of dawn a black cloud came from the horizon; it thundered
within where Adad, lord of the storm, was riding. In front over hill and plain
Shullat and Hanish, heralds of the storm, led on. Then the gods of the abyss
rose up; Nergal pulled out the dams of the nether waters, Ninurta the war-lord
threw down the dykes, and the seven judges of hell, the Annunaki, raised their
torches, lighting the land with their livid flame. A stupor of despair went up to
heaven when the god of the storm turned daylight to darkness, when he smashed
the land like a cup. One whole day the tempest raged gathering fury as it went,
it poured over the people like the tides of battle; a man could not see his brother
nor the people be seen from heaven. Even the gods were terrified at the flood,
they fled to the highest heaven, the firmament of Anu; they crouched against the
walls, cowering like curs. Then Ishtar the sweet-voiced Queen of Heaven cried
out like a woman in travail: "Alas the days of old are turned to dust because I
commanded evil; why did I command this evil in the council of all the gods? I
commanded wars to destroy the people, but are they not my people, for I

brought them forth. Now like the spawn of fish they float in the ocean." The great gods of heaven and of hell wept, they covered their mouths.

For six days and six nights the winds blew, torrent and tempest and flood overwhelmed the world, tempest and flood raged together like warring hosts. When the seventh day dawned the storm from the south subsided, the sea grew calm, the flood was stilled; I looked at the face of the world and there was silence, all mankind was turned to clay. The surface of the sea stretched as flat as a rooftop; I opened a hatch and the light fell on my face. Then I bowed low, I sat down and I wept, the tears streamed down my face, for on every side was the waste of water. I looked for land in vain, but fourteen leagues distant there appeared a mountain, and there the boat grounded; on the mountain of Nisir the boat held fast, she held fast and did not budge. One day she held, and a second day on the mountain of Nisir she held fast and did not budge. A third day and a fourth day she held fast on the mountain and did not budge; a fifth day and a sixth day she held fast on the mountain. When the seventh day dawned I loosed a dove and let her go. She flew away, but finding no resting-place she returned. Then I loosed a swallow, and she flew away but finding no resting-place she returned. I loosed a raven, she saw that the waters had retreated, she ate, she flew around, she cawed, and she did not come back. Then I threw everything open to the four winds, I made a sacrifice and poured out a libation on the mountain top. Seven and again seven cauldrons I set up on their stands, I heaped up wood and cane and cedar and myrtle. When the gods smelled the sweet savour, they gathered like flies over the sacrifice. Then, at last, Ishtar also came, she lifted her necklace with the jewels of heaven that once Anu had made to please her. "O you gods here present, by the lapis lazuli round my neck I shall remember these days as I remember the jewels of my throat; these last days I shall not forget. Let all the gods gather round the sacrifice, except Enlil. He shall not approach this offering, for without reflection he brought the flood; he consigned my people to destruction."[2]

The study of history involves the scrutiny of documents; the reading of journals, letters, and epics; and the examination of the arguments and ideas that men have proposed regarding the affairs of Then and There. In this activity, students may explore their skill at inquiry and experience a measure of human contact with other times and cultures. They may also discover the stuff of human knowledge. This knowledge precludes ultimate certitude, but it does demonstrate the validity of a reason that establishes its tentative truths on the basis of that which can be tested by an appropriate appeal to experience. The purpose of the study of the Then and There is to provide this human contact and to promote this experience with human knowing.

The responsibility of teaching something of the history and something of the "historying" of far-away places is one of the most difficult tasks faced

[2] From N. K. Sandars (trans.), *The Epic of Gilgamesh* (Maryland: Penguin, 1960), pp. 105–109. Reprinted by permission of the publisher.

by teachers of social studies. There are many technical problems: the search for, and acquisition of, relevant journals and documents, and speculation are not easy for a classroom teacher. There are intellectual problems: many teachers know little about the nature of historical knowledge or historical inquiry. There are a number of moral problems: in many districts, students are directed to read books; they are not expected to learn how to study history, nor is a teacher expected to demonstrate and nurture the capacity to study history. Any teacher, in meeting the challenge of teaching, will not only provide intellectual excitement for his students, but will be engaged in a profound adventure himself.

The following pages of this chapter will identify some basic features of historical knowledge; discuss some likely sources of primary documents of use in historical inquiry; discuss some interesting questions; and, finally, illustrate some approaches to the problem of teaching history.

What Is History?

The nature of history constitutes a profound question, discussed in the writings of E. H. Carr, Carl Becker, R. G. Collingwood, José Ortega y Gasset, and others. Each of them has devoted a great deal of attention to the question. Until he is fairly clear about his answer to this question, no teacher can hope to deal effectively with the challenge of teaching history.

Competent answers depend on a knowledge of the factors involved. It is not enough to say that history is concerned with events which have occurred in the past. One must also know that:

1. *All knowledge of these past events is inferred.*

What went on in the homes, in the streets, in the schools, on the battlefields, in the inns, and in the churches of ancient cultures in distant places is largely unknown. The records in history books are the guesses and impressions formulated by particular men, based on their observations of epic sagas, documents, journals, and the speculations of other men. Many school textbooks contain only parochial conjecture, treated as ultimate truth.

2. *All knowledge of the causes of events is inferred.*

One cannot see the *cause of an event* nor the *spirit of a time;* cause and spirit are explanatory notions that help to account for what can be seen. What can be seen are the words that have been written, the pictures that have been drawn, the buildings that still stand, and the artifacts that have survived. The notions of cause and spirit were invented to explain what can now be seen. More than thirty causes for the decline and fall of Rome have been put forth; all may be helpful, to some extent, in understanding

Roman civilization. Different notions concerning the causes of the American Civil War have been proposed; perhaps all of these, too, have some use. Some person must invent a notion of cause, and then seek to find out, on the basis of an appeal to experience, whether or not the notion is of some use. A notion of cause is of use only if it helps to account for the events that are being investigated.

3. *All knowledge of processes that are thought to go on within individuals or societies is inferred.*

Just as one cannot see *desire,* although one can infer it, he cannot see *growth, decline, failing morals, family disintegration,* or the *"rising specter of Communism."* None of these processes can be directly observed with the senses. These notions are invented to explain what can be observed. The problem for the student of history is to discover whether or not a notion is useful: does it help explain what can be observed? Are there other explanations?

4. *The past is always investigated in the light of some present interest.*

The past is infinite: men in many places and times have painted pictures, written poetry, made pots, married, constructed houses, studied plants, experimented with chemicals, worshiped gods, and gathered in groups and sought to kill each other. A historian engaging in history ignores a wide variety of events, selecting only certain events for exploration. Historical interests change: the history of Then and There is constantly being rewritten.

5. *The histories men write are influenced by the values they hold.*

The histories of Tudor England written by Tudor historians are very different from the histories of Tudor times written by later and modern historians. The Tudor historians tried to make Henry VII, the first Tudor king, legitimate, at the expense of Richard III, whom they depicted as a monster. Some later historians have tried to make Richard III a hero, and Henry VII, a villain. This is a gross case of biased historical writing, but there is always conflict in the accounts of controversial events. Consider the many views of the Reformation, the American Civil War, the Spanish-American War, and the treatment of the American Indians by the United States government. The writing of history is always an intensely personal activity.

6. *History is a search for tentative truths.*

The interpretations of past events proposed by historians are tentative truths. These truths can be constantly evaluated in the light of experience: they can be modified or abandoned. History is an illustration of the possibility for rationality; men can know on the basis of their capacity to invent explanatory notions and to test them in an appeal to experience. Reason can replace faith and custom as a basis of truth and knowledge.

7. *One who reads a history is obligated to rethink the historian's argument, test his facts, examine his inferences, and appraise the concepts that the writer has used.*

The historian is not just recounting past events; he is revealing himself, his interests, his willingness to test his ideas empirically, and his attitude toward his readers. Historical writing can be sorted into two general types: *personal writing* and *oracular writing.* Personal historical writing reports the thoughts and observations of a man who has engaged in inquiry and now shares his adventure. Oracular writing reports the observations of an "omniscient being" who only "relates the simple truth." Many school textbooks are oracular; most responsible historical writing is personal.

What is history? The teacher's answer to this question will determine what he teaches. History is an impression of past events. Students in school should be helped to form and criticize their own impressions of the past, and they should be given opportunities to read and evaluate the impressions of past events formulated by others. Reading history and "doing history" are complementary activities: each one facilitates skill at doing the other.

Historical Problems and Social Residue

Historical inquiry involves working with problems. A problem is a question that a student, on his own authority, based on his own thought and observation, poses to himself and answers or postpones answering. A question is not a problem if it is directed toward another person or if the answer to the question is what the other person said.

Students should be encouraged to identify interesting problems. An effective teacher of social inquiry can then guide his students in the pursuit and capture of appropriate epic stories, legal contracts, photographs, and journals, and demonstrate the manner in which scrutiny of these materials may lead the student to a solution to his problem.

A teacher of historical inquiry must know his sources. The nearest large library contains scholarly journals, standard source books, collections of letters, records, legal contracts, and the works of the great writers of antiquity; and the teacher should become familiar with them.

Contemporary Records

Bills, advertisements, contracts, journals, notebooks, and letters are useful contemporary records that survive from both ancient and modern cultures. The Hakluyt Society, as already pointed out, has published many, many volumes of contemporary records of travel and exploration. One of their recent volumes is titled *The Travels of Ibn Battuta, 1325–1354*. Marco Polo, Captain James Cook, and Alvar Nuñez Cabeza de Vaca were literate men who made extensive records of what they experienced. In 1527 Cabeza de Vaca was in Cuba; he was a member of an expedition commanded by Governor Panfilo de Narváez, which was directed to conquer and govern all the land between the Rio Grande and the Cape of Florida. The ships were being provisioned. One day, Cabeza de Vaca went ashore:

An hour after I left, the sea began to rise ominously and the north wind blow so violently that the two boats would not have dared come near land even if the head wind had not already made landing impossible. All hands labored severely under a heavy fall of water that entire day and until dark on Sunday. By then the rain and tempest had stepped up until there was as much agitation in the town as at sea. All the houses and churches went down. We had to walk seven or eight together, locking arms, to keep from being blown away. Walking in the woods gave us as much fear as the tumbling houses, for the trees were falling, too, and could have killed us. We wandered all night in this raging tempest without finding any place we could linger as long as half an hour in safety. Particularly from midnight on, we heard a great roaring and the sound of many voices, of little bells, also flutes, tambourines, and other instruments, most of which lasted till morning, when the storm ceased. Nothing so terrible as this [hurricane] had been seen in these parts before. I drew up an authenticated account of it and sent it back to Your Majesty.[3]

This day-by-day account of Cabeza de Vaca's activities presents a vivid description of the southeastern United States in the early sixteenth century. He describes the Indians; he recounts the enormous problems encountered by the explorers. The expedition was a total failure; four out of three hundred men survived. This exciting and useful document illustrates one kind of contemporary record that can easily be found in a library.

Another easily found contemporary record is a collection of letters. The Paston Letters are useful for the study of English manners and customs during the fifteenth century. *The Letters and Papers Relating to the Irish Rebellion,* edited by James Hogan, introduce the reader to the conflict between Great Britain and Ireland. These early seventeenth-century letters provide some insight into an antagonism that has endured to our own time. The *Letters of Pontius Pilate,* edited by W. P. Crozier, provide some interesting insights into the character of a famous figure in Christian history. He says:

[3] CABEZA DE VACA, *Adventures in the Unknown Interior of America,* trans. Cyclone Covey (New York: Collier, 1961), pp. 28–29.

Scratch a priest and find an autocrat. All the world over, if a man says that he will use his own intelligence about things divine, the priests prick up their ears and feel their knives. If he goes further and tells his fellow-men that they also are entitled to use their own intelligence—off with his head and there's an end of it![4]

Read a few of these letters, and many possible uses for them will become apparent.[5]

Contemporary Public Reports

Newspapers provide various social documents: works of fiction, advertisements, statements of opinion, and news dispatches. The news dispatches are important contemporary records, which, through microfilm, can be made available to students in school.

Memoirs and autobiographies are often useful personal documents. Many political, military, and literary figures have written interesting and lucid personal accounts that may be of some use to a student of history.

A number of memoirs reporting experiences in World War II have been published. Admiral Karl Doenitz, in charge of U-boat warfare for the Germans, discusses, in his *Memoirs,* the various military problems that he confronted. At one time, the race for an effective radar system was an important feature of the English war effort. On the basis of the experience of his U-boats, Doenitz decided that the English had finally perfected a system of finding submarines:

From the beginning of 1942 we observed that the British had strengthened their air patrols over the Bay of Biscay and were using faster aircraft. We presumed that attacks would occur on bright, moonlight nights, but in fact there then occurred an increasing number of surprise attacks by day. It was difficult to believe that these had been due to slackness on the part of the lookout, who ought to have spotted the aircraft sooner; the suspicion therefore grew that the British aircraft, which always launched their attacks out of the sun or out of cloud, must have located the U-boat beforehand and have taken up position for the delivery of their attack while still out of sight from the target. Our suspicions were confirmed in June, when for the first time U-boats in the Bay of Biscay were attacked from the air on a dark night. A searchlight had suddenly been flashed on at a range of 1,000 to 2,000 yards and had at once picked up the U-boat. The bombs followed immediately. In June three boats on their way to their operational areas were severely damaged in the Bay of Biscay in this

[4] From *Letters of Pontius Pilate,* ed. W. P. Crozier (London: Jonathan Cape, 1928), pp. 159-160.

[5] See Vincent Rogers, "Using Source Material with Children," in Part IV. The excerpt suggests some possible uses to which letters and similar documents may be put in the elementary classroom.

manner, rendered incapable of submerging and compelled to return to base.[6]

Filled with detailed reports on the conduct of war, these memoirs may be relevant to a number of the great debates that have developed regarding political and military decisions made during the war.

Contemporary historical writing provides another sort of document for students to examine. Some of the most famous contemporary historical writers of the Then and There are Herodotus, Thucydides, Tacitus, Bede, Voltaire, and Thiers—all worth exploring.

Government Documents

Census data, financial records, and other statistical information are available for Western European countries. A little effort will turn up considerable information from most of the non-Western countries.

Laws and regulations are another source of data regarding Then and There. The Code of Hammurabi, the Magna Charta, and the "laws of the barbarians" provide fundamental insight into the societies that produced these expressions of political and social regulation.

The "laws of the barbarians" were the laws of the Burgundians, Franks, Lombards, and West Goths. These "legal" procedures were the customs of the various peoples who gained ascendancy in Europe after the decline of Rome. Their laws, some of which survived through the Middle Ages, provide insight into the character of sixth-century European society. German law, for example, did not formulate procedures for weighing evidence and reaching reasoned decision. Instead, three alternatives were available when disputes arose:

1. Compurgation. A man could swear that he was telling the truth and get other men of his own class to swear that they believed that he was telling the truth. It was thought that divine vengeance would be visited upon any who swore falsely.
2. Wager of battle. Parties to a dispute could meet in combat. It was supposed that a just God would grant victory to the truthful.
3. Ordeal. A man could thrust his arm into hot water; or he could carry a piece of hot iron for some distance. If, at the end of three days, he showed no ill effects, then the case was decided in his favor. God, it was thought, would always establish the truth.

An examination of the laws by which men live tells much about the character and quality of their life.

[6] ADMIRAL KARL DOENITZ, *Memoirs,* trans. R. H. Stevens (Cleveland: World, 1948), p. 232.

Expressions of Opinion

Pamphlets, editorials, and speeches are useful sources of political and social opinions. The *Communist Manifesto* is one famous and provocative illustration of this sort of writing.

To some extent, school textbooks, because of the obvious, often sentimentalized, bias of their writing, might best be regarded as bland editorials. Here is a typical example of that style of textbook writing:

A Negro who had been giving trouble in a community might awake some night to find a ghost-clad figure standing by his bed. Or again a region might gain a reputation for ghosts if one of the white-robed members sat silently in a grave yard or by the roadside. Sometimes, when on a visit, the Klansmen would ask for water and then empty several buckets into bags concealed beneath their robes. If these attempts to frighten them did not change the Negroes, the Klansmen would resort to whippings and in extreme cases to killings. The organization helped the South at a difficult time, but when the Congress declared it illegal, it was disbanded.[7]

This selection from a Mississippi social-studies textbook for children illustrates the basic qualities of much social-studies textbook writing:
1. Statements of opinion are reported as if they were statements of fact about which there could be little dispute.
2. One perspective is presented, and the conflicts and issues are ignored.
3. The evidence that led the author to his judgment is not mentioned or discussed.
4. In general, social-studies textbooks present opinions and selected facts, as if they were the secure and only possible way in which to think about the situations and events being reported.[8]

Another source of opinion that sheds light on the period and the society that produced it is found in the more-or-less-philosophical writings that deal with men, morals, and the social order. Carefully selected portions of the writings of Plato might be examined to see what light they shed on Greek society. *The Apology* might be examined in order to identify the legal procedures of the Greeks. The issues explored in *The Apology* are relevant to contemporary society: their implications might be explored.

Opinions that were expressed and condemned may also be of some interest. Gracián was a seventeenth-century Spanish priest and university teacher. His writings came to the attention of the Church, and he was for-

[7] RICHARD AUBREY MCLEMORE, PH.D., and NANNIE PITTS MCLEMORE, M.A., *Mississippi Through Four Centuries* (Chicago: Laidlaw Brothers, 1945), pp. 247–248.

[8] See Martin Mayer, "The Trouble with Textbooks," in Part IV. This article deals critically with the blandness and the misinformation that are commonplace in textbooks for children.

bidden to write again. He was removed from the position of university rector. Finally, he was banished to the provinces, where he died. A letter was sent to the church official who was responsible for Gracián: "Watch him, keep him in sight, at unexpected moments look into his cell and his papers and allow him nothing under lock and key therein."[9]

One of Gracián's most famous works is called *A Truthtelling Manual and the Art of Worldly Wisdom*. It is interesting to speculate on why the Church sought to stop him from writing. Here is a sample of his thought:

Half the world laughs at the other half, even though the lot are fools. Either everything is good, or everything is bad, depending on the vote; what one sues, another pursues. An insufferable fool, he who wishes the universe regulated according to his plans. Bliss does not derive from the pleasure of any one man: for there are as many minds, as there are heads, and as different; there is no weakness without its admirer, so be not discomfited because your ways displease some, for they will not fail to be pleasing to others; nor let their approval of them make you vain, for still others will condemn them. Proper satisfaction may be taken only in the approval of men of authority, and by those who have standing in their fields. Do not live by the sanction of any one voice, or of any one custom, or of any single period.[10]

Fiction, Poetry, Epic, Myths, and Dramas

Fiction affords some insight into an author's hopes and fears, and it provides some description of prosaic details in everyday life. Something of the way of life of the ancient Sumerians may be inferred from *The Epic of Gilgamesh:* they regarded a flood of the region between two rivers as an attempt of the gods to destroy humankind—they had a very narrow spacial sense. Similarly, the fable of "Chicken Little" also misinterprets a personal or local tragedy for a world cataclysm.

Poetry is national expression; a poet must absorb, illuminate, and transcend the culture of which he is a part. Certainly, these two seventeenth-century writers live in different worlds:

> Now the swinging bridge
> Is quieted
> With creepers
> Like our tendrilled life.

> For a lovely bowl
> Let us arrange these
> Flowers . . .
> Since there is no rice.

[9] BALTASAR GRACIÁN, *A Truthtelling Manual and the Art of Worldly Wisdom* (Springfield, Ill.: Charles C. Thomas, 1934), p. 6.

[10] *Ibid.*, pp. 96–97.

White cloud of mist
Above white
Cherry-blossoms
Down-shining mountain.[11]

Shall I compare thee to a summer's day?
Thou art more lovely and more temperate:
Rough winds do shake the darling buds of May,
And summer's lease hath all too short a date;
Sometime too hot the eye of heaven shines,
And often is his gold complexion dimm'd;
And every fair from fair sometime declines,
By chance or nature's changing course untrimm'd:
But thy eternal summer shall not fade
Nor lose possession of that fair thou ow'st;
Nor shall Death brag thou wand'rest in his shade,
When in eternal lines to time thou grow'st;
    So long as men can breathe or eyes can see,
    So long lives this, and this gives life to thee.[12]

Both Basho and Shakespeare make much reference to the sense of sight. Huizinga, in his discussion of the late Middle Ages, relates a preoccupation with the sense of sight to the growth of science. The prescientific mode of thought regarded the sights and sounds of common experience as mere illustrations of fixed conceptions. The scientific mode of thought presupposes that words and conceptions are convenient ways to talk about what can be seen: "One of the fundamental traits of the mind of the declining Middle Ages is the predominance of the sense of sight, a predominance which is closely connected with the atrophy of thought."[13] By Shakespeare's time, the atrophy of traditional ways of thinking had led to the development of new scientific ways of thought. In his poetry, Shakespeare illustrates both visual orientation and predisposition to abstract, analyze, compare, and dramatize. A scientist is foremost an agent in the world: in a paraphrase of the words of Francis Bacon, he must "put nature to the test." Basho's poetry directs our thoughts and appreciation to what the eyes may encounter. His concern seems not to be to change or understand but to appreciate aesthetically the life that is given. Shakespeare, in this poem and others, appears to be a man of the world, a man of affairs in a world of innovation and scientific adventure. Basho, here and elsewhere, appears to accept life as he finds it and to discover what beauty may be found.

[11] From BASHO, *Japanese Haiku* (New York: Peter Pauper, 1955). By permission of the publisher.
[12] From William A. Nielson (ed.), *The Complete Plays and Poems of William Shakespeare* (Boston: Houghton Mifflin Company, 1942), p. 1374. By permission of the publisher.
[13] JOHAN HUIZINGA, *The Waning of the Middle Ages* (Garden City: Doubleday Anchor Books, Doubleday, 1954), p. 284.

Art, Architecture, and Artifact

Museums and books are rich sources of the creations of bygone times. An examination of twenty or so fourteenth-century Italian paintings will provide a view of the world and of man and his destiny that is totally different from the creations in sixteenth-century paintings. If one studies the differences, he is induced to speculate about the causes of these divergent styles of paintings and conceptions of social order. In the minor details, clues may be found that may be more useful than the manifest "message" and purpose of a work of art.

The artifact is probably one of the most useful of historical sources, and often one of the most aesthetically interesting. Etruscan art, for example, provides some insight into the role that women may have played in that society. At the same time, some of the Etruscan work is genuinely lovely.

Historical Writing

An obvious source of fact and conjecture is found in the writings of other students of the Then and There; recent thought and investigation are reported in the historical journals. *The Saturday Review* regularly surveys recent historical works; this popular journal is a useful source of information regarding contemporary historical scholarship. Books, such as Edward Schafer's *The Golden Peaches of Samarkand* and Kwang-chih Chang's *The Archaeology of Ancient China,* will be useful sources of information dealing with ancient China. Indeed, there is no culture or civilization that has not claimed the devoted attention of scholars, and their studies may prove very useful to historical inquiry in the classroom. Naturally, these books are not to be read through from cover to cover, or chapter to chapter; they are to be examined in the light of specific questions formulated by students.[14]

The sources of historical inquiry are infinite, but none of them is of any use until a student, in school or professionally, has invented a problem that transforms a work of art or a legal record into an object, the examination of which will lead to a solution of the problem.

Problems of Then and There

Three ways to approach historical inquiry in the elementary-school classroom are: (1) examine the commonplace; (2) examine artifacts; and (3) study situations.

[14] See R. G. Collingwood, "The Question," in Part IV. There Collingwood discusses some of the ramifications of the theory of historical method.

The Commonplace

Probably the easiest approach to historical study is to pose interesting questions about commonplace customs and ideas. The approach is not only easy, it is important. By asking historical questions about commonplace ideas, one will discover something of the antecedents of his own society.

The historical question is simply this: What is the origin of this custom, or attitude, or institution? The task of instruction is to get students to notice a commonplace feature of daily life, to pose careful historical questions about it, and to seek answers to their questions by observing appropriate documents and records.

WORDS IN COMMON USE

There are many fascinating words in the English language. To seek the origins and initial uses of such words is to engage in inquiry. Some words come from the Then and There, others have been invented recently. How, and on what basis, can one study the origins of words? A common reference work, perhaps Eric Partridge's *Origins,* is a useful start, but further inquiry must be pursued if students are to formulate an account of the way in which a particular word came into the language. Ancient writings, documents, and reports will have to be pursued with specific questions in mind.

The word "admiral" is a common English word—most children will have a fair idea of what it means. When did this word come into the language? Who was the first "admiral"? When was the first English use of this word? "Admir" is a variation of "emir" or "amir"; "emir," in Arabic, means "commander." The Arabic for "commander of the sea" is "amir-al-bahor." The English "admiral" is a shortened form of the Arabic word. What is the earliest date that this word could be used in English? What are likely documents in which to investigate the use of this word?

There is a multitude of words with interesting origins. The essential problem of inquiry is simply to be able to notice a word and pose a question about it. Here are some words that might be interesting to explore:

radar	pants	silly
maverick	boycott	jerkwater
hello	circus	leatherneck
jaywalker	licorice	Queen (in chess)
ok	dollar	science

The number of words that may be explored is enormous. Scientific words have interesting origins; so do words connected with business. And the jargon words that are associated with specialized social behavior are a rich source of modest historical inquiry.

CUSTOMS

Many of the customs practiced by students have origins and an antiquity of which the students are unaware. Christmas, for example, occupies much time in the elementary school. Often, the books that relate Christmas customs do not ask or answer historical questions. Some of the more interesting historical questions are:

1. When, and under what circumstances was Christmas first celebrated as a Christian holiday?
2. The celebration of Christmas had a beginning; what was that beginning? What conjectures can the class invent, test, and explore? What are the teacher's guesses, or those of the students, regarding the century in which Christmas was first celebrated? How could one test these guesses?
3. Why is Christmas celebrated on December 25th rather than December 21st?

There are many interesting documents that can be consulted in the pursuit of solutions of these problems. An extraordinary answer can be found in fourth-century papal encyclicals.

Similar questions can be asked about any of the following customs or attitudes:

Easter
Clapping to show approval
Marriage as a religious ceremony
Sunday
Men standing up when a lady walks into a room
The notion that woman's place is in the home.

The marriage ceremony, for example, is an interesting social occasion. Some marriages are secular, performed by civil authorities; some marriages in Christian societies have always been secular (read, for example, "The Wife of Bath's Tale" in Chaucer's *Canterbury Tales*). Was there a time in Christian societies when marriage was an entirely secular affair? The surprise answer to this question is "yes." Marriage became a religious concern only relatively recently in the history of Western Europe. Why and when did marriage become, for many people, a relationship that required the sanction of religious authority?

Various answers to the above question can be found that may prove interesting to students. How would a marriage ceremony be performed in Europe in the ninth century? What would happen on this secular occasion? What change in ceremony would have occurred one hundred years later? And another hundred years later? In seeking to answer these questions through the pursuit of relevant documents, students will not only engage in history, but will discover their own cultural heritage.

INSTITUTIONS

Social institutions—such as schools, cities, mayors, police, sheriffs, marshals, juries, grand juries, and hospitals—have antiquities that are fascinating to explore. Select any one of them, and the class will be led to discover the origins Then and There, of basic features of contemporary social organizations.

For example, most students have probably heard of a *grand jury;* with the help of TV, mystery fiction, and newspaper headlines, they may have some notion of the functions of a *grand jury.*

1. Why was the institution of the *grand jury* devised?
2. When was the first grand jury convened?
3. Is it a Roman invention?
4. Is it a Greek legal institution?
5. Did this useful social instrument come from the Arabs?

How can a student be helped to seek answers to such questions by confronting documents rather than by asking an authority to answer them for him? The use of standard source books for historical study will provide the experience of inquiry. Although the trail may have been explored before, the student will be on it for the first time. In seeking an answer to the question about juries, J. C. Ayer's *A Source Book of Ancient History,* A. Ogg's *A Source Book for Medieval History,* and J. T. Shotwell's *Records of Civilizations* may help. As a result of examining documents, students may formulate answers to the questions listed. They can check their answers with the ideas of other students, and they can seek to check their ideas by a further scrutiny of other materials.

PLACE NAMES

Names of cities, rivers, seas, and oceans are a record of people and events. The enduring name is often one of many; names and naming generate much excitement.[15]

1. *America.* How and why did this name come into the English language? Why not "Vinland," as some say the Vikings called it?
2. *The Tyrrhenian Sea.* What is the source of this name? Was there a time when this sea had another name?
3. *England.* When did England become "England"? What did the Romans call England?
4. *Nazareth*—a great name in Christian history. But what was Nazareth? A city? A region? Does anyone know?

Where did the following names come from? *Tokyo? Lima? Nineveh? Babylon?* The *Po?* The *Atlantic?* The *Pacific?* The *Red Sea?* The *Indian*

[15] See, for example, George R. Stewart, *Names on the Land* (New York: Random House, 1945).

Ocean? A study of maps will answer some of these questions. William R. Shepherd's *Historical Atlas* is one useful source of maps that have been made at various times and places. Many museums also have collections of interesting maps.

Contemporary records may also have to be consulted in the search for names. For example, according to Herodotus, some Lydians migrated to the Italian peninsula. These Lydians named themselves after their leader, Tyrrhenos. The Tyrrhenians were the Etruscans; the Etruscans were a maritime power in competition with the Phoenicians. Their portion of the Mediterranean was called the Tyrrhenian Sea.

BELIEFS

Children come to school with attitudes and beliefs regarding dating, dress, the purpose of life, the proper role and status of women, the proper relationship between parents and children, the importance of opinion.

To some extent, the articulated beliefs and opinions held by children can be explored historically. The purpose is not to discover why the child holds a particular belief; it is to discover how and why this belief has been held at different times and places.

It is a common belief among most young people in the United States today that each person should choose his own mate and that romantic love should be the basis of marriage. This attitude is regarded as bizarre by many Western and non-Western people today. How did this attitude toward personal selection in marriage develop? Many Europeans have argued that marriage and love are not compatible. Certainly, the institution of marriage is suffering from several difficulties. Perhaps inquiry into the antecedents of present beliefs might help young people to gain some insight into the character of the modern institution of marriage. T. Wright's *A History of Domestic Manners* may be of some use in pursuing this question, as may G. E. Howard's *A History of Matrimonial Institutions*. These are very old books, but they will prove interesting. G. Rattray Taylor's book, *Sex in History,* in spite of its somewhat lurid title is full of material that may help teachers and students form answers to these questions. This book has a particularly good bibliography.

The study that begins with the commonplace may take students into distant times and places; comprising more than adventurous inquiry, such a study will help students develop rational insight into their own present circumstances.

Artifacts

An artifact may initiate study simply by being in the classroom. A painting, a weapon, a photograph, a coin, a pot, or a statue may induce curiosity.

Curiosity, expressed in questions, is the beginning of study. When was the coin made? How was the weapon used? If students seek to answer their questions by scrutinizing the object, then they are beginning to study.

For example, the painting in figure 5 is an interesting, more or less realistic painting. One might ask the following questions about it:
1. What is happening in the picture?
2. In what country is this vendor selling his wares?
3. What is the earliest date on which the painting could have been made?
4. What conjectures might one make about the character and the life of the woman? Of the vendor?

To some extent, a work of art is a portrait of a culture; an artist, in his work, represents his conception of life and the human situation. In our contemporary, urban, complex, materialistic, "other-directed" culture, it is not surprising to find artists portraying flat, incomprehensible patterns of color; life itself, to many, is a flat, incomprehensible pattern.

Compare the painting in figure 5 with the painting in figure 6. The second painting is less realistic; the figures seem awkward, and the background is crude and childlike. The face seems very realistic; the painter could have painted the background with greater detail if he had wished to do so. Similar questions can be asked about this painting:
1. What is happening in the picture?
2. In what country is this action taking place?
3. What is the earliest date on which this picture might have been made?
4. What conjectures can one make about the character and the life of the figures in the picture?
5. Imagine their children, their wives, their sisters; what was their daily life?
6. How might such conjectures be checked?

The examination of artifacts, the effort to date them, relate them to a particular culture, formulate notions about the society that produced them, and checking these formulations is to engage in history.

Museums and libraries are full of artifacts which can be examined and studied. The art of such study is the ability to devise interesting questions concerning the origin, use, and significance of the object. This art can only be developed with practice; students will get this practice only if their teachers discover the many resources provided by museums and libraries and bring to their classroom appropriate objects for study.

Situations

With the commonplace and with artifacts, study begins with the examination of a specific object or notion. Noticing a real coin or a word can lead to historical investigation. The study of "situations," however, begins somewhat differently.

The study of situations begins with acquainting oneself with the facts and inferences that relate events that have occurred in the past. The inquiry regarding the Spartans[16] began with reading the familiar textbook accounts of Then and There. A question arose as a result of thinking about the available information.

Let us explore, by way of illustration, the facts and inferences related to the migrations that populated the Western Hemisphere. The hemisphere gets its culture and all of its people from Then and There. Consider the following questions:

1. Who were the first Americans?
2. Where did they come from?
3. When did they come?
4. How did they get here?
5. Did they float across the Pacific?
6. Did they flee from the "lost continent" of Mu?
7. Did they sail in open boats from Spain?
8. Were they immigrants from China?
9. Did they walk across the Bering Strait?

Most elementary-school textbooks will report the accepted conjectures: Asian migrants crossed the Bering Strait; some settled in Alaska, others moved south; they were nomadic cave dwellers with a very low level of technology. Examine any convenient elementary-school social-studies textbook dealing with this momentous migration, and it will probably give just such information.

What are the facts and what are the inferences in such stories? A statement of fact affirms an observation; a statement of inference reports a thought. No one saw this migration; there can be no report of a direct observation of it. On what facts are these conjectures based? How can one know about that ancient migration from Asia?

The obligation of a social-studies teacher is not just to affirm aloud or through the text that Asians migrated across the Bering Strait 1,000 years ago, or 10,000 years ago, or 25,000 years ago, or 37,000 years ago. The problem of instruction is to help students see how such things can be known.

When did they come? What are the facts? What are the inferences? The Big Question cannot be directly answered. Many small questions must be posed. The facts of the migration are few.

Up until 1925, no evidence had been found to support the notion that man had lived in the Western Hemisphere for more than 1,000 years. In 1925, however, a flint point, which came to be known as a Folsom point, because it was discovered near Folsom, N.M., was found amidst the bones of an animal. The bones were scratched; apparently, the point had been

16 See Chapter Four.

used to help kill or dress the animal. The bones had been covered with earth and were accidentally uncovered. They were identified as belonging to an extinct species of bison that had not lived in North America for some 7,000 to 10,000 years. The Folsom point appeared to be a human artifact. It could be argued, on the basis of the evidence of the bones and the Folsom point, that men had lived in the Western Hemisphere for at least 10,000 years.

Subsequent to this discovery and dating of the Folsom point, many identical flint points were found in different parts of the United States. One Folsom point was found in Alaska. It is because of such evidence that scientists guess that Folsom man migrated to the Western Hemisphere across the Bering Strait and followed his nomadic way of life in North America.

In 1936, evidence of even more ancient life in the Western Hemisphere was uncovered; a flint point which was more primitive than a Folsom point was found in a cave in New Mexico. The cave was named Sandia. A geologist determined that the Sandia points were discovered in a layer of the cave that was 25,000 years old. Subsequently, carbon-dating procedures confirmed the evidence of geology: a tusk in the cave, apparently carried there by Sandia man, proved to be about 25,000 years old.

The facts regarding early America are few, but interesting. Frank C. Hibben's book, *The Lost Americans,* provides a lucid account of how Sandia and Folsom were discovered and what the author believes is the significance of these findings.

But what of the men themselves? What did Sandia man look like? What language did he speak? No one knows! No skeletal remains of these early men have been found. The Sandia point, the Folsom point, and a few tusks of bison are all that have been found of that ancient time. We know that human artifacts were used in the New World at Sandia and Folsom, but we have no satisfactory account of the bewildering array of physical types and languages that are found among the Indians of the Americas.

Rather than a body of facts and assured conjecture, the discoveries have led only to unsolved problems, with which social scientists are working today. An examination of any recent anthropological journal might reveal a new discovery or a new interpretation of an old discovery. What seems like a commonplace account, occupying a half-dozen sentences in a textbook, may lead into a world of intellectual adventure.

The typical elementary-school textbook will mention that early migrants came from Asia across the Bering Straits. How is this known? Only one Folsom point has been found in Alaska. What facts and logic support the view that man came to the New World from Asia across the strait? They left no trail; they left no written record.

These questions can be explored by students in school. Identify the facts. Are there many or few? Identify the inferences. Can they be challenged? Consult the recent journals; see if any new discoveries regarding the travels

Figure 5
The Fruit Vendor, Circle of the Caravaggio, The Detroit Institute of Arts

Figure 6
The Resurrection (detail), Master of the Osservanza, The Detroit Institute of Arts

of ancient man have been made. Remember, the teacher's responsibility is not to affirm truths, but to help students discover how men come to know.

A study of the art of certain northeastern Indians and the art of prehistoric man in Europe has led some scholars to conjecture that it is possible that there was some migration from Europe, by way of Greenland, to the Western Hemisphere in very early times.[17] One can explore the evidence and the logic of this view in the anthropological journals.

The study of a situation involves acquainting students with information, identifying the facts, identifying the inferences, evaluating the facts and inferences, identifying large questions with which students may work, and pursuing inquiry through observation and the reports of observation.

The study of a situation involves acquainting students with information. The information presented by a textbook may initiate this study. The basic question that nurtures and sustains inquiry is this:

How do you know?

or

How can this be known?

or

On what basis is this known?

Did Richard III murder the boys in the Tower? Most books say he did. How can this be known? What is the evidence of contemporary records?

Did Europeans migrate to the New World from Europe? How can this be known? What would be relevant evidence?

As one reads the textual material in elementary social-studies textbooks, it becomes apparent that there is little effort to report facts. According to the narrow definition of a statement of fact that has been used in this book, it is very hard to find any facts at all in a textbook. What one finds there are opinions, thoughts, and conjectures that the textbook writer has chosen to share with students. Once the students have become acquainted with the material in a textbook, the teacher can initiate study by noticing a conjecture and posing the basic question:

How can this be known?

Some conjectures will turn out to be based on sound evidence; if so, the students will have learned something about the manner in which man goes about seeking and establishing knowledge. Other conjectures may turn out to be based on unsatisfactory evidence. The teacher can seek to modify the devices, or new opinions, or conjectures that more satisfactorily account for the available evidence. Recall the Mississippi textbook account of the Ku Klux Klan. What facts support the opinions reported there? What facts are in conflict with those opinions? How might the statement be written to represent the facts as a class finds them?

[17] E. F. GREENMAN, "The Upper Palaeolithic and the New World," *Current Anthropology*, IV, No. 1 (February 1963), 41–91.

The effort at inquiry will transform the dull experience of reading and believing a book into the high adventure of intellectual discovery. The teacher who introduces inquiry into the study of Then and There will provide students with honest tasks and will bring them into significant contact with the history of the far-away.

Possible Sources

Controversy provides much of the excitement of historical study. Here are some books that may initiate a class into the controversy regarding pre-Columbian explorations of the Western Hemisphere.

ARMSTRONG, ZELLA. *Who Discovered America? The Amazing Story of Madoc,* Chattanooga, Tenn.: The Lookout Publishing Company, 1950.

DONWORTH, ALBERT B., Sc.B. *Why Columbus Sailed,* New York: Exposition Press, 1953.

DUFF, CHARLES. *The Truth About Columbus and the Discovery of America,* New York: Random House, 1936.

GOODWIN, WILLIAM B. *The Ruins of Great Ireland in New England,* Boston: Meador Publishing Company, 1946.

GRAY, EDWARD F. *Leif Eriksson, Discoverer of America,* A.D. *1003,* New York: Oxford University Press, 1930.

HAWKE, DAVID. *The Colonial Experience,* Indianapolis: Bobbs-Merrill Co., Inc., 1966.

HOLAND, HJALMAR R. *A Pre-Columbian Crusade to America,* New York: Twayne Publishers, Inc., 1962.

HOLAND, HJALMAR R. *Westward From Vinland,* New York: Duell, Sloan & Pearce, 1940.

HOVGAARD, WILLIAM. *The Voyages of the Norsemen to America,* New York: The American-Scandinavian Foundation, 1914.

MERTZ, HENRIETTE. *Pale Ink. Two Ancient Records of Chinese Exploration in America,* Chicago: Ralph Fletcher Seymour, 1953.

OLESON, TRYGGVI J. *Early Voyages and Northern Approaches 1000-1632,* Toronto: McClelland and Stewart Limited, 1963.

POHL, FREDERICK J. *Atlantic Crossings Before Columbus,* New York: W. W. Norton & Company, Inc., 1961.

REMAN, EDWARD. *The Norse Discoveries and Explorations in America,* Berkeley and Los Angeles: University of California Press, 1949.

SKELTON, R. A., MARSTON, THOMAS E., and PAINTER, GEORGE D. *The Vinland Map and the Tartar Relation,* New Haven: Yale University Press, 1965.

THORDARSON, MATTHIAS. *The Vinland Voyages,* New York: American Geographical Society, 1930.

TORNOE, J. KR. *Early American History. Norsemen Before Columbus,* Oslo, Norway: Universitetsforlaget, 1964.

XIV

Ideas and Feelings

The first four chapters of this section have been preoccupied with the distance in time and space between children and the people and social events they are to study. This preoccupation is based upon the notion that study demands a confrontation with "things," that is, existing objects or messages. Confronting a "thing" is a process: observing it from many different points of view, asking questions about it, compelling it to answer these questions by further observations and thought, and taking some action. The action may be a search for more "things"; or a statement of relationship connecting observations from different vantage points into some pattern, or connecting observations of related "things" into some pattern; or a commitment on the part of children to act in a way that is consistent with the pattern they construct.

Words and Their Uses

In the study interludes scattered throughout Chapters Ten to Thirteen, one could see children learning how to use words when they examined such questions as: What is history? What is unemployment? What is a community? What is a grocery store? One could see them learning to define terms precisely, as they tried to test the truth of such statements as:
1. The speed limit is 45 m.p.h. on the freeway.
2. Using the freeway is faster than using city streets.
3. The freeway is a good thing to have.

And they could be observed learning to form intelligent statements on the basis of their experiences with words and documents: There are both large and small grocery stores in our town because each offers something to its customers that the customers are willing to pay for. Cities that are losing population tend to be cities with a higher rate of unemployment than cities that are gaining population.

This chapter pinpoints the problems confronting children as they attempt to learn to use and understand the many sorts of ideas or concepts that are important in social study and the words that are used to refer to these ideas.

In Chapter Five, it was suggested that words are of two general sorts: words that represent things and activities that one can observe in the external world, and words that represent ideas, feelings, and beliefs with which one regulates one's life.

Regardless of the time-space setting in which words are used, their study presents unique problems, partly because of their nature as symbols. A house is an object that is, or may be perceived to be, separate from any other object, even if many of the other objects are houses, and even if the other houses are identical to the first in size, color, materials, style, and most other measurable characteristics. The word "house" represents all the separate objects that may be thought of as houses. This word can represent all houses because there are characteristics or attributes that houses have but nonhouses do not have. The word "house" represents an abstraction or an idea that is illustrated by the many houses that we can observe. The notion of "houseness" exists as an abstraction; the word "house" exists as a symbol; neither exists in the same way a house exists.

Words represent abstractions; some words refer to objects that are readily identifiable; freight train, pyramids, roses. Some words refer to events and transactions that may be somewhat harder to identify; they deal with interactions among people and the objects around them: bargaining, irrigating, dancing, governing. Still other words refer to ideas, states of mind, or feelings. It may be extremely difficult to learn how to use the last-mentioned words because they refer to no particular objects or activities; one can learn how to use them only by finding out how various people talk about what such words mean. They always mean different things to different people: justice, beauty, democracy, learning, children's needs, intelligence, and power.

The experiences of a child with words and their referents will help him to develop intelligent strategies for word usage. Without some relevant experiences with the variety of talk about "democracy," or with the operations which give meaning to the word "parallel," or the processes related to the word "erosion," the development of intelligent word usage is unlikely.

Describing the External World

It is relatively easy for teachers to arrange for children to have relevant experiences with words whose referents are physical objects: children can look, or handle, or recall sense impressions. When words refer to ideas or feelings, teachers can often contrive activities through which the children can acquire sense impressions that help develop meanings for words. A verbal description can be transformed into actions or operations that can be observed, recorded, and recalled as the practical consequences of an idea.

Some of the ideas selected for study in the Greater Cleveland Social Science Program are contained in the following passage:[1]

An east-west line called the Equator is drawn around the globe halfway between the poles. Other east-west lines, drawn parallel to the Equator, are called parallels of latitude. These lines are numbered by degrees from the Equator to the poles.

A complete circle is 360°, and the distance from the Equator, which is 0°, to either pole is 90°. One degree of latitude equals approximately 70 miles.

A list of the words that a child would have to understand in order to comprehend the statements contained in these two paragraphs includes:

east	poles
west	parallel
east-west	latitude
line	parallels of latitude
called (by whom? why?)	are numbered
Equator	degree(s)
line is drawn (where? how?)	complete circle
globe	equals

An illustration of an activity contrived to help make one of these words clear, directs teachers to "have a pupil select an east-west line near the Equator. Measure with a strip of paper the distance from the Equator at several points. Make sure that the word parallel is understood by calling attention to other sets."[2] This is in the best tradition of modern experimental physics, in which words are defined in terms of operations. Lines are parallel as a result of measurements that discover them to be equidistant from one another at all the points measured. Children can recall the result of their measuring in order to understand the idea of parallel.

Children often bring prior experiences to the learning of a new idea. One of them may think he knows all about degrees because he has been using a thermometer since second grade. But then he may be puzzled to find that the numeral for degrees of latitude increases as one approaches the poles, because he also knows that, in general, temperatures get colder as one approaches the poles. Activities similar to measuring the distance between parallels may be needed to help children distinguish between degrees of temperature and degrees of latitude.

In the incident described below, a teacher and very young children try to come to grips with an elusive idea—the distance that separates people in different parts of our world.

[1] Educational Research Council of Greater Cleveland, Ohio, *Globe and Map Skills: Teachers' Guide* (Preliminary Edition, 1962–1963), p. 8.
[2] *Ibid.,* p. 9.

JAPAN IS FAR AWAY[3]

Akiko and her family are in the United States while her father is on a research appointment at the University. Akiko is in a kindergarten, where, with a little English and a little Japanese and many gestures, she has made herself a valuable member of the group. Mrs. Arnold thought it would be a valuable experience if the children could meet Akiko's mother and learn something about the country in which they lived and to which they planned soon to return. When she suggested that Mrs. Yoshida visit her classroom, Akiko's mother was reluctant to expose her meager English to such a test. Mrs. Arnold assured her that her children were more interested in seeing pictures and objects than in hearing about them and that her visit would be of great value in helping these very young children learn something about another country.

Mrs. Yoshida's visit was a great success. Both she and Akiko dressed in traditional Japanese clothing for their visit. They showed pictures of their home in Japan and of famous places in their country. Akiko showed some beautiful dolls which she had received on successive birthdays. When Mrs. Yoshida left, the class composed a little poem to thank her for her visit.

The next day Janey said, "When Akiko goes home, I am going to go with her and see all those places." Mrs. Arnold explained that Akiko lived a long ways away. To get to her home, Janey would have to cross a great ocean. Bob knew what an ocean was, "It was a lot of water. It was bigger than Lake Mendota or even bigger than Lake Michigan. You would have to spend all day on a boat in order to cross it. You might have to spend all week. Or maybe a year." Mrs. Arnold looked at Akiko and asked if she remembered how long it had taken to cross the ocean. Akiko smiled and shook her head. Mrs. Arnold explained that it might take many days for a boat to cross the ocean but it would not take as long as a year.

The next day the children were still talking about Akiko's house and how much they would like to visit it, and Mrs. Arnold was ready for them. In the days following Mrs. Yoshida's visit, Mrs. Arnold had been thinking about how much the children in her kindergarten could understand about the sweep and size of their country, about the vastness of an ocean, about the distance Akiko had traveled in order to be with them. She decided to make a try at helping these five- and six-year-olds extend their comprehension of the time and space that separate people.

When the expected comment about how nice it would be to visit Akiko's home was heard on Thursday, Mrs. Arnold suggested that if they could not

[3] Adapted from informal reports of a classroom teacher.

really visit Japan they might pretend to go on such a visit. She led the class to an open area on the floor where she had used masking tape in order to make a crude outline of North and South America, Hawaii, and Japan. A blue-colored piece of masking tape marked their city; another one marked Tokyo. Mrs. Arnold explained that on the floor they saw a picture that someone might see if he were high, high up in the air and looking down toward where we lived. Everything would look much smaller than it was when we were down on the ground. People and houses could not even be seen at all because they would look smaller than tiny specks of dust. They would find out just how far it was from where we lived to where Akiko lived as they measured how long it would take to travel to Akiko's home.

"How shall we go," Mrs. Arnold asked.

"Let's take a boat."

"We can't get a boat here. A boat won't go on land."

Mrs. Arnold suggested that they might drive to the place where the ocean began and get their boat there. They would start now. When they came to school tomorrow she would show them how far they had traveled. The next day the disappointingly short, stubby, red-painted strip of masking tape showed them that a day's driving had not taken them very far. Mrs. Arnold showed pictures of some of the countryside they might have seen by looking out of the window of the car. Children helped her to imagine the games they played while they rode along, the place they picnicked for lunch, the motel in which they stayed that night. When they came to school on Monday, they were delighted to see how far the red line had been pushed toward the ocean but they were not there yet. They saw more pictures of the country they had driven through over the week end; the Bad Lands of South Dakota, the great stone faces of Mount Rushmore, cowboys in Wyoming, and bears and geysers at Yellowstone Park. By Wednesday they were in San Francisco, catching their first glimpse of the ocean from the Golden Gate Bridge. Mrs. Arnold used pictures from the school's picture file, from a friend's slide collection, from current magazines, and from the personal collection of one of the travel agents in town. They saw pictures of the boat on which they were to travel. These pictures were to join the others on the back bulletin board; grouped under the appropriate heading of the day, such as: Monday, driving along; Tuesday, almost there; Wednesday, the ocean at last!

The next day, the red line had pushed out into the ocean. Children played at being ship's personnel and passengers, explored the engine room and the bridge, and swam in the ship's swimming pool. "Do you want to know what you would see if you looked out from the boat?" asked Mrs. Arnold. "In the morning you would see this," and she held up a picture of water and sky. "After lunch you might see this," she held up another picture—

more water. "And when it was time for bed, what is it that you think you would see from the porthole?"—the children knew!

They spent the week end in Hawaii. On Monday they saw the places they had visited in the Islands. Just before they left for home at lunch time they boarded an airplane at the Honolulu Airport. Some of the children sighed as they looked despairingly at the large space between Hawaii and Japan. "We sure been traveling a long time," someone said. "And we still have a long way to go."

Mrs. Arnold might have been a little disturbed by the shouts of excitement when the children discovered that overnight the airplane had carried them all the way to Akiko's home, except that she was so excited to get there herself.

Mrs. Arnold could not take the children in her class over the miles between their city and Japan. She transformed distance into time units, which she could control, and attempted to build an activity that might give some reality to the idea of the distance between their homes and Akiko's. It would be naïve to declare that these kindergartners now "really" understand how far it is to Tokyo. Many of them, however, if asked the question, might be able to say that it is further to Akiko's home than it is to Centerville, a large city about a three-hour drive away. And several, when asked why they think so, may be able to say something like, "We can drive to Centerville and go to the zoo there and get back home all on the same day. It took much longer than that to get to Japan." Many of these children will be able to deduce why the distance from Hawaii to Japan was covered so quickly while the shorter distance from their city to San Francisco took longer.

Representing Ideas, Feelings, and Beliefs

STATEMENTS OF EXPERIENCE

Words would have little value if they were not used in some way to achieve some intellectual purpose. Word-symbols are intellectually useful: they are devised so that one need not confront every new object or event as new and different (because it is separate) from every other event or object; new objects, situations, and emotional experiences can be related to others that are like it in some way through the use of a word, as a label for a category in which related objects, events, etc., can be contained.

The way in which we relate one experience to another, or one object to another, is to make statements that purport to represent our experience of love, fear, anxiety, and so forth or our perception of order in the social events that go on around us. We use the words we encounter or invent to pose questions and make statements concerning the world of our experience.

EMOTIONAL RESPONSES

Learning is a total and unified human experience. It is, therefore, an emotional, as well as an intellectual, experience. Words may carry a high, or medium, or low emotional charge. It is unlikely that they will evoke no emotional response at all. In order to talk about children's interaction with ideas, one must recognize the part that feelings play in the way words are used.

The positive or negative feelings evoked by a word may have little to do with its meaning and a great deal to do with the context in which it is learned. A boy who is punished with ridicule because he offers a garbled definition of "latitude" may make his feelings of shame or inadequacy an attribute of the word. Children learn to "love" or "hate" words like "arithmetic" and "social studies."

Apart from these conditions, a word may evoke more or less emotion than is closely related to its meanings. The word "house" may have very little emotional charge for a child, living in a suburban community, who has grown up in a house and has learned to take it for granted. The same word may carry highly positive emotional connotations for another child, who has heard his parents constantly plan and dream about the time when they can leave their trailer home and own a house of their own. Still another child may have a difficult time understanding the sheltering attributes of "house": his house is a prison to which he is sentenced for misdeeds, or the command, "Get in the house!" usually means he will shortly be spanked.

These different possible reactions to the word "house" suggest that one cannot always accurately predict the extent and kind of emotional charge a word may carry. Still, it is possible to anticipate, to some extent, the degree to which emotion will figure as an attribute in learning that word. Emotion may not figure much at all; it may interfere with understanding, for example, if it distorts perceptions of the word. It may be a crucial component in understanding such words as "love" or "honesty."

Every individual brings a unique set of previous experiences to new learning. Chapter Eleven showed how this caused a wide variety of impressions of India among a group of sixth graders, even though they had apparently shared the "common" experience of an illustrated discussion with an Indian student. A word "means" (to an individual) his patterning of all his experiences with referents of that word. Some of each person's meaning for any word is private or personal and very likely not sharable with anyone else.

Sometimes, the referent of a word can be made unambiguously sharable by public agreements about relatively stable ways to measure them. Several people can agree that the temperature on a particular day is 75° F. and the relative humidity 60 per cent, although one of them may assert that it is a trifle too cool, another that it is a bit too warm, and a third that it is a comfortably pleasant day. If parallel lines were determined by whether they *looked* equally distant from one another, one might expect considerable disagreement about whether or not two specific lines were parallel. If standard units of measure, such as those on a ruler or thermometer, were used, one can expect to find greater agreement about whether or not the lines are equidistant. Successive measurements with a ruler vary too, of course, but not so much as "looking" does.[4] The easier it is for the referents of a word to be determined by operations external to people, the more likely it is that they can agree about the nature of those referents. The easier it is to get agreement among different observers about what has been observed, the more "objective" their observations may be said to have been. When a word is used to refer to internal operations of people (assessing the results of looking, or feeling), it becomes more difficult to get agreement. These concepts are more subjective than objective—one cannot easily share his experiences of feeling or of applying personal measures.

A useful strategy for teachers is to try to predict whether children's feelings will be among the important responses to an idea. This kind of classifying may alert the teacher to the need to contrive activities that will help children resolve problems by sharing them. The kind of activity appropriate to examining feelings or ideas with a high degree of emotional content may be markedly different from the kind of activity appropriate to examining more "objective" ideas. Such a prediction may also permit the teacher to anticipate the degree to which he will have to contrive ways of involving children in learning. If the word is "communism," or if the statement to be formed is one that will connect the related words "parents," "children," "rewards," and "punishments," one might expect children to become deeply involved. Indeed, their emotional response to the words may interfere with their being able to think rationally about them. If the word to be used is "longitude," or if the statement to be formed is one that will relate the direction east and the direction north, children are not likely to be excited about it unless the teacher does something to excite them.

The remainder of this chapter is devoted to illustrations of methods used to teach children to form words and statements about matters that may be remote from their lives and interests, and about those that may be within their experience but too charged with emotion to deal with directly.

The first section is concerned with words and statements that carry a low emotional charge. These words represent ideas that are open to external measurement and outside of children's experience.

The second section is concerned with words and statements that carry a

---

[4] For a precise, though not overly technical, discussion of problems of definition, see Anatol Rapoport, *Operational Philosophy* (New York: Harper, 1953), Chapter 1, "The Problem of Definition: What is X?"

high emotional charge. Some of the responses to these words will be feelings about the ideas that the words represent, even though children are unlikely to have had much experience with instances of these ideas.

The third section concerns words and statements that carry a high emotional charge. Some of the responses to these words are the result of personal measurement and definition and of children's previous experiences with the events and ideas the words represent.

When Ideas Are Remote

Some ideas are like curiosities; they arouse interest for a short time but are too insignificant to produce the degree of involvement leading to prolonged effort. They seem a long, long way from everyday problems and concerns. An important facet of working with such an idea is getting children to care about whether they understand it or not.

The Use of Analogy

In the following classroom incident, a teacher builds a bridge between the experiences to which the words longitude and latitude refer and the experiences with which children are familiar.

LINES AND CROSS STREETS

The teacher began the hour by asking various children where they sat in the classroom.

CHILD: Where I sit?
TEACHER: Yes.
CHILD: Third row.
TEACHER: I see. Bill, where do you sit?
CHILD: Row five.
TEACHER: Exactly?
CHILD: Yeah, row five. That's all.
TEACHER: Mary?
CHILD: Row three.
TEACHER: But George said he sat in row three.
CHILD: Well, my desk is next to last. George is in the middle of the row.
    After questioning several students at random, the teacher changed tactics somewhat and began asking the class where they lived.
CHILD: 3503 Main Street.

CHILD: 370 Middlebury, Apt. 3.

TEACHER: Pretend I am a stranger in town. You'll have to give me further directions, if you want to help me save time. Main Street is seven or eight miles long and the numbers don't tell me very much.

CHILD: Well, 3503 is near the park.

TEACHER: Well, maybe so, but remember I am a stranger—I don't know where the park is.

CHILD: I live on Main between Maple and Orchard.

TEACHER: How will that help me find your house?

CHILD: There is only one place where Main Street crosses Maple, so if you find Maple you can follow it down to Main and then you will know just what part of the city I live in.

TEACHER: Yes, I see. That might save some time.

The class watched as the teacher began marking in chalk the seams of an old basketball. A large X was placed along one seam. He numbered the lines from one to six.

TEACHER: Where is this dot located?

CHILD: On line 3.

CHILD: Near the *top* of line 3.

TEACHER: (*pointing to several places near the top of the line but never to the X*) Here, here, or here on the line?

CHILD: Near the top! Near the top!

TEACHER: But I am pointing near the top.

CHILD: You gotta make some cross-streets.

The teacher was instructed to draw "cross-streets" on the basketball. These were given numbers, but that proved confusing when someone tried to say, "Near where one and two come together," since there were two ones and two twos. They decided to use another system and gave the cross-streets "letter" names. The class then located by intersection the dots or X's which the teacher placed on the basketball. It became something of a game.

The next day, the teacher brought in some city maps that used the same system for locating streets as the one they had developed together. Some children were quick to suggest that they had used maps like these, and were thinking about them when they developed their numbering system for the basketball. Step by step he led them to more and more sophisticated and precise statements of the problem until they were examining the meaning and use of longitude and latitude in navigation.

The device that this teacher used to make the problem both clear and motivating to children was to *transform it by analogy*. The analogy, though naïve, was direct and directly understandable by children. After encouraging his class to find direct, though naïve, solutions to a simple statement of the problem, he moved them from this level to increasingly more sophisticated forms of the same problem, ending with a precise problem and a precise solution. His purpose from the beginning had been to help children understand the meaning of the words "longitude" and "latitude."

The same teacher used this device with another class to help them confront a somewhat different idea.

THE PENNY[5]

"I wanted to impress a class with the importance and use of primary source materials. We were starting a unit on the caveman. I spoke about the author of our text. I asked how he found out about the caveman. Someone replied that he got his information from other books. I then asked where these authors got their information. "Did the caveman leave a written record? If he did not leave a written record, what did he leave? The obvious answer was, "Bones, bits of pottery, various stone artifacts, etc." "What can these artifacts, these dumb bits of clay, stone, and bone tell us? The archaeologist seems to be a kind of detective. He finds the evidence and then has to guess about what it could mean."

To give them the feeling of working with a primary source material and the problems that it presents, I gave each child a penny and the following directions: "Pretend that you are an archaeologist. You have just come across the ruins of a city that once was Detroit. It is 5,000 years from now. There are no buildings standing. In walking across the site, you have kicked this coin out of the soil with your foot. What will it tell you about the civilization that flourished here? Examine the coin carefully. Some of its story may be hidden unless you look and use your imagination as well as your eyes."

Some of the students saw the obvious and nothing more. Others saw a great deal more than the fact that we had an alphabet and a number system. Some saw that our economy had been based upon agriculture. (There is a sheaf of grain on the back of the coin.) Still others saw the existence of a religion (In God We Trust), and our connection with Latin (*E Pluribus Unum*). Some children guessed that this city belonged in some sort of federation, since they knew the meaning of the Latin phrase. Others, in comparing their coins, came to the conclusion that this ancient civilization must have developed the use of machinery to a high degree: the coins were almost exactly alike; the measurements were the same to a few thousandths of an inch. The makeup of the metal, the dress of Lincoln, all were com-

[5] Adapted from an informal report of a classroom teacher.

mented upon. Some of the reports written, some of the conclusions drawn, were truly amazing.[6]

As in the previous illustration, the teacher stated a problem in a naive but direct form and then encouraged children to project naive but direct solutions. One might question the value of such an experience had he stopped with that. However, their attempts at a solution helped them to comprehend more easily the complex problem of social scientists who must construct an analysis from fragmentary data.

Presenting children with *simpler forms of complicated problems* may be useful in helping teachers assess the extent to which children can transfer solutions to new but related contexts. Figures 7, 8, 9, and 10 present the results of a short test given by a teacher to her twenty-eight third graders. The results in Figure 7 show that most of these children can label the directions south, west, and east, when north is given. A surprisingly large number labeled the directions northeast, northwest, southeast, and southwest correctly. Figure 8 shows that most of these children can label directions cor-

Figure 7

Fill in the names of the other directions as on a compass.

North (Given)

17 Correct (Northwest)   16 Correct (Northeast)

18 Correct (West)   19 Correct (East)

19 Correct (Southwest)   16 Correct (Southeast)

23 Correct (South)

rectly when given a map of the United States. Figure 9 tells a somewhat different story, however, about the extent to which these children understand relative directions. Only eight children know that facing the sun early in the morning means that you are facing east. Nine know that facing the sun in the late afternoon means that you are facing west. Twelve children know that they should turn to the right if they are facing north and want to go east.

[6] We are indebted to Mr. Richard McBrein, social science teacher, Detroit Public Schools, Detroit, Mich., for this incident as well as for the description "Lines and Cross-Streets."

Figure 8

Fill in the directions on the outline map.

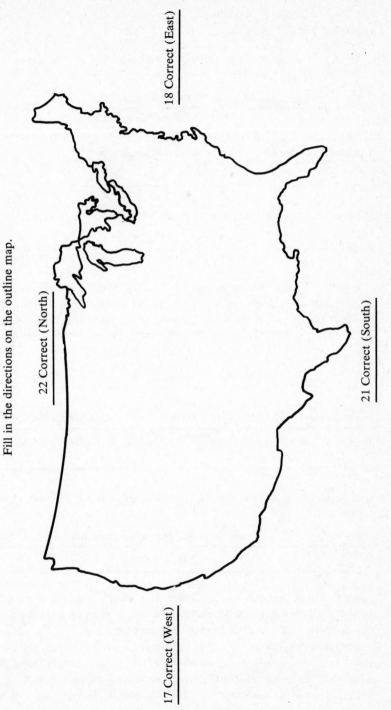

Figure 9

1. One day we got up early and went for a long walk. As we started walking I noticed the sun was shining in my eyes. In what direction were we walking?

8 Correct (east)

(west - east - south - north)

2. As we returned home late that afternoon, I again noticed the sun was shining in my eyes. In what direction were we walking now?

9 Correct (west)

(south - west - north - east)

3. How would you go if you were facing north and want to go east?

12 Correct (Go right)

(Go to my left—go to my right—turn around and go the opposite way)

Figure 10 presents the results of an interesting sequence of questions. Although twenty-three children are able to answer that the stars can help one find his direction on a clear night, only fifteen remember that part of the Big Dipper points to a star that is north. Seven children are able to answer a question about finding direction in a field on a clear night, by

Figure 10

1. On a clear night   23 Correct (stars)   will help you find direction.

---

2. You will always find that part of the Big Dipper points to a star which is
   15 Correct (north)

(west - north - south - east)

3. If you were in an open field on a clear night, how would you find the direction west?

2 Correct (find North Star, turn left)

---

7 Half Correct

---

suggesting that one can use an observation of the Big Dipper to tell where north is, but only two can go on from this to say that after discovering which way is north, one can find west by turning to the left.

The results of a test like this one provide invaluable information for a teacher. They help him to know when the facile manipulation of words represents thorough understanding, and when it represents only a hazy or surface idea of a concept or a generalization. These results can help the teacher plan to establish the meaning of words by contriving additional and relevant experiences for his pupils.

The Use of Dramatic Play

Another useful device in motivating children to learn the meaning of words referring to external or impersonal objects and situations in nature is the device of dramatic play. Its name often causes it to be misunderstood. Dramatics as an activity results in a drama or play. The drama is a work of art; it can exist for any of the reasons for which any work of art—painting, sculpture, short story, poem—exists. Its purpose is to amuse or entertain the observer, or possibly to inform him by examining some facet of human experience or the human condition. It can exist, if for no other reason, for its own sake. Dramatic play does not produce a drama; it is not an art form. It exists for the purpose of helping children identify and understand the ideas and actions to which words refer, and to form intelligent statements about these ideas and actions. It is not play in the sense of loose, unstructured, leisure-time activity. It is structured by the teacher and children in such a way as to make it likely that they will discover the meaning of words in which they are interested. In the following learning episode, a teacher of second graders found that the results of dramatic play helped him, first, to identify the extent to which children understood certain words and, later, to help children form intelligent statements.

THE LAUNDRY TRUCK

On the floor of a second grade room, streets have been marked off with masking tape. A number of vehicles are available to the children. They are of the type that normally travel on city streets: garbage trucks, delivery trucks, ordinary automobiles—and a laundry truck. With blocks, the children represent the houses and stores in their neighborhood and also their school.

In the first play session, the teacher noticed that the boy who has the laundry truck pushes it back and forth on one of the streets. It is not going anywhere in particular, just up and down the same street. In the discussion period following the play session, she asked him why he pushed his truck up and down the same street. She was surprised to discover that he believed that that was what trucks did, because that is what he had observed about trucks on his street. They just went up the street or else they went down the street. She asked whether he thought the truck had come from somewhere. Many children volunteered that it was a laundry truck, so it must be coming from a laundry. They established that a laundry cleaned clothes, and that the truck was possibly taking clean clothes to the people who had given soiled clothes to the laundry. It would stop at houses in order to pick up more soiled clothing to be cleaned at the laundry.

Before the next play session began, some of the blocks represented the laundry and others the houses at which the truck would stop. Some children were laundry workers and others were people who would send clothes to the laundry.

The dramatic-play opportunity helped the teacher discover an inadequate idea and then allowed him to help children begin to understand the way in which a truck connected people who were dependent upon one another in the community for services. In subsequent dramatic-play sessions, other trucks were introduced. Children established the fact that trucks move in a pattern that is in keeping with their function. Postal trucks stop at every mailbox. The cement truck moves back and forth from the source of cement to the place where it is needed. The dump truck moves back and forth from the source of whatever it might be carrying (gravel, dirt, refuse) to the delivery point where the materials are intended (driveway, highway, garbage dump, or fill-point).

The Technique of Dramatic Play

Dramatic play offers a teacher a setting in which he can measure the effectiveness of his teaching by observing the extent to which children can make sensible statements and use information appropriately, transferring learning from one context to another. For example, having formed a statement connecting the function of a laundry truck with its pattern of movement, the teacher introduces other, similar, vehicles. In the discussion preceding dramatic play, he can raise a question about materials or arrangement needed to use these new trucks in a realistic way. Children who ask or comment about a new truck's function, and who set up "rules" for its movements that are related to its function, are able to transfer the ideas. That is, they can make plausible statements out of new situations. If no questions or comments come from the children, the teacher can prompt them with questions about what the truck is supposed to do, and what beginning and stopping points will mark its path through their "city." Questions or comments may indicate that children know too little about some new element to incorporate it realistically into the dramatic play. Such a discovery leads to a search for information in books, or from people whose experience makes them knowledgeable. The information gathered is used to make subsequent sessions true-to-life.

A typical organizational pattern for dramatic play follows some such sequence as this:

1. Raising questions and discussing possible answers; gathering information; seeing some possibilities for dramatic play to use information or test generalizations. ("Just how big is a cabin if it is 10 feet by 16 feet? How much room would there be for furniture? Maybe we could understand what living in a log cabin was like if we marked off that area and tried to live in it.")

2. Preparing to act out a problem by anticipating needs for:
   a. Objects ("We'll have to put some blocks to show the laundry and we'll need the houses where the truck stops.") Sometimes there is a call for objects that must be built, such as walls for a cabin or a stop light for a city intersection.
   b. People ("What people do we need?" "We need the truck driver, and the mothers where he stops to give them clean clothes." "Why can't we have some people who work in the laundry cleaning up the dirty clothes?")
   c. Rules, related to relevant ideas that determine the actions of the players ("What side of the road do cars drive on?" "Yes, so remember to keep your cars and trucks on the right side of the center line.")
   d. Rules that contribute to an orderly but pleasant learning environment ("Do you remember Jerry's saying, yesterday, that everyone noticed the signal to stop, so the clean-up went very quickly? Most of you thought that was a good thing to happen because we had more time to talk about what we did, and then to make some extra houses that we needed. Let us see if we can get that extra time today, too." "Everyone used very quiet voices yesterday. When I was talking to Mrs. Bricker in the hall, we could hardly hear you. Do you think you can remember to use your quiet voices today, too?") A clear signal for stopping (blinking the lights, playing a tune on the piano, or part of a record) may prove very useful.

3. The dramatic-play session itself. The first few play sessions are usually intended to help in discovering and clarifying a problem and the kind of information useful for solving it. They may be somewhat ragged, especially if the children have had little previous experience with this technique. Although they should be long enough to give the children time to use the created environment, beginning play sessions may be fairly short, sometimes only five or ten minutes long, so that the focus of action does not blur into aimlessness. As the children become skillful in using the technique, the sessions may become longer. They should never become so long that there is too little time left for an analytic review of what took place. During dramatic play, the teacher records instances of the action which it would be valuable to discuss. He may select a few children to join him in looking at the total play and in recording actions that are worth discussing or questioning.

4. Post-session analysis. This is an essential adjunct to dramatic play. Since the purpose of dramatic play is to help children learn concepts and test generalizations, the emphasis in this analytic session is on the *content* of the play session. Whatever questions or tentative problem solutions prompted the dramatic play, they are now re-examined in light of what the players have just experienced.

As children become involved, they are often aware only of the action in which they took part. Minor incidents that demonstrate clearly the significance of ideas may be repeated during the analytic session, so that everyone can observe them.

Dramatic play becomes a powerful teaching technique to the extent that it allows children to form generalizations that do not merely connect words with other words, but instead permits them to use words to refer to experiences with which children are familiar and whose consequences they can share meaningfully.

When Emotion Is Strong and Experience Is Lacking

Certain terms cause people to react positively, while equivalent terms referring to the same thing, notion, or feeling produce a neutral or negative reaction. Real estate brokers have a hard time selling "houses"; it is easier to sell "homes." A practice or product which has "withstood the test of time" is clearly better than one that is "old-fashioned," even if they happen to be exactly the same practice or thing. The same word can even shift in connotation from context to context. "Gentle," when applied to women, has a positive connotation; when applied to men, it implies weakness, and is not nearly so positive.

Children often bring feelings about some idea to its study. This prior experience may have taught them how to feel about a concept without having taught them what the concept means; their experience includes no contact with instances of its attributes. An assembly line, to one child, is a fine thing, because his mother works on one. Another child knows it is bad, because his father is always complaining about it. But what is it? He may be puzzled because what he seems to know about a term does not fit the way it is being used. He gets into line to go to assembly every Friday, but no one gives him any money for that.

In the following episode, the nature of the community in which a teacher worked permitted her to anticipate a higher level of interest in learning about facets of factory life than might be present in other communities. Feelings might be associated with these ideas, but firsthand experiences might likely be missing.

FACTORY LIFE[7]

I teach in an industrial city and most of my children have heard such terms as assembly line, shift, foreman, plant, die, etc., but do not quite know what they mean. I decided to stress the importance of the factory because our school district does a great deal with "Our Community" in the first three grades, and this particular phase (factory life) seems to be such a fundamental part of our city.

The children made a study of factory life, aided by film strips and numerous pictures. We also prepared a mural showing different types of factories. (*This* project was a trifle hectic—poster painting can get messy.) They learned that many products are manufactured on an assembly line. And, in assembling products, each work-station and subassembly line is important. Parents were able to give extra background material, because most were factory employees.

A display of brightly colored place mats constructed of woven strips of paper had appeared in the hall. Several children commented that these would make fine Valentine's Day gifts for parents. One boy made the happy suggestion that if we produced the place mats by turning the class into an assembly line we might be able to make enough for every member of every family. We tried making one place mat and kept a record of the time that each operation took. Since it took longer to weave a mat than to cut up the strips we needed, we would need more weavers than strip-cutters. It took even less time to tape the ends, so we would need fewer end-tapers than either strip-cutters or weavers. The class sat at three long tables and pretended these were different factory buildings. Jobs and work-stations were decided upon. Each child had a task to perform—cutting paper, weaving a certain colored strip, being plant manager, taping the ends, and so forth. This approach seemed to enhance our community study. At least, certain household words came to have a little more meaning to these children. They continue to tell events or bring in pictures that refer to the factories of our city.

Had this been an upper-middle-class suburban community or a small farm town, the major problem would have been the one identified in the preceding section: contriving some way to interest children in dealing with the ideas. The nature of this community made it likely that the interest would already be present. The major problem was that of helping the children have ap-

[7] Adapted from informal reports of a classroom teacher.

propriate experiences with illustrations of the idea. Studying a simplified model of a factory constructed within a classroom helps children identify essential characteristics of a factory or assembly line. If they follow this experience with a visit to an actual factory to observe an assembly line in operation, they may be less likely to confuse characteristics that happen to be present in the specific factory they visit with essential referents of the word "factory."[8]

Some notions are so abstract that the appropriate experience with them may be discussion rather than acting something out or taking a study trip. Children may react emotionally—positively or negatively—to certain ideas; yet they may never have thought very deeply about the implications of these ideas. The teacher in the following episode encouraged children to dig beneath the surface meaning of the word "equality."

EQUALITY[9]

About four years ago, I was conducting an eighth-grade class in American government. We were in the process of discussing the United States Constitution, and we quite naturally started with the Preamble. We discussed the meaning of each line and were stopped at once by the statement, "All men are created equal. . . ." I asked what the line meant. I was given the answer that all men were in fact the same in every respect. My opening here was beautiful, and I asked if we all drew pictures equally well. Did we all sing or play a musical instrument equally well? Did we all play football or baseball equally well? Did we all get the same scores on our tests or the same marks on our report cards? Some of the children were quite shocked that such a sacred tenet would be attacked with such vigor. The fundamentalists and die-hards leaped to their guns to do battle. I was trying to develop the difference between equal abilities and equality of opportunity for justice and self-realization in a democracy. I was trying, in addition, to examine the notion of the equality of man in the eyes of God.

The fundamentalists (about six) would have none of it. The Bible was quoted and misquoted (mostly the latter) as an authority. The discussion became very enthusiastic and even heated. We had to call time on our initial discussion because the period ended. I invited my opponents to return to the battle after school. Much to my surprise, almost the entire class came back, and the engagement resumed. It was, all things considered, a

---

[8] See Frederick J. McDonald, *Educational Psychology* (Belmont, Calif.: Wadsworth, 1959), pp. 146-148, for an analysis of research and theory related to the value of realistic experiences in forming concepts.

[9] Adapted from informal reports of a classroom teacher.

very enjoyable afternoon. Ideas were presented, discussed, torn apart, and rebuilt.

One word of caution, however. It was perhaps a little heady for eighth graders. Care must be taken also that religious beliefs are not assailed. Thank heaven for tenure!

In the effort to get his class to think about the meaning of the words "All men are created equal," this teacher used the device of the provocative or belligerent question.

Such statements as, "Democracy depends upon a belief in the dignity of the individual," or "Common problems can be settled cooperatively in a democratic community," have emerged from a process of intellectual struggle. Their defense requires intellectual as well as physical risk and effort. Mouthed without thought, they degenerate into clichés and have the intellectual vulnerability of clichés. The provocative question makes it necessary to examine the consequences of looking at something "the other way 'round." This kind of question forces one to examine and defend assertions assumed to need no defense. This examination can result in modifying an assertion so that it can be better defended; or it can lead to the reaffirmation of an assertion, for reasons that are clearly understood and able to withstand challenge.

When Emotion Is Strong and Experience May Be Painful

Learning About Feelings

The preceding paragraphs have referred to feelings as important responses to words. Feelings in this sense are impulsive, spontaneous responses of an individual to an object or person or idea. Within the repertoire of feelings available to a person, certain responses may be encouraged, because their consequences are somehow rewarding or protecting, and other responses may be discouraged, because they result in "punishment." The experience of individuals in groups teaches them that some feelings can be freely and safely expressed, but others must be controlled or guarded in order to avoid disapproval. It may not be possible to prevent feelings from occurring even if it is possible to inhibit their expression. Two general types of responses resulting from feelings are those of avoidance or adherence: one's feelings about some object tend to move him away from it (avoidance) or toward it (adherence).

Feelings result in behavior. When the behavior can be observed, it can be used to make inferences about the feelings that produced it. One can not observe feelings in any direct way.

Feelings about specific objects are learned. Children are not born afraid of fire or heights, or ashamed of parts of their bodies, or disgusted by certain habits, or liking sugar. Different experiences with any of these can result in two individuals with quite different feelings about the same objects. The arrival of sea snails brings joyful anticipation to some Polynesians as they splash into the surf to gather a favorite food. Merely the touch of a sea snail makes some Westerners shudder with disgust; they would not think of eating one.

An attitude may be thought of as a predisposition to act in a particular way. Attitudes are like feelings in that they are directed toward some object, person, or idea; they may be thought of as if they form part of a continuum from highly positive or highly negative—they may be more or less intense. Unlike feelings, however, attitudes may be thought of as generalized, stable, consistent responses toward some attitude-object. Feelings may be thought to be more variable or fleeting, as well as highly specific, responses.[10]

People act toward one another in certain ways because of their feelings as well as because of their judgment. Sometimes feeling follows reason. A businessman employs a blind telephone-switchboard operator when it is demonstrated that her disability will not interfere with her adequate performance of this job. His feelings of pity or protectiveness toward blind people may undergo some change when they are joined by feelings of admiration or respect for the skill with which a particular blind employee performs her job. Often "reason" follows feelings, arguments being constructed to support a feeling. One man, who believed that Africans were childlike and incapable of self-government, listened to an account of an administrative tangle created by some people in Africa. He remarked, "It is impossible to understand the African mind." His colleague looked at him in surprise and said, "Those weren't Africans I was telling about. They were Americans, the members of a United States diplomatic mission." The first man shook his head sadly, "My goodness, they are taking on the characteristics of the Africans." One might infer from his comments that this man had feelings of contempt for Africans or at least for the administrative abilities of Africans. When Africans mix things up, it is only to be expected; if Americans do so, it is because they are acting like Africans.

This section has emphasized helping children to examine feelings and the part played by feelings in directing the behavior of people. One can know little about such concepts as love, loyalty, friendship, and honesty without having the experiences and the emotions that are inextricably a part of their meanings. Listening to descriptions or reading about feelings are pale substitutes for feeling itself.

[10] See the discussion of attitudes in W. E. Vinacke, *The Psychology of Thinking* (New York: McGraw-Hill, 1952), Chapters 13, 14, 15; and F. J. McDonald, *Educational Psychology*, Chapters Seven and Eight.

The intensity of emotion generated by some words may make children eager to explore their meaning. The rewards for knowing what friendship is and how it operates may be both immediate and direct, as may be also the punishments for misunderstanding. Intensity of feeling may also operate as a motivating force against examining some concepts. Discussing "friends" and "friendship," for example, may make public a child's carefully guarded "secret," that he longs for friends he does not have and cannot seem to get.

The Use of Role-Playing

Role-playing has much in common with dramatic play. Like the latter, it is often confused with dramatics, although the purpose of role-playing is not to produce a work of dramatic art, but an understanding of the feelings that words may assume, or a setting in which children can tentatively test solutions to problems of social interaction. Role-playing provides a protected setting in which children can "try on" feelings. Children are protected, by the "masks" of the roles they play, from the anxiety of self-exposure and from the hurtful consequences of the choices made by the characters portrayed.

One of the clearest descriptions of the uses and potentialities of role-playing in schools appears in a pamphlet, *Role-Playing the Problem Story,* by George and Fannie R. Shaftel.[11] The discussion that follows borrows heavily from this source.

Role-playing begins with an introduction to a problem to be examined. The "warming-up" period may use a discussion or a story that is not finished, or the ending of which is calculated to stimulate children's comments in defense or rejection of the problem-solution presented. Children who seem to have identified with the characters and are eager to offer problem-solutions are selected to enact their own endings. The following episode records a fifth-grade experience in role-playing a problem story.

CLUBHOUSE BOAT[12]

ACTION

TEACHER: "Do you remember, the other day, we had a discussion about Janey's lunch money? Because she had put her money in her pocket and

Children are used to the "happy ending" pattern. The satisfaction that comes with increased

---

[11] GEORGE and FANNIE R. SHAFTEL, *Role-Playing the Problem Story* (New York: National Conference of Christians and Jews, 1952), pamphlet. Reprinted by permission of the authors.

[12] *Ibid.,* pp. 13–19.

had not given it to me when she came into the
room, it was lost. We had quite a talk about finding money: whether to keep it or turn it in.

"Sometimes it's not easy to decide what to do.
Do you ever have times when you just don't know
what to do? (*There are nods in the group.*)

"I would like to read you a story this afternoon
about a boy who found himself in just such a spot.
He really didn't know how to decide.

"This will be one of those problem stories which
stop, but are not finished."

A PUPIL: "Like the one we did last week?

TEACHER: "Yes."

A PUPIL: "Oh! but can't you give us one with
an ending?"

TEACHER: "When you get into 'a jam, does
someone always come along and tell you how your
problem will end?"

PUPILS: "Oh, no! Not very often."

TEACHER: "In life, we usually have to make our
own endings—we have to solve our problems ourselves. That's why I'm reading you these problem
stories—so that we can practice endings—try out
many different ones to see which work the best
for us.

"As I read this story, you might be thinking of
what you would do if you were in Tommy Haine's
place."

Teacher reads the story, entitled "Clubhouse
Boat." (In summary):

Tommy Haines belongs to a club which the boys
have organized in the neighborhood, the Mountain Lions. An uncle of one of the boys agrees to
give them a houseboat for a club if they will have
it repaired and docked in the town's yacht harbor.

Tommy agrees to pay his share of the repair
bill, twenty dollars. He is confident that he can
manage this, because he is earning money as delivery boy for a drugstore.

To his dismay, his father refuses to let him participate, insisting that he must put his earnings in
the bank.

This places Tommy in difficulty with his gang.

Marginal notes:

ability to tackle and solve
problems develops slowly,
and only through
opportunity to face
problems.

Preparing the class to
listen purposefully. This is
a very important part of
the process.

The story constitutes an
extended warm-up or
preparation for
role-playing. Characters
and actions are delineated
and the problem situation
is developed to its critical
point.

They have had the boat repaired and owe money
for it. Pete "borrows" the money for Tommy out
of a purse which had been left in his Dad's taxicab
by a patron.

Tommy, frantic to get together the amount he
owes his gang, resorts to small subterfuges, deliberately working to talk people into giving him tips,
not telling his folks that he has earned tips, or that
he has been given a raise in pay, and even keeping
several small sums given him in overpayment on
orders.

Finally, the boys are in difficulty. The woman
returns for her purse, and Pete's parents learn that
he took money from it. They threaten to go to all
the boys' fathers unless the money is returned by
the next morning.

The boys manage to chip in some more money,
but cannot raise enough. They insist that Tommy
find the balance needed.

Tommy worries. Then, after delivering a package for the druggist, Tommy discovers that the
customer had made a mistake and overpaid him
$5.00. Enough to clear the debt to the gang!

Tommy is deeply tempted. He stands in front
of the customer's closed door. Shall he knock and
return the money?—or shall he leave and keep the
money he needs so badly?

TEACHER: "What do you think Tommy will
do?"

Stimulating the class to
explore possible solutions.

A PUPIL: "I think he'll keep the money!"

A spontaneous expression
which probably reveals
an impulse.

TEACHER: "Yes?—"

A PUPIL: "Because he needs to pay the club."

Analyzing the problem.

A PUPIL: "Oh, no, he won't. He'll get found out,
and he knows it."

Anticipating consequences.

A PUPIL: "How can he? Nobody can prove anything."

Expressing a personal
philosophy.

TEACHER: (to this last student) "Would you
like to come up here, Jerry, and be Tommy? (Jerry
comes to the front of the room.) Jerry, whom will
you need to help you?"

The teacher deliberately
chooses the boy who
expresses an anti-social
solution.

JERRY: "I'll need somebody to be the customer.
And I'll need boys to be the gang."

Encouraging the pupil to
describe his solution and
situation himself.

(Players are chosen)

The teacher invites several children to participate. The setting is arranged. One corner of the classroom is the school where the gang is waiting for Tommy to come with the needed money. A chair is placed in another corner to represent the door of the house to which the package is delivered.

TEACHER: "Where are you going to start, Jerry?"

JERRY: "I'll deliver the package."

TEACHER: "Very well. Now, you people, as you watch, consider whether Jerry's way of ending the story is the way you think it would end. Perhaps you'll have different ideas about it; and when Jerry's finished, we can try your ideas."

While children are never urged to play roles which they do not "feel," occasionally a child needs to be encouraged to participate.

Setting the stage.

The teacher helps describe the furnishings needed and helps arrange them quickly.

Preparing the class to be participating observers.

FIRST ENACTMENT

(Tommy knocks on door. The boy playing role of old man "opens" the door).

TOMMY: "Delivery from Central Drugstore, sir. Eleven dollars and twenty-eight cents due."

MAN: "Here you are. And here's a quarter. Buy yourself a Cadillac." *(Man closes door. Tommy counts money. Discovers he has been overpaid $5. Raises hand to knock on door and call man back— then turns away. Walks across the classroom to the waiting gang.)*

TOMMY: "Hey, guys, look! I got the money we need. Here!"

EDDY: "Swell! Now we can pay for the boat. Come on, gang!"

This boy chooses to "get away with it." His enactment is an expression of the ethical values and the anti-social behavior which has been causing concern among the school faculty.

END OF ENACTMENT

TEACHER: "Well, Jerry has given us one solution. What do you think of it?"

A PUPIL: "Oh—uh! It won't work!"

JERRY: "Why not?"

A PUPIL: "That man is going to remember how much money he had. He'll phone the druggist about it."

Encouraging an evaluation. The teacher is careful to be non-committal.

A judgment.

It happens that Jerry was a boy of low mental ability; he was quite

JERRY: "So what? He can't prove anything on me. I'll just say he didn't overpay me."

A PUPIL: "You'll lose your job."

JERRY: "When they can't prove it?"

ANOTHER PUPIL: "Yes. Even if they can't prove it."

TEACHER: "Why do you think so, John?"

JOHN: "Because the druggist has to be on the side of his customer. He can fire Tommy and hire another boy. But he doesn't want his customers mad at him."

A PUPIL: "He's going to feel pretty bad inside. If he keeps the money."

TEACHER: "What do you mean?"

A PUPIL: "Well, it bothers you when you know you've done something wrong."

TEACHER: "Do you have any other way to solve this problem?"

A PUPIL: "Yes. Tommy should knock on the door and tell the customer about being overpaid. Maybe the man'll let Tommy keep the money."

TEACHER: "All right, let's try it your way, Dick." (*New role-players are selected and the scene is set.*)

SECOND ENACTMENT

(*Tommy delivers the parcel, is paid; the door is shut. He discovers that he has been overpaid $5.00*)

TOMMY: "Gosh, I better knock and call that man back!"

(*He knocks*)

MAN: (*opening door*) "What is it, son?"

TOMMY: "Sir, you overpaid me five dollars."

MAN: "I did! Well—you're an honest boy. Tell you what—you keep the change."

END OF ENACTMENT

sure of himself.

An analysis of consequences.

Other consequences are here foreseen—anxiety and guilt. Encouraging further expression.

Exploring for other solutions.

A proposal with wishful (fantasy) solution.

The teacher follows through. The consequences of fantasy solutions should be explored.

1.

These two enactments were followed by a third, after the children's comments suggested that the fantasy solution was not acceptable to them. In the third version, Tommy's parents help him out of his difficulty, but he is punished in the process.

The Technique of Role-Playing

Several important characteristics of role-playing are illustrated in this episode. An enactment may be very short; length is not a factor in usefulness. The teacher encourages exploration of several different solutions. She is careful not to commit herself through obviously approving or disapproving comments. If the teacher made it clear that she would accept one solution only, children would quickly learn to look for that one and give it to her. This would shut off any opportunity for children to examine their own solutions to problems and the consequences of those solutions.

Since role-playing invites children to expose their feelings in an attempt to help them understand how feelings shape behavior, a teacher must assume some responsibility for guaranteeing the "safety" of the setting.

Tact is an important attribute of the person directing role-playing. Young people of minority groups are especially sensitive—though they may mask it very well—to comments about their characteristics. Teachers need to plan carefully for these children.

If it is a different sort of problem, such as that of honesty, and one of the students in the room has been questioned on suspicion of looting lockers, obviously it is necessary to safeguard him from being openly talked about and condemned. The problem should be examined in terms that remove it from the immediate situation. In fact, it may be wise to postpone such a discussion until the actual incident has been largely forgotton.

Another risk is that of self-exposure.

In any group enterprise of this sort—in dramatic play, in sociodrama, even in mere discussion—it may happen that an individual will expose himself to ridicule or rejection by being too frank about himself. In the heat of argument, when a permissive atmosphere has been established, a young person may reveal some past behavior which will hurt his status among his peers. The alert teacher will try to play down such revelations. In starting discussion, it is wise to ask, "Do you know anyone to whom this sort of thing has happened?" This is a wiser device than asking, "Has this sort of thing ever happened to you?" Also, the careful teacher will not push a student to elaborate upon a comment when to do so may cause him to betray that the example he's telling about is himself. When the teacher senses resistance, she should move on to another student or topic in a casual manner so that no attention is drawn to the pupil's retreat from self-exposure.[13]

[13] *Ibid.*, pp. 35–36.

Analyzing the Consequences of Ideas

Earlier in this book, it was suggested that in studying ideas children can confront variety in writings and variety in their personal experiences with the ideas.[14] Teachers will probably have written materials readily available to them. This chapter, then, has chosen to illustrate ways in which children can analyze the intellectual and emotional consequences of their experiences with ideas. Both activities, however, are important facets of the study of ideas. Examining writing puts children in touch with the continuing process through which men make use of words and relate them to one another in interesting statements. Examining experience develops referents for ideas that are close-at-hand and sharable, making it more likely that verbal statements about social events will have some intelligent basis upon which to rest.

In this book we have written about the significance of primary sources in the conduct of inquiry, suggesting and illustrating several fundamental ideas:

(1) inquiry involves a person directing questions to himself and seeking to answer them on the basis of observations of what is happening or the residue of what has happened in the world;

(2) in elementary school the study of Now and Here, Now and There, Then and Here, Then and There and Ideas and Feelings pose distinctly different practical problems of inquiry that students and teachers must face;

(3) encouraging a student to write and talk about what he experiences and believes is a very significant school activity; writing of this sort calls upon a student to be "somebody," to have an opinion, to defend his views.

In these final paragraphs of our contribution to this book, we would like to focus attention upon what is often the final experience of a social studies program: testing. An appropriate question that a teacher might ask himself regarding an achievement test in social studies is this: How can I judge if this test is one that will serve students and not subvert their respect for ideas and their own intellectual abilities? This is a question for which there is no routine answer. But any teacher can seek to maintain an intelligent attitude toward the tests that children are compelled to take. The following questions may be helpful: (1) does the test deal honestly with ideas? (2) does the test help students become aware of the challenges and excitement of intellectual work? (3) does the test help students become aware of the development of their intellectual powers? An achievement test is an affirmation that a teacher supports by decision or default.

[14] See Chapter Five.

PART FOUR

Speculative Resources:
Writings of Scholars and Educators

———

With the exception of the last four selections, these excerpts are the writings of scholars and educators that have been selected to complement the discussions of the authors of this book. Some of the selections are the reflective comments of scholars on the character and method of their work. Some of the articles discuss the educational use to which scholarly findings can be put. A few of the articles present information that is relevant to elementary-school social-studies programs. These various resources illustrate the ideas and thought that teachers must seek and evaluate if they are to avoid triviality in their work with children.

The Question

R. G. COLLINGWOOD

Most historians of science would assign a prominent place to Francis Bacon, because he, more than any other man, formulated what is and remains the scientific method: *Put nature to the test.*

History, in this general sense, is a science; it is the effort to pose and answer questions through observation.

The classroom student confronts the same intellectual problem faced by any scientific worker: he must decide what he wants to know, and then he must form questions that can be answered through observation. Hopefully, these preliminary questions and the observations called for lead to the piecing together of plausible answers to questions of greater magnitude. R. G. Collingwood is concerned here with the importance of the question in the process of inquiry.

Francis Bacon, lawyer and philosopher, laid it down in one of his memorable phrases that the natural scientist must 'put Nature to the question.' What he was denying, when he wrote this, was that the scientist's attitude towards nature should be one of respectful attentiveness, waiting upon her utterances and building his theories on the basis of what she chose to vouchsafe him. What he was asserting was two things at once: first, that the scientist must take the initiative, deciding for himself what he wants to know and formulating this in his own mind in the shape of a question; and secondly, that he must find means of compelling nature to answer, devising tortures under which she can no longer hold her tongue. Here, in a single brief epigram, Bacon laid down once for all the true theory of experimental science.

It is also, though Bacon did not know this, the true theory of historical method. In scissors-and-paste history the historian takes up a pre-Baconian position. His attitude towards his authorities, as the very word shows, is one of respectful attentiveness. He waits to hear what they choose to tell him, and lets them tell it in their own way and at their own time. Even when he has invented historical criticism, and his authorities have become mere sources, this attitude is at bottom unchanged. There is a change, but it is only superficial. It consists merely in the adoption of a technique for dividing witnesses into sheep and goats. One class is disqualified from giving testimony; the other is treated exactly as authorities were treated under the old dispensation. But in scientific history, or history proper, the Baconian revolution has been accomplished. The scientific historian no doubt spends a great deal of time reading the same books that the scissors-and-paste historian used to read—

Herodotus, Thucydides, Livy, Tacitus, and so forth—but he reads them in an entirely different spirit; in fact, a Baconian spirit. The scissors-and-paste historian reads them in a simply receptive spirit, to find out what they said. The scientific historian reads them with a question in his mind, having taken the initiative by deciding for himself what he wants to find out from them. Further, the scissors-and-paste historian reads them on the understanding that what they did not tell him in so many words he would never find out from them at all; the scientific historian puts them to the torture, twisting a passage ostensibly about something quite different into an answer to the question he has decided to ask. Where the scissors-and-paste historian said quite confidently 'There is nothing in such-and-such an author about such-and-such a subject', the scientific or Baconian historian will reply 'Oh, isn't there? Do you not see that in this passage about a totally different matter it is implied that the author took such-and-such a view of the subject about which you say his text contains nothing?' . . .

. . . I have gone to some length in this analysis because I wish to bring home to the reader the following points about the questioning activity which is the dominant factor in history, as it is in all scientific work.

(1) Every step in the argument depends on asking a question. The question is the charge of gas, exploded in the cylinder-head, which is the motive force of every piston-stroke. But the metaphor is not adequate, because each new piston-stroke is produced not by exploding another charge of the same old mixture but by exploding a charge of a new kind. No one with any grasp of method will go on asking the same question all the time, 'Who killed John Doe?' He asks a new question every time. And it is not enough to cover the ground by having a catalogue of all the questions that have to be asked, and asking every one of them sooner or later: they must be asked in the right order. Descartes, one of the three great masters of the Logic of Questioning (the other two being Socrates and Bacon), insisted upon this as a cardinal point in scientific method, but so far as modern works on logic are concerned, Descartes might never have lived. Modern logicians are in a conspiracy to pretend that a scientist's business is to 'make judgments', or 'assert propositions', or 'apprehend facts', and also to 'assert' or 'apprehend' the relations between them; suggesting that they have no experience whatever of scientific thinking, and wish to palm off, as an account of science, an account of their own haphazard, unsystematic, unscientific consciousness.

(2) These questions are not put by one man to another man, in the hope that the second man will enlighten the first man's ignorance by answering them. They are put, like all scientific questions, to the scientist by himself. This is the Socratic idea which Plato was to express by defining thought as 'the dialogue of the soul with itself', where Plato's own literary practice makes it clear that by dialogue he meant a process of question and answer. When Socrates taught his young pupils by asking them questions, he was teaching them how to ask questions of themselves, and showing them by

examples how amazingly the obscurest subjects can be illuminated by asking oneself intelligent questions about them instead of simply gaping at them, according to the prescription of our modern anti-scientific epistemologists, in the hope that when we have made our minds a perfect blank we shall 'apprehend the facts.' . . .

The Cherokees

JOHN COLLIER

A nation, like man, has a varied past—with much to be proud of and some things to be ashamed of. A competent man knows and faces the mistakes he has made. Because he can face them and because he is aware of his capacity for error, he may improve in his ability to avoid mistakes.

In the conduct of national policy, the leaders of any sovereign state, including our own, cannot make an unending succession of wise decisions. Citizens should be conscious of the capacity for error, for cruelty, and for injustice within their own system of government. Men in government, aware of this capacity for error, can do much to avoid it.

John Collier, former United States Commissioner of Indian Affairs, relates, below, some of the events associated with the relations between our government and the Cherokee Indians. Much of it is a catalogue of mistakes and cruelty.

Students, during the course of their schooling, should encounter the noble and the ignoble. Without an awareness of both, they will lack a full capacity for intelligent citizenship, and they will underestimate the arduousness of the search for justice.

More than any other tribe, the Cherokee nation furnished the crystallizing thread of United States government policy and action in Indian affairs. The Cherokees were the largest of the Iroquoian tribes; but they never joined the Confederacy, and we never think of them as being Iroquois. In the years before Great Britain's power ended, the British Crown had intervened repeatedly to check the seizure of Cherokee lands by the "borderers." Thus it came about that in the war of the Revolution the Cherokees allied themselves with the British.

Not until 1794 did they stop fighting. The treaty which they then made with the United States was kept by them as a sacred thing.

The Cherokees met every test of peacefulness, of practicality, of Christian profession and conduct, of industry and productiveness, of out-going friend-

From *Indians of the Americas* by John Collier, copyright 1947 by John Collier, published by arrangement with The New American Library of World Literature, Inc., New York.

liness to the whites, of "progress" in domestic order and in education. They
even offered little resistance to marriages between young men of the whites
and their young girls. One of their great men, whom we know as Sequoia,
and whom we have idealized, invented an alphabet considered second only
to our European system in the various schemes of symbolic thought representation, and the tribe quickly became literate in our European sense. The
Cherokees wrote a constitution of the American white man's kind. They
established a legislature, a judiciary and an executive branch. A free press
and public schools were set up. Again and again the tribe surrendered great
areas of its treaty-held land. Over and over again, however hard pressed, it
kept the faith.

Yet, in the years that followed, the treaty was breached both in the letter
and in the spirit by the United States over and over again. And it is clear
that nothing the Indians could have been or not been, could have done or
not done, would have changed the white man's heart and will. The remnant
of their lands included seven million acres, mostly mountain country in the
region where Georgia, North Carolina and Tennessee converge, what is now
called the highland country. The Cherokees had to be removed even from
these last fastnesses.

In 1828 Andrew Jackson was elected president. He was a "borderer"
and had been a famous Indian fighter. Immediately he put through Congress
an act called the Indian Removal Act which placed in his own hands the
task of leading or driving all Indian tribes to some place west of the Mississippi River. At about the same time gold was discovered in the Cherokee
country. The Georgia Legislature passed an act annexing—confiscating—
all Cherokee lands within the state, declaring all laws of the Cherokee Nation to be null and void, and forbidding Indians to testify in any state court
against white men. The Cherokee lands were distributed to whites through
a lottery system.

In 1830, through John Ross, its chief, the tribe vainly appealed to President Jackson. Then it appealed to the Supreme Court. The Court refused to
take jurisdiction; the tribe, it ruled, was not a foreign nation. "If it be true,"
said the Court, "that the Cherokee Nation has rights, this is not the tribunal
in which these rights are to be asserted. If it be true that wrongs have been
inflicted, and that still greater are to be apprehended, this is not the tribunal
which can redress the past or prevent the future."

The conscience of the Court was troubled by this Pilate-like decision.
Two years later, it had an opportunity to reconsider. Three white missionaries refused to swear the oath of allegiance to Georgia while resident
in the defined country of the Cherokee Nation. They were arrested, chained
together, and forced to walk twenty-one miles behind a wagon to jail. Two
Methodist preachers intervened against the brutality; they were chained with
the others and thrown into jail with them. The missionaries were tried and
sentenced to four years' hard labor in the state penitentiary. The case came

up before the Supreme Court, and the Court, in effect reversing itself, ruled that Indian tribes or nations "had always been considered as distinct, independent, political communities, retaining their original natural rights . . . and the settled doctrine of the law of nations is, that a weaker power does not surrender its independence—its right to self-government—by associating with a stronger, and taking its protection.

"The Cherokee nation, then, is a distinct community, occupying its own territory, with boundaries accurately described, in which the laws of Georgia can have no force, and which the citizens of Georgia have no right to enter, but with the assent of the Cherokees themselves, or in conformity with treaties, and with the acts of Congress."

President Jackson retorted to the Court: "John Marshall (the Chief Justice) has rendered his decision; now let him enforce it."

So Georgia, and the whole of the Federal Government apart from the helpless Court, continued their policies toward the Cherokees. The whites could prospect for gold anywhere, the Indians not at all, though the land was their own. The President's commissioners harried some of the Cherokees into signing a treaty giving up the 7,000,000 acres still theirs for $4,500,000 which would be deposited "to their credit" in the United States treasury. The leaders and people had been immovable, but in an arranged meeting attended by some 400 of the tribe's 17,000 members, the fictional treaty was extorted. The Senate quickly ratified this "treaty."

Three years passed and the Cherokees were still upon their land. Then came General Winfield Scott with 7,000 troops and a non-military rabble of followers to invade the Cherokee domain. Cherokee men, women, and children were seized wherever found and without notice removed to concentration camps. Livestock, household goods, farm implements, everything went to the white camp-followers; the homes usually were burned. After this the long trek to Arkansas in mid-winter was begun. An eye-witness in Kentucky reported: "Even aged females, apparently nearly ready to drop into the grave, were travelling with heavy burdens attached to their backs, sometimes on frozen ground and sometimes on muddy streets, with no covering for their feet."

Of about 14,000 who were herded onto this "trail of tears," as it came to to be called, 4,000 died on the way. While a hundred Cherokees a day were perishing of exhaustion and cold on that dreadful road, President Van Buren on December 3, 1838 addressed Congress: "The measures [for Cherokee removal] authorized by Congress at its last session have had the happiest effects . . . The Cherokees have emigrated without any apparent reluctance." The financial costs of the trail of tears were charged by the government against the funds credited to the tribe pursuant to the fraudulent treaty.

As the final company of the Cherokees started on the long trail, their leaders held the last council they would ever hold on their home ground.

They adopted a resolution which ought to be remembered forever. They did not ask pity for their people, because they knew there would be no pity, and asking pity was never the Indian's way. They did not reproach or condemn Georgia or the United States government. They did not quote John Marshall's decision, since that decision, for them, had been written on water. To the violated treaties and fraudulent treaties they made no reference; for they had now learned that which General Francis C. Walker was to phrase immortally when, in 1871, writing as Commissioner of Indian Affairs, he described the white man's view concerning honor toward Indians: "When dealing with savage men, as with savage beasts, no question of national honor can arise. Whether to fight, to run away, or to employ a ruse, is solely a question of expediency." Their treaties, the Cherokees had learned, had been "ruses" of the white man. So the resolution, passed in what then seemed to be their final hour, was addressed to no man, and leaned on no consideration, except the principle of justice which they believed was undying:

"The title of the Cherokee people to their lands is the most ancient, pure and absolute known to man; its date is beyond the reach of human record; its validity confirmed by possession and enjoyment antecedent to all pretense of claim by any portion of the human race.

"The free consent of the Cherokee people is indispensable to a valid transfer of the Cherokee title. The Cherokee people have neither by themselves nor their representatives given such consent. It follows that the original title and ownership of lands still rests in the Cherokee Nation, unimpaired and absolute. The Cherokee people have existed as a distinct national community for a period extending into antiquity beyond the dates and records and memory of man. These attributes have never been relinquished by the Cherokee people, and cannot be dissolved by the expulsion of the Nation from its territory by the power of the United States government."

That was all. Then these men of true greatness, through fraud and violence stripped of everything, set forth on the bitter trail to a place which was to be no lasting home. . . .

History's Nature, Object, Method, and Value

R. G. COLLINGWOOD

One can benefit from the advances of the natural sciences whether or not he understands anything at all about physics or mathematics: he can eat winter

Reprinted from *The Idea of History* by R. G. Collingwood. By permission of Oxford University Press. Copyright 1946 by Oxford University Press.

corn, or he can undergo radiation treatment. But no one can benefit from the insights that develop in the social sciences unless he can, to some extent, adopt the social scientist's mode of thinking. The social scientist offers a way of thinking about the world; he offers no product that can be manufactured and marketed.

In the following selection, R. G. Collingwood, one of the most distinguished British historians of the twentieth century, poses to himself the question, "What is the nature, purpose, method and value of history?" After reading some of the great writers in the various disciplines, a teacher could pose similar questions regarding political science, geography, sociology, and anthropology. Only after he can answer such questions is the teacher ready to confront the challenge of teaching social study.

What history is, what it is about, how it proceeds, and what it is for, are questions which to some extent different people would answer in different ways. But in spite of differences there is a large measure of agreement between the answers. And this agreement becomes closer if the answers are subjected to scrutiny with a view to discarding those which proceed from unqualified witnesses. History, like theology or natural science, is a special form of thought. If that is so, questions about the nature, object, method, and value of this form of thought must be answered by persons having two qualifications.

First, they must have experience of that form of thought. They must be historians. In a sense we are all historians nowadays. All educated persons have gone through a process of education which has included a certain amount of historical thinking. But this does not qualify them to give an opinion about the nature, object, method, and value of historical thinking. For in the first place, the experience of historical thinking which they have thus acquired is probably very superficial; and the opinions based on it are therefore no better grounded than a man's opinion of the French people based on a single week-end visit to Paris. In the second place, experience of anything whatever gained through the ordinary educational channels, as well as being superficial, is invariably out of date. Experience of historical thinking, so gained, is modelled on text-books, and text-books always describe not what is now being thought by real live historians, but what was thought by real live historians at some time in the past when the raw material was being created out of which the text-book has been put together. And it is not only the results of historical thought which are out of date by the time they get into the text-book. It is also the principles of historical thought: that is, the ideas as to the nature, object, method, and value of historical thinking. In the third place, and connected with this, there is a peculiar illusion incidental to all knowledge acquired in the way of education: the illusion of finality. When a student is *in statu pupillari* with respect to any subject whatever, he has to believe that things are settled because the text-books and his teachers regard them as settled. When he emerges from that state and goes on studying the subject for himself he finds that nothing is settled. The dogmatism which is an invariable mark of immaturity drops away from him. He looks at so-called facts with a new eye. He says to himself: 'My teacher and text-books told me that such and such was true; but is it true? What reasons had they for thinking it true, and were these reasons adequate?' On the other hand, if he emerges from the status of pupil without continuing to pursue the subject he never rids himself of this dogmatic attitude. And this makes him a person peculiarly unfitted to answer the questions I have mentioned. No one, for example, is likely to answer them worse than an Oxford philosopher who, having read Greats in his youth, was once a student of history and thinks that this youthful experience of historical thinking entitles him to say what history is, what it is about, how it proceeds, and what it is for.

The second qualification for answering these questions is that a man should not only have experience of historical thinking but should also have reflected upon that experience. He must be not only an historian but a philosopher; and in particular his philosophical thought must have included special attention to the problems of historical thought. Now it is possible to be a quite good historian (though not an historian of the highest order) without thus reflecting upon one's own historical thinking. It is even easier to be a quite good teacher of history (though not the very best kind of teacher) without such reflection. At the same time, it is important to remember that experience comes first, and reflection on that experience second. Even the least reflective historian has the first qualification. He possesses the experience on which to reflect; and when he is asked to reflect on it his reflections have a good chance of being to the point. An historian who has never worked much at philosophy will probably answer our four questions in a more intelligent and valuable way than a philosopher who has never worked much at history.

I shall therefore propound answers to my four questions such as I think any present-day historian would accept. Here they will be rough and ready answers, but they will serve for a provisional definition of our subject-matter and they will be defended and elaborated as the argument proceeds.

(a) The definition of history. Every historian would agree, I think, that history is a kind of research or inquiry. What kind of inquiry it is I do not yet ask. The point is that generically it belongs to what we call the sciences: that is, the forms of thought whereby we ask questions and try to answer them. Science in general, it is important to realize, does not consist in collecting what we already know and arranging it in this or that kind of pattern. It consists in fastening upon something we do not know, and trying to discover it. Playing patience with things we already know may be a useful means towards this end, but it is not the end itself. It is at best only the means. It is scientifically valuable only in so far as the new arrangement gives us the answer to a question we have already decided to ask. That is why all science begins from the knowledge of our own ignorance: not our ignorance of everything, but our ignorance of some definite thing—the origin of parliament, the cause of cancer, the chemical composition of the sun, the way to make a pump work without muscular exertion on the part of a man or a horse or some other docile animal. Science is finding things out: and in that sense history is a science.

(b) The object of history. One science differs from another in that it finds out things of a different kind. What kind of things does history find out? I answer, *res gestae:* actions of human beings that have been done in the past. Although this answer raises all kinds of further questions many of which are controversial, still, however they may be answered, the answers do not discredit the proposition that history is the science of *res gestae,* the attempt to answer questions about human actions done in the past.

(c) How does history proceed? History proceeds by the interpretation of evidence: where evidence is a collective name for things which singly are called documents, and a document is a thing existing here and now, of such a kind that the historian, by thinking about it, can get answers to the questions he asks about past events. Here again there are plenty of difficult questions to ask as to what the characteristics of evidence are and how it is interpreted. But there is no need for us to raise them at this stage. However they are answered, historians will agree that historical procedure, or method, consists essentially of interpreting evidence.

(d) Lastly, *what is history for?* This is perhaps a harder question than the others; a man who answers it will have to reflect rather more widely than a man who answers the three we have answered already. He must reflect not only on historical thinking but on other things as well, because to say that something is 'for' something implies a distinction between A and B, where A is good for something and B is that for which something is good. But I will suggest an answer, and express the opinion that no historian would reject it, although the further questions to which it gives rise are numerous and difficult.

My answer is that history is 'for' human self-knowledge. It is generally thought to be of importance to man that he should know himself: where knowing himself means knowing not his merely personal peculiarities, the things that distinguish him from other men, but his nature as man. Knowing yourself means knowing, first, what it is to be a man; secondly, knowing what it is to be the kind of man you are; and thirdly, knowing what it is to be the man *you* are and nobody else is. Knowing yourself means knowing what you can do; and since nobody knows what he can do until he tries, the only clue to what man can do is what man has done. The value of history, then, is that it teaches us what man has done and thus what man is. . . .

Three Observations About Language

H. MILLARD CLEMENTS

Any particular language is a specific mode of representing human experience. The distinctions of one's own language appear to be plausible, even necessary or inevitable. But languages differ widely. They differ in their structures: some languages have no nouns. They differ in the provision of available concepts: an English-speaking parent tells his child to *be good;* a French-speaking parent tells his child to *be wise.* The dictates of language exert important and subtle influences upon values and beliefs.

The following discussion is a brief introduction to the conception of a language as a set of presuppositions; the various footnotes provide a further guide to language study.

Most people seldom think about the language they speak. A language is usually regarded as a more or less neutral instrument which represents, in a fairly satisfactory way, the real character of the world. Languages, however, are not just neutral instruments. They have many interesting qualities which influence the ways in which men regard themselves and the world and what they know.

It takes unusual effort to examine the commonplace: it has been often said that fish would be the last form of life which might discover water. Water is everywhere for fish. Language is everywhere for human beings. The following three observations which can be made about language may suggest to the reader some possibilities of directing his curiosity towards a commonplace aspect of his world.

What human beings know is always stated in some language. That which distinguishes men from the other animals is his capacity for symbolization:

Not higher sensitivity, not longer memory or even quicker association sets man so far above other animals that he can regard them as denizens of a lower world: no, it is the power of using symbols . . . that makes him lord of the earth.[1]

The capacity for symbolization is the basis for the invention and use of language; in the use of language is the unique aspect of the human act of knowing.

From *Educational Theory*, XIII, No. 2 (April 1963), 149–154. By permission of the publisher.

[1] SUSANNE K. LANGER, *Philosophy in a New Key* (New York: Penguin Books, 1948), p. 20.

To know in the sense that rats know does not involve the use of language: rats may learn how to run in mazes; in this sense, they know. Both men and rats may learn how to run in mazes; the rat can only interpret signs which may lead him to his goal. The man, however, not only can interpret the signs of mazes, he can represent and in a sense objectify his maze experience to himself and others with symbols, that is, with a language. The capacity to represent experience in the symbols of a language is the essential attribute of knowing. Examine every facet of human knowing; no one of them is divorced from language.

Languages have important attributes which influence what it means to know. It may seem queer to think of languages as having any attributes at all:

. . . while it [language] may be looked upon as a symbolic system which reports or refers to or otherwise substitutes for direct experience, it does not as a matter of actual behavior stand apart or run parallel to direct experience but completely interpenetrates with it.[2]

The result of this interpretation is that despite the obvious role language plays in thinking and knowing it appears to be without attributes:

It is difficult to see adequately the functions of language, because it is so deeply rooted in the whole of human behavior . . .[3]

Languages differ in the way they structure the world which is known to men. Whorf reports that the "natural" logic, the grammar of any given language, is usually unknown to the speakers of the language and is dissimilar to the "natural" logics of other languages:

First, it [natural logic] does not see that the phenomena of a language are to its own speakers largely of a background character and so are outside the critical consciousness and control of the speaker who is expounding the natural logic. Hence, when any one, as a natural logician, is talking about reason, logic, and the laws of correct thinking, he is apt to be simply marching in step with purely grammatical facts that have somewhat of a background character in his own language or family of languages but are by no means universal in all languages and in no sense a common substratum of reason.[4]

As pointed out by Whorf above, there are characteristics of the language we speak which influence how we think in ways of which we are unaware. For example, the distinction between *substance* and *form* which is fundamental in Aristotle's thought may be conceived to be predictable of the

[2] EDWARD SAPIR, *Culture, Language and Personality: Selected Essays,* ed. David G. Mandelbaum (Berkeley and Los Angeles: University of California Press, 1958), p. 8.

[3] *Ibid.,* p. 15.

[4] BENJAMIN LEE WHORF, *Language, Thought and Reality,* ed. John B. Carroll (New York: John Wiley and Technology Press of Massachusetts Institute of Technology, 1956), p. 211.

grammar of Indo-European languages rather than of any "reality" to which they may refer.

And yet, what have the metaphysicians done? Plato unwittingly discovered that Greek, like all the other Indo-European languages, is a noun-language—and then thought that the *logos* or the noun created all the particulars of the real world! . . . The sorry fact is that our unconscious linguistic habits shape our religions and our philosophies, imprison our scientific statements about the world, are of the essence of the conflict of postulated culture with postulated culture, are involved with our wars and other human misunderstandings. . . .[5]

The impact of the structure of language on thought has also been investigated by Dorothy Lee.[6] She studied the Wintu language. Her investigations reveal that the Wintu language neglects entirely a distinction which is fundamental in the English language: there are no distinctions of number in Wintu. The nominal categories of Wintu are universals; the particular is not an attribute of nature but a focus of consciousness: one may not say in Wintu, "This is bread," but rather, "I call this bread."

The fundamental distinction in Wintu is not between singular and plural but between the particular and the generic: that which exists in the Wintu language are wholes not classes of particulars. The particular in Wintu reflects only a relationship to a speaker which lasts only as long as he is speaking; as soon as he ceases speaking the particular ceases to exist.

The ways in which the Wintu know are vastly different from the ways in which English-speaking people know. Translating from one way of knowing to another is difficult:

From the anthropological point of view there are as many different worlds upon the earth as there are languages. Each language is an instrument which guides people in observing, in expressing themselves in a special way. The pie of experience can be sliced in many different ways, and language is the principal directive force in the background. . . . Chinese gives priority to 'how?' and nonexclusive categories; European languages to 'what?' and exclusive categories. In English we have both real plurals and imaginary plurals, 'ten men' and 'ten days'; in Hopi plurals and cardinal numbers may be used only for things that can be seen together as an objective group. . . .[7]

Not only do languages differ with regard to their structures, they differ with regard to their array of available concepts. Men know the answers to the questions they can ask; they can ask only the questions which are possible

[5] WESTON LABARRE, *The Human Animal* (Chicago: University of Chicago Press, 1954), p. 171.

[6] DOROTHY LEE, *Freedom and Culture* (Englewood Cliffs, N. J.: Prentice-Hall, A Spectrum Book, 1959), pp. 121–130.

[7] CLYDE KLUCKHOHN, *Mirror for Man* (Greenwich, Connecticut: Fawcett Publications, A Premier Book, 1957), p. 129.

in their language. The possibility of a question depends upon the presuppositions imbedded in language. Presuppositions do not reflect inevitable distinction. They reflect prevailing notion whose validity depends upon belief:

Such a statement as, 'The word *cat* stands for a certain small mammal' is not either true or false. Its truth depends upon agreement between the speakers that it be true.[8]

This "agreement" holds true not only for *cats* but for all of the conventions of communication and categorization which inhere in language. These implicit beliefs make communication possible; they are fundamental instruments of knowing.

The categories which a language may symbolize are human inventions. The influence of this sort of invention on the human act of knowing may be studied.

Attributes of language may be studied and their influence on what it means to know may be examined, criticized and explicitly acknowledged. Archaic presuppositions, imbedded in language, in terms of which men know are sometimes charming. They may be clearly "visible." Robert Graves' translation of *The Iliad* provides a vivid picture of the world in which the ancient Greeks lived; for example:

Teucrus took careful aim at Hector, and if he had shot, the battle would have ended suddenly. *But Zeus, who was guarding Hector, denied Teucrus any such glory by snapping his bowstring.* The bronze-headed arrow fled wide, and the bow dropped on deck. 'Alas!' he cried, trembling for disappointment. *'Heaven is against us; Some God tore the bow from my grasp and broke the fresh, well-twisted bowstring with which I fitted it,* only this morning, in expectation of a hard day's work.'[9] (italics mine)

By examining the literature of the early Greeks we may discover "instruments" of thought in terms of which the Greeks knew their world. We may discover the questions which they could ask and, thereby, what they knew.

Understanding the ways in which people know is difficult. In *The Heavenly City of the Eighteenth-Century Philosophers,* Becker quotes a perplexing definition of St. Thomas and then makes this remark:

What renders . . . St. Thomas' definition meaningless to us is not bad logic or want of intelligence, but the medieval climate of opinion—those instinctively held preconceptions in the broad sense, that *Weltanschauung* or world pattern—which imposed upon . . . St. Thomas a peculiar use of the intelligence and a special type of logic. To understand why we cannot easily follow . . . St. Thomas it

---

[8] JURGEN RUESCH and GREGORY BATESON, *Communication: The Social Matrix of Psychiatry* (New York: W. W. Norton, 1951), p. 228.

[9] ROBERT GRAVES, *The Anger of Achilles* (A Translation of *The Iliad;* Garden City, New York: Doubleday & Company, Inc., 1959), p. 257.

is necessary to understand (as well as may be) the nature of this climate of opinion.[10]

What Becker calls the "climate of opinion," the "instinctively held pre-conceptions" of the men of St. Thomas' day are the presuppositions which make communication possible. Becker then affirms that prerequisite to understanding the thought of that period is an identification and study of the prevailing presuppositions in terms of which men knew. He identifies one such presupposition in this way.

Existence was regarded by the medieval man as a cosmic drama, composed by the master dramatist according to a central theme and on a rational plan.[11]

This presupposition was imbedded in the symbols in terms of which 18th century men represented their experience. An analysis of *what was knowledge* for 18th century men would necessarily require a study of the presuppositions of that age.

In a similar fashion, a study of *what is knowledge* in any age or language requires an examination of the preconceptions in terms of which men know.

David Riesman has made just this kind of fascinating study of the works of Freud. Sigmund Freud's great contribution to modern psychology was a system of hypotheses concerning human motivation. Although Freud was a scientist concerned with studying human behavior more or less independently of time and place, he brought to the time and place of his study the "climate of opinion" or the preconceptions of his culture which made communication and language possible. Riesman studied the influence of these presuppositions on the structure of Freud's thought. Riesman found that Freud's theories are permeated with presuppositions regarding the concepts of work, sex, play, authority and reality.[12]

In Freud's view, "man's lot", to use Hobbes' phrase, is "nasty, brutish, and short." The need for food compels him to work; the need for sex bribes him to be social. Work is the price of civilization: work is an agony to be endured; it is the male burden. The role of women is to be desirable: a decoration of the evening hours of men; women are trophies. Thus, women who seek to enter the workaday world of men are compensating for their genital loss.

Work is the tragic necessity and play is the bribe. The adequate man must be economically productive, and he must partake of the consolations of sex.

---

[10] CARL L. BECKER, *The Heavenly City of the Eighteenth-Century Philosophers* (New Haven: Yale University Press, 1957), p. 2.

[11] *Ibid.*, p. 7.

[12] DAVID RIESMAN, "The Themes of Work and Play in the Structure of Freud's Thought"; "Authority and Liberty in the Structure of Freud's Thought"; "The Themes of Heroism and Weakness in the Structure of Freud's Thought", *Psychiatry*, Vol. 13 (1950), pp. 1–16; 167–187; 301–315.

The serious work and standards of business life is the paradigm of reality in terms of which the ego must operate. Concern with art connotes homosexuality: it is an evasion of responsibility. Only work that is exacting, arduous, and unpleasant is worthy of men: all else is escape from reality. Thus did Freud incorporate into his theories presuppositions of his middle-class culture.

Freud's presupposition was that *work* possesses a constant meaning in human society. He did not see that the meaning of work or sex arises out of human decisions within particular cultures. *Work* means many things in the different human societies: it may mean an opportunity for creativity; an escape from the stress of domesticity; an escape from boredom; or an expression of manhood.

Associated with Freud's notion of work is his presupposition regarding what might be called "the human condition." By nature man is slothful; every expenditure of energy must be explained because energy conservation is the natural predisposition of men. Essentially, the need for food and sex is responsible for whatever men do. Dream and symptom analysis amounts to finding out why energy is expended: why did the individual invest energy in the ornate dream? In the bizarre symptomology?

Basic presuppositions about man and his world, however, influence the kinds of explanations which are generated and the kinds of empirical research which are pursued. As one alternative to Freud's presupposition, it might be assumed that growth or activity or energy expenditure is the natural human condition. With this presupposition, considerable change in Freudian theory would ensue. The ornate, richly imagined dream in the Freudian view must be explained, for it is not normal; the flat, uneventful dream of Freud's normal man, in the alternative view, must be explained, for it is not normal.

The *pattern* of any given culture determines the meaning of work or sex or authority in that society. There is nothing in the genital or "work" equipment of men which demands that any particular meaning be given to work or to sex. The meanings which are given men *choose* to give. They have chosen different meanings at different times and places.

Riesman does not suggest in his discussion that Freud's theories should be rejected because of their cultural bias. He does suggest that a proper understanding of Freud's explanations is dependent upon an awareness of the extent to which Freud's views are themselves dependent upon cultural presuppositions implicit in language.

Language does even more than "carry" the *values* of a culture: it interprets reality. Resisting this interpretation of language is a major task of scholars which the following discussion will illustrate.

The "revolution" in physics, frequently associated with Einstein's work, is essentially a revolt against the dictates of language. Prior to the "revolution," elements of language, such as, "time," "distance" and "mass" were assumed to represent absolutely measurable categories of the real world; they were thought to reflect independent categories of existence:

The giant machine (the causal world) was not only causal and determinate; it was objective in the sense that no human act or intervention qualified its behavior.[13]

Physicists discovered, however, that precise measurement of these categories revealed contradictions. They found that the dichotomies of language and nature may also be dependent upon a frame of reference, a language, a system of beliefs of which it is part.

It became apparent to physicists that physical measurement may be thought to be dependent upon units of time, distance and mass.[14] For example, measurement of force may depend upon units of time, distance and mass; measurement of velocity may depend upon units of time and distance. A prevailing cultural presupposition was that these units were measurable in an absolute sense, that is, independently of one another and of the frame of reference of any particular procedure of measurement or of observation.

The discovery upon which innovation in physics is based is that the length of an object may be known in a new way: length is not a fact about an object independent of the person and procedure of measurement. The length of an object may be known as a relationship between object and observer. This relationship makes the description of length dependent upon the velocity of the observer with respect to the object.

The classical physicists' "possible world" was a cultural phenomenon; it was a codification of experience in a particular system of symbols. The presuppositions upon which this possible world was based went unnoticed because they were implicit in the language in terms of which the physicists knew. Innovation occurred when the metaphysics of a language was examined and criticized. The result of this examination gave a new possibility: what is known may be determined by how it is known. A new set of presuppositions replaced the old; the new were conscious and criticized; the old were implicit and unnoticed.

Human beings do not live in the objective world alone, nor alone in the world of social activity as ordinarily understood, but are very much at the mercy of the particular language which has become the medium of expression for their society. It is quite an illusion to imagine that one adjusts to reality essentially without the use of language and that language is merely an incidental means of solving specific problems of communications or reflections. The fact of the matter is that the 'real world' is to a large extent unconsciously built up on the

13 J. ROBERT OPPENHEIMER, *Science and the Common Understanding* (New York: Simon and Schuster, 1953), p. 13.

14 LILLIAN R. LIEBER and HUGH G. LIEBER, *The Einstein Theory of Relativity* (New York: Rinehart, 1936), chapters 3–5.

language habits of the group . . . We see and hear and otherwise experience very largely as we do because the language habits of our community predispose certain choices of interpretation.[15]

In conclusion, it has been suggested that whatever men know is formulated in some language, that the character of a language influences whatever men may say that they know, and that the influence of language upon knowing may be deliberately confronted. If, as it has been suggested, men are born into a language which may impose upon them constraint of which they are unaware, then the obligation of education is to aid each man to become aware of these impositions from without. A human being exercises his humanity when he chooses himself rather than being chosen by accidents which birth or fortuitous circumstances may thrust upon him.

A Word About Method

JURGEN RUESCH and GREGORY BATESON

How does one go about the task of studying men and their affairs? Ruesch and Bateson, in the following selection, point out that there are astonishingly few things a person can do in this type of study. Most of these things can be done by students in the classroom. The most learned anthropologist, it appears, can ask only the more subtle question; he cannot encounter any mysterious data which is unavailable to even the youngest students.

It is well to remember that regardless of whether the scientist studies psychiatric, social, or cultural phenomena, sooner or later he has to consider the individual. The only thing that differs is the data obtained from individuals. Therefore in carrying out this study we have found it convenient and necessary to keep clear in our thinking the differences between the various sorts of data with which we have had to deal. Especially is this true of the differences between participant experience and experimental operation, and between observation of behavioral acts and introspective reports. The fact must be faced that when a culture or subculture is studied as an integrated communication system, it is necessary to consider in the scheme of scientific operations the following circumstances:

(a) That the members of the population studied make generalizations about their own culture.

Reprinted from *Communication* by Jurgen Ruesch, M.D., and Gregory Bateson. By permission of W. W. Norton & Company, Inc. Copyright 1951 by W. W. Norton & Company, Inc.

[15] KLUCKHOHN, *Mirror for Man,* p. 129.

(b) That the investigator observes interaction and communication between the members of the population as a neutral spectator.

(c) That each member of the population has his own view of his own roles and can in some measure report these to the observer.

(d) Lastly, that the investigator obtains important insight from his own personal interaction with members of the population.

Each of these circumstances determines a particular way of collecting data, and it is necessary to insist that the data collected in any one of these ways are not the same, either in their order of abstraction or in the distortions which they introduce, as the data collected in one of the other ways. In general, it may be said that these four types of data are mutually corrective and that an undue specialization in any one of the four leads to a distorted picture. The sorts of distortion which result from over-specialization in each type of data collecting may here be mentioned:

If the investigator overspecializes in his attention to what people say about their own culture, he will arrive at an idealized or stereotyped picture of that culture; he will collect a system of social generalizations which ignore the actual behavior of actual people. His picture will be a function of the culture which he is studying, because he will collect stereotypes which are themselves culturally determined; but it will be a distorted function. Further, if the investigator is sociologically minded, he may be guilty of the sort of oversimplification which occurs in organizational charts, forgetting the human individuals and seeing only their defined functions.

Similarly, if the investigator specializes in being a neutral observer of interaction between members of a population, he may build up a picture of customs and character types from which human individuality and the idiosyncrasies of motivation will be lacking. He might, for example, arrive at the position common in anthropology of paying attention to individual behavior, only to use his observations of people's reactions to point up their culturally stylized attitudes.

If, on the other hand, the investigator specializes in collecting personal introspective reports, he will arrive at the distortions characteristic of the overspecialized therapist; he may see the individuals as isolated entities, not related to each other or to himself. He will be limited to a discussion of their internal structure and dynamics, not seeing the structure and dynamisms of the larger social whole.

Finally, the scientist who overspecializes in participant experience will perceive individual trends and interaction but will tend to ignore the more static phenomena of convention, social organization, and other social determinants. His picture will resemble one which might be drawn by an overspecialized psychiatrist who sees the unique dynamics and flux of an individual's responses to himself without seeing that individual's life as socially determined.

Also, it is of interest to note that the systematic differences and distortions which follow when the investigator takes a particular view of the system which he is studying, or when he specializes in a particular method of collecting data, are themselves clues to his value system. The nature or slant of his knowledge is determined by his methods of obtaining that knowledge and by his notions of what knowledge is. If we describe his selective awareness—his structuring of perception—we shall, in fact, be describing his system of values. . . .

Approaches to Study

OSCAR LEWIS

On occasion, during the school year, the teacher will wish to engage his students in a study of the people in their own community. Chapter Ten calls this the study of the *Now and Here*. How can one go about the task of studying nearby people? What is there to look at?

The following discussion presents Oscar Lewis' thoughts about methods of studying people by means of participant observation.

To understand the culture of the poor it is necessary to live with them, to learn their language and customs, and to identify with their problems and aspirations. The anthropologist, trained in the methods of direct observation and participation, is well prepared for this job, whether in his own or in a foreign country. Unfortunately, in many of the underdeveloped countries the educated native elite generally have little first-hand knowledge of the culture of their own poor, for the hierarchical nature of their society inhibits communication across class lines. In Mexico, for example, practically nothing of a scientific nature is known about lower-class family life. In one of the few recently published studies on the Mexican family (Bermudez 1955), the author had to rely almost entirely upon data from novels. This is not to minimize the insights of novelists; but there have been very few great contemporary novels dealing with the lower classes of underdeveloped countries.

This new subject matter calls for some modifications in the conventional research designs of anthropologists. Peasant villages cannot be studied as isolates apart from the national culture; city dwellers cannot be studied as members of little communities. New approaches are necessary, new techniques, new units of study, and new ways of reporting the data so that they can be understood by the nonspecialist.

From *Five Families* by Oscar Lewis (New York: Basic Books, Inc., 1959), pp. 2–5. By permission of the author and publisher.

The present study of five Mexican families is a frank experiment in anthropological research design and reporting. Unlike earlier anthropological studies, the major focus of this study is the family rather than the community or the individual. The intensive study of families has many methodological advantages. Because the family is a small social system, it lends itself to the holistic approach of anthropology. The family is a natural unit of study, particularly in a large metropolis like Mexico City. Moreover, in describing a family we see individuals as they live and work together rather than as the averages and stereotypes implicit in reports on culture patterns. In studying a culture through the intensive analysis of specific families we learn what institutions mean to individuals. It helps us get beyond form and structure to the realities of human life, or, to use Malinowski's terms, it puts flesh and blood on the skeleton. Whole family studies bridge the gap between the conceptual extremes of culture at one pole and the individual at the other; we see both culture and personality as they are interrelated in real life.

In my studies of families in Mexico over the past fifteen years, I have used four separate but related approaches which, when combined, provide a rounded and integrated study of family life. The first or topical approach applies most of the conceptual categories used in the study of an entire community to a single family. The data on the family are organized and presented under the headings of material culture, economic life, social relations, religious life, interpersonal relations, and so on. From a great mass of information based upon living with the family, interviews, and extended observation, the various aspects of the family and of the individual members of the family are reconstructed. This approach is analytical and has the advantage of permitting comparisons between the family culture and the larger culture outside the family.

A second approach is the Rashomon-like technique of seeing the family through the eyes of each of its members. This is done through long, intensive autobiographies of each member of the family. This gives more insight into the individual psychology and feeling tone as well as an indirect, subjective view of family dynamics. This type of material would probably be most useful to the psychologist. Its methodological advantage derives from the independent versions of similar incidents in family life which amount to a check on the validity and reliability of the data.

The third approach is to select for intensive study a problem or a special event or crisis to which the family reacts. The way a family meets new situations is revealing particularly of many latent aspects of family psychodynamics; it also points up individual differences.

A fourth approach to the study of a family as a whole is through detailed observation of a typical day in the life of the family. To give depth and meaning to this approach it must be combined with the other three. This is what I have done to some extent in the present volume.

The selection of a day as the unit of study has been a common device of the novelist. However, it has rarely been used and certainly never exploited by the anthropologist. Actually it has as many advantages for science as for literature and provides an excellent medium for combining the scientific and humanistic aspects of anthropology. The day universally orders family life; it is a small enough time unit to allow for intensive and uninterrupted study by the method of direct observation, and it is ideally suited for controlled comparisons. It makes possible a quantitative analysis of almost any aspect of family life. For example, one can study the amount of time devoted to the preparation of food in different families, the amount of conversation between husband and wife or between parents and children, the amount of laughter, the extent and kind of table talk, etc. One can also study the more subtle and qualitative aspects of interpersonal family relations.

The study of days presented here attempts to give some of the immediacy and wholeness of life which is portrayed by the novelist. Its major commitment, nevertheless, is to social science with all of its strengths and weaknesses. Any resemblance between these family portraits and fiction is purely accidental. Indeed, it is difficult to classify these portraits. They are neither fiction nor conventional anthropology. For want of a better term I would call them ethnographic realism, in contrast to literary realism. These days are not composites; they are real days. And the individuals are not constructed types but are real people. In a sense, these portraits of contemporary Mexican life are historical documents which may be useful for cross-cultural comparisons now and in the future. How many controversies might have been avoided and precious hours of research time saved if historians had had comparable records of ordinary days in the lives of families of ancient Egypt, Rome, or feudal Europe! . . .

What Is Meant by Geography?

RICHARD HARTSHORNE

Geography was once thought to be the business of describing the land and the uses to which it was put. The first geographers were travelers. They wrote notes and drew pictures or sketches upon them in order to represent the problems of land, vegetation, animals, and hostile inhabitants that they encountered. The writings of Herodotus provide an ancient example of a geographer at work; a somewhat more recent example of this sort of geography may be found in *The Journals of Lewis and Clark,* edited by Bernard De Voto.

From *Perspective on the Nature of Geography* by Richard Hartshorne (Chicago: Rand McNally & Company, 1959), pp. 12–15 and 49–55. By permission of the publisher.

But the geographer has altered his view of himself and his works. Description is not enough; one must also explain what has been described and the way in which the charted features are associated. The following discussion presents a sophisticated commentary on the purpose and character of geographical inquiry.

Many students have found difficulty with the statement of geography as "the science of areal differentiation."

Hettner expressed the concept numerous times in statements varying somewhat in form but little in meaning. Thus in 1898 he found that "the distinctive subject of geography, from the most ancient times to the present, was the knowledge of earth areas as they differ from each other," that man was included as an integral part of the nature of an area (*Landesnatur*), and that with the general advance of science "mere description has been replaced in all branches of geography by search for causes."[1] . . .

. . . Cholley [writes] in his excellent *Guide to the Student of Geography:* "The object of geography is to know the earth," in its total character, not in terms of individual categories of phenomena, physical, biological, and human arranged in a series, but rather in terms of "the combinations produced among them, because it is these combinations which create the different physical and human aspects which the surface of the earth reveals to us. . . . It is an astonishing variety of aspects which this cover reveals to us: oceans, continents, and, overlying them, all the diversity of vegetational landscapes, of systems of culture, forms of settlement and the organization of area (*espace*) by the human groups."[2] . . .

. . . Very early in human development, man discovered that his world varied greatly from place to place. It was to satisfy man's curiosity concerning such differences that geography developed as a subject of popular interest. From earliest times travelers returning from "foreign" parts were expected to tell the stay-at-homes what things and people were like in the places they had seen, whether in adjoining, but relatively inaccessible, districts or in more remote parts.

This universal curiosity of man about the world beyond his immediate horizon, a world known to differ in varying degrees from the home area, is the foundation of all geography. Among the innumerable geographers of divers countries who have stated this principle explicitly we may mention Strabo, Vidal de la Blache, Volz, Sauer, and Darby.

The fact that all the areas of the earth differ from each other leads also to a special interest in any cases in which separate areas appear to be alike.

---

[1] ALFRED HETTNER, "Die Entwicklung der Geographie im 19. Jahrhundert," *Geographische Zeitschrift*, IV (1898), p. 320.

[2] Cholley's writing undoubtedly owes much to that of Vidal de la Blache. It is not possible to determine from his book whether the similarity of his viewpoint to that of Hettner and other German geographers represents independent thought or the influence of their writings, either direct or through intermediary sources.

Closer examination reveals that they are never exactly alike, certainly not remotely as much alike as "two peas in a pod," nor even as two individuals of completely European ancestry may be alike in physical characteristics though born and raised on opposite sides of the Atlantic Ocean. Nevertheless, the ways in which separate areas are alike is no less significant than the ways in which they differ. Comparative study of such areas permits geography to approach the methods of laboratory sciences, in which certain facts are controlled as constants, while others vary.

This purpose may appear to be excluded from a geography defined as "the study of areal differentiation" if one omits the phrase "the study of" and thus reads "differentiation" in the active sense—that is, "to differentiate." The purpose of close examination of areas which are somewhat alike is not to demonstrate that they differ, which we know must be the case without need of examination, but rather to determine how small or large the specific differences are. If such examination shows that in respect to certain individual features or groups of closely related features—for example, atmospheric conditions determining rainfall, temperature, cloudiness, etc., which we group together as climate—the differences among several areas are very slight, we say that such areas are "similar" in climate. We may then consider these areas, and all other areas of the world in which climatic conditions are "similar" in contrast to "dissimilar" conditions of other areas—that is, areas differing in minor degree in contrast to those differing in major degree—as specimen areas of the same type. . . .

. . . "Similarity" is not the opposite of "difference," but merely a generalization under which differences deemed minor are ignored, those deemed major are emphasized. Some writers seek to avoid misunderstanding by speaking always of "differences and similarities," without recognizing that the phrase is redundant. It may well be also that the repeated use of the term "differences" gives undue emphasis to the search for "contrasts." It therefore seems advisable to use the more neutral word, "variations." . . .

. . . If it is the role of geography to analyze all the kinds of interrelations among the diverse factors whose total interrelationship forms the existing reality of any area, the insistence on distinguishing between two particular groups of factors, human and nonhuman, introduces a number of handicaps to progress in research.

. . . The first step in analysis is to break down the complexity of all that is within an area into readily recognizable composite features existing in some degree of interrelation with each other, as, for example, vegetation and soil, transportation and waterways, urban structures and the landforms on which they stand. If it were universally, or even generally, true that each such feature was a composite of exclusively human factors or of exclusively natural factors, it would be in order to classify these features in the two groups. . . .

. . . But this is in direct disregard of reality, which recognizes no distinction between "human" and "natural." As Hettner put it, as early as 1905: "Both nature and man are intrinsic to the particular character of the areas, and indeed in such intimate union that they cannot be separated from each other." . . .[3]

. . . No research in geography can hope to make a complete investigation of all the interrelationships of the diverse factors. To disentangle completely the human and nonhuman elements in a particular situation, the student may need to dig back through centuries of human history, even to times earlier than recorded history. But if the study is made with the purpose of determining the relation between human and natural factors, no sound conclusions can be drawn until the study is complete, which will generally be impossible. Hence, even studies of relatively simple elementary problems can yield only hypotheses of low reliability. Successively more penetrating investigations reveal errors in the preceding studies, but do not establish a greater degree of reliability, since they likewise introduce, even at the elementary level, uncertainties of their own.

Thus the accumulation of studies carried on by geographers under the "environmentalist" concept did not progress toward increasing approximations of accuracy and certainty. The most that could be said of more thorough studies was that they appeared more convincing, but one knew that later still more thorough research might appear to demonstrate entirely different conclusions.

If, in contrast, we recognize the fundamental rule of science of starting with observation of the naively given phenomena, we know that in geography these, the earth features, are neither purely human nor purely natural, but composite in character. We must begin, then, by considering these earth features, as we find them, as element-complexes distinct from each other, whether composed of human or nonhuman elements or both. The first step is to describe these features according to their characteristics as significant to man and to seek to establish the interrelations among them.

Thus a geographer studying an area in China may accept the existing soil as a single factor to be measured in terms of its present composition, without attempting to unravel the determinants—bedrock, climate, vegetation, insects, and man—that have made it what it is. . . . Likewise he can accept the existing character and pattern of surface waters without attempting to unravel the degree to which men over the centuries have altered its original features. In analyzing relationships of these existing features to crops, farms, roads, and villages, he can work with the assurance that he knows what he is talking about and can evaluate the degree to which his findings, at

---

[3] ALFRED HETTNER, *Die Geographie, ihre Geschichte, ihr Wesen und ihre Methoden* (Breslau, 1927).

whatever level of analysis he is working, are complete, accurate, and certain.

He may find that his analysis, say, of the relation of village location to other features, will not be complete unless he digs back into past conditions. Ultimately he will reach problems that are either insoluble or for which he can offer only very uncertain hypotheses. But, however incomplete his study may be, he will have accomplished the purpose of increasing our comprehension of the place under study, and to the extent that his analysis of the relationships between existing features has been sound, he will have established a base from which later students may be able to advance.

What Are Historical Facts?

CARL BECKER

In Chapter Five we made the distinction between words that refer to things we can see, smell, and taste, such as "flower," "boy," and "sugar," and words about which we can only talk in order to give them meaning, such as "love," "justice," and "facts."

This selection from Carl Becker's writings presents one man's efforts to make sense out of the word "fact." Carl Becker was one of America's most distinguished historians. His intellectual efforts should illustrate the profound complexity of what may appear to be a very simple affair.

. . . When anyone says "facts" we are all there. The word gives us a sense of stability. We know where we are when, as we say, we "get down to the facts"—as, for example, we know where we are when we get down to the facts of the structure of the atom, or the incredible movement of the electron as it jumps from one orbit to another. It is the same with history. Historians feel safe when dealing with the facts. We talk much about the "hard facts" and the "cold facts," about "not being able to get around the facts," and about the necessity of basing our narrative on a "solid foundation of fact." By virtue of talking in this way, the facts of history come in the end to seem something solid, something substantial like physical matter (I mean matter in the common sense, not matter defined as "a series of events in the ether"), something possessing definite shape, and clear persistent outline— like bricks or scantlings; so that we can easily picture the historian as he stumbles about in the past, stubbing his toe on the hard facts if he doesn't watch out. That is his affair of course, a danger he runs; for his business is

From *Detachment and the Writing of History,* by Carl Becker (Ithaca, N.Y.: Cornell University Press, 1958), pp. 43–61 (with omissions).

to dig out the facts and pile them up for someone to use. Perhaps he may use them himself; but at all events he must arrange them conveniently so that someone—perhaps the sociologist or the economist—may easily carry them away for use in some structural enterprise.

Such (with no doubt a little, but not much, exaggeration to give point to the matter) are the common connotations of the words historical facts, as used by historians and other people. Now, when I meet a word with which I am entirely unfamiliar, I find it a good plan to look it up in the dictionary and find out what someone thinks it means. But when I have frequently to use words with which everyone is perfectly familiar—words like "cause" and "liberty" and "progress" and "government"—when I have to use words of this sort which everyone knows perfectly well, the wise thing to do is to take a week off and think about them. The result is often astonishing; for as often as not I find that I have been talking about words instead of real things. Well, "historical fact" is such a word; and I suspect it would be worthwhile for us historians at least to think about this word more than we have done. For the moment therefore, leaving the historian moving about in the past piling up the cold facts, I wish to inquire whether the historical fact is really as hard and stable as it is often supposed to be.

And this inquiry I will throw into the form of three simple questions. I will ask the questions, I can't promise to answer them. The questions are: (1) What is the historical fact? (2) Where is the historical fact? (3) When is the historical fact? Mind I say *is* not *was*. I take it for granted that if we are interested in, let us say, the fact of the Magna Carta, we are interested in it for our own sake and not for its sake; and since we are living now and not in 1215 we must be interested in the Magna Carta, if at all, for what it is and not for what it was.

First then, What is the historical fact? Let us take a simple fact, as simple as the historian often deals with, viz.: "In the year 49 B.C. Caesar crossed the Rubicon." A familiar fact this is, known to all, and obviously of some importance since it is mentioned in every history of the great Caesar. But is this fact as simple as it sounds? Has it the clear, persistent outline which we commonly attribute to simple historical facts? When we say that Caesar crossed the Rubicon we do not of course mean that Caesar crossed it alone, but with his army. The Rubicon is a small river, and I don't know how long it took Caesar's army to cross it; but the crossing must surely have been accompanied by many acts and many words and many thoughts of many men. That is to say, a thousand and one lesser "facts" went to make up the one simple fact that Caesar crossed the Rubicon; and if we had someone, say James Joyce, to know and relate all these facts, it would no doubt require a book of 794 pages to present this one fact that Caesar crossed the Rubicon. Thus the simple fact turns out to be not a simple fact at all. It is the statement that is simple—a simple generalization of a thousand and one facts. . . .

. . . Thus the simple historical fact turns out to be not a hard, cold something with clear outline, and measurable pressure, like a brick. It is so far as we can know it, only a *symbol,* a simple statement which is a generalization of a thousand and one simpler facts which we do not for the moment care to use, and this generalization itself we cannot use apart from the wider facts and generalizations which it symbolizes. And generally speaking, the more simple an historical fact is, the more clear and definite and provable it is, the less use it is to us in and for itself.

Less simple facts illustrate all this equally well, even better perhaps. For example, the fact that "Indulgences were sold in Germany in 1517." This fact can be proved down to the ground. No one doubts it. But taken by itself the fact is nothing, means nothing. It also is a generalization of a thousand and one facts, a thousand and one actions of innumerable sellers and buyers of indulgences all over Germany at many different times; and this also acquires significance and meaning only as it is related to other facts and wider generalizations. . . .

. . . What then is the historical fact? Far be it from me to define so illusive and intangible a thing! But provisionally I will say this: the historian may be interested in anything that has to do with the life of man in the past—any act or event, any emotion which men have expressed, any idea, true or false, which they have entertained. Very well, the historian is interested in some event of this sort. Yet he cannot deal directly with this event itself, since the event itself has disappeared. What he can deal with directly is a *statement about the event.* He deals in short not with the event, but with a statement which affirms *the fact that the event occurred.* When we really get down to the hard facts, what the historian is always dealing with is an *affirmation*—an affirmation of the fact that something is true. There is thus a distinction of capital importance to be made: the distinction between the ephemeral event which disappears, and the affirmation about the event which persists. For all practical purposes it is this affirmation about the event that constitutes for us the historical fact. If so the historical fact is not the past event, but a symbol which enables us to recreate it imaginatively. Of a symbol it is hardly worthwhile to say that it is cold or hard. It is dangerous to say even that it is true or false. The safest thing to say about a symbol is that it is more or less appropriate.

This brings me to the second question—Where is the historical fact? I will say at once, however brash it sounds, that the historical fact is in someone's mind or it is nowhere. To illustrate this statement I will take an event familiar to all. "Abraham Lincoln was assassinated in Ford's Theater in Washington on the 14th of April, 1865." That *was* an actual event, occurrence, fact at the moment of happening. But speaking now, in the year 1926, we say it *is* an historical fact. We don't say that it *was* an historical fact, for that would imply that it no longer is one. We say that it *was* an actual event, but *is now* an historical fact. The actual occurrence and the historical fact, however closely connected, are two different things. Very well, if the assassination of Lincoln is an historical fact, where is this fact now? Lincoln is not being assassinated now in Ford's Theater, or anywhere else (except perhaps in propagandist literature!). The actual occurrence, the event, has passed, is gone forever, never to be repeated, never to be again experienced or witnessed by any living person. Yet this is precisely the sort of thing the historian is concerned with—events, acts, thoughts, emotions that have forever vanished as actual occurrences. How can the historian deal with vanished realities? He can deal with them because these vanished realities give place to pale reflections, impalpable images or ideas of themselves, and these pale reflections, and impalpable images which cannot be touched or handled are all that is left of the actual occurrence. These are therefore what the historian deals with. These are his "material." He has to be satisfied with these, for the very good reason that he has nothing else. Well then, where are they—these pale reflections and impalpable images of the actual? Where are these facts? They are, as I said before, in his mind, or in somebody's mind, or they are nowhere. . . .

. . . Now for the third question—When is the historical fact? If you agree with what has been said (which is extremely doubtful) the answer seems simple enough. If the historical fact is present, imaginatively, in someone's mind, then it is now, a part of the present. But the word *present* is a slippery word, and the thing itself is worse than the word. The present is an indefinable point in time, gone before you can think it; the image or idea which I have now present in mind slips instantly into the past. But images or ideas of past events are often, perhaps always, inseparable from images or ideas of the future. Take an illustration. I awake this morning, and among the things my memory drags in to enlighten or distress me is a vague notion that there was something I needed particularly to remember but cannot—a common experience surely. What it is that I needed to remember I cannot recall; but I can recall that I made a note of it in order to jog my memory. So I consult my little pocket memorandum book—a little Private Record Office which I carry about, filled with historical sources. I take out my memorandum book in order to do a little historical research; and there I find (Vol. I, p. 20) the dead historical fact—"Pay Smith's coal bill today: $1,016." The image of the memorandum book now drops out of mind, and is replaced by another image—an image of what? Why an image, an idea, a picture (call it what you will) made up of three things more or less inseparable. First the image of myself ordering coal from Smith last summer; second, the image of myself holding the idea in mind that I must pay the bill; third, the image of myself going down to Smith's office at four o'clock to pay it. The image is partly of things done in the past, and partly of things to be done in the future; but it is more or less all one image now present in mind.

Someone may ask, "Are you talking of history or of the ordinary ills of every day that men are heir to?" Well, perhaps Smith's coal bill is only my personal affair, of no concern to anyone else, except Smith to be sure. Take then another example. I am thinking of the Congress of Berlin, and that is without doubt history—the real thing. The historical facts of the Congress of Berlin I bring alive in memory, imaginatively. But I am making an image of the Congress of Berlin for a purpose; and indeed without a purpose no one would take the trouble to bring historical facts to mind. My purpose happens to be to convey this image of the Congress of Berlin to my class in History 42, in Room C, tomorrow afternoon at 3 o'clock. Now I find that insepar-able from this image of the Congress of Berlin, which occurred in the past, are flittering images of myself conveying this image of the Congress of Berlin to my class tomorrow in Room C. I picture myself standing there monoton-ously talking, I hear the labored sentences painfully issuing forth, I picture the students' faces alert or bored as the case may be; so that images of this future event enter into the imagined picture of the Congress of Berlin, a past event; enter into it, coloring and shaping it too, to the end that the performance may do credit to me, or be intelligible to immature minds, or be compressed within the limits of fifty minutes, or to accomplish some other desired end. Well, this living historical fact, this mixed image of the coal bill or the Congress of Berlin—is it past, present, or future? I cannot say. Perhaps it moves with the velocity of light, and is timeless. At all events it is real history to me, which I hope to make convincing and real to Smith, or to the class in Room C.

I have now asked my three questions, and have made some remarks about them all. I don't know whether these remarks will strike you as quite beside the mark, or as merely obvious, or as novel. If there is any novelty in them, it arises, I think, from our inveterate habit of thinking of the world of history as part of the external world, and of historical facts as actual events. In truth the actual past is gone; and the world of history is an intangible world, re-created imaginatively, and present in our minds. If, as I think, this is true, then there are certain important implications growing out of it; and if you are not already exhausted I should like to touch upon a few of these implications. I will present them "firstly," "secondly," and so on, like the points of a sermon, without any attempt at co-ordination.

One implication is that by no possibility can the historian present in its entirety any actual event, even the simplest. You may think this a com-monplace, and I do too; but still it needs to be often repeated because one of the fondest illusions of nineteenth century historians was that the historian,

the "scientific" historian, would do just that: he would "present all the facts
and let them speak for themselves." The historian would contribute nothing
himself, except the sensitive plate of his mind, upon which the objective
facts would register their own unimpeachable meaning. . . .

. . . Well, for twenty years I have taken it for granted that no one could
longer believe so preposterous an idea. But the notion continues to bob up
regularly; and only the other day, riding on the train to the meeting of the
Historical Association, Mr. A. J. Beveridge, eminent and honored historian,
assured me dogmatically (it would be dogmatically) that the historian has
nothing to do but "present all the facts and let them speak for themselves."
And so I repeat, what I have been teaching for twenty years, that this notion
is preposterous; first, because it is impossible to present all the facts; and
second, because even if you could present all the facts the miserable things
wouldn't say anything, would say just nothing at all.

Let us return to the simple fact: "Lincoln was assassinated in Ford's
Theater in Washington, April 14, 1865." This is not all the facts. It is, if
you like, a *representation* of all the facts, and a representation that perhaps
satisfies one historian. But another historian, for some reason, is not satisfied.
He says: "On April 14, 1865, in Washington, Lincoln, sitting in a private
box in Ford's Theater watching a play, was shot by John Wilkes Booth,
who then jumped to the stage crying out, *'Sic semper tyrannis!'* " That is a
true affirmation about the event also. It represents, if you like, all the facts
too. But its form and content (one and the same thing in literary discourse)
is different, because it contains more of the facts than the other. Well, the
point is that any number of affirmations (an infinite number if the sources
were sufficient) could be made about the actual event, all true, all representing the event, but some containing more and some less of the factual aspects
of the total event. But by no possibility can the historian make affirmations
describing all of the facts—all of the acts, thoughts, emotions of all of the
persons who contributed to the actual event in its entirety. One historian
will therefore necessarily *choose* certain affirmations about the event, and
relate them in a certain way, rejecting other affirmations and other ways of
relating them. Another historian will necessarily make a different choice.
Why? What is it that leads one historian to make, out of all the possible
true affirmations about the given event, certain affirmations and not others?
Why, the purpose he has in his mind will determine the precise meaning
which he derives from the event. The event itself, the facts, do not say anything, do not impose any meaning. It is the historian who speaks, who imposes a meaning.

A second implication follows from this. It is that the historian cannot
eliminate the personal equation. Of course, no one can; not even, I think,
the natural scientist. The universe speaks to us only in response to our purposes; and even the most objective constructions, those, let us say, of the

theoretical physicist, are not the sole possible constructions, but only such as are found most convenient for some human need or purpose. Nevertheless, the physicist can eliminate the personal equation to a greater extent, or at least in a different way, than the historian, because he deals, as the historian does not, with an external world directly. The physicist presides at the living event, the historian presides only at the inquest of its remains. If I were alone in the universe and gashed my finger on a sharp rock, I could never be certain that there was anything there but my consciousness of the rock and gashed finger. But if ten other men in precisely the same way gash their fingers on the same sharp rock, we can, by comparing impressions, infer that there is something there besides consciousness. There is an external world there. The physicist can gash his finger on the rock as many times as he likes, and get others to do it, until they are all certain of the facts. He can, as Eddington says, make pointer-readings of the behavior of the physical world as many times as he likes for a given phenomenon, until he and his colleagues are satisfied. When their minds all rest satisfied, they have an explanation, what is called the truth. But suppose the physicist had to reach his conclusions from miscellaneous records, made by all sorts of people, of experiments that had been made in the past, each experiment made only once, and none of them capable of being repeated. The external world he would then have to deal with would be the records. That is the case of the historian. The only external world he has to deal with is the records. He can indeed look at the records as often as he likes, and he can get dozens of others to look at them: and some things, some "facts," can in this way be established and agreed upon, as, for example, the fact that the document known as the Declaration of Independence was voted on July 4, 1776. But the meaning and significance of this fact cannot be thus agreed upon, because the series of events in which it has a place cannot be enacted again and again, under varying conditions, in order to see what effect the variations would have. The historian has to judge the significance of the series of events from the one single performance, never to be repeated, and never, since the records are incomplete and imperfect, capable of being fully known or fully affirmed. Thus into the imagined facts and their meaning there enters the personal equation. The history of any event is never precisely the same thing to two different persons; and it is well known that every generation writes the same history in a new way, and puts upon it a new construction.

The reason why this is so—why the same series of vanished events is differently imagined in each succeeding generation—is that our imagined picture of the actual event is always determined by two things: (1) by the actual event itself insofar as we know something about it; and (2) by our own present purposes, desires, prepossessions, and prejudices, all of which enter into the process of knowing it. The actual event contributes something to the imagined picture; but the mind that holds the imagined picture always contributes something too. This is why there is no more fascinating or illuminating phase of history than historiography—the history of history: the history, that is, of what successive generations have imagined the past to be like. It is impossible to understand the history of certain great events without knowing what the actors in those events themselves thought about history. For example, it helps immensely to understand why the leaders of the American and French Revolutions acted and thought as they did if we know what their idea of classical history was. They desired, to put it simply, to be virtuous republicans, and to act the part. Well, they were able to act the part of virtuous republicans much more effectively because they carried around in their heads an idea, or ideal if you prefer, of Greek republicanism and Roman virtue. But of course their own desire to be virtuous republicans had a great influence in making them think the Greeks and Romans, whom they had been taught to admire by reading the classics in school, were virtuous republicans too. Their image of the present and future and their image of the classical past were inseparable, bound together—were really one and the same thing.

In this way the present influences our idea of the past, and our idea of the past influences the present. We are accustomed to say that "the present is the product of all the past"; and this is what is ordinarily meant by the historian's doctrine of "historical continuity." But it is only a half truth. It is equally true, and no mere paradox, to say that the past (our imagined picture of it) is the product of all the present. We build our conceptions of history partly out of our present needs and purposes. The past is a kind of screen upon which we project our vision of the future; and it is indeed a moving picture, borrowing much of its form and color from our fears and aspirations. The doctrine of historical continuity is badly in need of overhauling in the light of these suggestions; for that doctrine was itself one of those pictures which the early nineteenth century threw upon the screen of the past in order to quiet its deep-seated fears—fears occasioned by the French Revolution and the Napoleonic wars.

A third implication is that no one can profit by historical research, or not much, unless he does some for himself. Historical knowledge, however richly stored in books or in the minds of professors of history, is no good to me unless I have some of it. In this respect, historical research differs profoundly from research in the natural sciences, at least in some of them. For example, I know no physics, but I profit from physical researches every night by the simple act of pressing an electric light button. And everyone can profit in this way from researches in physics without knowing any physics, without knowing even that there is such a thing as physics. But with history it is different. Henry Ford, for example, can't profit from all the historical researches of two thousand years, because he knows so little history himself.

By no pressing of any button can he flood the spare rooms of his mind with the light of human experience.

A fourth implication is more important than the others. It is that every normal person does know some history, a good deal in fact. Of course we often hear someone say: "I don't know any history; I wish I knew some history; I must improve my mind by learning some history." We know what is meant. This person means that he has never read any history books, or studied history in college; and so he thinks he knows no history. But it is precisely this conventional notion of history as something external to us, as a body of dull knowledge locked up in books, that obscures its real meaning. For, I repeat (it will bear repeating) every normal person—every man, woman, and child—does know some history, enough for his immediate purposes; otherwise he would be a lost soul indeed. I suppose myself, for example, to have awakened this morning with loss of memory. I am all right otherwise; but I can't remember anything that happened in the past. What is the result? The result is that I don't know who I am, where I am, where to go, or what to do. I can't attend to my duties at the university, I can't read this paper before the Research Club. In short, my present would be unintelligible and my future meaningless. Why? Why, because I had suddenly ceased to know any history. What happens when I wake up in the morning is that my memory reaches out into the past and gathers together those images of past events, of objects seen, of words spoken and of thoughts thought in the past, which are necessary to give me an ordered world to live in, necessary to orient me in my personal world. Well, this collection of images and ideas of things past is history, my command of living history, a series of images of the past which shifts and reforms at every moment of the day in response to the exigencies of my daily living. Every man has a knowledge of history in this sense, which is the only vital sense in which he can have a knowledge of history. Every man has some knowledge of past events, more or less accurate; knowledge enough, and accurate enough, for his purposes, or what he regards as such. How much and how accurate, will depend on the man and his purposes. Now, the point is that history in the formal sense, history as we commonly think of it, is only an extension of memory. Knowledge or history, insofar as it is living history and not dead knowledge locked up in notebooks, is only an enrichment of our minds with the multiplied images of events, places, peoples, ideas, emotions outside our personal experience, an enrichment of our experience by bringing into our minds memories of the experience of the community, the nation, the race. Its chief value, for the individual, is doubtless that it enables a man to orient himself in a larger world than the merely personal, has the effect for him of placing the petty and intolerable present in a longer perspective, thus enabling him to judge the acts and thoughts of men, his own included, on the basis of an experience less immediate and restricted. . . .

Using Anthropological Materials

JACK L. ELLISON

When a teacher leads his students into the study of their own community, he can help them to make use of anthropological and sociological techniques of inquiry: they can talk to people and visit courtrooms, railway stations, city council meetings, and banks. But a study of distant contemporary cultures is dependent upon the scientific work of others. We have called this sort of investigation the study of the *Now and There*.

Elementary-school students cannot visit the South Pacific, France, or the Arctic Circle. They might simply read the information found in the books available in the classroom—textbooks, encyclopedias, and so forth. A better alternative is to consult reports that researchers have made regarding far-away places. Scientists learn to make use of the investigations of others. Children, too, can learn that real people engage themselves in many sorts of investigations. Often, the bland overgeneralizations encountered in many textbooks are far different in quality and interest from the reports made by serious investigators.

The following discussion suggests uses for anthropological writings. Chapter Eleven, on the Now and There, presents a more extended discussion of these possibilities.

For twelfth graders to embark on a serious study of the Eskimo and Iroquois of North America, the Samoans of the South Seas, the Aranda of Australia and the Todas of Southern India may seem, at first glance, an odd way to spend the first semester of senior-year social studies when there is the "insistent present" (to use Whitehead's phrase) all around us. How, you might ask, can such a study illuminate the concerns of today's young people? . . .

. . . [One] value of this material is that it is concerned with the most basic human relationships and institutions; parent-child relationships, the family, marriage, death, growing up, man and the unknown, man and the physical environment, man's relationship to other men. A cross-cultural study of societies which have developed outside the orbit of Western civilization enables the students to see how differently various societies have structured these relationships and, at the same time, to observe the recurrent individual and social needs which must be met.

Take the area called "Growing Up." It is fascinating to look at societies

From "Anthropology Brings Human Nature into the Classroom," by Jack L. Ellison, *Social Education*, XXIV (November 1960), 313–316 (with omissions). By permission of author and publisher.

where, as Robert Redfield says, "What one man knows and believes, all men know and believe." Grandparents understand their grandchildren because the same skills and the same values are being taught. Puberty ceremonials, found so frequently in elaborate form in these societies, tell the boy what he must adhere to so that the society will be strong and he will be assured that he is a man. Learning is closely related to doing, and doing is closely related to survival: an Eskimo boy is not confused as to why he must pay attention when lessons in catching the walrus are being offered. These clarities of agreed-upon customs and values present such a different picture from the complexities of choice our young people face that the contrast, along with the universal similarities of growing up, enables the students to talk about themselves in a more objective and useful way.

With a variety of societies to draw upon, societies so seemingly remote from ours, it is possible in the discussions of how others face growing up, marriage, and death, to talk about one's own wonderings and feelings without appearing to do so, an opportunity greatly desired by adolescents. It should not be hard to see how rich and meaningful discussion can grow out of such subject matter, provided that there is always new "objective" material being introduced, and provided that the teacher respects the circumlocutions of the students.

Another value of studying primitive societies grows out of the fact that their populations are, compared to ours, small in number and relatively homogeneous in custom and belief. One can, therefore, see the culture as a whole and observe the interrelationships among the various parts. A well-known example can be taken from a Plains Indian tribe, the Crow. Central to their way of life were the war-like exploits of the men; counting coup, leading a successful war party, untethering a horse from an enemy's encampment, stealing an enemy's bow. In order to lead a successful war party, a man needs to have a Vision, usually acquired by going to a solitary place, fasting, and physically mutilating himself. Thus a central aspect of their religious life is closely related to their military. Those who achieve these four deeds become chiefs who, in their Councils, give some direction to the tribe. Thus social organization or politics is added to the picture. To accomplish these deeds one must be skilled on horseback, possess physical courage and individual daring; and thus we arrive at the personality type most admired by the society and encouraged by the elders in the growing up of the young.

One could demonstrate in many other ways the manner in which certain central themes appear in varied aspects or institutions of a society. Our modern urban society, on the other hand, has become more complex. Not only is economics a specialized field but the study of depressions is a specialization within a specialization. The growing ability of the students to become more sensitive to these interrelationships leads them to look at the subcultures of their own society more holistically.

"After all, it's only human nature . . ." to have wars, to be greedy, to be competitive rather than cooperative, to be lazy; and "You can't change human nature, you know." These are assumptions which the material of cultural anthropology critically challenges. Just because the students come to observe such a broad panorama of ways of behaving, they come to recognize one of the most important concepts anthropology has to offer: that much which may seem to be "human nature" is only one's accustomed way of thinking and behaving. There are societies, like the Todas, which live in peace with their neighbors, whereas other societies, like the Plains Indians, give great status to warlike pursuits. There are societies like the Hopi and Zuni who emphasize cooperation and underplay competition, whereas among the Dobu each man's hand is against his neighbor. The most highly valued quality of an Indian chief is liberality with his possessions; the refrigerated caches of food of the Polar Eskimo are available to anyone who is hungry, even if "undeserving." Thus man appears to be a more flexible being than the rigid human nature school would lead us to believe. This is a very hopeful concept for young people whose idealism leads them to want to improve the world they live in. If culture is man-made (which it is), it can be altered by man. Man is the "creature" and the "creator" of his culture. . . .

. . . "Our Hero: A Study of the Ideal Male Type" is the somewhat facetious title of a written assignment given after we have studied four or five societies.[1] The students are expected to describe as best they can the personality characteristics of the ideal male in three of the societies (or two of the societies and either the Homeric hero, since they have been reading the *Iliad* in English, or an American subcultural hero). As they compare the aggressive, boasting, highly status-aware Haida chief with the passive, self-abnegating, highly ritual-aware Hopi chief or the physically agile, individualistic Crow chief with his mind filled with martial exploits, they become aware of the degree to which varying cultures admire quite opposite types of personality. The paper is also expected to include their findings about how the society encourages the boys and young men to strive toward this ideal. Each of the coveted positions carries its symbols whether they be totemic crests, eagle feathers, or Cadillacs. Some of these positions are wholly or partially ascribed, i.e., inherited; others are achieved, i.e., gained by the individual himself or with the help of others. Once in this position, certain types of behavior are expected of the individual by the community. Walter Goldschmidt in an article named "Arete," which the students read, summarizes these ideas in a very stimulating fashion. Two additional points which he makes and which very much interest the class are: (1) that in a

---

[1] Of necessity, in a brief article there is oversimplification. Let it be said for those who are acquainted with anthropological literature and who may raise a scholarly eyebrow, that in class we develop such topics as "Ideal Types" more fully than would appear here, though not sufficiently, perchance, to satisfy the most exacting.

society like those of the Plains Indians where the qualities necessary for the ideal are exceedingly demanding and require basic physical skills, the society creates a secondary acceptable role for the men, that of a berdache who does women's work but better than women do it; (2) that though a relationship can usually be found between the economic needs of a society and its ideal type, yet highest status is very often gained in ways which are economically wasteful. An example of the latter can be found among the Trobriand Islanders where yams are piled up in as great quantities as possible—to rot; at the same time good yam farming is encouraged in order to accumulate such a display, and the good farmer is essential to the society's economy. All these ideas, along with the examples from the students' reading and their papers, lead to absorbing discussions; and the relevance to their own society and subculture is understood—in part explicitly, and in part implicitly. Adolescents are often wondering about themselves in relation to the honored roles in their society. They often experiment with being different kinds of people just to see what it feels like. To repeat a point made earlier in this discussion, a new perspective is gained by looking at one's own society and oneself via seemingly remote, markedly different societies. . . .

School History and the Historical Method

HENRY JOHNSON

To some extent, the following selection has been an important inspiration for much of this book. In his 1940 revision, Johnson proposed an idea that may well have been twenty-five years ahead of his time. A statement like this one is not unusual today; but his ideas are as provocative now as they were then.

Johnson's basic point is simply this: history is something to do; an important part of studying history is learning how to do it.

To most teachers, most of the time, history for school purposes presents itself as a body of assured knowledge, selected portions of which are to be interpreted, learned, and, so far as possible, applied to life in the present. Some teachers seem to believe that history may literally set forth the truth and nothing but the truth. For this there is distinguished precedent. Eighteenth century Johnson, according to Macaulay, with a touch of the literary critic's contempt for historians, put the case very simply. "The historian tells either what is false or what is true: in the former case he is no historian: in the

From *The Teaching of History* (rev. ed.) by Henry Johnson (New York: The Macmillan Company, 1940), Chapter XV (abridged). By permission of the publisher.

latter he has no opportunity for displaying his abilities: for truth is one: and all who tell the truth must tell it alike."[1] In a vein not altogether different it is related of Fustel de Coulanges, nineteenth century critical historian, that one day when he was lecturing and his students broke into applause, he stopped them with the remark, "Do not applaud me, it is not I who address you; it is history which speaks through me."[2]

That there is a residuum of assured historical knowledge is not to be denied. Without it history could have little claim to differentiation from fiction. The residuum is in fact so large that the idea of drawing exclusively upon it for school purposes may seem entirely feasible. In practice that idea has, however, not been realized. If many of the textbooks and some of the popular histories used in school convey a different impression, if they are in general pervaded by an atmosphere of undisputed verity, the effect is, in large part, achieved by the arbitrary device of elevating opinions based upon incomplete evidence to the rank of clearly established truth. It is by means of this device that some of the most familiar personages, conditions, and events have, for school purposes, been withdrawn from the realm of controversy. Take the case of Columbus. In a well-known and deservedly popular textbook we read:

Christopher Columbus, the great discoverer, was born in Genoa, Italy, about 1436. He spent most of his early life at sea, and became an experienced navigator. He was a man who read widely, and intelligently. When on shore, his trade was the designing and making of maps. This occupation led him to think much about the shape of the earth, and he came to agree with those men who held that the earth is round like a globe. This belief led him to conclude that Asia could be reached by sailing westward and that a new route to India could be opened.

The account is accompanied by a portrait, labeled "Christopher Columbus."

The facts sum up in a typical manner the Columbus of our elementary schools, and, as here presented, make a very simple and reasonable kind of history. It is interesting to know how Columbus looked, where he came from, and how he made up his mind that India could be reached by sailing westward. But is the assurance warranted? A larger and more critical history informs us that while a number of portraits exist with claims to the honor of representing Columbus, "there is no likeness whose claim is indisputable."[3] Concerning the date of birth and the genesis of the ideas that lead to the discovery of America, another critical historian writes:

Christopher Columbus was born at some time between 1430 and 1456, the precise date of this event being of slight importance nowadays, save to him who

[1] T. B. MACAULAY, *Critical, Historical and Miscellaneous Essays and Poems,* Boston, 1880, 3 Volumes, I, 276.

[2] *Congress of Arts and Sciences,* St. Louis, 1940, II, 158.

[3] JUSTIN WINSOR, *Narrative and Critical History of America,* Boston, 1886, II, 69.

seeks to conjure up a picture of the great seaman as he paced the deck of his flagship off San Salvador on that pregnant October night in 1492. Henry Harisse and Justin Winsor unite in giving the date as 1446-47, and when these two agree one may as well follow them without more ado. Eighteen places claim Columbus as a native, but scholars unite in giving that honor to Genoa or its immediate vicinity. At an early age he shipped on his first voyage, and kept on sailing the seas until, some years later, he found himself in Portugal, the fifteenth century meeting place of adventurous and scientific seamen.

Exactly how or when Columbus made up his mind as to the shape of the earth, the feasibility of sailing westward to India, and determined to do it, is not clear. Ferdinand Columbus, for instance, tells us that the admiral was influenced by the works of Arab astronomers and by Ptolemy and the ancients. But whether this should be taken in more than a general sense may be doubted. Another theory is that Columbus, studying the *Imago Mundi* of Pierre D'Ailly, Bishop of Cambray, came across the old ideas which that compiler had borrowed from Roger Bacon. The first printed copy of the *Imago Mundi* was made at Louvain not before 1480; but Columbus thought that the earth was round before that time and there is no evidence that he ever read the Bishop of Cambray's work in manuscript. It is true that in the report of his third voyage (1498) he quoted a sentence from this book, and there still exists a copy of it with marginal notes in his handwriting, or in that of his brother, Bartholomew, for the writing of the two was much alike. But none of these things proves that he had read the work in manuscript, nor is there reason to suppose that the theories of the ancients had much, if any, direct influence upon him. If he had known of the Bishop of Cambray's book before 1492, it is most probable that he would have used it as an authority to reinforce his ideas; but there is no evidence that he did this. Another way to account for Columbus's opinions is to attribute great influence to the letters of Paolo dal Pozzo Toscanelli of Florence. Sir Clements R. Markham even goes so far as to print them as the "sailing directions of Columbus." A more recent writer, Henry Vignaud, has gone to the other extreme and has denied that such letters ever existed.[4]

Many teachers who habitually treat history in school as assured knowledge are, of course, aware of doubts lurking behind, not only individual facts, but behind the selection and organization of facts. They know that individual facts, even when true, may yet in combination fail to convey the truth. They agree with Macaulay that one writer may even tell less truth than another by telling more truths. But school conditions seem to them to render dogmatism both necessary and desirable. There is, in the first place, the question of what is possible. History of the kind in which an author writes as if he really knows presents difficulties. History of the kind in which an author writes as if nobody really knows introduces complications which many teachers consider unsuitable for children, beyond their range of interests, and confusing, even to the average adult. To be told in substance that there was once a man by the name of Christopher Columbus who made

[4] EDWARD CHANNING, *History of the United States,* New York, 1905–1925, I, 14–15.

up his mind that India could be reached by sailing westward, and that considerable energy, most of it vain, has been expended in trying to find out when and where he was born and how he reached his epoch-making conclusion may be satisfying to historical experts; it neither can nor ought to be satisfying to others. Both for children and for the general reading public, history, to be read at all, must be something definite to believe about the past and not something to be doubted or argued about. If there are controversies, they must, therefore, be forcibly suppressed.

There are, in the second place, uses of history to which, it is often urged, the subject must at any cost be subordinated. Balanced opinions, and arguments that lead chiefly to doubt, are, even if manageable, at best uninspiring and at worst positively harmful to childhood and youth. They are, therefore, to be avoided, and even resented. "There is a certain meddlesome spirit," says Washington Irving, at the end of his account of the early years of Columbus and of the origin of the idea of a western voyage, "which, in the garb of learned research, goes prying about the traces of history, casting down its monuments, and marring and mutilating its fairest trophies. Care should be taken to vindicate great names from such pernicious erudition. It defeats one of the most salutary purposes of history, that of furnishing examples of what human genius and laudable enterprise may accomplish."[5] Many teachers find in the "salutary purposes of history" a justification for eliminating controversy.

There is, in the third place, a feeling that such exaggeration of historical probability as may result from a dogmatic treatment need excite no special concern. School history, it is argued, is in most cases destined to an early oblivion, and if, in some cases, remnants do survive, it is at worst better to go through life with a few definite errors than to think of history as something that might have been either this or that, and was probably neither. "It's all in confidence," says a delightful essayist, protesting, on behalf of the "Gentle Reader," against the ways of the critical historian, "speak out as one gentleman to another under a friendly roof! What do you think about it? No matter if you make a mistake or two, I'll forget most that you say anyway."[6]

Shall doubts, then, be suppressed? Shall mere personal opinions, mere guesses, and sometimes mere fancies be combined on terms of complete equality with indisputable facts? Shall the study of history concern itself only with the meaning of an author? Shall there be no distinction between *his story,* with the emphasis upon the *his,* and *history?* In the opinion of a growing minority of history teachers, both in Europe and in America, to ask such questions is in effect to ask whether the school view of history shall be intelligent or unintelligent. . . .

[5] WASHINGTON IRVING, *The Life and Voyages of Christopher Columbus,* author's revised edition, New York, 1850, 3 volumes, I, 55–56.

[6] SAMUEL MCCHORD CROTHERS, *The Gentle Reader,* Boston, 1903, p. 173.

. . . Not all of us read histories, but all of us begin with the first dawning of intelligence to use facts known to us historically and not directly. It is a commonplace that most of our conversation is narrative and historical, whether the subject be what we, our friends, or some other person, said or did this morning, or what was said or done a hundred or a thousand years ago. It is a commonplace that data historical in character enter into most of the thinking and planning of life from childhood to the grave. It ought to be a commonplace that schoolroom history should give the pupil some consciousness of what historical knowledge is and some training in the method by which historical knowledge is established. It ought to be a commonplace that there are "salutary purposes" to be served by history as a process of determining, selecting, and arranging facts, not less important than those to be served by history as the organized result.

Training in the historical method of study is a somewhat formidable expression difficult to dissociate from university work. But the teacher must not be frightened by what may appear to be pretentious terminology. We speak of history in the elementary school and history in the university, without prejudice to either. It is convenient, and it ought to be possible, to speak of the historical method in both, without prejudice to either. Certainly the processes thus described—the search for material, the classification and criticism of material, the determination of particular facts, the selection and arrangement of facts—present elementary aspects. A first grade can be led to see that something is learned about the Indians from things dug up out of the ground, something from writings of white men who reported what they saw, and something from stories told by Indians about themselves and later reported by white men. First-grade children will themselves often suggest that the Indians did not write books. A fourth grade can be led to think of different ways of knowing about people, and of the relative merits of the different ways of knowing about them. A sixth grade can be taught the use of indexes and tables of contents and something of the significance of references to authorities. A seventh grade can be led to solve some simple problems in criticism. From the first, there can be exercises in putting facts together, and, above the seventh grade, exercises involving essential aspects of the historical method of study from the search for material to the organization and exposition of results. . . .

. . . School history must, in the main, be presented as ready-made information. But there can be, and should be, illustrations of the historical method sufficient to indicate the general nature of the problems behind organized history, and sufficient to give some definite training in the solution of such problems. How shall this be accomplished?

Here, let us say, is a teacher of a fourth or fifth grade who is called upon by the course of study to discuss with her class some of the peoples of antiquity. She has discovered that for certain subjects Herodotus seems to be a mine of information, and that somehow he has mastered the art of telling a story so as to be interesting even in a translation. He is to be used mainly for information, but the teacher believes that the children's interest will not be lessened by raising here and there the question of how Herodotus gathered his information. The rôle of father of history, which he has played so long, lends, it may be, a peculiar sense of fitness to the idea of raising the question first with him. She begins with a few preliminary questions: What people are there in the world besides Americans? How do you know? Who are the oldest people in the world?

On one occasion a girl knew that there were Germans in the world because she had heard her mother speak of a German woman. The teacher wrote on the blackboard: "We may know of people by hearing about them." A boy knew that there were Indians in the world because he had read about them in a book. The teacher wrote: "We may know of people by reading about them." Another boy knew that there were Chinese in the world because he had seen a Chinese. He spoke with an air of conviction that seemed to express disapproval of hearsay or books as evidence, and a new look of intelligence swept over the class. They had all seen a Chinese. The teacher wrote: "We may know of people by seeing them." Before this last statement had been put on the board the children were discussing the relative merits of the three ways that had been suggested of knowing about people. It was unanimously agreed that the Indians were the oldest people in the world, on the ground, as one member of the class put it, that "they are the first people we read about in school." This was the crudest piece of reasoning developed during the lesson. The children were told that the question was one which appeared to have been raised a long time ago in Egypt, for a traveler who went there has told us a story about it. A line was drawn on the blackboard to represent ten years, the average age of the pupils. With this as a unit, the line was continued to represent a century. It was then extended century by century across the blackboard of three sides of the room until the twenty-five centuries back to Herodotus had been measured. In this way the children were at least made conscious that Herodotus lived a very long time ago. They had already heard of Egypt and had formed some impression of where Egypt is. The story as told by Herodotus was then read.

The Egyptians before the reign of their king Psammetichus believed themselves to be the oldest of mankind. Psammetichus, however, wished to find out if this was true. So he took two children of the common sort and gave them over to a herdsman to bring up, charging him to let no one speak a word in their presence, but to keep them in a cottage by themselves, and take to them food and look after them in other respects. His object herein was to know, after the first babblings of infancy were over, what word they would speak first. The herdsman did as he was told for two years, and at the end of that time on his opening the door of their room and going in, the children both ran up to him with outstretched arms and called, "Becos." When this first happened, the herdsman took no notice; but afterwards when he observed on coming often to see them that the word was constantly in their mouths, he told the King and by his command brought the children into the King's presence. Psammetichus himself then heard them say the word, upon which he proceeded to ask what people there were who had anything they called "Becos." Hereupon he learned that Becos was the Phrygian word for bread. The Egyptians then gave up claiming that they were the oldest people in the world and agreed that the Phrygians were older than they.

Children, even in a fourth grade, will readily anticipate the later steps in this story, if given the opportunity. In a fifth or sixth grade they are almost sure to raise on their own motion objections to the conclusion which the Egyptians are alleged to have drawn from the experiment. Discussion is almost sure to lead some one to suggest that the story is probably not true, and to ask if Herodotus really thought it was true, or expected anybody else to think so. This naturally raises the question of where Herodotus got the story anyway. The reading is resumed:

That these were the real facts, I learned at Memphis from the priests of Vulcan. The Greeks told other stories of how the children were brought up, but the priests said that the bringing up was as I have stated it. I got much other information from conversation with these priests while I was at Memphis and I even went to Heliopolis and to Thebes expressly to try whether the priests of those places would agree in their accounts with the priests at Memphis.[7]

The children thus see at once that Herodotus knew of the experiment credited to Psammetichus only through "hearing about it." With this introduction children so fortunate as to be allowed to travel for some weeks afterward with Herodotus are found to be more or less on the alert to discover when he is talking about things that he has really seen and when he is talking about things that he has merely heard or read. . . .

. . . When the stage is reached at which children begin to use formal textbooks, these may serve as the point of departure for occasional illustration of how histories are made. It is the duty of teachers to point out recognized errors. Incidentally, this may be turned to account in showing what is really involved in getting at the truth about a matter in history. In the seventh grade the colonial period is usually treated for the first time with some degree of seriousness. Probably no subject of equal importance in that period has been dealt with so carelessly by textbook writers as that of colonial boundaries. This subject is as likely as any to furnish ground in need of being cleared up by the teacher. It may therefore be allowed to supply an illustration.

A well-known textbook has the following account of the boundary provisions of the charter of 1606:

---

[7] HERODOTUS, Book II, 2, 3. Slightly adapted.

To the London Company the king granted the coast of North America about from Cape Fear to the mouth of the Potomac; to the Plymouth Company he granted the coast about from Long Island to Nova Scotia. These grants were to go in straight strips, or zones, across the continent from the Atlantic Ocean to the Pacific (for so little was known about North American geography that a good many people believed the continent up here to be no wider than in Mexico). As for the middle strip, starting from the coast between the Potomac and the Hudson, it was open to the two companies, with the understanding that neither was to plant a colony within 100 miles of any settlement already begun by the other. This meant practically that it was likely to be controlled by whichever company should first come into the field with a flourishing colony. This made it worth while to act promptly.

An average seventh grade can read and interpret this paragraph. Several textbooks have maps showing the parallel strips running across the continent. If the particular text in use does not contain such a map, pupils can readily work one out on the board with the assistance of the teacher. How did the writer of this paragraph know that the boundaries were as he has described them? Let the class make suggestions. A little discussion will prepare the way for reference to the charter itself. The charter may then be studied in the manner indicated in the chapter on the use of maps.

The study will naturally conclude with a comparison of the two maps. Can both be right? Which is wrong? Compare with the map, if there is one in the textbook that may be in the hands of the class. It should be said that the textbook quoted has a footnote explaining that the sea to sea provision was added by the charter of 1609. But even that charter did not provide for "straight strips, or zones."

Whether a textbook is right or wrong in the matter, the difference between taking the textbook conclusion ready-made and taking our own conclusions worked out from the charter itself is the difference between learning the answer to a problem and working the problem. . . .

. . . But is there not danger of making children skeptical beyond their years, unduly wise, and even "bumptious"? Apparently not. The usual lesson which they seem to learn is that one must work very hard to find out the truth about the past. It is besides not at all necessary that every look behind a history should open up a controversy. It is, in fact, desirable that some of the stories investigated should be found indisputably true. The question of how we know requires illustration of what we really know as well as of what we ought really only to suspect or openly to doubt. . . .

. . . The history learned in school unquestionably makes its heaviest contribution to oblivion. But there are some results which endure. The treatment of history as assured knowledge prepares for the treatment of history as assured knowledge. The tendency of pupils accustomed in school to accept facts as facts without discrimination is to continue in after life to accept and to use facts without discrimination. The tendency of pupils accustomed in school to look upon the printed page itself as evidence of the truth of what is printed is to continue in after life in subjection to the tyranny of the printed page.

Communism
BARBARA WARD

Much of the hatred that characterizes our time centers on notions concerning the regulation of political power. The acts of many men—acts of desperate faith and terrible bluster, promises of fearful retaliation—are entwined in the passions of ideology.

A teacher seeking to avoid the constraint of ignorance must be something more than a practicing ideologist when he deals with political and economic thought. He must pursue his own understanding of such ideas. To do otherwise is to risk a small and unwitting role in maintaining the supply of ideologists, and, thus, the hard lump of anxiety within Everyman.

The Communist ideology is probably one of the most hated and one of the most loved political faiths in competition for the minds of modern men. Intelligent citizenship requires an understanding of this faith. Barbara Ward, a British economist, writer, and lecturer, has written clearly and without intemperate rancor about communism in the following selection. This discussion was written in 1959; since then there have been many changes in political geography, but the basic problems she explores remain the same today.

To understand the modern impact of Communism we have to take up again some of the facts that have been outlined on earlier pages. One is the process by which enough capital was saved to set the industrial revolution in motion, another the effect of that revolution when it spread beyond the Atlantic Ocean to embrace all the peoples of mankind. In both cases, as we have seen, the process involved much that was brutal, haphazard, and catastrophic; to these upheavals Communism is the response, brutal in its turn, catastrophic too, and—for all its claim to have deciphered the "objective" laws of history—in very large measure equally haphazard and blind.

The capital—or saving—which launched the new system was provided in part by the men and women who already possessed some wealth—traders, bankers, landowners, artisans with a little money put by. They put these savings in promising undertakings—or lost them in mistakes and bankruptcies. Where the new technique proved successful, they remained sharers in the new wealth and part-owners of the new means of production.

But the great bulk of the saving was provided—as in all subsequent industrial revolutions—by the workers themselves, by the men streaming in from farms and fields to the new cities, working inhumanly long hours for wages that barely kept them and their families alive. The wealth which their efforts created was the source of further investment and of a wider expansion in the power to produce still more goods. Yet in the first decades of industrialism, the workers saw precious little of the new wealth. It enriched the owners and was reinvested by them, but the mass of the people—the laborers working a seventy-hour week, the children of five and six sitting at the looms, or the women who crawled underground, half naked, dragging coal baskets —slaved on in unrelieved conditions of urban squalor.

Today, when we read of the conditions revealed in official Blue Books or described with wrathful realism in such novels as Dickens' *Bleak House* and *Hard Times,* we wonder how such things were allowed to come to pass or, once known, to continue unreformed. Were there no men of conscience? Was it not supposedly a Christian country? Yet every day crimes that in the great tradition of the Bible call to heaven for vengeance—oppressing the poor and defrauding the laborer of his hire—were not simply tolerated. They were in some degree the basis of the system.

The reason was not all wickedness and avarice and greed—although, as in any human order, these played their part. We have to remember the degree to which the whole new process of industrialism was highly mysterious to contemporary thought. Men were not clear how it had started and gathered momentum. There had been no master plan. On the contrary, the origins had lain in a series of independent efforts by entrepreneurs and capitalists, all in a sense working in the dark. They were pursuing profits—that they could see—but they were not consciously taking part in a vast economic and industrial revolution. This was occurring all around them without design or direction and when you consider how strange the new techniques were, how widespread the social upheaval that they brought about, it is not surprising that many people gave the new system the almost magical respect we give to things which seem wholly mysterious.

There was, of course, a rationalization of the mystery. In the eighteenth century the idea had been popular that the Creator had set the whole universe to work as a clockmaker sets a clock. Thus men's instincts, implanted by Nature, were bound to be in tune with Nature's general plan. To pursue one's own interests could not, on this theory, contradict the public weal. On the contrary, private profit equaled public good.

From this, it was an easy step to argue that the "hidden hand" which held all in harmony could be interfered with only at peril to the whole system. To check it or restrain it or divert it might pull out the mainspring and risk the running down of the entire industrial experiment.

This ignorance helps to explain an attitude towards government intervention which seems fantastic to us now. The idea was almost universal that if the government extended its functions beyond those of preserving law and order, it might, in some catastrophic way, bring the whole new, precarious industrial system to collapse. Men of good will, honor, and integrity such as Richard Cobden and John Bright of England were prepared to argue with almost religious fervor that you could not intervene in the economy without ruining it. Even attempts to regulate the hours of work in factories or to stop little children from going into factories and mines would, in some way, impair the harmony of the system and lead, therefore, to the collapse of the whole economy.

Here, then, was a fearsome combination. Change of a revolutionary order was thrust forward by men who were very largely ignorant of the full consequences of what they were doing and at a time when attempts to introduce measures of rational control were regarded as more menacing than the obvious evils they were designed to remove.

In any circumstances, these conditions would have created outrage and protest. And indeed they did. In England, for example, a great manifestation of popular discontent boiled up—and fizzled out—in the Chartist Movement in the 1840's; and all through Europe, 1848 was a year of revolution. True, the main aims of these upheavals were political—to end dynastic absolutism and introduce the franchise. But in each of them a more radical left wing demanded not simply political change but a complete remolding of economic conditions and property relations which were felt to be intolerable. Of all the demands and programs put forward at that time, none was more cogent, hard-hitting, all-embracing, radical, yet visionary than Marx's *Communist Manifesto* published just as the revolutionary wave in Europe began to flow strongly toward the crest of 1848.

It is one more of the many paradoxes of history that Communism, which was to draw its strength from the miseries and aspirations of the masses, was the product not of any working-class leader but of a middle-class German intellectual of Jewish stock. The miseries were apparent to any one who cared to look, the aspirations were normal human aspirations—to live and eat and perhaps prosper. What turned the churning eddies of hate and hope into one of the greatest revolutionary forces of all time was the imagination and intellectual formulation provided by a single man. Marx found a world in the striving confusion of early industrialism and imposed upon it the order of his Communist idea.

And here we see, in all its force, what the idea, working in history, can bring about. A pattern of thought is derived by human imagination from certain given conditions—in Marx's case, the early decades of industrial growth. But once the pattern is established, it cuts loose from any necessary connections with reality. It exists in its own right. It can long survive the conditions which prompted it. It becomes a creator or a destroyer in all manner of new conditions, many of which it has helped to bring about. And so we have another paradox. One of the basic ideas of Communism is that environment and economic substructure create ideas. Yet no system of thought has ever so conclusively shown that, on the contrary, ideas modify and transform the economic and social substructure.

This potency of ideas to transform reality is one dimension of human freedom. But like all mankind's greatest gifts, it carries an opposite risk—that ideas become prisons in which people isolate themselves from any reality that does not fit into their own preconceived pattern. Presented with the choice between their theories and the facts, the blinded ideologues chose the theory and let the facts go hang.

Communism is already a hundred years old. Yet its fundamental presuppositions about industrial society have not changed in spite of all the radical changes that have occurred in industrial society. The gap between the Communist view of the world and the world as it actually is thus widens every day. It is a rift in which humanity itself may founder.

What are these presuppositions? Perhaps before I outline them, I should allow for one possibility. Are we conceivably living in the final decades of pure Communist orthodoxy? The appearance of Titoism on the world stage and all the current discussions of "different roads to socialism" may presage the beginnings of a whole spectrum of Communist faiths, allied yet different, as are the sects of Christianity. We can still talk of Communist orthodoxy today. But in twenty years' time, shall we be able to say so emphatically what Communism is? This I hold to be one of the most encouraging signs that we shall not all be drawn over the edge of the ideological abyss.

But today we can still discern an orthodoxy worked out by Marx and by his friend Engels during the period of nascent industrialism. Communism is thus permeated through and through with reflections from early industrial Britain. There are other influences—German philosophy, French sociology, eighteenth-century rationalism. But the solid underpinning of factual study and social experience is provided in large measure by the reactions of Engels and Marx to industrial England in the Victorian period. It is much easier to grasp some of the key factors in Communism if one realizes the extent to which they reflect this environment of a hundred years ago.

I cannot hope in a brief essay to give any idea of the full scale of Communist theory. I can only hope to pick out one or two points which are relevant to its subsequent development and to its growth as a world force.

The starting point is a theory of the dynamics of history. Marx believed, as we have seen, that the decisive element in human destiny is the material condition under which people work for their living. All else—politics, philosophy, religion—consists of so many reflections or projections of underlying material relationships—of the way property is divided, of techniques of production, and methods of exchange. There is a religion, an art, a system of government for communal, tribal agriculture, another for slave-owning society, another for feudalism and again another for capitalism, as each order of production gives way, by the dialectic of history, to its successor.

I do not think we need to elaborate this question of the dialectic which Marx took over from Hegel. It is roughly the idea that each condition tends to produce its opposite and out of this tension, a new synthesis arises. In the unfolding of history one set of economic relationships, say, feudalism with its dominant landowners, gives rise to the opposite and conflicting interest of merchants and bankers and nascent industrialists. The next stage of society is already foreshadowed in the struggles over power and privilege and economic control—in other words the class struggle—of the previous epoch. The new class wins and the stage is set for the next phase of development.

In Marx's own day, Communism, he thought, was already stirring in the womb of early capitalism and however terrible and prolonged the convulsions attending its birth, it would triumph because it represented the irresistible force of determined history. But at this point, the dialectic would have done its work and history could cease. All previous class struggles had, in Marx's definition, been based upon the exclusive control of property by privileged groups. But if all ownership became public, if separate economic classes could no longer manipulate the levers of economic power in their own interest, all tension would die away; and with tension, change; and with change, history itself.

There is, one must admit, a certain magnificence in this picture of human destiny unfolding ineluctably through stage after stage of economic and social development to its appointed end in the classless millennium. The fact that most of the human race had not in fact traversed the great Marxian cycle from tribalism to slavery to feudalism to capitalism was not allowed to disturb the general harmony of this vast historical vision. At one time, Marx did consider "the Asian mode of production" as a possible variant to the general rule, but later on the concept was swept under the rug.

This point has more significance than Marxists care to admit. For what is this "Asian mode of production" but that method of large-scale, centralized, planned production which, as we have seen, underlay many of the great despotisms of the past? It is thus arguable that the kind of collective structure established in such societies as Russia or China has nothing whatsoever to do with the Marxian dialectic but is simply the adaptation to modern industry of an economic structure normal to Eastern society.

But there was a more immediate flaw in Marx's analysis. His picture of socialism struggling to be born as capitalism destroyed itself by its own contradictions was profoundly influenced by the first phase of capital accumulation in the West. He drew from the first five or six decades of industrialism conclusions which he generalized to cover the whole development of industry under more or less private ownership. In fact, as the century advanced the conditions in Western industrial society were to change, leaving the theory high and dry above the receding facts. Needless to say, Marx kept the theory, not the facts.

The most vulnerable point in the theory, as it turned out, was the "progressive immiseration of the workers"—in other words, the claim that as industry developed, the workers would grow steadily poorer and more wretched. How did Marx come upon this idea? Actually it is not an impossible conclusion to draw from the first brutal phase of capital growth—it was certainly true later on, for instance, of the period of the first Five Year Plan in Russia. During this phase, the workers coming in from the country, unused to industrial conditions, ignorant, brutalized, dwelling miserably in slums hastily run up for the purpose, work at a bare minimum necessary for survival while the entire increment is removed to create more capital, more machines, more enterprise. In a private society, private entrepreneurs make this transfer and reward themselves and their backers handsomely in the process. In a collective society, the Commissars do the transferring and look after themselves quite adequately, too. And in both cases, it does seem as though the misery of the masses is increasing as the capital for tomorrow's wealth is squeezed out of their labor.

Marx further remarked that competition between industrialists was beginning to produce mergers, larger units, even monopolies. From this he concluded that while the misery of the masses deepened, the number of men directly profiting at the top would steadily decrease. More and more miserable workers would face fewer and fewer rapacious monopolists. The day would come when the masses, fully class-conscious at last, would realize their strength, drive out the few owners, and transfer to the people the means of production whose control by private interests had led to the enrichment of the few at the expense of the many. In Marx's limpid phrase, "the expropriators would be expropriated," and the golden age would begin.

All this was, of course, to come about automatically. The inescapable dialectic of history—an unbending goddess of iron countenance—cannot be revoked. Yet Marx was not above giving history a bit of a nudge. However inevitably Communism would emerge from capitalism, he realized that some of the "expropriators" would probably object to their own elimination and it might therefore be necessary to give history a little help. The change could, in short, be violent and during the interim period, which fits rather uneasily into the precise pattern of the dialectic, the workers might need to consolidate their power by maintaining a dictatorship of the proletariat. This, however, would be a temporary phenomenon and with the full establishment of Communism—of the public ownership of all the means of production—not simply the dictatorship of the proletariat but the state itself would "wither away."

One does not need to be a constitutional specialist to be amazed at the blithe way in which Marx waves away the risk of continued despotism. In time and space, absolute government is the customary method of exercising political power. No other tradition is known in Asia. Europe's own history of freedom is checked with relapses into absolutism and in our own day produced the most extreme variants of dictatorship known to man. But we have to understand Marx's special angle of constitutional vision. He was very Victorian in his approach to government. Like Cobden and Bright, he did not think it had much function beyond that of preserving law and order and, as such, he saw it simply as a "managing committee of the bourgeoisie," as an instrument of class interest and class protection.

One can see why. The task of preserving law and order in Victorian times very often did mean sitting hard on the heads of those who wanted to change the order and were not too keen on the law—which, whatever else it did, certainly ensured the sanctity of property. If the state is seen chiefly in this policemen's role, protecting private property and interests, it is not illogical to assume that it will wither away when there is no more private property to protect. The government has in fact a thousand other functions, and so the logic seems to us to have the inner coherence and external fantasy of the lunatic. But many of the state's functions have been added since Marx's day. His political theory—like many of his economic theories—reflects conditions which are now a century out of date.

It did not take many decades to show that Marx's fundamental law of increasing misery was somehow failing to work out. For one thing, the industrial system was beginning to produce goods so much more effectively and cheaply that the new prosperity did in fact "trickle down." Between the 1860's and the early 1900's, prices fell, real wages rose, there was a noticeable increase in working-class prosperity.

Nor were the changes solely due to industrial expansion. Marx dismissed the influence of political institutions. They were derivative, he thought, and could not alter the substance of society. He therefore completely misunderstood the significance for Western industrial society of adult suffrage. One thing certain in any industrial system is that there will tend to be a majority of workers. If you extend the vote to all adults, this large group is bound to have some say in what is to happen. They are unlikely to be attracted by the proposal of steady general impoverishment and have no inhibitions about using the government they are beginning to influence in order to avoid such a gloomy outcome. It is no coincidence that in Britain with every extension of the franchise to the general body of voters, the state began to intervene more directly in the community's activities. Disraeli came to office in 1874 with the slogan: "Sanitas, sanitas, omnia sanitatum"—which might be interpreted not as "bread and circuses" but as "drains and housing" —and with him begins the welfare state.

Once the government is pledged to the provision of more and more services for the mass of the community, its sources of revenue have to increase. Progressive taxation makes its appearance and becomes steadily heavier. The rich become poorer and the poor become richer—as direct a contradiction of Marx's axiom as human reason can conceive. In short, under the impact of democracy and the vote, politics did what they had no right to do —altered the economic underpinning of the community.

This was not the only disobliging failure of society to conform to Marx's pattern. Another deviation could be found in the growing power of independent trade unions. Far from being content with the old Iron Law of Wages—which held that competition between workers always thrusts wages down to the minimum necessary to keep a working class in being—the trade unions began to agitate steadily for increased wages, for better working conditions, and for shorter hours—aims in which they were supported by the more enlightened sectors of public opinion. In fact, Christian men of the stamp of Lord Shaftesbury led the campaign for factory reform even before the trade unions had the necessary influence to work for it themselves.

Successful trade union activity had more than economic consequences. To the disgust of the Marxists, some of the most active and "class conscious" of the new working-class leaders drew from their experience the political conclusion that industrial society needed not so much overthrow as reform. They wanted to advance toward a society in which wealth would be shared, in which brotherhood would be the rule of life, and in which great social differences would be abolished. But they believed that their vision of a socialist society could be achieved by peaceful argument and by the ballot box.

No belief has roused Marxists to greater fury. As in some forms of religious controversy, you can forgive a man who does not share your faith but there is no pardon for someone who claims to have a better variant. Communists have a quite special virulence for Socialists who say in effect: "We can do everything you can do better." The dispute still rages today. "Revisionism" is the crime of Socialists who, like Tito, believe that there may be more than one road—and some of them peaceful—to socialist society. In unalloyed Marxist theory—as interpreted today by Moscow and Peking—the notion of different paths is still anathema.

To return to the Law of Increasing Poverty—by the beginning of the twentieth century it took a good deal of swallowing. Economically, no facts were available to demonstrate it. Politically, it had been nullified by the emergence in the working class of cautious, reformist, antirevolutionary leaders who felt they had a real stake in industrial society. Clearly the theory had either to be explained or explained away.

It was at this point that Lenin made his most significant contribution to the development of the Marxist canon. From scattered hints and comments of the master he elaborated a new theory to cover the obstinate refusal of Europe's workers to grow poorer and at the same time extended the whole range of Communist tactics and activity. Marx had always seen his theory as encompassing all mankind, but his chief focus had been Europe at the time of its industrialization. Lenin outlined more concretely the manner in which a worldwide revolution could be brought about.

The *Communist Manifesto* cannot be understood apart from the conditions of early industrialism; nor can Lenin's *Imperialism: The Highest Stage of Capitalism* be grasped out of context. When it was published in 1916 the major industrial Powers were at war or on the brink of it. Millions in Europe were fighting and dying to preserve, as they believed, their national independence and identity. Since between them they held in colonial control virtually the whole of Asia and Africa, the repercussions of the struggle stretched to the ends of the earth. From this vast maelstrom of war, nationalism, and colonialism, Lenin drew out a single pattern of interpretation which, because it seemed to explain everything, gained power over men's minds—just as Marx's hypnotic simplicities had done forty or fifty years before.

Briefly put, the Leninist theory of imperialism amounts to this: Since capitalism does not share its wealth with the workers, the home market soon reaches saturation and industrialists are bound to seek for fresh markets and new areas of profitable investment elsewhere. These in turn—in India, in Indonesia, in Africa—are ruthlessly exploited under colonial control. However, the wealth squeezed from them has percolated in some degree to the workers at home. Thus the law of increasing misery in Europe was mitigated by its application to colonial lands. British workers as well as capitalists waxed fat on profits sweated from the Indian coolie.

Yet the number of colonial markets available is limited. The industrialists must struggle to control them and their rivalry must lead inevitably to imperialist war. If, however, the colonial peoples could become conscious of their national rights and cast out the colonial expropriators and exploiters, their revolt would begin to break capitalism where its organization was most frail and could lead from nationalist to Communist revolution. Incidentally, capitalism in this theory did not need to exercise actual political control in order to be "imperialist." Simple foreign investment created exploitation. Thus in 1914 Russia was held to be a semicolonial dependency of Western finance capital because of the scale of foreign investment under Czarism.

You can see that this theory explained far more than Europe's failure to grow poorer. It explained why wars were inevitably caused by capitalism. It explained why capitalists had to have colonies. It explained why the Communist revolution could begin in such industrially backward countries as Russia—or China—whereas Marx seems to have expected the first breakthrough to occur in a fully developed industrial society. But after the Leninist definition of imperialism, it could be claimed that Russia was simply the "weakest link" in the capitalist chain. Later, the same explanation could serve for China.

The fact is, of course, that in both Russia and China, the Communist seizure of power had little or nothing to do with capitalism. In both countries, leaders of tactical genius had the sense to abandon the Marxist strategy of revolt based upon a developed industrial working class—which did not exist—and to exploit the two real sources of revolutionary ferment which did—war-weariness and the peasants' longing for land. It is a revealing sidelight on Marxist perspicuity that Stalin so misunderstood the lessons of Lenin's success in 1917 that he almost destroyed Chinese Communism by advising it to strike first in the cities through the almost minute urban working class. Only when Mao Tse-Tung took Communism to the peasants was it possible for Chinese Communism to find its road to victory.

Even in 1916, there were a lot of flaws in the Leninist argument. Most colonies had been acquired long before industrialism began and even where capitalism and colonialism appeared together, as in Africa, the Great Powers' rivalry there after 1880 had more to do with prestige and strategy than with the search for markets. Although colonial and maritime rivalry added something to the estrangement of Britain and Germany between 1880 and 1914, World War I was primarily fought, like all Europe's pre-industrial wars, to preserve the Balance of Power—in other words, to safeguard national survival.

The incongruities of Lenin's theory were not confined to Europe. America, the area where capitalism at that time was becoming most "monopolist," passed through and left behind a short fever of external intervention—in the Caribbean and the Pacific—invested marginally overseas and derived its growing prosperity from within its own wide boundaries. In fact, virtually every industrial country gained more of its wealth by conducting trade with developed industrial partners than by any colonial activity. Western Europe was a more valuable market for Britain than all Asia and Africa combined.

Yet in the twenties and thirties, this Leninist version of the Communist faith exercised a profound influence upon thought and policy. For one thing, the human mind, especially in a scientific era, has a bias against two explanations where one will do. Marxism-Leninism answers a profound instinct: to find a single pattern of explanation for everything—and there were enough facts available in the interwar years to fit the theory without too much violence.

Colonial control was a fact and, as we have already remarked, the economic policies of the European powers disrupted some Asian economies and failed to create conditions of dynamic expansion in others. There was enough discontent and frustration about for the charge of exploitation to be eagerly accepted. The discontent increased when in 1929 the capitalist world underwent a supreme crisis of overproduction and in the consequent depression, widespread dislocation and unemployment almost suggested that the law of increasing misery was at work after all.

Above all, the Marxists scored a master stroke in identifying "late-capitalism" with Fascism and using this identification to "prove" that capitalists must be war-mongers and imperialists. In fact, Fascism is the extreme point not of capitalism but of nationalism. Mussolini built the first working model in Italy, one of the least industrialized nations in Europe. The mature capitalist economies, Britain and America, which, if there is any such thing as late-capitalists, were undoubtedly the latest of all, remained immune to the supposed fatalities of their stage of economic development. Fascism sprang up in Italy and Germany, two nations distinguished not by the advanced stage of their capitalism but by the early stage of their nationalism. Both had waited longest to achieve that coincidence of frontiers and language which is one of the strongest roots of modern nationalism. Belated nationalism, not late capitalism, was their trouble. Their sense of nationhood was still febrile and insecure. Nationalist grievances, great-power illusions, the memory of military humiliation—these fevers, and not any hidden economic motives, drove the dictators on to war.

In spite of these obvious incongruities, Marxist-Leninist theory still kept a vestigial anchorage in the facts between the wars. It is since 1945 that the last link with reality has been broken and Communism has become a source of almost pure unreason in the world. Remember that its world picture has not changed. Advanced capitalist countries are still portrayed as ravening imperialists driven by the fear of overproduction at home to fight each other for control of markets abroad. They are still seeking to check the rise of local nationalism and to enslave the rest of the world either by direct domination or by the sinister economic control exercised through their overseas investments. They are still plotting war against the peace-loving guardians of the new Socialist order in Russia and China—even though it is not yet two decades since they fought at Russia's side.

These are the staple themes of Communist propaganda. Worse, this is the world of fantasy Communist leaders apparently inhabit and from which they draw their conclusions about policy. It is a sobering thought that for all their force and shrewdness men like Khrushchev and Chou En-lai may well be alienated from reality to a degree which would probably consign them, in private society, to a mental asylum.

Consider the actual, factual condition of the world today. The Western industrial powers have undergone no violent convulsions of overproduction. Mild recessions there have been, and these have had some repercussions abroad; but in general the upward surge of production in the mature industrial societies has actually exceeded earlier phases of industrial growth. We cannot say that the inherent tendency of capitalist economies to proceed by slump and boom—by alternations of under- and overproduction—has been entirely overcome. Perhaps this last Marxian contradiction is still with us. But at least, Western governments are now committed politically to policies which prevent the cycle from becoming catastrophic. The popular vote and Keynesian economics have made "full employment" the formal policy of Western democracy.

As a consequence of this economic expansion at home, there are no vast sums of capital competing for overseas markets and investment. On the contrary, America's foreign ventures are barely one-fifth of Britain's in the heyday of foreign lending and Britain itself is tempted to concentrate its investment at home. Shortage of capital is the world's trouble today, not the struggles of rival capitalists to go out and invest. Even where there are heavy Western investments—of which, of course, the chief is in oil—no Western Power is carving out oil territories under its own colonial control. On the contrary, Western policy in the Middle East can best be understood as a fumbling rearguard action to obtain even minimum safeguards for existing investment.

Nowhere is the gap between the Communists' world picture and the actual reality of things greater than in their political analysis of imperialism. Today, outside Africa, there are only pockets left of Western colonial control— tiny enclaves like Hongkong or Goa or Macao. In Africa itself Ghana's achievement of freedom is only the first act in an unfolding drama of African independence. Save in the Union of South Africa, even the communities of mixed racial stock are moving, however hesitantly, towards the eventual enfranchisement of the African majority. In the Arab world, only Algeria— another plural society—is still directly controlled from Europe. Yet in 1945 virtually the whole of Asia, Africa, and the Middle East was under Western colonial administration.

An earthquake, a cataclysm on a global scale, has occurred in the disappearance of so vast a dominion. The peacefulness of most of this gigantic transfer of power may have blinded people to its revolutionary character. Even so, there is a staggering unreality in the Communists' cries of imperialism and colonialism. The Law of Increasing Imperialism—if one may so paraphrase their insistent propaganda—is as ludicrous as the old Law of Increasing Misery.

Yet it confronts the world with a disturbing dilemma. It is perfectly possible to argue that the Communists' use of imperialism as a stick to beat the West is quite cynical. They believe that nationalist regimes emerging from a long period of colonial control are likely to be weak, divided and uncertain. The experience of Indonesia or Burma has done nothing to modify this judgment. In the new fluid situation, the Communists can hope to gain ground and sooner rather than later replace the nationalist regime that immediately succeeded the old imperial regime. They have everything to gain by pressing for independence and by continuing to paint a picture of a Western Imperialism that is ever ready to pounce again and reimpose the old control. Anti-imperialist propaganda is thus a simple instrument of ultimate Communist domination and non-Communist nationalist leaders—a Nasser or a Nehru or an Nkrumah—simply act as unwitting precursors to full Communist "liberation."

But it is also possible that the Communists' propaganda is not entirely cynical. They may be victims of it themselves. They may not simply find it more convenient to see the retreating West as the advance guard of imperialism. They may actually believe in a world-wide imperialist plot. Driven not by opportunism but by fear, they may move within a lurid global vision of Western menace and aggression, in a state of perpetual military preparedness, heavily armed, massively mobilized, scaring the death out of most other Powers and keeping the world for ever on the dreadful brink that overlooks Armageddon.

This state is not incompatible with what we know of mental alienation. Fear and aggression are twin sides of the same coin of hallucination. The Communists may fear the West, but they have not abandoned the original Marxist goal of a total Communist world order. How, then, can one distinguish the offensive from the defensive aspects of their policy, how determine whether conciliation designed to check Communist fears will not be interpreted as softness inviting a Communist assault? Western diplomacy may have been something less than skillful in handling the Communist phenomenon, but let no one suppose that there is any easy, straightforward method of dealing with the rulers of nine hundred million people who behave as though they believed that men stand on their heads or that the sun goes round the earth—or the equivalent, that the Western Powers are plotting imperialist war and world dominion.

Communism, in short, is the tragedy of ideas working free from the reasonable restraint of fact. In Marx's own day, its entire analysis and strategy were based upon the first phase of capitalist accumulation—a grim period in any society. In the Leninist aftermath, its doctrines were fashioned in the last phase of Western colonialism. Today, both phases are a matter of history. Western capitalism has evolved far beyond its painful beginnings. Western imperialism is being liquidated more rapidly—and on the whole more peacefully—than any comparable dominion in the human record. But Communism keeps pounding along, repeating the same slogans and proclaiming the same myths as though the whole march of events had been arrested at the moment at which Marx and then Lenin turned a baleful eye on Western society. The gap between ideology and fact thus grows wider every hour, and like all demonstrations of unreality, it grows more dangerous. Unanchored in anything save power, fear, ambition, and fantasy, who can say to what risks and follies it may not seduce the leaders of the Communist world?

How, then, has an order of ideas, a doctrine, an ideology patently at variance with the facts contrived to become one of the greatest revolutionary forces ever known to man? The answer, I believe, has very little to do with Communist orthodoxy but everything to do with the concrete experience of the Soviet state. In 1914, Russia was about to go through the "sound barrier" of modern capitalism. The fearsome privations and turmoil of early industrialism still lay heavily on the country, and the degree of capital accumulation was not yet sufficient to transform industrialization from an iron penance for all save the few to a means of greater prosperity for everyone.

The First World War ruined what had been begun. By 1917, the whole fragile structure of Czarist Russia, caught between a dying and an unborn order of society, collapsed. The universal confusion gave Lenin and his determined Bolshevik minority the opportunity to seize power. Then they found themselves in charge of a vast country but with no doctrines that seemed to apply. Marx had expected revolution to occur only when a full-scale industrial apparatus, created by the bourgeoisie, was already in being. None existed in Russia in 1918. The Bolsheviks tried pure Communism for a time, putting workers in charge of factories. It did not work. To keep some feeble pulse stirring in the country Lenin had to restore a measure of free enterprise under his New Economic Policy, and I think one can safely say that if Russian policy had advanced no further than the confusions of its first decade, we should have heard little of Communism as a worldwide force.

Stalin's contribution was the forced-draft industrialization of Russia. He combined two traditions—the industrial experience and techniques worked out under private enterprise in the West and the traditional "Asian method of production" based upon centralized control, state planning, and a vast bureaucracy. Under such stringent political control, there seemed no limit to the amount of saving that could be shorn from the people. The thirties were a time of bloody oppression and misery for millions of Russians. But the basis of a vast industrial apparatus was laid—and laid in time to resist the Nazi invasion.

Nor was it simply a physical achievement. Communism provided the element of zeal, discipline, and almost Puritanical fervor which had distinguished the earlier Calvinist attitude toward the creation of wealth. In the great drive to modernize the country, no resources—either human or material—were neglected. Education was made universal, the curriculum redesigned for modern scientific society; able children were forced forward up the ladder of learning, the university became the entry to the new elite.

For thousands of workers, for the ignorant peasants coming in from the countryside, for the bewildered tribesmen of Uzbekistan or Khirgizia, the new industrial world was as alien and hideous as the worst slum in Glasgow or Pittsburgh. According to one estimate, as many workers were killed in the building of Magnitogorsk as in the Battle of the Marne. But for their children there was the chance for a new existence, and by clearing away the old aristocratic Czarist superstructure, the Communist leaders had thrown open these chances to more people than had any previous way of life.

The appeal of Communism is not so much its dialectic or its metaphysics —save to a minute group of intellectuals in search of a new faith—but its ability to carry backward countries speedily through the tremendous crisis of modernization. It offers a successful pattern of industrial saving and it provides the drive and discipline without which saving, particularly in poor countries, cannot be achieved. It also promises that the fruits of the transformation will ultimately be enjoyed "by each according to his need."

This last promise cannot yet be judged. Those who control the means of production—whether they are capitalists or bureaucrats—tend to reward themselves rather more handsomely than the mass of the people. Certainly, the gap between the Commissar and the day laborer in Russia is greater than between the average American manager and trade unionist. But compared with the gulf between rich and poor customary in preindustrial society, the results of Communism already show it to be an instrument of radical justice as well as of technical innovation. We should not forget that Marx, for all his scientific jargon, was a prophet in the great Hebrew tradition, putting down the mighty from their seats and exalting them of low degree. In the misery and confusion of our present worldwide economic revolution, there are millions who will listen to his prophetic promises of justice who never heard of the dialectic and would not recognize a synthesis if they saw one.

It is not, therefore, difficult to grasp the appeal of Communism to backward areas of the world, to lands still living in misery and economic stagnation, plagued by ambitions toward a better lot, restrained by the traditions of preindustrial society and the authority of older modes of leadership. In China, as we have seen, the wreck of the old Manchu system was followed by forty years of almost continuous war, during which the industrial transformation of society could hardly be carried through under middle-class leadership on the Western model, weakened as it was by inflation and by its association with "colonial" foreign capital. Communism was therefore able to repeat the Bolshevik tactic. It based itself on peasant discontent in a country sickened with war and destruction and, once in power, began to thrust through, with comparable rigor, the total modernization of the economy.

Must we, then, assume that the driving vigors and simplicities of Communism offer the future pattern of modernization and that, at least outside the older industrial West, we face in Communism "the wave of the future"? There are, I believe, solid grounds for believing that the future is not so rigidly determined. Russia and China are great powers, the greatest powers in numbers and soon perhaps in resources that the world has seen. Communism in their powerful system does not entail being subjugated to anyone else, does not, in short, entail imperialism. But the fate of Eastern Europe suggests that Communism for smaller powers carries no such guarantee of independence and elbow room.

I do not myself believe that imperialism at this late day is going to become more attractive simply by calling itself "international proletarian solidarity." Hungary stands as the tragic proof that national independence and international Communism are not yet compatible. I suggest that this lesson is not lost on the nationalist leaders around the world who are supposed to be preparing Communism's advance.

Again, I do not believe that Communism as a system has yet shown us that it can do more than drive societies at breakneck speed through the "sound barrier" of modernization. But out on the other side, a thousand problems remain—above all, the problem of an economy flexible enough and sensitive enough to provide ordinary people with the things they really want. For this, the market economy is a much better instrument than bureaucratic planning. Yet one may question whether the Communists will dare risk the step of making the consumer supreme, for this change might also enhance his position as a voter. How much choice can you admit economically without awkward questions of political choice arising too?

And here we touch on what, surely, remains the greatest failure and potential weakness of Communism. It is politically inflexible. It enshrines the principle of despotic authority in a world now shot through with the dreams, hopes, and experiences of free government. You cannot cancel this pressure and this ferment, any more than you can turn imperialism into something else by inventing new names for it. And this failure to confront the realities of politics has been, I believe, the fundamental flaw in Marx's thought from the very first hour.

He dismissed as irrelevant trappings the political traditions of Western life—the rule of law, constitutional practice, the vote, supremacy of parliament, the hard-won rights and liberties of the individual. But these were the means whereby Western industrial society eased itself through the crises of early industrialism, sloughed off its colonial past and began, by trial and error and innovation and experiment, to turn industrialism into an instrument of well-being for more and more of its citizens while leaving them to enjoy the supreme good of individual rights and ordered liberty.

Communism misunderstands totally the central problem of power. By relying on such puerile fantasies as the "withering away of the state," it has allowed a concentration of political and economic power to come about in the Communist state which goes even beyond the oriental tyrannies that are its model. Power still corrupts; absolute power still corrupts absolutely, and Khrushchev's recital of Stalin's iniquities at the 20th Party Congress was only one more dreary record of the despot's traditional cruelties and crimes.

Nor is it only the domestic community which bears the terrible risks and penalties of unfettered power. The Government which respects no limits on its internal authority tends to be equally lawless in its external relations. The Soviet and Chinese governments, for all their internationalist protestations, stand firm on the principle of unlimited sovereignty and state power. And they do so in the atomic age when the unbridled right of all states to do exactly what they wish can lead inexorably to the holocaust that destroys them all.

Using Source Material with Children

VINCENT R. ROGERS

In the following discussion, Rogers identifies some problems and some advantages in using the residue of social activity as a basis for social study in the classroom. His discussion illustrates the significance of *questions* and *things* when one inquires about the past. Until a student identifies a specific ignorance that the scrutiny of objects will answer, study cannot take place.

The use of original sources in the teaching of American history has had, to say the least, a rather stormy past. Some have seen it as a veritable panacea —a cure-all for all of the educational ills of the times. Others have roundly condemned the technique as narrow, arid, and vague.[1]

In any event, the use of sources with children *below* the senior high school level seems to have been at best neglected, and at worst, totally ignored even by those who favor the technique. Before we wonder why, it might be wise to think a little about the possible uses of original source material at any age level. Keohane pulls them together for us very effectively,

From "Using Source Material with Children," by Vincent R. Rogers, *Social Education*, XXIV (November 1960), pp. 307–309 (with omissions). By permission of the publisher.
    [1] ROBERT E. KEOHANE. "Historical Method and Primary Sources." Chapter 25 in Richard E. Thursfield, editor, *The Study and Teaching of American History*. Seventeenth Yearbook of the National Council for the Social Studies. Washington, D.C.: The Council, 1946.

I think.[2] Check this list for any additions or deletions you might want to make.

1. Inspirational
2. "Making history live"—giving it warmth, color, and the flavor of the times
3. Reinforcing knowledge about important persons, events, laws, institutions, and problems
4. Gaining firsthand knowledge of significant documents
5. Developing habits of critical reading and thinking
6. Gaining familiarity with some creative ideas in U.S. history through analysis of some classic statements of American social thought.

As one who has taught in the intermediate elementary grades, junior high school *and* senior high school, it seems to me that these "objectives" are both valid and, at least to some degree, achievable at each of these levels. If so, can relatively young children use original source material to aid in the achievement of these objectives? If you've given a positive answer to this question (as, of course, I have) you'll have to face up immediately to certain harsh realities:

1. Usable sources *are* hard to find—and it takes time to locate, browse and extract.
2. If poorly chosen, original sources can be deader than the deadest text.
3. Sources do not always fit the vocabulary level deemed appropriate for grade by the writers of the basal readers.

The first objection can be overcome by diligence, persistence, and perhaps to some extent, by the brief bibliography which follows this article. Dealing with the second is somewhat more difficult. Overcoming it depends largely upon each teacher's understanding of both his students *and* his subject. The third can be, at least partially, ignored.

Perhaps, then, this is the time to examine some sources which I have used effectively with sixth-, seventh-, and eighth-grade children.

These are excerpts from a letter written by Lewis B. Williams of Orange, Virginia, to his sister, Miss Lucy P. Williams of Richmond, on July 12, 1836. It concerns an unusual slave called Polly.

. . . On last Monday week, I had to whip Polly for her impudence to me, since which she has continued in a pet, not treating myself or any of the family with the slightest respect, and continually telling me that she did not wish to stay with me as she could not please me and alleging that she was willing to be sold, in fact anxious even to the Southern traders. . . .

. . . She has been now for eight days in a continual ill humor, speaking roughly

---

[2] ROBERT E. KEOHANE. "Use of Primary Sources in United States History for High School Pupils." *School Review,* December 1945, p. 580.

and rudely to every member of the family and continually throwing it in my teeth, that she could not please me, ever since and altho' I told her that she should never be sold, as long as I was able to keep her, provided she would behave herself and that I would sell her, if she did not, she still tells me that she is perfectly willing to go and that she cares not about staying with me. Upon this I have informed her that she must make up her mind, take her choice to be in a good humor and behave herself or be sold and I am resolved that one or the other must be done. I regret it very much, but there must be one master in a family or there can be no peace. I told her that I did not wish to sell her, and particularly to separate her from her husband, father, mother, and brother, that I was opposed to it except in case of necessity and that she could take her choice. She still persists in saying that she is willing to be sold and that she cannot please me and that she had as soon be sold to the negro traders as to anyone else, and I am satisfied that I will have to sell her in the course of the week. . . .

This seems to me to be a most devastating challenge to a stereotyped concept of the master-to-slave relationship. Here is an impudent Polly, literally sassing her master and the rest of the family, and, what's more (temporarily, at least), getting away with it. Students might be asked to dwell a little on the lines, "I regret it very much, but there must be *one* master in a family or there can be no peace." Children can be asked such questions as: What kind of a person *was* Polly? Why didn't Lewis Williams simply sell her immediately? Why was he so concerned? What was Polly's "status" or "position" in the Williams family? Do you suppose all slaves owned by the Williams were thought of in the same way? Who were the "Negro traders"? Was Polly treated differently from other slaves?

Obviously, this material cannot be used in isolation. Its value depends entirely on what preceded its use and what will follow it. This source can be used most effectively to challenge, to raise questions, and to encourage further study.

Prospective settlers in Jamestown were given advice concerning what equipment was necessary for survival in the New World. Excerpts from a document published in 1622 appear below.

	Apparell.		*Tooles.*
	One Monmouth Cap		Five broad howes
	Three shirts		Five narrow howes
	One waist-coate		Two broad Axes
	One Suite of Frize		Five felling Axes
Apparell	One suite of cloth	For a	Two steele hand sawes
for	Three paire of Irish	family	Two two-hand sawes
one	stockings	of 6	One whip-saw
man	Foure paire of shooes	persons	Two hammers
	One paire of garters		Three shovels
	One paire of sheets		Two spades

(*Apparell.*)
One Rug for a bed
Five ells coarse canvas,
   to make a bed at Sea
   for two men, to be
   filled with straw
One coarse Rug at Sea
   for two men

Victuall.
Eight bushels of Meale

For a   Two bushels of pease
whole   Two bushels of Oatemeale
yeare   One gallon of Aquavite
for   One gallon of Oyle
one man   Two gallons of Vinegar

Armes.
One Armour, Compleat,
   light
One long Peece, five foot
   or five and a halfe,
   neere Musket bore
One sword
One belt
One bandaleere
Twenty pound of powder
Sixty pound of shot or
   lead, Pistoll and
   Goose shot

(*Tooles.*)
Two augers
Sixe chissels
Two percers stocked
Three gimlets
Two hatchets
Two hand bills
One grindstone
Nailes of all sorts
Two pickaxes

Household Implements.
One Iron Pot
One kettle
One large frying pan
One gridiron
Two skillets
One spit
Platters, dishes,
   spoones of wood

For a
family
of 6
persons

Most of us who teach American history are concerned with helping children develop an understanding of the bitter realities of life in the colonies during these trying times. Intelligent use of this document, it seems to me, can contribute a great deal towards developing that understanding. A comparison, for example, of the household implements brought here "for a family of six" with the implements found in the children's own kitchens would certainly be revealing. A comparison of the diets of these early settlers with the diets of contemporary Americans would be equally revealing. Teachers might, before using the document, ask children to make a list of things they thought would be absolutely essential for survival if they were to make a similar voyage. These lists could then be compared with the document.

The settlement of the West was often encouraged by posters like this one, distributed in 1867.

Farms and Homes in Kansas
EMIGRANTS
Look to Your
INTEREST
Farms at $3. Per Acre!
And Not a Foot of Waste Land.
And on Purchase No Portion of the Principal Required!!
LANDS NOT TAXABLE FOR SIX YEARS!
FARMING LANDS IN
EASTERN KANSAS
The Central Branch
UNION PACIFIC RAILROAD CO.,
Offer For Sale Their Lands in the Celebrated
KICKAPOO INDIAN RESERVATION
152,417 acres
Schools and Churches

This was certainly a vivid, dramatic chapter in our history. Intelligent use of this poster may raise such questions as these: "Why did so many people move west?" "Was it mostly a matter of adventure (as many of our TV oriented children must believe) or were there other motivating factors?" "Why did this poster attract settlers?" "How could the Union Pacific Railroad sell lands in the Kickapoo Indian reservation?"

The sources used in this article were chosen because of their unusually challenging, thought provoking, and dramatic nature. There are, of course, many similar items tucked away in seldom used corners of most libraries. Perhaps the following bibliography will give the reader a start toward beginning his own collection of original source material.

BIBLIOGRAPHY

PAUL M. ANGLE. *The American Reader.* New York: Rand McNally, 1958.

B. H. BOTKIN, editor. *Lay My Burden Down, A Folk History of Slavery.* Chicago: University of Chicago Press, 1945.

BRUCE CATTON, editor. *American Heritage, The Magazine of History.* New York: *American Heritage,* Bi-monthly.

HENRY STEELE COMMAGER. *Blue and Gray: The Story of the Civil War as Told by Participants.* Indianapolis: Bobbs-Merrill, 1954.

HENRY STEELE COMMAGER. *Documents of American History.* New York: Appleton-Century-Crofts, 1949.

HENRY STEELE COMMAGER and ALLAN NEVINS. *The Heritage of America.* Boston, Mass.: Little, Brown, 1947.

MARSHALL DAVIDSON. *Life in America.* Volumes I, II. Boston, Mass.: Houghton Mifflin, 1951.

HOWARD R. DRIGGS. *The Pony Express Goes Through: An American Saga Told by Its Heroes.* New York: Stokes, 1935.

OTTO EISENSCHIML and R. NEWMAN. *The American Iliad.* Indianapolis: Bobbs-Merrill, 1947.

ALBERT B. HART. *American History Told by Contemporaries.* Volumes I–V. New York: Macmillan, 1924.

Log of Christopher Columbus' First Voyage to America in the Year 1492. New York: Scott, 1938.

P. A. ROLLINS. *The Discovery of the Oregon Trail: Robert Stuart's Narratives of His Overland Trip Eastward from Astoria in 1812–1813.* New York: Scribner's, 1935.

VILHJALMUR STEFANSSON. *Great Adventures and Explorations.* New York: Dial, 1947.

The Trouble with Textbooks

MARTIN MAYER

The social-studies textbook is a ubiquitous feature of the elementary-school classroom. Often these books have pretty pictures, to make them attractive to children, and a teacher's manual, to make them attractive to teachers.

The unimaginative teacher may assume that his most important job is to get all his students to read—and remember, on fill-in-the-blanks tests—what the textbook has to say. Any teacher, however, must give serious attention to the school-supplied textbook, in order to decide upon its proper use. One possible use for even the worst textbook is as a source of misinformation, overgeneralization, and sentimentalization that could be an important document for classroom study.

The following selection may provide some insight into how and why textbooks are made. In itself a controversial view, commented upon by educators, reviewers, and publishers when it first appeared in print, the selection may be helpful in making the necessary decisions about textbook use.

Textbooks, curiously, receive less public criticism than any other kind of writing. They are never reviewed in the general press, and even the educational press gives them no more than perfunctory notice. A few noisy pressure groups, usually of the Radical Right, make a business of attacking textbooks on ideological grounds, but no major citizens' organization has

From "The Trouble with Textbooks," by Martin Mayer, *Harper's Magazine* (July 1962), pp. 65–71 (with omissions). Reprinted by permission of the author. Copyright © 1962, by Harper & Row, Publishers, Incorporated.

ever paid systematic attention to the *quality* of the books used in our schools.

Yet nobody would deny their importance. These texts—casually ignored or given merely statistical treatment in the recent controversies over American education—must influence what gets into the heads of all our children. When the books are poor, they can lead to a contempt for education, and even for the printed page. (Many a boy leaves school with an ingrained conviction that *all* books must be a bore, because the books the school takes most seriously are nothing but a bore.)

Moreover, textbooks are big business, both to their producers and to the taxpayer. (Just as the school budget dominates the economy of a small town, so the textbook dominates the small industry of book publishing. Profits are greater in this field, and risks smaller. Promotion occurs, as at school itself, mostly through seniority; a firm's position acquired in one generation tends to sustain itself into the next, provided the publisher keeps up with slight changes in fashion. The books look much alike; mostly, they read alike. Competition is stabilized on a basis of personal salesmanship, elaborateness of product, and marginal difference in the handling of materials. (Thus it was, also, in cigarettes in the late 1940s and automobiles in the mid-1950s; such situations seem inevitably to foreshadow big changes in an industry.)

But in textbooks the change has not yet come. The schools are still waiting, in their typical attitude of inarticulate patience, for publishers to supply the great variety of text materials required by the great variety of children in the nation's classrooms. Textbooks are still, as Scarsdale Superintendent of Schools Harold Howe II recently told a publisher who tried to hire him, "the dead hand holding down American public education."

There are some stirrings in the ooze. There is, for example, the Addison-Wesley Publishing Company, the fastest-growing textbook publishing house in the United States, fashionably located off Route 128 outside Boston. Most of the company's gain of 80 per cent over the last two years came from expansion of its established business—college- and graduate-level texts in mathematics, science, and engineering. But an increasing fraction derives from new ventures in high-school mathematics—textbooks in algebra and geometry significantly different from the others on the market.

In spirit and often in the flesh, the American algebra text displays a cover with a four-color lithograph of an incredibly handsome young man, staring straight ahead with firmly American determination; and from the cauldron between his temples emerge rockets, atom bombs, television sets, and skyscrapers. In contrast, the Addison-Wesley text has a solid red die-stamp cover, no illustration at all. Inside, there are no photographs of eminent scientists solving problems at the consoles of giant calculators, no colored drawings, no cute cartoons of Mr. Mathematics explaining to awed boys and girls how you make money with numbers. The level of discourse in these texts (which come from the hands of Charles Brumfiel and Robert Eicholz of Ball State Teachers College, and Merrill Shanks of Purdue) assumes a respect for and interest in mathematics: the "motivation" is in the material. And while there is a teacher's manual explaining carefully what the text hopes to accomplish, the "answer key" does not give the teacher worked-out answers to all the problems in the books. "We felt," says Stuart Brewster, the young editor of the firm's new elementary and high-school division, "that our market would be in strong schools." And in strong schools, of course, math teachers would never dream of assigning textbook problems they had not worked (or, in the ultimate horror, were unable to work) for themselves. . . .

. . . Mathematics education is a field in wild agitation, and the Addison-Wesley texts are inevitably something less than perfect. Everybody who writes on this subject, for text or other uses, has hobbyhorses to ride and compromises to defend. There are other "modern algebra" texts on the market. What sets off the Addison-Wesley books is, simply, their seriousness of attitude, their respect for both students and teachers. What makes them significant is the fact that they show a profit. It seems there are more "strong schools" than the rest of the textbook industry believed.

Some other departures from the textbook norm are also making money. D. C. Heath has made available to high schools the interesting Amherst series of source-material pamphlets in American history; and the same firm is blanketing the country with the physics text prepared by the Physical Sciences Study Committee, which spent $5 million of National Science Foundation money—and months of the time of "physicists of Nobel laureate quality," to quote Jerrold Zacharias, who ran the committee—to develop a spectacular, all-new high-school program. . . . Macmillan has allowed Preston James of Syracuse to write the geography text he wanted to write, and is selling the unconventional result quite well, thank you. Row, Peterson and Company has finally come out of the woods on its ten-year-old program of pamphlets about science for elementary and junior-high use. These pamphlets vary vastly in quality, but nobody can quarrel with the idea behind them—the idea of making materials available in brief, adaptable, topic-by-topic morsels rather than in the monstrous dog biscuit of the predigested "course." . . .

Where the Money Is

These stirrings and heavings may break the smooth surface of textbook publishing some day, but not yet. By and large, textbooks for any given subject at any given age are still homogenized and padded, and so lavishly produced that they will break even only if they can be sold to thousands of schools for hundreds of thousands of youngsters to use in dozens of different educational programs. And the textbook publishers, all claiming to be educators, make one simple (very possibly inaccurate) defense of these procedures: that's where the money is.

In 1960, the last year for which full figures are available, some fifty-odd publishers sold some $230 million worth of elementary and high school textbooks—almost exactly $100 million more than they had sold in 1954. This rise does not come from the purchase of more texts per student—in 1954, the average number of new books per elementary student was 2.01, and in 1960 it was only 2.05. But enrollment in the schools was up 26 per cent and the price per book was up 29 per cent, so expenditure went up 65 per cent. Wall Street brokers began to regard textbook publishing as one of the nation's "growth industries," and investment bankers underwrote the sale of publishing stocks to the public at prices only remotely related to current earning or dividends. . . .

. . . By and large, each publisher puts one salesman in the field for every $70,000 to $120,000 of sales. The salesman is a man who once had a strong interest in education and sometimes still does—almost all textbook salesmen are former teachers or school administrators. But his primary interest is now concentrated on selling his employer's product. Occasionally, though not nearly as frequently as in past years, he may even try his luck at kickbacks and a spot of bribery.

What made corruption profitable in the old days was the purchase by state governments of a single "basal" textbook for each child in each subject. This procedure was obvious nonsense—there is no state (or city or town or school) so small or homogeneous that every fifth-grade child in it should be using the same book. Reason prevailed, and by 1961 only North Carolina was still buying from publishers in 100,000-book lots. Eighteen states still approve only a limited number of texts per subject (usually three to five), but "adoption" by such a state is a hunting license rather than a sale, and thus less likely to be worth a bribe. Even political influence is no longer so valuable as it used to be, though one publisher brags of a salesman "really more powerful than the governor."

Today, textbook selection in most places has passed into the hands of committees of teachers. Salesmen must sell their wares in the open (though there is still, unfortunately, virtually no press coverage of the sessions at which purchasing committees hear pitches from textbook salesmen). They must knock on doors, see teachers, even give demonstration lessons before they can make a sale. In some cities, each high school now chooses its own texts, and there are even a few school systems which have had the wisdom to allow each elementary school to spend its own textbook budget for its own needs.

Yet the shift to more sedate selling procedures may have hurt rather than helped the quality of textbooks. When a salesman could work by bribery or influence, he did not care greatly about the book itself; once he had to sell a product, he became considerable of a nosy Parker about what was printed on the pages. Editors began to lose control over their books. Every salesman knows what he *can't* sell, and will insist that such things be kept out of his satchel. In the obvious case, nobody who works a Southern territory can tolerate anything that smacks of integration. Rand McNally, showing more courage than most firms, printed two versions of a social-studies text, one of them with a picture of a New York chemistry class which showed some Puerto Rican faces at the lab tables (for Northern distribution), the other with a picture of a lily-white chemistry class (for Southern distribution). Most publishers simply avoid any picture of the races together. A Macmillan civics text got into final proof with a picture of an integrated playground; a salesman spotted it and screamed; and Macmillan, with a gesture of rebuke to the editor responsible, remade the book with a different picture. Row, Peterson's American history text, complete through the 1960 election, deals with Southern resistance to the Supreme Court in a single sentence: "Many states, believing the ruling of the Supreme Court was an infringement on state authority and on the rights of its citizens, employed legal devices to prevent integration of the public schools."

Even where pressures from part of the national community do not give a plausible excuse for fuzziness, most salesmen want to be sure no book contains an idea most teachers have not already learned to love, and to teach. "The three magic words in selling a textbook," says Maynard Hites, "are 'easy–new–free.' In that order." Thus, there must be the manual that takes all the drudgery out of teaching, the lovely teacher aids that will make your classroom the envy of your friends, the objective tests prepared by modern scientists in our own laboratories, all absolutely up-to-the-minute yet tested and proved coast-to-coast. The books must be weighed on almost meaningless "readability scales," though everybody but the *Lumpenproletariat* of "language-arts specialists" knows that children and adolescents read what interests them on one level and what doesn't interest them on another. To prove it is "easy," the salesman must show that his eleventh-grade American history text measures tenth-grade on the "readability scale."

Alfred North Whitehead once said that "Whenever a book is written of real educational worth, you may be quite certain that some reviewer will say that it will be difficult to teach from it. Of course it will be difficult to teach from it. If it were easy, the book ought to be burned, for it cannot be educational." But Whitehead was a philosopher, not a textbook salesman. He did not understand how important it is (to sales) that a teacher (*any* teacher) be "comfortable" with the textbook. He was not "in touch with the market."

Who Writes Them?

The textbook is the original "non-book"—the book that someone feels he must publish rather than the book that someone feels he must write. Except on the college level, textbooks rarely grow out of an initiative from the author. Letters come to publishers all the time from teachers who would like to write textbooks—but these teachers have been goaded to this ambition by their dislike for existing texts, their desire to present something quite unusual in the field, and salesmen know that the market wants the usual because the market is buying the usual. Occasionally, an original idea does win approval from the front office, but everybody is relieved to find, once the manuscript has gone through the meat grinder, that the result is really not very different from what is selling right now.

Still, the books must be changed, if only because a committee adopting a textbook looks first of all at the copyright date, to see whether the book is "up-to-date"—and you cannot get a new copyright unless you make some changes. Most textbook publishers, too, do want to improve their product, provided they are sure the improvements won't bother anybody. Editors attend teacher conferences, get in touch with people who write articles in education magazines, consult with administrators and professors of education. Salesmen feed back reports from the field on why schools are buying other books, what features would help sell a new book, what reputations are being made and unmade in the little worlds of "subject matter" and theory of education.

The ideal team of authors for a textbook series (very few textbooks are admittedly the work of a single author) includes a university professor who is an expert on the "subject matter," a professor of education who is an expert on how to teach it, and one or more teachers who are actually wrestling with the problem here and now. For elementary texts, the "subject matter" expert is usually omitted—if only because so few university people have the faintest interest in the fascinating problems of elementary education. In a few cases, authors are chosen because they have a political position that will sell books; they are head of some national council or other, or they are spokesmen for a school of thought. Usually, though, textbook editors honestly try to get the best people they can to write their books. Most of the time, they fail. Textbook writing is hard work, and first-rate people find it dull—especially when committees of editors and fellow authors are virtually certain to remove from the manuscript anything that smacks of personal communication from writer to reader.

On the rare occasions when a first-rate scholar is persuaded to work on a text, the results are often highly disappointing. He goes at it, usually, with a view to himself when young, and tends to teach what was taught to him. He forgets the work he and his colleagues have done recently, because this is by definition "advanced" work. A decade ago, for example, Oliver Dickerson demonstrated that the transfer of colonial customs control from London to Boston in 1767 had profoundly influenced the events leading to the Revolution; few American history texts yet mention this transfer. Even routine factual errors remain embedded in the texts—it is now known, for example, that the slogan "Fifty-four forty, or Fight!" was not coined until 1845, but a brand-new high-school text by a former president of the American Historical Association still proclaims that Polk won the 1844 election on this platform.

In science and mathematics, these inhibitions are gradually disappearing, because some curious mathematicians and physicists discovered that certain notions basic to their own recent work could be taught directly, without massive prior preparation, to young children. This discovery was probably as important as Sputnik, and the rockets of cash that followed in revitalizing these areas of American education. Such procedures may be possible in other fields of inquiry, too—but nobody yet knows how to develop them, and the textbook publishers, though they always want the name of the innovator on their book, are not always very much interested in the work. . . .

. . . Editors of "trade" books—novels and general non-fiction sold through bookstores—are usually midwives: their job is to get out of an author what may be in him. Editors of textbooks, however, on the elementary and often on the high-school level are usually progenitors. They have suggested the book and the angle, they have picked the author, and they will probably rewrite the prose. . . . Some houses have been known to prepare elementary texts in the shop, then get an eminent professor of education to go over the results and put his name on the cover for a one per cent royalty.

Most textbook editors started life as teachers (it is extremely rare for any of them to have been a scholar or a writer) and put in some years as salesmen before they were allowed to settle down in the home office. They are, notoriously, experts in what cannot be done.

"The National Council of Teachers of English is a wonderful group," says Lee Deighton of Macmillan, "but you can't rely on their opinion of what books will go. They'll get you into trouble. The books they want are a lot better than what you can sell, because they're much more ambitious than the ordinary teacher."

So-and-so won't like this; you can't sell this in that state; how many thirteen-year-olds will know that word? Worse yet, they know what cannot be *omitted:* they have all the "curriculum guides" that keep the duplicating machines busy in the educational provinces, and they insist on the insertion of every little unrelated or wrongheaded bit of "subject matter" that any local school politician has picked up on his travels. "In this office," an editor says rather proudly, "we are all salesmen."

Controls on Quality

What emerges from this machinery is usually shoddy and sometimes scandalous. Many books lack distinction, integrity, and style. The teachers' manuals that accompany them are commonly an insult to the professional competence and common sense (let alone intelligence) of the teachers to whom they are delivered. Even when a book is aimed at a special market, rather than at a standard "course," the publisher and authors may be unwilling to concede that the material it contains could interest anyone. For example, Holt's text on "Space Science" begins with the sentence, "There was no World Series game on October 4, 1957"—presumably because no student would take an interest in the launching of the first satellite unless the event were linked to baseball.

Errors abound. Chicago had to instruct its teachers to avoid certain errors contained in all biology texts on the market. Elementary texts dealing with geography typically teach the nonsense of "frigid, temperate, and torrid zones," which has been out of date for roughly four centuries. (There is no point along the Equator anywhere near so hot as Death Valley, which is in the "temperate zone," and much of the Arctic never gets as cold as Missoula, Montana.) The prose is vague, characterless at best, cluttered with chatty avoidance of the issue. ("The cow has many uses," runs a caption in Allyn & Bacon's *Our World and Its Peoples,* "so Hindus refuse to kill it, and there is always a shortage of meat in India.") One of the reasons students write so poorly is their constant contact with the glue that passes for English in their textbooks. . . .

. . . Yet the materials for major improvements are certainly present. Most informed people who do not have a vested interest in current textbooks are fairly sure that American teachers, for all the poverty of their training, are better than the materials with which they must work. (And, at worst, can be successfully retrained to teach specific materials once the materials have been developed.) Where a book or a series dominates a market, it is always among the better and usually the best available version (keeping in mind that questions of "better" in this context may be like Samuel Johnson's famous "question of precedence between a louse and flea"). The Harcourt literature anthologies are available in two "tracks" for better and weaker students; the "high" track has enormously outsold the "low" track. Rand McNally has stolen the largest single chunk of the American history market with a text most observers regard as marginally more serious than its rivals —and has done so, by the way, without "adoptions" in backward states, which other publishers say they must have. Where the product at the top of a homogeneous cluster is garnering the largest share of the market, there is sound business reason to cut in on top of it. Natural competitive forces should be driving textbooks to improvement.

Unfortunately, the system contains a number of built-in brakes against advancing quality. Far too many school systems still "adopt" a single book for use in every school in the city, preventing what may be a fairly large adventurous minority of teachers from rewarding the publisher with the courage to put out an original book. The argument that a book is "too difficult" for teachers or students is always a reason for rejection by a purchasing committee—which by definition regards itself as a group superior to teachers not on the committee and feels obliged to defend them against "difficult" books. Nobody ever argues that a book is "too easy," because one can always provide "enrichment" for above-average students—and, of course, your first-rank teacher typically throws the textbook out the window anyway. The notion that bad textbooks teach children contempt for the materials of learning is simply too rude a thought for a well-mannered committee, and ill-mannered people somehow never get asked to join committees.

Within the publishing houses, the tradition of compromise (to give the thing its kindest name) is deeply rooted. Many of the men who work on textbooks—particularly at the top level in their firms—are far more interesting and distinguished than their product. They retain their self-respect by arguing that the pap they dump on the schools is the very best and purest pap, and the only nourishment teachers are able to ingest. Many of them have made a psychological commitment to the publishing of bad books, as cigarette manufacturers have made a commitment to the wholesomeness of smoking; they could not live with themselves otherwise.

Effective pressure from the outside has been brought to bear only by the Modern Language Association for "audio-lingual" elementary-school foreign-language materials, and by the National Science Foundation through the various "study groups" of scientists and mathematicians, who have created guaranteed markets for new material. Even here, however, one of the two major publishers without a textbook division (Doubleday) bid more than any textbook publisher for the Physical Science Study Committee collateral reading materials. Pressure from the teacher organizations, all of which are more or less dissatisfied with existing texts, has accomplished almost exactly nothing. The only other source of organized influence is the Radical Right, which is no longer quite so idiotic as it used to be, and often mixes with its paranoiac complaints ("anti-American and anti-Christ" for a definition in a school dictionary) a certain number of perceptive objections. But there is, of course, an obvious danger in a situation where only Right-wing extremists read textbooks seriously.

What Will Draw Talent?

Public interest touches textbook publishing at every point. More than four-fifths of the elementary and high-school texts are bought with tax moneys; and, on a more serious level, what is available in text form often determines the limits of what can be studied in an ordinary school. The sameness of existing text materials restricts all but the brightest teachers and children, or the richest communities, to a "national curriculum" accidental in origin, disabling in effect, and incredibly slow-moving. There has been no major change in a quarter of a century in the grade-levels at which elementary textbooks introduce ideas about history, language, math, etc. With more than a hundred thousand teachers and four million children now working on each grade level in the elementary school, it is nonsense to say that the tiny range of difference among the existing text series can cover the natural range of needs in the schools.

There are many areas where textbooks are probably undesirable, however good they may be. "I don't see why we have 'readers,'" says William Spaulding, who publishes such stuff himself. "I don't know why we don't have a lot of books for children to read." Physical equipment for experiments is probably more important than books in elementary science; source documents and passages from the work of real historians, economists, *et al.,* are probably more valuable than four-pound textbooks in high-school social studies. Even where text materials are necessary, the teacher's ability to supplement and interpret are vital to the creation of interest—and the incredibly unimaginative publisher-supplied manuals murder interest in both teachers and students.

If the current furor over American education is to produce more than mounds of unread committee reports and self-congratulatory messages from the Fund for the Advancement of Education, something must be done to provide more stimulating written materials for use in the schools. Despite the bits of encouraging evidence dredged up for the beginning of this article, despite the occasional crusades of individual publishers (Harcourt for structural linguistics, Heath for direct-method foreign-language films and records), despite the obvious economic logic of a more ambitious effort, it is doubtful that the established houses will pull up their own socks.

New materials must be independently created, by groups of scholars and teachers working together with minimal interference from the educational bureaucracy—and published, probably by the university presses, which have learned to break even on low sales figures. (Distribution rights for the more successful items could be licensed to the textbook publishers, if desired.) Not all these materials—probably not many of them—need be "textbooks." Both quality and variety would be served better by the use of relatively short, deliberately incomplete pamphlets and paperbacks that might draw the talents of people who are repelled by the tedious crutch-making of textbook construction. (There is also a desperate need for quality films, a need which has been hidden, almost deliberately, under the noisy propaganda for educational television, which is cheap to produce by comparison.)

Obviously, the job is important—far too important to leave in the not-highly-skilled, not-very-ambitious, not-always-clean hands of the textbook publisher.

Students Prepare for Teaching:

SAMPLE STUDY PLANS

The following readings are quite different from those presented earlier. The Speculative Resources presented here were written by students preparing for teaching. They represent various efforts to invent study possibilities within the context of elementary-school instruction.

An American philosopher once observed that human beings characteristically display four kinds of behavior in attempting to deal with the problematic. Some-times, men engage social problems on the basis of intuition or by following the dictates of their conscience. Sometimes, they follow tradition, applying orthodox solutions to new and unorthodox problems. At other times, they resolve matters of doubt by appealing to authority—in one way or another, men are in fre-quent and intimate consultation with soothsayers. Finally, they use methods of inquiry. It is this fourth type of behavior that these young teachers have tried to encourage in their students.

On Trial*

Proposed Study for 5th and 6th Grade Social Studies
Elvehjem School, Madison

. . . the historian requires, above all, evidence. It is
the character of the evidence which establishes the
framework within which he writes. He cannot imagine

From unpublished materials, reprinted by permission of the authors: "On Trial," by Jean Selk; "There and Now: Angola, Africa," by Alice Sherman; "Jobs and Places of Employment," by Jean O. Roark; "The Monroe Doctrine—Why?" by Lynn Bolton.
* By permission of Jean M. Selk, Madison, Wisconsin.

scenes for which he has no citation, invent dialog for
which he has no text, assume relationships for which
he has no warrant. Fact is his raw material, and the
farther he strays from his evidence, the more contentious his history becomes.

—Arthur M. Schlesinger, Jr.,
writing in the *Atlantic*

This study possibility uses a court trial as the jumping off point for an
investigation into the notion of authoritative sources of knowledge and into
an historical examination of the American system of law and justice.

It is designed to develop a more closely defined concept of "authority,"
as well as to provide a study into the here and then.

The Issue in Focus

Social studies textbooks and classroom discussions—strongly aided and
abetted by popular fiction, the movies and television series such as "Perry
Mason," and "the Defenders"—do a fairly good job, it seems to me, of
promulgating such basic American judicial concepts as those that a person
is "innocent until proved guilty" or that the accused, in most cases anyway,
is guaranteed the "right of trial by jury."

This study would not ignore the over-all concept of impartial justice for
all. But the major emphasis would be on the necessity, as illustrated by a
court of law in action, to test evidence for its reliability whenever we are
gathering information to support, discount or modify our hypotheses. Wit-
nessing first hand the application of judicial safeguards in the gathering of
information would, it is hoped, offer insights into the means of gathering
information for historical and other types of studies.

How to Proceed

A civil rather than a criminal trial, it seems to me, would be the best
vehicle for starting this study. Civil trials have the virtue, for our purposes,
of being on the whole less sensational and less prolonged than criminal
trials. The advance scheduling of civil actions also lends itself to planning
ahead for class attendance.

In Dane County the vast majority of civil trials are conducted in one of
the three Circuit Court branches located in the City-County Building. Trials
in these courts normally are scheduled months in advance when the seasonal
court calendars are prepared. The teacher, however, would have to stay in
touch with the office of the court clerk to learn of possible postponements
or delays in trial dates.

I would propose to select for this initiating study a trial involving a suit
seeking damages for alleged injuries suffered in an automobile accident.
These type suits are probably the most prevalent of those heard in the Dane

County Circuit Courts. They also, commonly, are "classic" trials involving many of the safeguarding procedures we will examine.

To be most effective, the suit should be one in which not only the plaintiff has filed a complaint (as is required in all such cases), but also one in which the defendant has filed an answer to the complaint. I also would choose a case in which a jury trial has been requested.

Complaints and answers normally are available and on file at the court clerk's office at least several weeks before the trial date. Photostatic copies of complaints and answers can be obtained for a nominal charge in the City-County Building.

Many trials for auto injury damages involve sharply divergent interpretations of causes, effects and even of the so-called "facts" involved. An examination of complaints and answers would assist the teacher in selecting a trial which promises to unfold such differing interpretations, thus assuring a fairly wide testing ground for the validity of conflicting evidence.

I would propose to obtain photostatic copies of both the plaintiff's complaint and the defendant's answer, divide the class into two groups and furnish one group with the complaint and the other with the answer. In addition, each class member would receive a copy of the 25-page booklet, "Law and Courts in the News," a layman's handbook of court procedures which also contains a glossary of legal terminology. This booklet is distributed free by the American Bar Association and is written in quite easy-to-understand terms.

The booklet, along with other resources which might prove necessary, would help the two groups decipher the legal terminology contained in the documents and also help each of the groups gain an understanding of "their side" of the dispute.

A classroom discussion would serve to acquaint both groups with the issues at stake, the differences in interpretation of facts and perhaps actual variance in the facts themselves as presented in the two documents. The discussion undoubtedly also would raise a number of unresolved questions and a variety of hypotheses about the case.

The discussion would help the teacher uncover possible gaps in knowledge and understanding of the case. Efforts thus could be made to breach these gaps through further research, reading and so on before the class attends the trial.

The class also should have a basic acquaintanceship with the court system and with court procedure in order to aid their comprehension of the trial as it is in progress. But minute probings into the whys and hows, I think, could most profitably await the discussion, analysis and further study which will follow the trial.

The class goes off to the trial, with eyes and ears sharply attuned for discovering how information is gathered and authenticated for the official court record.

Issues at Stake

It would be foolhardy to predict what sort of questions will arise or events occur during the trial, but I think it's safe to assume that most if not all the following rules will be invoked in the course of taking testimony or receiving evidence:

1. Physical evidence and testimony offered by witnesses must be *relevant*. That is, it must be applicable to the issue involved in the trial.
2. Testimony and other evidence must be *material*. That is, it must have some consequence or meaning in resolving the issue at hand.
3. Witnesses must be *competent* to testify. For instance, a doctor who testifies as to the plaintiff's injuries must establish that he, in fact, is a qualified physician and that he has, in fact, examined and/or treated the plaintiff.
4. The *authenticity* of physical evidence also must be established. For instance, a photograph of the accident scene must be established by the person who took it as being a photograph of the accident in question.
5. *Hearsay* testimony by witnesses is not permitted in the record. Hence, second-hand testimony in which a witness attempts to relate what another person told him about a fact or event in question is not allowed.
6. Witnesses must testify only to their version of the facts and are not permitted to draw conclusions or state opinions about the meaning of these facts.
7. Each side will give greatest emphasis to the *direct evidence* (that is, the testimony by witnesses who actually saw acts committed or events occur) on its side. Each side, on the other hand, can be expected to disparage the *circumstantial* or indirect evidence offered by the other side in presenting facts or testimony from which it hopes the jury will draw inferences or presumptions.
8. The judge, in all likelihood, will ask the jury to decide in favor of the side which jury members believe has presented the *preponderance of evidence*. That is, the decision must be based on the quality, not the quantity, of evidence.

As soon as the jury begins its deliberations, students rush back to their classroom to begin a lively and thought-provoking discussion of the trial. (A considerate teacher will not insist that her class be "locked up" overnight with the jury if deliberations are prolonged, but she will stay in touch with the court clerk's office so she can inform the class of the jury's verdict.)

The verdict, however, is not all-important—for our purposes, anyway. The vital issue at hand is the method of gathering information upon which the jury has been asked to reach its verdict.

Do members of the class, after having heard the evidence presented at the trial, have the same impressions, knowledge and opinions about the case that they had before entering the courtroom?

The classroom discussion could begin at this point and proceed to probe more deeply into the rules by which information and facts were gathered and used at the trial.

I do not believe students should be left with the impression that they can or should employ all of the arduous, and tortuous rules governing the admissibility of courtroom evidence in their own classroom inquiries. But I think some inferences can be drawn (adroitly, if need be, through helpful suggestions by all-knowing teacher) about how methods of authenticating evidence can be used by students in social "studies" and in other learning activities within and outside the classroom.

If this project is undertaken early in the school year, I believe many instances would occur during the course of the year when students could harken back (or be gently harkened by same all-knowing teacher) to courtroom examples and their broad implications.

The study would move now into "historying" the origin and the whys of judicial safeguards and other features of our American court and legal system. Hopefully, student interest would be highly piqued at this point.

Some directions the study might take:

An examination of the sources of law (morals, canons, customs, statutes, judicial precedents, etc.)

How and why much of American judicial practice and legal system was derived from English common law. How this differs from the more rigid legal system which originated in Continental Europe. What effect has our adoption of English common law had on other aspects of American life?

What significant changes have occurred in our laws and judicial system and what prompted them? What have been the results? (For example, Wisconsin is one of a minority of states without capital punishment. Has this always been the case? Inquiring students will find the answer to be "no." Why did Wisconsin abolish capital punishment? Inquiring students will learn of a 19th century case in which a man was executed for murder and, later when the actual culprit was found and confessed, the Legislature promptly abolished capital punishment.)

What effect do laws and the actions of courts have on our life today (an endless inquiry)?

There and Now: Angola, Africa

The sixth grade social studies curriculum undertakes the imposing task of covering Ancient Civilizations to the present, and then branching out into

By permission of Mrs. Alice Sherman, Madison, Wisconsin.

a "survey" of the various countries of the Eastern Hemisphere. As I understand it, the time traditionally spent on Africa has been relatively short. My plan would be to adjust curriculum so that less time is spent on places such as Australia, and more time devoted to the study of Africa. I feel this is justified by the current importance of Africa on the world scene and by the fact that Africa is an example of a country in the midst of observable change which provides many study possibilities for students.

I am assuming that the students have previously studied "civilizations" and that they will be able to apply their understanding to the position Africa is in today. The study possibility, as I envision it, would introduce the study of Africa, and most probably, due to the time element, would become the major portion of their study. Because the African continent is so large and a great variety of peoples, situations, and environments exist within its borders, I have decided that the study must focus on a particular area; I choose Angola because I have at hand many interesting resources for the students to use in their study, and I feel that their learning to handle these resources would be an important objective of the study.

To initiate the study, I would bring in thirty or so art objects made by natives of Angola. These can be obtained from a collection at the First Methodist Church, Madison. There would be at least as many articles as there are students in the class. These would be displayed around the room along with bulletin board displays raising the question, "What is Africa like today?" (This might include a picture of a tribal scene, city scenes, schools, primitive farms, etc.—as many contrasts as possible.) Hopefully this will draw their attention and spark some curiosity about the articles around the room. (Truthfully, I will be surprised and most disappointed if it doesn't, because the art articles range from a crude small axe used by a witch doctor, to carvings of natives in Western dress carrying books.)

When class begins, I plan to let each student choose one of these "things" to take (carefully!) to his desk to examine freely, with instructions to the effect that we are going to act in a sense as anthropologists and try, through the examination of articles, to speculate and predict as much as we can about the people who created these articles. (If this meets blank looks, discussion will be necessary at this point, but hopefully they will be so curious about what they are holding that they will want to do this naturally.) The idea here would be to present them with object things about which they can think, and then proceed to infer information from these things. In addition to "speculation" they will be encouraged to jot down the questions that arise as they examine the objects, i.e., what types of information cannot be inferred, yet would be important to understanding these people? In addition to the content value, and the "study" value, I feel that these initial observations concerning the objects will give me, as teacher, an important clue as to their level of thinking at the present time and could help direct the remaining part of the study.

My husband and I attempted this ourselves to try to get an idea of what sorts of information or questions the objects raise. Samples of the articles available and our observations follow. (I would predict that the responses of the children will be greatly varied, from the most obvious to extreme speculation. This would be fine and hopefully they will see things we missed!)

SAMPLES:

Article	*Possible Observations*
1. Decorative ivory tusk	The people obviously had a source of ivory-elephants; they must have had sharp cutting tools and polishing tools; fish, hippopotami and crocodiles are pictured indicating a proximity to water and perhaps that these are prominent animals in the environment; the detailed work would indicate that time must be allowed in this society for art work and some value must be placed on the decorative. In one part of the carving there is a string of elephants faced by a lion, indicating one of the problems of the jungle.
2. Wood rattles	Demonstrates precise carving skill; indicates that rhythm is a component of their music and causes one to wonder about their music, what it is used for, type, etc.
3. Carved male musician	Again makes one think of a very rhythmic music because the musician is playing a percussion instrument which shows a type of musical scale of at least seven tones. It is quite different from one we know, with the vibration resonating from hollow gourds. The dress can also be observed from this carving.
4. Wooden spoons	The people must eat with utensils; shows carving skills particularly in the bowl of the spoon. The wood is a soft wood and fire has been used for some of the decoration perhaps indicating that they like decoration, but had to use natural means to obtain the effect.
5. Reed baskets	Shows that the people are near a source of grasses and reeds; they have the techniques and skills of bending and shaping reeds, weaving, plus a designing capacity. The baskets are designed for carrying and for storage of food or

	grains. They seem to combine practicality and beauty. Makes one wonder if these would be the sole means for storage compared with our cans, boxes, etc.
6. Metal tipped walking cane	Says something about the fact that some metal must be available and used; could at least raise the question about the old or sick people in that society; might indicate the height of some. Might raise a question of who would use such a cane as contrasted to a walking stick.
7. Toy wood truck	Looks like a toy model of a large truck; might indicate that the children of their society play with toys and that there must be the presence of trucks, or knowledge of trucks for this to have been carved. This might indicate a degree of modernity in transportation and would raise questions of their availability and use.
8. Carvings of people	One is of a lady in native dress carrying jug on her head—shows what the native dress looks like, use of prints in materials would cause speculation as to weaving, beads are worn (is this a native product or acquired through trade?), the hair styles can be observed and one gets an idea of the way water is carried. Another carving shows a native boy dressed in shorts and shirt, carrying school books and lunch. This makes one think of the influence of the west in his dress, and causes speculation about education. The fact that this was an object for carving might indicate some value of literacy.
9. African elementary school book	"O Livro da Segunda Classe." From the pictures in the book one can guess at the age group, what kind of book it is, what they study. It raises many questions as to who goes to school, what are their schools like, etc.
10. Crude Axe	There is a note on this object saying that it was used by witch doctors. It can be seen how a simple tool was made, and raises questions about the witch doctor's place today, what about religion and superstitions, how old is this axe, what was the witch doctor's place in their society.

These were just some of the observations that came to our minds; I am sure students would see others probably more astute! Other possible objects for study include pieces of colorful cloth, beads, alligator leather purse, carved antelope head, bracelets, straw fan, clay dishes, etc.

After the students have written down their impressions and observations, a class discussion could be held to compile their ideas in an attempt to form some sort of picture of the people, their environment and life. Hopefully questions would arise as to how certain articles were made, who uses them? Is it currently in use? How is it used? It will be interesting to see if their discussion brings out, "Can we really tell 'that' from the spoon?" "Couldn't it also mean . . . ?" If this question does not come from one of the students, I feel that the teacher might throw in the belligerent question at this point to make sure they are thinking and not just guessing off the tops of their heads. Because of the nature of the articles, the comments should raise some question as to the seeming "mixture of the old and the new" in Africa. What does this say about the current African situation?—I see this discussion as whetting their taste to see how close they have come to actually describing the people and society in this particular section of Africa.

The question could then be thrown out as to where we might go check our description with the observations of others. I think the students will first suggest books, then maps and films. I think this would be a valid beginning, and I would encourage this, but I have found after investigating these sources myself, that they present only the most obvious information, much of which the students will have arrived at themselves through their observations and discussions. (i.e., crops, climate, dress, etc.)

I think that we would soon discover that the big area we really don't know anything about would be the present status of the people in Angola. I have at my disposal several contradictory sources of information concerning this topic. I would have to give these to the students to use, as I have not found them available from the library. I think they would be able to handle this material well after their initial study of the people, their way of life, etc. It could be used in several ways (and the students could express a preference) but tentatively I would plan to have some of the students read about Angola from the viewpoint of Portugal, and others from the "native" point of view. Both sources are written very persuasively. Then in discussion the students could weigh and evaluate the various points of view and grapple with the problem of different sources supposedly speaking authoritatively and truthfully, yet seeming at opposite poles. "How do we know whom to believe?" "Must we accept one view?" "What does this tell us about the problem?"

Some of these resources are:

1) A 14-page document submitted to the United Nations in November 1961 by Domingos Francisco da Silva, a native of Angola, asking for support of the natives: *Report On The Events In Angola.* In this document there is a report on the historical background, labor, poll taxes, schools,

revolution, abuses, etc. It is definitely native oriented. I think there is a lot of meat here and the children could really become involved in it.

2) *Portugal and Her Overseas Provinces,* a pamphlet put out by the Portuguese-American Committee on Foreign Affairs. This is prepared as a defense of Angola as a province and states quite succinctly the Portuguese point of view.

3) "I Saw the Horror in Angola"—*Saturday Evening Post,* May 12, 1962. This is an article written by an American agricultural missionary supporting the native viewpoint.

4) *Reforms*—a four-page brochure put out by the Portuguese public relations office.

5) *Angola Interview*—a record recording an interview made by three Americans who had been imprisoned in Portugal as a result of their having been in Angola during the native uprisings; the interview was held at the United Nations.

6) "Wars of 'Liberation' In Africa—What They Mean"—from *U.S. News & World Report,* October 30, 1961. Written by Pedro Theotonio Pereira, Ambassador of Portugal to Washington.

After doing some of this reading, an Angolan student from the university could be invited in to speak and answer questions or someone from the department of African Studies (the husband of one of the interns is in this department and would be available).

I think that a study of this nature can accomplish several things: 1) It can confront the students with an authentic problematic situation about which there is no *one* authority to appeal to for "the answer." The students will have to seek out the varying opinions and weigh them against each other in order to draw their own conclusions or form an opinion. 2) The study can provide a situation in which the students can deal with "things" from which they must speculate as to their message value. 3) The students can realize that information is written from some point of view and that the reader must take this into consideration when evaluating his source material. 4) The students can have the opportunity to work with first-hand materials concerning the "changing Africa" rather than simply accepting "authoritative" reports such as those found in textbooks, etc. And finally, 5) I think this approach can give the students a more acute understanding of the history, development and current position of a native people who have quite recently joined in the nationalistic fervor covering the African nations.

Though this may seem to be an unreasonable amount of time to spend on such a small part of Africa and a part which has problems which are unique to it, as teacher I have made a value choice to deal as thoroughly as possible with one particular area in Africa. I realize that the students can briefly survey all Africa (as they have done in the past) and probably come out with a fund of informational bits of knowledge, but this doesn't touch on the importance of Africa *today* and predictably tomorrow. This traditional survey gives them no sense of the changing Africa and the unusual heritage it has had when viewed in relationship to other countries and continents. Angola was chosen because of the resources available and the students' learning to handle these resources is considered an important objective of the study as well as the information imparted. (It could have been the Congo, Ghana . . . as well, but Angola held these study possibilities here in Madison.)

As I see it, though this study plan takes pages to explain, it could be done in a classroom within a two (depending on the class) week period. I would follow this study with an overview of Africa, applying their learning about Angola to the other nations, noting their similarities and differences. Even if time limited this, I would still feel justified in spending the time available becoming well acquainted with one country rather than in getting a scanty introduction to all of them.

Jobs and Places of Employment

The social studies program in the first few grades of the elementary school is largely devoted to studying the community. As Madison schools are no exception the students typically take a trip to the local fire department, perhaps to a farm, study the milkman, postman and other obvious "community helpers" in an attempt to get to know their city. One might question whether or not the horizons of the young student are so narrow that a superficial study of the corner policeman and the like are the extent of the youngsters' interests. However, as no great break-throughs in the curriculum are imminent, probably the next best thing is to acquaint the boys and girls with a more accurate and realistic view of their city. After all most of their fathers are not milkmen, policemen, or farmers, and probably a good percentage of their mothers are employed outside their homes. Just where are their parents and other Madisonians employed and what are their jobs like?

A logical way to begin this study would be to ask the children where their parents and other people they know work and what they do. Perhaps they could make a guess as to what the major jobs are in the community. Quite likely the students would feel that whatever their particular parents did was the most common occupation. Chances are slim that the children would be aware of the employment and occupational patterns of Madison. Having no teaching experience I can only guess as to whether or not

By permission of Jean O. Roark, Madison, Wisconsin.

the children could figure out on their own where to hunt for some information. Possibly they would suggest some good sources for likely answers. If the students lack imagination suggestions from the teacher would be necessary.

In my investigations I found it no simple matter to get hold of some "official" facts and figures offering pat answers to the questions of where Madisonians work and what they do. (These two questions are not completely separable of course. In some cases the place of employment fairly well defines the type of job. For instance a production man at Oscar Mayers is very likely concerned with meat processing, although the company has a specific job title for him. For other cases the title of the employer tells little. At the University of Wisconsin can be found electricians, janitors, maids, professors, etc.) Thinking the Madison Chamber of Commerce would be a ready source of such information I was surprised to find they had nothing to offer other than the 1962 City Directory. Theoretically I could have plowed through scores of pages and totaled up the various jobs. For many individuals the actual employer was not listed. Deciding I'd use a sample technique I turned to the name Smith and noted the occupations of 36 consecutive listings. I chose the surname Smith because I felt it would be less likely to give related individuals than many of Madison's Norwegian and German names. Therefore I hoped there would be less of this type of bias. Non-jobholding housewives were not included. Of the 35 five were widowed or retired people, and two were students. (Only individuals over 18 are listed.) The occupations of the 29 remaining people were:

> associate professor—UW
> market manager
> research assistant—UW
> accountant
> domestic worker
> group manager—Gimbels
> elementary school teacher
> medical secretary
> physician
> assistant field director—Red Cross
> grocery store clerk
> mechanic—Oscar Mayer
> tire salesman
> representative for life insurance company
> stenographer
> cashier
> professor—UW
> nurse's aide
> resident director—UW
> engineer—Telephone Company

housekeeper
apprentice carpenter
accountant
fellow—UW
teaching assistant—UW
used car reconditioner
sheet metal worker
lab technician
electrician

A study of these sample occupations allows for a lot of interesting speculation and further investigation. Even young children should be able to
detect (aided by some translation by the teacher) that farmers, firemen, etc.
do not dominate the list. Class discussion could help explain the work of a
nurse's aide, an insurance salesman, an electrician, and so forth. For very
young children no doubt some of these occupations would be difficult to
understand. Perhaps the children would notice that six of the people plus
the two students are connected with the University of Wisconsin. This might
be their first inkling of the importance of the university in the Madison
community. I'm struck by the variety of jobs listed; except for the two
students and the two accountants there are no exact duplications. Another
observation the children might make is that many of the jobs are of a
"white-collar" nature. These are probably least familiar to most of the children and the most difficult for them to comprehend.

The city directory turned out to be the best, and in fact only, source for
a run-down of typical Madison occupations. No doubt a more extensive
sampling list could be compiled giving additional jobs.

The Madison Public Library had no available figures of the places of
employment. However, they did hand me a 1963 Classified Directory of
Wisconsin Manufacturers. Although I was unable to determine the exact
criteria for inclusion in the directory, I noted that most of the businesses
had salable products, and a few services. Only one bank was listed; for what
reason I don't know. Madison is credited with 168 of Wisconsin's manufacturers of surprising diversity. I jotted down 25 of them, trying to include
all the larger employers and some of the unusual ones. They are:

Dairy Equipment Co. Average Wis. Employment: 300 men, 50 women
Democrat Printing Co. 135, 50
Fauerbach Brewing Co. 73, 2
First Nat. Bank 50, 160
Gardner Baking Co. (No figures given)
Gisholt Machine Co. 850, 60
Grimm Book Bindery 11, 4
Litho Productions, Inc. 35, 5
Henry Town Labs (pest control) 5

Madison Kipp (die castings, mechanical lubricators, air grinders) 450, 50
Madison Silos 75
Mautz Paint and Varnish 90, 35
Oscar Mayer 2,947, 748
Stefan Mittler Monuments (No figures given)
Ohio Chemical and Surgical (medical gases, therapy oxygen, pipeline systems for hospitals) 223, 100
Olds Seed Co. 20, 10
Ray-O-Vac (batteries, flash light cases, etc.) 511, 464
Research Products (humidifiers, air filters, etc.) 110, 110
F. S. Royster Guano Co. (fertilizers) 72, 8
Schoeps Ice Cream Co., 30, 10
Sprague-Dawley Inc. (albino rats) 42, 2
Sub-Zero Freezers (No figures given)
Bob White Candy Co. 4, 4
Wis. Foundry and Machine Co. (crane booms, conveyors, castings) 91, 5
Wis. Power and Light Co. 1,400, 300

My sampling technique was strictly biased in the hopes of providing students with material for discussion as to the major employers and the interesting products available. A study of these businesses would give a more accurate picture of a modern American city with its wide range of businesses. Many of these are quite recent in development, such as the Ohio Chemical Company with its medical equipment. Litho Products is dependent upon 20th-century advances in photography and duplicating processes; a good comparison could be made between it and the more conventional printing company.

The Oscar Mayer meat packing company is the biggest private employer in town. Their public relations department was quite willing to supply me with information I needed and gave me a good résumé of its present operations and recent developments. At present the company employs about 3,700 people, averaging $7,600 to $7,700 per year, who work a single shift. Of the 3,700 approximately 3,000 are in production and 700 in managerial, clerical and sales work. 1953 was the peak year so far as the number of people employed—8,500 working two shifts. The number has gone steadily down although wages and production are up due to better equipment and methods. I was assured that no layoffs had occurred—personnel who retired or quit were not replaced. The Oscar Mayer Company considers itself a pioneer in the development of vacuum packed Saran-wrapped sausages, cut meats, sandwich spreads and smoked meats and hence concentrates production in this area. They concede their second-place position in fresh meat production. A survey of this company would illustrate two typical features of present business operations: (1) The trend towards automation and (2) increased specialization. This first aspect might very well have affected the lives of some of the children in the classroom.

Madison's two largest employers do not appear in the manufacturers' guide however. Any resident of the city could hardly escape observing the fact that Madison is the capitol of the state and the seat of the University. Nevertheless I think it would come as a surprise to most children (and probably some adults) to learn the extent to which they touch the lives of the people here. The University employs over 11,000 people and the state about 10,000. At the personnel department at the University I found out that there are 4,500 to 5,000 regular permanent civil service employees. The personnel department could not provide me with a breakdown of this figure into the many categories of secretaries, typists, janitors, painters, plumbers, etc. The office of the Secretary of the Faculty was able to provide the numbers of people in the various academic levels. Their total of about 6,600 is subdivided accordingly:

administrators 135
full professors 652
associate professors 344
assistant professors 497
instructors 419
lecturers 147
associate and project supervisors 241
teaching assistants 1,004
fellows 821
research assistants 1,140
project assistants 874
resident MD's 147
Wisconsin High teachers 39
miscellaneous 158

The Bureau of Personnel for the state employees informed me that about 60% of the state workers live in the Madison area and at present it includes about 10,000 people. The various categories of employees could not be readily supplied.

At City Hall I met with obvious reluctance to supply me with the information I sought. The Personnel Department was short-handed due to vacations and as I couldn't provide a particularly pressing need for monopolizing their time I left without pursuing the matter further.

Ideally, with proper teacher direction the children will have thought up the pertinent questions, discovered the proper resource areas and have gained some knowledge about jobs and employers in Madison. Obviously a lot depends upon the level of the children. For the early elementary grades a good deal of teacher guidance, research and translation would be required. For the upper grades more self-exploration should be forthcoming. With different methods and emphasis this type of study should be appropriate for any grade level, and I think the children would see Madison in a new light after such an endeavor.

Once the types of jobs and major employees have been pinpointed the question arises of what to do about it. Since it would be impossible to make a complete study there would have to be a selection process. Some jobs and businesses could be studied from books, parents could be brought into the classroom to explain their jobs, and field trips could be made. Unfortunately the largest employers are not particularly good for field trips. Although the students are free to visit parts of the State Capitol, State Office Building, and the City County Building, a superficial tour doesn't really explain very much. The majority of the work done in these places is of such an unspectacular and uninteresting nature that not much can be gained by first hand contact with them. Older children would of course be more interested in their local and state governments. A walk around the University campus would at least provide the students with a notion of the size of the institution. Parts of the College of Agriculture, a lab or classroom or two could be explored perhaps.

The Oscar Mayer Company has regular field trips and a number of other businesses are willing to have visits on a limited basis. The Sprague-Dawley Company which produces experimental albino rats explained the impossibility of visitors because of the need for sterile laboratory conditions. Many of the smaller businesses have no regular procedures for tours but try to be as accommodating as possible.

Hopefully, at the conclusion of this study the children would have a better understanding of the occupations of Madisonians in 1963. The absence of heavy industry, the predominance of "white-collar" work and other unique features of our community ought to become apparent. Reliance on a textbook or on pleasant little field trips for the main source of information would probably not result in an accurate picture of "community helpers."

This type of study would probably be a good starting-off point for many other studies. What might appear as deceptively simple survey stuff could really be material for deep sociological probing, probably for the most part, way beyond the elementary school level. The study of socio-economic classes, educational opportunities, job mobility, family life and many other subjects could be a natural outcome of such an investigation. Elementary school children would probably be better equipped to compare Madison with other communities in the types of jobs and industries. An excellent question requiring a look into state history would be "why are the Capitol and the University of Wisconsin located here?" After ascertaining the types of employment one might ask, "How do the people who hold these jobs live? What are their living conditions, their salaries, etc?" Perhaps using the various resources might make some children ask why we have a Chamber of Commerce, a City Directory, a manufacturers' directory, etc. Another possibility would be a further look into the multitude of products and services people create with their jobs.

The Monroe Doctrine—Why?

On page 122 of *Exploring American Neighbors,* the textbook we will be using for 6th grade social studies next year, mention is made of the Monroe Doctrine. It is included under a section entitled "The United States helped the Latin American Republics preserve their independence." Later on, on the same page appears the statement, "The Monroe Doctrine has helped Venezuela and other Latin American countries in the past." These over-simplified and perhaps misleading statements would provide a good opportunity for challenging the authority of the textbook and of pointing up the interpretive nature of history (i.e., history is not objective fact, but the way men have seen and interpreted events).

What I would do is have the children read some of the many different accounts of the motives behind the Monroe Doctrine. Was it proclaimed to help our Latin American neighbors? Or, were we afraid of our security being threatened by Spanish take-over of the newly independent Latin American countries? Many prominent historians think not.

I first went to the encyclopedias because I think children could read and understand them most easily. I found two different accounts or interpretations of Monroe's original message to Congress in 1823. The *Encyclopedia Americana* article states that the Doctrine was based on the grounds of national security (which did not really seem to be threatened) and that it shows the general tendency of American diplomacy towards sweeping generalization which captures the imagination of the mass of people and becomes a focus for popular support. In other words, the Doctrine was a warning to European powers to refrain from threatening our security— and threat to our security was generalized to include threat to any independent nation in the Western Hemisphere. *Collier's Encyclopedia,* on the other hand, says that the Doctrine implied that America wanted merely to keep these areas intact until it could colonize them itself. In another book, Whitaker—*The Western Hemisphere Idea,* I found a third interpretation. Whitaker felt that the Doctrine was actually a hemispheric projection of the national American policy of isolation laid down in Washington's Farewell Address. Great Britain had suggested a joint U.S.-British resolution on the same subject as the Doctrine. Monroe chose to make the declaration alone, choosing the lesser of the two evils (U.S. defense of the Western Hemisphere) as the only alternative to the even more far-reaching departure from

By permission of Lynn Bolton, Madison, Wisconsin.

isolationism a joint declaration with Britain would mean. The main evidence cited for this conclusion is some documents written by John Quincy Adams, the Secretary of State, which pointed to his extreme isolationist position. Other documents show that President Monroe was favorable to the joint resolution. Yet, he made the statement of the Monroe Doctrine alone. Could it be that John Quincy Adams influenced him on this matter? In the *World Book Encyclopedia* article on the Monroe Doctrine I found the statement that isolationism was no part of the Monroe Doctrine. It was merely meant to warn Europe against interfering in American affairs.

Which of these accounts is right? Or are any of them to be considered either right or wrong? An interesting way to present these different interpretations to the class would be to assign a few children to do the reading in the encyclopedias and each report to the class. After seeing the discrepancies the class could battle it out as to whose report was right or whether any of them could be considered right. We would probably conclude (I hope) that it was necessary to look at the Doctrine and at some of the original documents the historians have cited as evidence for their conclusions. We could then see what we thought might have been intended. In the documents I have been able to locate, I have found some evidence to indicate that the U.S. did indeed think that it could eventually colonize some of these areas, that the threat to our security was not imminent, and that the U.S. considered the North American continent its exclusive possession even though none of the land had been explored and claimed.

There are many other "study" possibilities in this topic. For example, we might look at interpretations other U.S. presidents have made of the Doctrine—the Roosevelt Corollary, American intervention in Cuba, etc. We could also see what the European and Latin American countries thought of the Doctrine.

This study interlude would, I think, clearly challenge the authority and perhaps the competency with which the textbook was written. It would also show the process which historians go through in making conclusions about historical happenings and the idea that history is written as men see it and that no two men will see the same thing when looking at the same event.

One difficulty we might encounter in this study is obtaining the original documents. Sometimes, we would have to satisfy ourselves with quotes given in the secondary sources rather than the original documents. I think I would have to do much of the tracking down of sources and give a lot of help to the children in reading and understanding them. The one documentary source book I have found contains some of the original documents we'd need, especially the writings of Secretary of State John Quincy Adams. In spite of these difficulties, though, I think this study interlude would have much value.

SOURCES

Collier's Encyclopedia, Vol. 14. New York: Collier, 1959.

Encyclopedia Americana, Vol. 19. New York: Americana, 1962.

GANTENBEIN, JAMES W., *The Evolution of Our Latin-American Policy: A Documentary Record.* New York: The Columbia University Press, 1950.

GRAY, WILLIAM H., et al., *Exploring American Neighbors.* New York: Follett, 1961.

PERKINS, DEXTER, *Hands Off: A History of the Monroe Doctrine.* Boston: Little, Brown, 1941.

WHITAKER, ARTHUR P., *The Western Hemisphere Idea: Its Rise and Decline.* Ithaca: The Cornell University Press, 1954.

World Book Encyclopedia, Vol. 11. Chicago: Field, 1958.

Appendix

SOCIAL SCIENCE JOURNALS[1]

The following journals illustrate the variety of writings that may facilitate a social studies program that calls upon students to engage in social study. The list is by no means exhaustive. Some journals are foreign, some have a political orientation, and some are scholarly; many sorts of writing are required if social study is to be encouraged.

American Slavic and East European Review. American Association for the Advancement of Slavic Studies, Inc. Columbia University Press, 2960 Broadway, New York 27, New York. Quarterly, $6.00.
  Content: Essays, articles, editorials, written, for the most part, by professors of American universities. Political and literary situations or movements in Eastern European and Slavic countries. Past and current.
  Style: Fairly informal, nontechnical.
  Use: A source of opinion and interpretation of Eastern Europe.
Chicago Review. University of Chicago, Chicago 37, Illinois. Quarterly, $3.00.
  Content: Essays, poetry, book reviews, illustrations, art work. Literature, philosophy, history. Past and current.
  Style: Sophisticated, literary.
  Use: Interesting source of opinion regarding contemporary social and intellectual life.
Comparative Studies in Society and History. Mounton & Co., Printers, The Hague, Netherlands. Quarterly. $6.00.
  Content: Essays, book reviews, letters to the editor. Sociological and political issues on an international basis.
  Style: Erudite, dry.
  Use: A source of opinions and interpretations on world affairs.
Confluence: An International Forum. Summer School of Arts and Sciences and of Education, Harvard University, 10 Weld Hall, Cambridge 38, Massachusetts. Quarterly. $3.00 or $1.00 per copy.
  Content: Essays and letters. Socio-cultural, politico-cultural affairs: each issue deals with one topic—e.g., religion, relation of underdeveloped to advanced countries.
  Style: Formal, scholarly.
  Use: A useful source of opinions and interpretation of contemporary social affairs.

[1] Data concerning address, time of publication, and price taken from *Ulrich's Periodicals Directory,* ed. Eileen C. Graves (9th ed., New York: R. R. Bowker, 1959).

Crisis. The Crisis Publishing Co., Inc., 20 West 40th Street, New York 18, New York. Monthly (October–May), bimonthly (June–September). $1.50.
Content: Articles, book reviews, illustrations, sketches, editorials. American Negroes and some of their present dilemmas. Current.
Style: Serious, informal.
Use: Opinions and arguments on contemporary social problems.

Diogenes: An International Review of Philosophy and Humanistic Studies. International Council for Philosophy and Humanistic Studies, University of Chicago Press, 5750 Ellis Avenue, Chicago 37, Illinois. Quarterly. $4.00.
Content: Essays and discussions. Sociology, economics, the arts, and politics.
Style: Sophisticated, literary.
Use: Opinions, inference, and interpretation on contemporary affairs.

Economica. London School of Economics and Political Science, Houghton Street, Aldwych, London W.C.2, England. Quarterly. 30 shillings.
Content: Essays, book reviews, scientific reports.
Style: Serious, erudite, technical.
Use: Opinion, examples of scientific writing.

Etc. International Society for General Semantics, 217 West Jefferson Street, Bloomington, Illinois. Quarterly. $4.00.
Content: Articles, essays, book reviews, verse, correspondence. Semantics.
Style: Informal, editorial.
Use: Important source of ideas on problems of language and meaning.

European Productivity. European Productivity Agency of the Organization for European Economic Co-operation, 3 Rue André-Pascal, Paris 16ᵉ, France. Trimonthly.
Content: Book reviews, publications lists, articles, graphs, charts. European business trends and industrial, marketing, or mechanical innovations and their productive effects. Mainly current.
Style: Serious, formal, journalistic in parts.
Use: Important source of data and inference on European economic development.

External Affairs. Department of External Affairs, Queen's Printer, Ottawa, Canada. Monthly. $1.00.
Content: Articles, graphs, charts, photographs. Information on Canada's economic, social, and political foreign relations. Current.
Style: Serious, formal, journalistic in parts.
Use: Interesting source of Canadian opinion on contemporary international affairs.

Foreign Affairs Record. External Publicity Division, Ministry of External Affairs, New Delhi, India. Monthly.
Content: Reports and verbatim records of addresses. International, national, foreign, economic, political policies; speakers are listed, but authors of reports and articles are not. Current.
Style: Serious, journalistic, formal.
Use: Interesting source of Indian opinion and inference on international affairs.

Geographical Magazine. Geographical Magazine, Ltd., Friars Bridge House, Queen Victoria Street, London, England. Monthly. $6.00.

Content: Highly illustrated (many black-and-white and color photographs) reports, accounts, and descriptions. Various cities, countries, and "wonders" of the world; written from a travelogue orientation. Past and current.

Style: Nontechnical, informal.

Use: An excellent English perspective on contemporary affairs.

Geography. Geographical Association, G. Philip and Son Ltd., 32 Fleet Street, London, England. Quarterly. 6 shillings per copy (nonmembers).

Content: Essays, sketch-maps, diagrams, graphs, research reports, book reviews, photographs, obituaries, society reports and news (Geographical Association). Physical, applied economic geography and climatology, teaching of geography in the public schools; international scope. Current.

Style: Serious, formal.

Use: Provides examples of contemporary scientific writing.

Historical Journal. Cambridge University Press, Bentley House, Euston Road, London N.W. 1, England. Semiannually. $4.25.

Content: Articles, book reviews, "notes and communications." Religion, economics, government, political movements of England. Ancient and recent past.

Style: Scholarly.

Use: Examples of historic scholarship.

Human Relations. Tavistock Publications, Ltd., 2 Beaumont Street, London W.1, England. Quarterly. $8.00.

Content: "Studies toward the integration of the Social Sciences" (title page), reports of experiments on human behavior in a variety of situations—industrial jobs, university work as a student, resistance to propaganda, measurement of aggression increase or reduction in given situations, group decisions; group situations and group action and interaction. Recent past and current.

Style: The (1) problem, (2) method, (3) results, (4) discussion, and (5) summary are presented in each article. For the most part, these five divisions comprise the entirety of an article. The writing is scientific, or technical.

Use: Example of contemporary social scientific study and scientific writing.

Italian Affairs: Documents and Notes. 56 Via Veneto, Rome, Italy. Bimonthly. $1.00.

Content: Articles, photographs, maps, tables, graphs. Developments and trends in Italian education, industry, trade, economic situations, agriculture, etc. Some recent past, but mainly current.

Style: Journalistic, sometimes technical-statistical.

Use: Information and inference relating to Italian affairs.

Japan Quarterly. Asahi Shimbun-Sha, Yurakucho, Chiyodku, Tokyo, Japan. Quarterly. $5.50.

Content: Essays, short stories, book reviews, chronological tabulation of news events, plates (black-and-white and color), graphs, art work (sketches). Some past, but mainly current.

Style: Informal, journalistic.

Use: Interesting information and inference from a Japanese perspective.

Journal of International Affairs. School of International Affairs, Columbia University, 429 West 117th Street, New York 27, New York. Semiannually. $1.00 per copy.

Content: Articles, book reviews, editor's forewords. National and international foreign relations, foreign policies—political and economic; attempts also to react to events in the recent past that have affected world politics (each issue pertains to one topic only). Recent past and current.

Style: Literary, not overly technical.

Use: An excellent source of discussion of contemporary affairs.

Labour Monthly. Trinity Trust, 134 Ballards Lane, London N.3, England. Monthly. 1 shilling, 6d. per copy.

Content: Articles, essays, some prints (of art work), photographs, book reviews, "news and notes," advertisements, verse, verbatim records of discussions, list of publications received. International labor issues, political and economic situations and their effects on labor organization and employment; unions, etc. Recent past and current.

Style: Serious in part, satirically humorous in part, informal.

Use: Information and interpretation from the point of view of English labour.

Listener. British Broadcasting Corp., Publications, 35 Marylebone High Street, London W.1, England. Weekly. $7.50.

Content: Essays, articles, letters to the editor, poetry, art prints, photographs, advertisements, book reviews, cartoons. The arts, literature, current affairs, travel, and gardening; international scope. Past and current.

Style: Sophisticated, literary.

Use: Fascinating examples of thought and argument reflecting a wide range of views.

Mainstream. Masses and Mainstream, Inc., 832 Broadway, New York 3, New York. Monthly. $5.00, or 50¢ per copy.

Content: Articles, stories, poetry, book reviews, illustrations. The arts, political, economic, and sociological situations; it reflects the views of American Communists. Mainly current.

Style: Informal, journalistic, analytical.

Use: Here one can find American Communists' views on many contemporary topics.

Middle East Journal. Middle East Institute, 1761 "N" Street, N.W., Washington 6, D.C. Quarterly. $6.00.

Content: Essays, articles, chronological reports, book reviews, economic reviews, letters to the editor, tables, charts, bibliography. Political, governmental, social, and economic trends, movements, and problems in the Middle East. Mainly current.

Style: Serious, journalistic.

Use: Information, interpretation, and argument relating to Middle Eastern Affairs.

Midwest Journal of Political Science. Midwest Conference of Political Scientists, Wayne State University Press, 4841 Cass Avenue, Detroit 2, Michigan. Quarterly. $6.00 (nonmembers).

Content: Essays, published research, tables, charts, book reviews and notes, lists of books received, index. Comparative government, problems related to governmental systems, political ideology, characteristics of bureaucracies, trade unions, and political parties; international scope. Recent past and current.

Style: Considerable jargon, dry, statistical.

Use: Useful source of scientific writing in the style of political science.

Monthly Review: An Independent Socialist Magazine. 218 West 10th Street, New York 14, New York. Monthly (September–June), bimonthly (July–August). $4.00.

Content: Essays, critiques, reports, verbatim records of speeches, synopses of current events, book reviews. Labor organization, the Cuban Revolution, economic planning, music, government organization, events, or situations; it reflects American Socialist thinking; international scope. Current.

Style: Serious, nontechnical.

Use: An interesting source of argument and discussion that frequently expresses support for various Communist governments and notions. One can find sympathetic articles dealing with North Vietnam, China, and the Soviet Union.

National Review. 150 East 35th Street, New York 16, New York. Weekly. $16.00.

Content: Essays, articles, book reviews, verse, illustrations (art work). Topics of sociological and political nature.

Style: Informal.

Use: Useful source of opinion and interpretation from the conservative viewpoint.

New Leader. American Labor Conference on International Affairs, Inc., 7 East 15th Street, New York 3, New York. Weekly (September–June), biweekly (July–August). $6.00.

Content: Articles, book reviews, letters to the editor, art work, photographs, stage and art reviews. Comment mainly on current political movements on the international level.

Style: Journalistic.

Use: Useful source of comment from the non-Communist American Socialist viewpoint.

New Outlook: Middle East Monthly. Tazpioth, Ltd., Box 11269, Tel Aviv, Israel. Monthly. $5.50.

Content: Essays, articles, poetry, book reviews, tables, news, and reports. Middle Eastern countries and their political, economic, governmental, educational developments and trends. Recent past and current.

Style: Technical, scholarly.

Use: Information and inference from the Israeli perspective.

Philosophy East and West: A Quarterly Journal of Oriental and Comparative Thought. University of Hawaii Press, Honolulu 14, Hawaii. Quarterly. $4.00, or $1.25 per copy.

Content: Essays. Philosophical and spiritual, or religious, concepts of Oriental civilization; Western and Eastern thought; ethics, economics, political thought.

Style: Sophisticated, literary.

Use: Thought and comment that relate to Far Eastern perspective.

Queen's Quarterly; A Canadian Review. Queen's University, Kingston, Canada. Quarterly. $4.00.

Content: Essays, poems, book reviews, stories. Literature, economics, politics, contemporary Canadian situations and events, education.

Style: Editorial, journalistic.

Use: Useful source of Canadian thought.

Saturday Review. Saturday Review, Inc., 25 West 45th Street, New York 36, New York. Weekly. $7.00.

Content: Articles, editorials, book reviews, verse, poetry, illustrations. The humanities and politics. Current.

Style: Informal, usually literary.

Use: Excellent source of thought and discussion regarding contemporary affairs.

Social Forces; A Scientific Medium of Social Study and Interpretation. Williams and Wilkins Company, 428 East Preston Street, Baltimore, Maryland. Quarterly. $6.00.

Content: Scientific articles, book reviews. Sociological phenomena: social participation, contact pattern in the city, satellites, and suburbs, adjustment of migrants to cities, interracial marriage, religion and secularization, segregation; mainly national (most contributors are from United States universities and most studies are conducted within United States boundaries). Recent past and current.

Style: Somewhat technical, often jargonese. Format of reports follows, in varying degrees, this general outline: (1) introduction, (2) method with discussion, (3) conclusions and summary.

Use: Excellent source of scientific writing and useful illustrations of contemporary social scientific interests.

Social Order. Institute of Social Order, 3908 Westminster Place, St. Louis 8, Missouri. Monthly (September–June). $4.00.

Content: Articles, book reviews, letters, tables, graphs, small sketches. Labor, social change, farm problems, and political and economic problems; international scope. Recent past and current.

Style: Informal, somewhat jargonese.

Use: Information and interpretation regarding contemporary United States and international affairs.

Soviet Liturature. Union of Soviet Writers, Mechdunarodnaya Kniga, Moscow 200, U.S.S.R. Monthly.

Content: Stories, critiques, interviews, poetry, prints (paintings), book reviews, letters to and from the editor, illustrations. Soviet literature and the arts (contributors are from the Soviet Union).

Style: Informal.

Use: Excellent source of Soviet opinion.

Spectator. Spectator, Ltd., 99 Gower Street, London W.C. 1, England. Weekly. 50 shillings.

Content: Essays, book reviews, cartoons. The arts, political, economic, educational situations; resembles *The Nation* in format. Fairly current.

Style: Literary, journalistic.

Use: Interesting source of social and political interpretation from an English perspective.

Word. The Linguistic Circle of New York, Columbia University, New York 27, New York. Thrice annually. $5.00, or $3.00 per copy.

Content: Essays. Grammar, meaning, syntax, and dialects.

Style: Erudite, technical.

Use: Provides examples of contemporary linguistic scholarship. May provide teacher with opportunities to extend his own understanding of language, and relate that understanding to classroom affairs.

Index